Across the Revolutionary Divide

The Blackwell History of Russia

General Editor: Simon M. Dixon

This series provides a provocative reinterpretation of fundamental questions in Russian history. Integrating the wave of new scholarship that followed the collapse of the Soviet Union, it focuses on Russia's development from the mid-seventeenth century to the present day, exploring the interplay of continuity and change. Volumes in the series demonstrate how new sources of information have reshaped traditional debates and present clear, stimulating overviews for students, scholars and general readers.

Published

Russia's Age of Serfdom, 1649–1861
Elise Kimerling Wirtschafter

Across the Revolutionary Divide: Russia and the USSR, 1861–1945
Theodore R. Weeks

Forthcoming

The Shadow of War: Russia and the USSR, 1941 to the present
Stephen Lovell

Across the Revolutionary Divide
Russia and the USSR, 1861–1945
Theodore R. Weeks

WILEY-BLACKWELL

A John Wiley & Sons, Ltd., Publication

This edition first published 2011
© Theodore R. Weeks 2011

Blackwell Publishing was acquired by John Wiley & Sons in February 2007. Blackwell's publishing program has been merged with Wiley's global Scientific, Technical, and Medical business to form Wiley-Blackwell.

Registered Office
John Wiley & Sons Ltd, The Atrium, Southern Gate, Chichester, West Sussex, PO19 8SQ, United Kingdom

Editorial Offices
350 Main Street, Malden, MA 02148-5020, USA
9600 Garsington Road, Oxford, OX4 2DQ, UK
The Atrium, Southern Gate, Chichester, West Sussex, PO19 8SQ, UK

For details of our global editorial offices, for customer services, and for information about how to apply for permission to reuse the copyright material in this book please see our website at www.wiley.com/wiley-blackwell.

The right of Theodore R. Weeks to be identified as the author of this work has been asserted in accordance with the UK Copyright, Designs and Patents Act 1988.

Library of Congress Cataloging-in-Publication Data

Weeks, Theodore R.
  Across the revolutionary divide : Russia and the USSR, 1861–1945 / Theodore R. Weeks.
      p. cm. – (Blackwell history of Russia)
  Includes bibliographical references and index.
  ISBN 978-1-4051-6961-5 (hardcover : alk. paper)–ISBN 978-1-4051-6960-8 (pbk. : alk. paper) 1. Russia–History–Alexander II, 1855–1881. 2. Russia–History–Alexander III, 1881–1894. 3. Russia–History–Nicholas II, 1894–1917. 4. Soviet Union–History–1917–1936. 5. Soviet Union–History–1925–1953. 6. Soviet Union–History–1939–1945. 7. Social change–Russia–History. 8. Social change–Soviet Union–History. I. Title.
  DK189.W44 2011
  947.08–dc22
                                                                      2010003197

A catalogue record for this book is available from the British Library.

Set in 10/12.5pt Minion by Toppan Best-set Premedia Limited
Printed in Singapore by Ho Printing Singapore Pte Ltd

1 2011

To my students: Past, present, and future

Contents

Illustrations

Series Editor's Preface

The Blackwell History of Russia aims to present a wide readership with a fresh synthesis in which new approaches to Russian history stimulated by research in recently opened archives are integrated with fundamental information familiar to earlier generations. Whatever the period under review, new discoveries have thrown into question some persistent assumptions about the nature of Russian government and society. Censorship and surveillance remain important subjects for investigation. However, now that social activity in Russia is no longer instinctively conceived in terms of resistance to a repressive, centralized state, there is room not only to investigate the more normal contours of everyday life, but also to consider its kaleidoscopic variety in the thousands of provincial villages and towns that make up the multinational polity. Religion, gender, and culture (in its widest sense) are all more prominent in the writings of contemporary scholars than they were in the work of previous generations. Historians once preoccupied with pig-iron production are now more inclined to focus on pilgrimages, icon veneration, and incest. No longer so overwhelmingly materialist in their approach, they are more likely to take "the linguistic turn"; the changing meanings of imagery, ritual, and ceremonial are all being reinterpreted.

The challenge is to take account of "extra" dimensions of the subject such as these (the list could easily be extended), and, where appropriate, to allow them to reshape our understanding, without risking a descent into modishness and without neglecting fundamental questions of political economy. One way of squaring the circle is to adopt an unconventional chronological framework in which familiar subjects can be explored in less familiar contexts. Each of the three volumes in the series therefore crosses a significant caesura in Russian history. The first, examined by Elise Kimerling Wirtschafter in *Russia's Age of Serfdom, 1649–1861*, is the physical and cultural move from Moscow to St Petersburg at the beginning of the eighteenth century; the last, explored by Stephen Lovell in *The Shadow of War: Russia and the USSR, 1941 to the present,* is the collapse of the USSR in 1991. In this middle volume, Ted Weeks ranges "across the revolutionary divide" of the year 1917.

For much of the twentieth century, 1917 seemed to mark the most significant of historical ruptures and there are naturally good reasons for continuing to regard the revolutionary cataclysm as a fracture between radically different worlds. Autocracy and Marxism-Leninism were ideological poles apart; so were the aims of their respective proponents. Indeed, it is hard to exaggerate the ambition of the Bolsheviks who came to power in October to transform the world in which they lived. They attempted not only to supplant the monarchy and to extend the dictatorship of the proletariat far beyond Russia's borders, but also to forge a new civilization, ultimately to be peopled by a different sort of human being: New Soviet Man and New Soviet Woman.

For all these reasons, it is no surprise that the Soviet and tsarist periods should have tended until recently to attract historians of different backgrounds, different temperaments, and different preoccupations. While some were fascinated by the decline of an increasingly inflexible tsarist regime, whose attempts to strengthen the Romanov dynasty paradoxically served only to make its own government more brittle, others were drawn to explain why a Bolshevik vision apparently so suffused with optimism should have corrupted within less than a generation into the horrors of the Stalinist Terror. Even basic logistics militated against scholarly efforts to "cross the revolutionary divide," for while the Soviet government stored its principal papers in Moscow, the richest archival collections relating to the late-imperial period remained in Leningrad.

Nearly 20 years after the collapse of the USSR, however, 1917 no longer seems quite such a total rupture. After all, as governors of a sprawling multiethnic state, the Bolsheviks faced many of the same geopolitical challenges as their tsarist predecessors. How were they to balance the security of multinational *Rossiia* against ethnic and cultural *Rus'*? Some of the most fertile research of the last generation has been devoted to precisely this question and to related dilemmas of imperial expansion. Himself an acclaimed authority on the history of the Polish-Lithuanian borderlands both before and after 1917, Weeks draws on this literature to offer a brilliant analysis of the nationalities question in one of the most striking chapters of his new book. Continuities are no less striking when one turns to the economy. The last three tsars and the early Soviet leaders were all struggling to manage the politics of industrialization in an overwhelmingly agrarian empire. All of them ran up against the risk-averse peasantry's stubborn attachment to the small-scale communal organization that had helped them to survive for centuries. Peasant obstinacy was to prove just as exasperating to Stalin at the end of the 1920s as it had to Stolypin between 1906 and 1911. Their solutions, of course, were radically different. Whereas Stolypin hoped to foster a new generation of prosperous (and politically loyal) farmers by encouraging the wealthiest peasants ("kulaks"), Stalin set out to annihilate them. Nevertheless, it would be misleading to suppose that the Bolsheviks had a monopoly on state violence. In many ways, the key turning point was not 1917, but, rather, World War I, described with characteristic prescience by Norman Stone in 1975 as "a first experiment in Stalinist tactics for modernization." More recently, Peter Holquist has traced the development of a wartime consensus in favor of planning that stretched across the political spectrum, including among liberals in government who regarded themselves as a supra-class elite with the best interests of the state at heart. And just as liberal planners' commitment to forcible state intervention in the food supply chain during World War I marked the first stage in a continuum of state violence that stretched beyond 1917, so Daniel Beer has demonstrated the ways in which psychiatrists and other liberal intellectuals anticipated some of the controlling instincts of the Soviet regime by seeking to combat a perceived threat of moral degeneration well before 1917.

Not that violence and surveillance were the only tools at the state's disposal. Russia has always derived much of its stability and flexibility from time-honored ways of doing things. The sorts of informal patronage network that had overlain the tsarist bureaucracy for centuries at both central and local levels soon wove their way into a powerful Soviet *nomenklatura*. Nor should we confine our interest in continuity to matters of geopolitics and the state. Most aspects of the distinctive form of Soviet consumer society that emerged in the aftermath of the Russian Civil War – tourism, the cinema and so on – had their origins in the commercial explosion of late-imperial Russia. Many of the reformist impulses in Russian Orthodoxy that emerged in the first decade of the twentieth century found expression only after the October Revolution, when the nascent Soviet regime tried to exploit them as a way of splitting the church. There is no need to stress the virtues of writing cultural history "across the revolutionary divide": it is the *only* way to write about Russian modernism, itself part of a European cultural movement with deep roots before World War I.

In other words, while no one would sensibly seek to minimize the impact of the October Revolution, the lived experience of Stalin's generation only partly confirms the impression of 1917 as a fundamental caesura. Drawing on recent writings which have enriched our understanding of the 1920s and 1930s as never before, Ted Weeks explores a vital period in Russian history, culminating in the "Great Patriotic War" that served as the ultimate test of the nascent Soviet regime.

Simon M. Dixon
School of Slavonic and East European Studies
University College London

Acknowledgments

Writing a textbook is truly a case, as medieval writers liked to say, of a "dwarf standing on the shoulders of giants." Among the giants among Russian historians that I have known and learned from over the years are my *Doktorväter*, Nicholas Riasanovsky and the too-soon departed and sorely missed Reggie Zelnik. My wonderful colleagues in graduate school at the University of California, Berkeley, here at Southern Illinois University, and throughout the world, have also been important teachers. Probably most vital of all for a textbook writer is the interaction with students who are constantly reminding me to be clear, precise, and concise.

Many people helped improve this book. My sincere thanks to colleagues who took time from their busy schedules to read and critique chapters: Peter Blitsein, Chris Chulos, Adrienne Edgar, Brian Horowitz, Stephen Lovell, Kevin O'Connor, David Schimmelpenninck van der Oye, and Christine Worobec. Brad Woodworth, Pierre Holquist, and Clayton Black helped with specific queries. Chapter 5 is much improved after the thorough critique provided by the Midwest Russian Historians Workshop. My sincere gratitude to all of these people and all others whom I have neglected to mention specifically. All remaining weaknesses, errors, and infelicities are entirely *mea culpa*.

 A Note on Calendars

Unlike most European countries, which had adopted the Gregorian calendar ("new style": "n.s.") by the eighteenth century, imperial Russia continued to use the Julian calendar ("old style": "o.s.") well into the twentieth century. This meant that the calendar used in Russia was 12 days behind in the nineteenth century, 13 days behind in the twentieth. Thus October 1, 1901, in Russia was October 14 in, say, London. This fact is important in understanding why this book speaks of the "October" (old style) Revolution whereas a general European history would speak of the "November" (new style). This confusion was cleared up when the Bolsheviks adopted the Gregorian calendar in February 1918.

Introduction

Why a New Russian History?

The Russia of today is an entirely different place than the one I read about in college textbooks and experienced as a college student in the 1980s. In the past generation Russia has gone from being, in the guise of the USSR, one of two superstates whose policies affected millions around the globe to a still powerful but insecure state no longer certain of its preeminence on the global scene. This enormous change took place almost literally overnight in the early 1990s and left millions of Russians baffled, frustrated, and angry. One cannot understand the politics and culture of the Russian Federation in the twenty-first century without a good grasp of the past – in particular of the crucial period between serf emancipation (1861) and victory in the second World War (1945). In that quite short period – essentially one long lifetime – Russia became a world power as it had never been before in history. Now, once again, Russia has returned more or less to its pre-World War I power status: important but not one of the two superpowers engaged in power projection around the globe. At the same time many Russians continue to feel that their country is not receiving proper respect in the world. The broad discrepancy between Russia's actual military and economic power and the role that Russians think their country should play in world politics stems mainly from the memory of a powerful USSR – the country built in the years we will consider here.

Despite the transformations of the 1990s and the resulting reduction in Russian military might, Russia continues to aspire to a global role – to the great consternation of many of its European neighbors. With its large energy reserves, nuclear capabilities, and geographical sweep covering nearly half of the globe, Russia remains vitally important in world politics. One should also never forget that the

MAP 0.1   Russian Empire.
Source: based on map in Dominic Lieven, *Empire*, Yale University Press, 2000, "The Russian Empire at its Greatest Extent, 1914."

Arctic Ocean

Bering
Straits

R. Anadyr

KAMCHATKA

R. Indigirka

R. Kolyma

R. Lena

SIBERIAN PLAINS

Okhotsk

R U S S I A N

Yakutsk

Sea of
Okhotsk

LOWER TUNGUSKA

E M P I R E

R. Aldan

SAKHALIN

Yeniseysk

R. Angara

R. Lena

AMUR REGION

Gained by
Japan, 1905

Krasnoyarsk

Lake
Baikal

Nerchinsk

Irkutsk

MANCHURIA

R. Yenisey

Kharbin

Vladivostok

MONGOLIA

CHINA

KOREA

JAPAN

	Russian Empire, 1796
	Acquisitions, 1796–1855
	Acquisitions, 1856–1914
	Russian Sphere of Influence
——	Boundary of Russian Empire, 1914
+++	Trans-Siberian Railway

Russian nuclear arsenal is still capable of ending all life on earth. So Russia continues to "matter," just as Germany and Britain after 1945 remain significant in world politics, economy, and culture. Up to now, all histories of Russia written have consciously or unconsciously been histories of a world power. The challenge of a survey of Russian history in the twenty-first century is to present the history of a country whose importance can no longer be taken for granted.

The present-day importance of Russia derives from geographical, military, cultural, and historical factors. The largest country in the world from the seventeenth century to the present day, its borders stretch from the European Union to China, from the Middle East (Iran) to Korea, from the Black and Baltic Seas to the Pacific. The huge oil and natural gas reserves located on its territory allow Russia to exert serious – and often much resented – influence in Europe where many countries are overwhelmingly dependent on energy delivered from the east. With its nuclear arms and new-found assertiveness under President Vladimir Putin and his successors, Russia cannot be dismissed as "yesterday's news." Of course, for a historian, the news of yesterday is vitally significant, even more so, perhaps, for Russia more than any other present-day country. While Germans or Japanese no longer regard their countries as world powers (and, crucially, have no great desire to take on that role) and the British Empire has been transformed into the Commonwealth that has relinquished any pretensions of a geopolitical role, the Russian Federation and Russian citizens in the early twenty-first century often regard their country in terms of world political power. Thus Russia expects to be respected as a power of the first rank; neither government nor populace is yet content to accept a reduced role on the international scene in the way that former world powers like Great Britain, France, or Japan have. This view, which clashes with many aspects of post-1992 political reality, can only be understood through a sympathetic examination of Russia's past experience.

In the early twenty-first century, with the USSR a fading memory, the triumph of the Bolshevik party in 1917 remains an important historical event, but only one among many. In the past decades western historians have attempted to look across and beyond the revolutionary year, pointing to continuities before and afterwards rather than stressing the total break with tradition that the creation of the world's first socialist state represented. This book will reflect that historiography. Nobody would deny the importance of the communist victory in October 1917 as a crucial event in world history. At the same time the Bolsheviks were building on an already-existing revolutionary tradition that dated from the Great Reforms of the 1860s and early 1870s. After the communist victory, moreover, Lenin and his party comrades had to deal with many of the same issues that had plagued pre-revolutionary Russian rulers: developing the economy, raising the education level, dealing with Russia's multiethnic and multilingual population, defending Russia from internal and external threats, and justifying the revolution not just in practical but in moral terms. This volume's narrative will be structured around some of these major themes.

The period covered in this book, from the emancipation of the serfs in 1861 to the victory over Hitler's Germany in 1945, represents a critical and unique era in Russian history. Serf emancipation formed the cornerstone of the Great Reforms that aimed to modernize Russia, in effect, to preserve Russia's great power status. The impressive industrial development of Russia that began approximately a generation after the Great Reforms appeared to prove that Russia was indeed successfully modernizing. But economic development could not prevent revolutions in 1905 and 1917, the final of which brought down the tsarist regime. The new communist government dedicated itself to creating an entirely new kind of state – modern, secular, socialist, and a model for the world. The social and economic convulsions of the 1930s shook the Soviet state to its foundations but also helped to pave the way to victory in 1945. Thus in a sense the defeat of Nazi Germany at the hands of the Red Army can be seen as the culmination of a modernizing process begun with the emancipation of serfs three generations earlier.

Main Events and Arguments

A common definition of history is "the study of change over time." In this book we will certainly witness enormous changes as Russia went from being a politically conservative, peasant-dominated, religious country to the world's first socialist state, officially atheist and dominated – at least in principle – by the industrial working class. Vastly more of the population lived in cities in 1945 than in 1861, and women occupied a far more prominent place in public life. Still, much remained of the past. Religion lived on in official and unofficial forms; women continued to raise children and carry out nearly all household work even while working outside the home; vodka still provided important tax revenues for the state as well as pleasure and pain for ordinary Russians. Certainly from 1861 to 1945 Russia became more modern: industrialized, literate, urban, secular.

We start in 1861 with the emancipation of the serfs, the most important act of the "Great Reforms" that would stretch into the 1870s. These reforms, as we will see, were a major step toward creating a modern Russia, at least on the social and economic planes. We end in 1945 with the Soviet victory against Nazi Germany not because the USSR was a truly modern and prosperous country by that date – the opposite was in many ways true – but because the peculiar path of modernization that had been followed since 1861 had proved itself in one vital respect successful: the USSR was able to take on a major military threat and emerge victorious. The role of World War II in legitimating the Soviet regime is so vital that this conflict will figure both here and in the next, final, volume of this history that will take the story up to our own days. Furthermore, in a sense the type of centrally planned, state-dominated modernization followed since 1917 reached its logical limits in the decade or two after 1945; the future economic difficulties of the USSR were thus a function of the structures set up in the first generation after 1917.

Major political developments will be treated in some detail in chapter 1, but a quick overview may be helpful. In 1861 Russia was ruled by an autocrat, without any parliament or even a cabinet of ministers, and its economic and social life was dominated by the institution of serfdom. The Great Reforms of 1861–76 abolished serfdom, set up institutions of limited local autonomy in cities and the countryside (the *zemstva*), modernized the legal system, and reformed the army. However, the Russian political system remained entirely dominated by the tsar, whose rule was unfettered by either a constitution or a legislature of any kind. Neither the peasantry nor educated society were satisfied with the reforms and this unhappiness – especially among young educated people – developed in a violent direction that culminated in the assassination of Tsar Alexander II in 1881.

From 1881 until the end of the old regime in the midst of World War I, Russia's rulers understood the need to modernize the empire to finance an army, but stubbornly assumed that they could do this without relinquishing autocratic authority. Without modernization, Russia would have fallen into the status of a second-rate power, something the Russian tsars refused to consider. Tsar Alexander III (reigned 1881–94) was relatively successful in allowing industrial development without conceding political reform. The failure of his unfortunate son, Nicholas II (reigned 1894–1917), can be seen in two revolutions, one in 1905 (which the tsarist regime survived, though after conceding a parliament, the Duma) and one in February 1917, which ended tsarist rule.

The Bolsheviks, led by Vladimir Ilyich Lenin, took power in late 1917 and aimed at a complete transformation of Russia – and the world. Not only economic and political relations were to be transformed: social relations, spiritual beliefs, even the family and gender relations were to be completely changed. A new human being was to be created! The first years of communist rule coincided with a bloody civil war, which ended with a devastating famine in which millions perished. The shattering experience of the civil war convinced the communist leadership that some concession had to be made with the market and private property. During the 1920s this period of the "New Economic Policy" (NEP) saw economic recovery and cultural innovations, but no political liberalization. At decade's end the NEP was eclipsed by a more radical – and more socialist – economic policy of the first Five Year Plan (for industrial growth) and agricultural collectivization (to neutralize the peasants as possible threats to Soviet power and to guarantee a reliable supply of grain to the industrial cities). This period of "socialist construction" which lasted at least until 1939 was brutal and inhumane, but also impressive: entire new industries and even new cities rose in the space of a decade. The 1930s also saw mass arrests, the so-called Great Terror, and enormous growth in the coercive labor camp system (the Gulag).

The feeling of insecurity engendered by the dislocations of the "Great Terror" – thousands of military officers and the majority of the politburo were purged – may have contributed to Stalin's decision to sign a pact with Adolf Hitler in August 1939. Thus when the Nazi invasion of Poland set off World War II, the USSR was Hitler's ally (and quickly occupied the eastern half of Poland). The enormous ideological differences between the USSR and Nazi Germany made further conflict inevitable; the Nazi attack of 21/22 June 1941 should have come as no surprise to Stalin. Unfortunately Stalin had convinced himself that the Germans could not – yet – attack, a faulty judgment that would cost millions of Soviet lives. By fall 1941 German armies were on the outskirts of Leningrad and Moscow and it appeared that the USSR's last days had come. But appearances deceive: after four years of almost unbearable suffering the Red Army took Berlin. The Soviet Union, despite the huge devastation its western and southern territories had suffered, found its international prestige at an all-time high.

Why a Thematic Approach?

Such were some of the major events of this formative period in Russian history. Yet this quick sketch leaves out vast areas of human experience – family life, social identities, the ethnic diversity of Russia/USSR, urbanization, religion, foreign affairs, culture and education. Politics influences – in a sense provides the setting for – all of these things, but in a traditional history political events tend to overwhelm and "push out" social, cultural, and everyday developments. Here we will begin with a political overview and will then cover six other broad themes in separate chapters. In this way crucial issues like ethnic-national policy, everyday life, culture, and religious feeling can be considered in their own right rather than as a function of larger political trends.

In the past generation or two, professional historians and students have become increasingly impatient with traditional political narratives. Readers demand less emphasis on the inner workings of cabinets, diplomatic intrigue, and great men, and more focus on the lived experience of everyday people. This is not to say, obviously, that politics is entirely divorced from everyday life. For instance, censorship laws had a direct effect on literature and journalism. Laws in imperial Russia restricting the movement, educational opportunities, and professional rights of Jews influenced many younger Jews to oppose the old regime – sometimes violently. Marriage and divorce laws – utterly different before and after the October 1917 revolution – had profound consequences for family life, inheritance, and relations between the genders. Similarly the two World Wars had an enormous and devastating impact on culture, economics, and gender relations throughout Russia/USSR. Accordingly this book starts with the traditional theme of politics as a framework and context for the other chapters.

The themes we will cover are seven: Politics, Society, Nations, Modernization, Belief, World, and Culture. Politics is more or less self-explanatory: political events, wars, administrative and legal changes, revolutions, rulers. In the chapter on society we will consider how the Russians perceived their own social order and how both perceptions and social realities changed over the four generations of our study. In this context we will consider the term "intelligentsia" as the nucleus for a developing Russian civil society that would, eventually, include the entire nation. In 1861, to be sure, the vast majority of Russia's population – the peasantry – still remained outside "society." Thus an important part of our story examines how serfs became peasants and these later became collective farmers, while also tracing the path of millions of other peasants who left the countryside to become wage laborers in the growing cities.

Half of society is made up of women, but in the past they were rarely considered men's intellectual or legal equals. The "Woman Question" was a fundamental social issue from the mid-nineteenth century into the Soviet period and challenged basic assumptions about society. If the peasantry and women often remained outside "society," following the Russian use of the word, at least in the first part of our period, the state bureaucracy and the men (nearly all men) who worked in it were seen as society's antithesis. In fact, of course, clerks and bureaucrats both formed part of society and – particularly in the Soviet period – helped mold the contours of a changing and newly developing social organism. Finally we will look at peripheral groups in society, including criminals, "deviants," prostitutes, and homosexuals. These groups had little in common aside from the consternation they caused in "respectable" society both before and after the revolution.

The next chapter focuses on "nations" in Russian history. While the word "nation" in English is ambiguous, referring sometimes to a group of people and sometimes to a political entity ("our nation's capital"), in Russian *narod* or *natsiia* can only be a group of people or ethnicity. Throughout the period of this textbook, ethnic Russians made up not quite half of the empire's (or USSR's) total population. What strategies were employed by tsarist and Soviet decision-makers to deal with such ethnic, religious, and linguistic diversity? The great differences between so-called nationality policy before and after 1917 stem from the very different natures of the imperial and Soviet state. While imperial Russia could be very harsh in crushing rebellions and punishing rebel groups – including perceived "rebel nations" like the Poles – the empire was by its nature more likely to react than to act, was suspicious of change (even such a change as assimilation to Russian culture) while having no fundamental respect for ethnic or linguistic diversity. Thus Poles and Jews could be respected as the bearers of centuries-old cultures, while peasant or nomadic nations whose culture existed mainly in oral form (e.g., Ukrainians, Kyrgyz, Lithuanians) were not particularly esteemed.

Under Soviet rule, on the other hand, great efforts were expended to introduce alphabets, standardize languages, and to oblige each individual to adopt a single national identity (e.g., Russian, Uzbek, Jewish). One troubling nation for both imperial rulers and the Soviets were the Jews: Stalin initially denied them any status as a nation (in a pre-revolutionary theoretical work), but in the USSR Jews came to enjoy – if that is the word – the status of separate nation even as thousands of Jewish individuals migrated to the cities, brought their children up speaking Russian (not Yiddish), and abandoned the religious practices of their ancestors. Although official Judeophobia and legal restrictions of the imperial era were abolished in 1917, antisemitism did not die – despite Soviet laws forbidding it – and remained a powerful social force throughout the Soviet period.

Modernization forms the focus of chapter 4. Here the main focus will be on economic development, industrialization, and urbanization. At the same time modernization also implies social transformation toward a mobile (both geographically and in class terms), flexible, and relatively homogenous society. Indeed Soviet society in 1945 was relatively – and that is a key word – more homogenous than Russian society in 1861. The industrial development of the generation or two before 1917 inadvertently helped put in place the preconditions for revolution by creating an industrial proletariat dissatisfied with long hours, dangerous work, and inadequate pay. Certainly the Bolsheviks wished to create a modern, prosperous, literate, and socialist country. To a great extent they succeeded. The gap between city and village remained important even in 1945, but education, improved transport, and new technologies such as the radio meant that Soviet citizens could perceive themselves as part of a greater whole by the 1930s in a way that subjects of the tsar could not 70 years earlier. Bolshevism (and Marxism) is all about modernity: we will weigh the positive and negative outcomes of the modernizing path taken in the generations between the rapid industrialization of the 1890s and the crash industrializing programs of the 1930s.

"Belief" is the title of chapter 5. I use this term in a broad sense, including organized religions, ideologies, and dissenting "sects," but also belief in the sense of "worldviews," such as anarchism or Marxist communism. In the Russian Empire the "ruling role" of the Russian Orthodox Church was part of Russian law: both the tsar and his wife had to be of that denomination (though born into Lutheran families, the Danish and German wives of the last three tsars all converted to Orthodoxy before marriage). However, other religions from Islam to Buddhism to Catholicism were tolerated within the Russian Empire. Jews (and, to a lesser extent, all non-Christians) were subject to a number of legal restrictions, but were never forbidden to follow their religions. Besides religious beliefs, political convictions were important in the imperial period, with liberals and socialists (of different parties) putting forth different arguments about the proper future of the Russian state. After the Bolshevik revolution the range of permitted opinions became considerably narrower, with liberals (and of course conservatives) deprived of a public voice. Within a few years of 1917 even non-Bolshevik socialists found their freedom of expression tightly circumscribed. Religious beliefs were even more directly attacked by the communist rulers and yet continued to exist both in legal and underground forms. Despite these attacks of the 1920s and 1930s, during World War II the Soviet state did not hesitate to use religious (and Russian patriotic) themes to bolster the war effort.

For generations Russian intellectuals have pondered to what extent Russia is part of Europe. In chapter 6 Russia's role in the world is examined. Here we consider foreign policy, national prestige on the international scene, but also "mentality": is Russia unique in world history or must she follow the same historical path as other countries? The country's unique geographical position, stretching from the Pacific Ocean to the Baltic Sea, meant that the bulk of Russian territory was actually located in Asia, while the centers of Russian culture were in Europe. Perhaps Russia's geography meant that it had a special role to play in world history? More prosaically the Russian Empire was vitally concerned in preserving its great power status – this had been, after all, one of the main motivations behind the Great Reforms. Concern for international prestige also explains Russia's plunge into war in late July 1914 when Austria-Hungary appeared to threaten its ally and fellow Orthodox state, Serbia.

After 1917 the USSR promoted another kind of historical uniqueness as the world's first socialist state and harbinger of world revolution. At the same time Russian émigré communities from Kharbin (China) to Berlin to Los Angeles preserved customs and culture of the old regime intelligentsia. Just as the "capitalist world" was getting accustomed to the continued existence of the USSR, the world economic crisis occurred and Hitler's Nazi party in German threatened to end communism (and, indeed, liberalism) once and for all. World War II nearly caused the collapse of the Soviet state, but the USSR's eventual triumph – at enormous cost – gave it a prestige and importance on the world stage never enjoyed by the Russian Empire.

The last theme covered in this book will be culture, from education and scientific achievements to painting, popular entertainment, propaganda, and literature. The strains and upheavals in Russian society are well documented in the classic novels of Ivan Turgenev, Fyodor Dostoevsky, and Lev Tolstoy. At the same time new technologies and growing literacy were encouraging the publication of adventure stories for peasants as well as the adornment of the walls of rural dwellings with brightly colored lithographs of popular myths or fairytales. Russian realist painting glorified history and revealed present injustices. Russian scientists such as psychologist Ivan Pavlov and chemist Dmitry Mendeleev became world-renowned for, respectively, drooling dogs and the periodic table of elements. Under Soviet rule many writers and artists emigrated, but many others continued their work in word, sound, and image to entertain and uplift their Soviet compatriots. Like everything else under communism, culture was to serve as a tool of revolution – informing, admonishing, and spreading enthusiasm for socialism. In the 1920s radical experiments were undertaken to "lift" proletarian culture and integrate it into Russian high culture. As the 1930s progressed, however, official views of culture became increasingly conservative, with poet Alexander Pushkin, composer Peter Tchaikovsky, and other old regime artists winning out over artistic experimentation. The Bolsheviks took culture seriously and used it in novel and exciting ways, from poster art to paintings to the so-called Agitprop (agitational propaganda) trains that brought music, visual arts, and speeches to the countryside.

Two Snapshots: 1861 and 1945

To set the stage for what will follow, let us consider two moments in time: the Russia of January 1861, just before the serf emancipation, and the USSR of June 1945, just after the end of World War II. These two snapshots will allow us to gauge the enormous differences that had taken place over the course of a long lifetime or, to put it another way, four short generations. Looking at the starting and end point of our narrative will also give the reader a framework to "fill in" with more details from the chapters that follow.

At the beginning of 1861, Tsar Alexander II ruled over an empire stretching from Finland to Alaska (which would be sold to the USA in 1867), the largest country in the world. In this enormous expanse lived hundreds of different peoples, from Poles and Jews to pagan Udmurts, Buddhist Kalmyks, and Muslim Tatars and Kazakhs. All were ruled from the capital of St Petersburg, in the extreme west of the empire, a city barely one and a half centuries old, having been founded by Peter the Great in the early eighteenth century on land taken from Sweden. But the tsar was always crowned in Moscow and traditional Russians looked upon St Petersburg with disdain and suspicion. The tsar ruled absolutely; there was no parliament of any kind and his word (in the form of an imperial order or *ukaz*) was literally law. At the same time laws and administrative practices differed hugely in various regions of the empire. The Finns had their own diet (legislature) and constitution, German elites dominated over Estonian and Latvian peasants in the Baltic provinces (today's Estonia and Latvia), and in peripheral regions on the western, southern, and south-eastern frontiers, governors general ruled with a minimum of interference from the center.

Economically the empire rested on an agrarian economy supported by serfdom. Serfs made up nearly half of the Russian peasantry (44.5 percent of the total population around 1860) and generally lived in poverty. Their landlords, mainly of noble birth, were not much better off, often in debt to the government and without the means of incentives to modernize their estates. The primitive state of Russian agriculture was not just a problem for peasants and landlords: it also severely restricted the government's ability to finance state expenditures, especially for the military. Serfdom and the primitive agricultural economy based on it had to be reformed if the Russian Empire was to afford the military outlays necessary to remain a major power.

In general, industrialization had barely touched Russia by 1861. To be sure, a textile industry existed in central Russia but the lack of a modern railroad net made it impossible to sell these textiles widely, and much of the production was bought up by the government (for military uniforms). The first major Russian railroad, connecting Moscow and St Petersburg, had only been completed in 1851, and Russians had to wait until 1862 and the completion of the St Petersburg–Warsaw line to be linked by rail with the rest of Europe. Although telegraph lines had been constructed in Russia already in the late 1830s, many provincial towns lacked access to the telegraph decades later, considerably complicating administration. In per capita income, railroad lines, literacy, and many other measures of modernization Russia lagged behind western and central European countries. If Russia was to be a great power, it would have to catch up or at the very least not allow the rest of Europe to get even further ahead.

In 1861 most subjects of the tsar lived traditional and religious lives. Whether pagan, Catholic, Lutheran, Russian Orthodox, Jewish, or Muslim, behavior and everyday life were governed by religious practices and holidays. While Russian Orthodoxy enjoyed privileges as the official and "ruling" religion in the empire, other religions were tolerated and protected. To be sure, "tolerated" did not necessarily mean respected or treated equally. Since the 1830 Polish Insurrection at least, the Russian government had looked on the Catholic clergy as seditious, nationalist Poles just waiting for a chance to oppose or even rise up against Russian rule. Jews were viewed as economically pernicious and religiously retrograde; with extremely rare exceptions they were not allowed to reside outside the so-called Pale of Settlement, those territories taken by Russia during the Polish Partitions of the late eighteenth century. Muslims did not serve in the Russian army (unlike Jews), although some Muslim landholding nobles, especially among Tatars, enjoyed wealth and prestige. Nearly all Russians followed the traditions of the Russian Orthodox Church, though significant numbers – so-called Old Believers – were alienated from the official church and continued, despite persecution, to follow the rituals prevalent before the religious reform of the later seventeenth century. But all Orthodox believers shared a number of similar customs and practices, such as having an icon in the "red corner" of each room, fasting nearly half of the year (at different levels of severity), and celebrating Easter (Paskha) in the spring as the most significant religious holiday.

The situation in summer 1945 was on the surface radically different from that of eighty-four years earlier. Having just defeated Nazi Germany after four years of intense and bloody fighting, the population of the USSR was exhausted but also jubilant. Now more than any previous moment in history, the USSR dominated on the international scene, as one of the two "superpowers" with the United States. While the USSR no longer ruled over some territories held by the Russian Empire in 1861 – most notably Alaska to the far east and Finland to the far west – the territory of the USSR was far more tightly controlled than the Russian Empire had ever been. Railroads, telegraphs, telephone, surface roads, mechanized armed forces, and air transport meant that Stalin's orders could be carried out far more efficiently than the tsar's could. The empire's ethnic and linguistic diversity was every bit as great in 1945 as under the tsar but now it was far more likely that non-Russians would know at least the rudiments of the Russian language. Besides "national languages" (e.g., Kazakh, Ukrainian, Georgian) Russian was taught throughout the USSR as the "common language" of all Soviet citizens. And for anyone wishing to rise to the top levels of a profession – and all the more so for ambitious party members – fluency in Russian was an absolute requirement.

On the international scene the USSR enjoyed prestige (and was feared) considerably more than Alexander II's Russia had been. The Soviet Red Army far exceeded in troop numbers any other country's military force. To be sure, the Russian army in 1861 had also been the largest in Europe, but Stalin's troops were much better equipped with modern weapons. Russian troops were stationed in Berlin and throughout Eastern Europe. While no one could say for sure what the next few years would bring, already in 1945 it was very clear that the USSR would not allow hostile governments to come to power in any countries it had liberated from the Nazis. To the east, Japan was in ruins and China was in the throes of a vicious civil war. To the south, the British Empire was in retreat from India and elsewhere and the USSR had every reason to think that the newly decolonized states would be pro-Soviet: after all, the USSR had consistently opposed capitalism and imperialism. So despite the devastation caused by the war, the Soviet leadership could look with optimism on the international scene. At the same time Moscow could not help but be troubled by the fact that the other superpower, the USA, possessed a thriving economy, large and well-equipped military forces, and the atomic bomb. Still, in summer 1945 the Americans were still – officially at least – allies of the Soviet Union and did not pose any immediate threat.

Economically the USSR in 1945 was vastly more developed than the Russia of 1861. Railroads connected east and west, north and south. Suburban trains

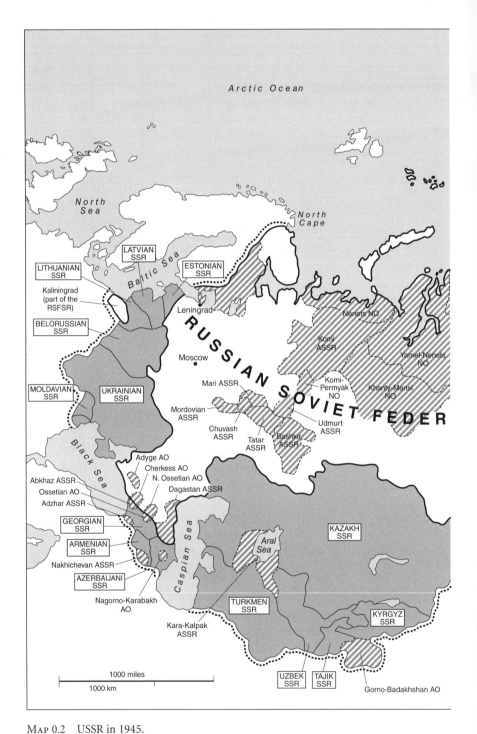

MAP 0.2 USSR in 1945.

Source: based on map in Dominic Lieven, *Empire*, Yale University Press, 2000, "Republics and Autonomous Regions of the Soviet Union, 1970."

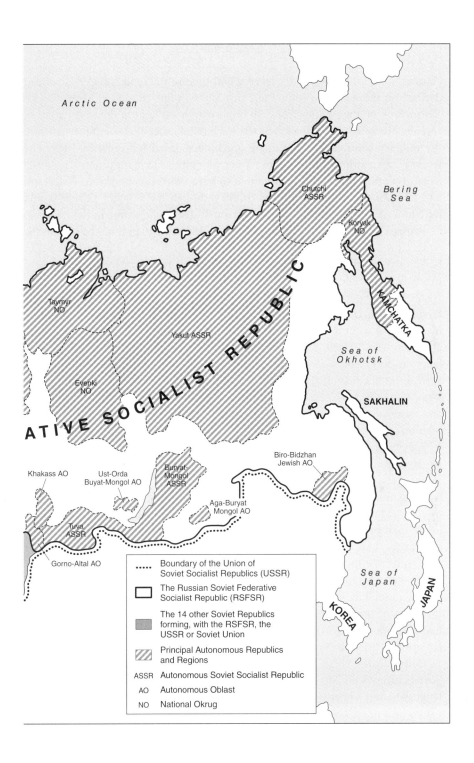

Arctic Ocean

Chutchi
ASSR

Bering
Sea

Koryak
NO

KAMCHATKA

Taymyr
NO

Yakut ASSR

Sea of
Okhotsk

Evenki
NO

SAKHALIN

ATIVE SOCIALIST REPUBLIC

Biro-Bidzhan
Jewish AO

Khakass AO

Ust-Orda
Buyat-Mongol AO

Buryat-
Mongol
ASSR

Aga-Buryat
Mongol AO

Tuva
ASSR

Gorno-Altai AO

Sea of
Japan

JAPAN

KOREA

..... Boundary of the Union of
Soviet Socialist Republics (USSR)

☐ The Russian Soviet Federative
Socialist Republic (RSFSR)

■ The 14 other Soviet Republics
forming, with the RSFSR, the
USSR or Soviet Union

▨ Principal Autonomous Republics
and Regions

ASSR Autonomous Soviet Socialist Republic

AO Autonomous Oblast

NO National Okrug

allowed millions of Soviet citizens to spend time in weekend cottages (so-called dachas) on the outskirts, while the Trans-Siberian line connected Moscow with Vladivostok on the Pacific Ocean. To be sure, railroad lines in the west had been severely disrupted and damaged by the war, rolling stock was overburdened, and the military continued to dominate much of railroad transport in 1945. The world's largest airline, Aeroflot, served all major cities and many points (especially in Siberia and the Far East) too remote to have railroad connections. Telegraph and telephone lines connected the country, though most Soviet citizens would have to wait several decades more to get a private telephone line in their homes.

Perhaps the most obvious change between 1861 and 1945 could be seen in the cities. Cities like Leningrad (formerly St Petersburg), Moscow, Kiev, and Tashkent had grown enormously over those decades. Even more impressive was the growth in smaller cities and the number of completely new industrial cities like the steel center Magnitogorsk. While most Soviet citizens continued to live in the countryside (only in the 1960s would the majority of Soviet citizens be urban dwellers), by 1945 over a third of the population lived in cities. And the countryside had also been transformed: gone were the landowner's estate houses and peasant villages of 1861, replaced by collective farms. Still, while some modernization of agricultural methods had occurred over these generations, Soviet peasants – now known as *kolkhozniki*, collective farmers – remained much poorer, less educated, and more isolated (they could not leave the collective farm without special permission) than other Soviet citizens.

Society had also changed dramatically. Soviet power had educated vast numbers of engineers, technological experts, doctors, and teachers. Thus the educated middle class of 1945 was far larger than its counterpart of 1861. The industrial working class had also grown enormously. Some groups, on the other hand, had disappeared nearly completely: landowners had been expropriated decades before, no shopkeepers or capitalists remained – except perhaps as managers in the enterprises they once owned, and the clerical estate had shrunk radically. Tens of thousands of educated middle-class Russians – the flower of the *intelligentsia* – had fled or been forced out of the country in the first decade of Soviet power and a new, rawer but more numerous educated class had taken their place. Some members of the old intelligentsia had remained, like scientist Ivan Pavlov who had died not ten years earlier in Leningrad, but thousands of others now lived as émigrés in Paris, San Francisco, and elsewhere.

Culturally the USSR had made enormous strides. By 1945 over 80 percent of Soviet citizens were literate, millions of books were published yearly in dozens of languages, and Soviet citizens could choose among thousands of periodicals (or would be able to, once wartime shortages ended, freeing up paper and journalists). Still, one cannot point to any novel of 1945 – or probably of the entire decade of the 1940s – that would be recognizable to western readers in the way that

Tolstoy's major novels (e.g., *Anna Karenina, War and Peace*) were and are. Censorship had certainly existed under the tsars, but since the early 1930s Soviet censors not only prohibited certain topics; they also demanded that Soviet writers present reality in a positive, progressive way. Similarly in the visual and even musical arts, Soviet artists operated in a far more constricted intellectual climate than the artists of 1861. Experiments like atonal music or abstract art were simply not allowed. With the Soviet state as the sole employer, artists or writers whose works were not deemed suitable had to find another way of earning their living. On the other hand, the expansion of literacy and publications meant that Soviet citizens could enjoy translations of works of world literature (in Russian and dozens of other languages from Ukrainian to Kazakh, many of which had lacked a standard written form in 1861), educate themselves and their children about the world and the latest scientific discoveries, and keep abreast of developments around the world.

We have seen here some of the major transformations that occurred over the nine decades from 1861 to 1945 and have also noticed certain continuing problems and continuities. In the chapters that follow we will examine in more detail how these changes came about over time, who caused or suffered them, who won and who lost. It is a story at once exhilarating and melancholy, fascinating and repugnant, full of glorious deeds and terrible crimes, development and destruction. Let us embark.

Chapter 1
Politics

In the modern world, politics forms the backdrop – perhaps the skeleton – of everyday life. The modern state taxes, conscripts, arrests or, to stress more positive matters, assures security, funds education, subsidizes culture, builds hospitals. Throughout Russian history, the state has played a strong role: classical *laissez-faire* liberalism never took root here. No Russian constitution ever proclaimed the right for "life, liberty, and the pursuit of happiness." Rather the Russian Empire and Soviet Union aimed to protect its citizenry but at the same time to preserve the political leadership from the mainly uninformed and possibly seditious masses. This dynamic between, on the one hand, state policies sincerely aiming at the betterment of economic and social conditions and, on the other, policies restricting basic freedoms (the exercise of which seemed potentially dangerous for state order and stability) will be seen throughout the pages that follow. Both Russian and Soviet politics was often "for the people" but almost never "through the people."

The Great Reforms: 1861–1876

The Great Reforms aimed to reform Russia's social and economic structure in the wake of the stunning defeat in the Crimean War (1854–6). Despite having the largest army in Europe and fighting on Russian territory (though, to be sure, a great distance from central Russia: the Crimean Peninsula is closer to Istanbul than to St Petersburg), Russia suffered a string of military setbacks at the hands of British and French forces. The failure of the army to protect Russian territory convinced even the most conservative Russians that fundamental reforms were necessary, if only to preserve Russia's military power and international prestige.

Yet there were other long-term causes for the reforms. The existence of serfdom, a form of unfree labor wherein peasants are not free to move and must give up a significant part of their labor and/or produce to the landowner, had long been seen as economically retrograde and morally repugnant. Liberal economists argued that serfdom (and unfree labor in general) stifled initiative and retarded economic development. Certainly industrial growth demanded a more fluid labor market than serfdom allowed. Many were disturbed by the moral implications of serfdom: arch-conservative Tsar Nicholas I (reigned 1825–55) reportedly feared divine retribution for presiding over such an immoral system, but at the same time dreaded the social upheaval that liberation might unleash. The obviously enormous complications of liberating nearly half of the Russian population (44.5 percent on the eve of emancipation, or even 80 percent if one includes "state peasants" owned by the imperial family and the Russian state) from serfdom prevented any significant reform from occurring during Nicholas I's reign. The fear of serf rebellion always formed the background to discussions about serf emancipation. The number of disturbances on the countryside had been growing from the 1830s to 1850s and it was feared that trying to reform the system might touch off a general serf revolt.

The death of Nicholas I in the midst of the Crimean War brought to the throne his son Alexander II (reigned 1855–81) who was neither very young (born 1818) nor particularly liberal, but enough of a realist to recognize the need for major reform. Still, Alexander proceeded cautiously. In 1856 he famously announced at a gathering of Moscow nobles that while he had no plans for the immediate emancipation, it would be better to abolish serfdom from above than to wait for it "to abolish itself spontaneously from below." The tsar called on landowners (in other words, the nobility) to discuss the details of emancipation and report to him. Perhaps predictably the nobles submitted proposals very favorable to their own interests, in particular keeping the best land and demanding payment from the freed serfs for any arable land they would thereby obtain. Frustrated with the unwillingness of landowners to sacrifice some of their landed wealth for the greater good of the Russian state, Alexander set up a Secret Committee on Peasant Affairs (later known as the "Main Committee") in January 1857 to consider concrete measures. Provincial committees of the nobility were allowed to submit proposals but these did not have to be accepted or even acknowledged by the Main Committee or the Editing Commission set up in 1859 to draft the actual emancipation statutes. The result was a compromise that satisfied few and disappointed nearly everyone.

One group that warmly welcomed emancipation was educated society, that is, the *intelligentsia* (see discussion in chapter 2, "Society," pp. 64–8). From abroad the radical writer Alexander Herzen hailed the tsar's planned reform in his influential newspaper *Kolokol* (The Bell). Within Russia the press eagerly discussed the plans for reform, taking advantage of a less stringent censorship regime. Alexander in part encouraged these discussions, seeing *glasnost* (a word used at the time referring to public debate) as a means of gauging public opinions. On the other hand, proposals seen as too extreme or infringing on the tsar's power would bring a reprimand or worse. Alexander II wanted, indeed needed, the help of educated Russians to help craft and carry through the reforms, but fearing for his own unlimited power, he was constantly apprehensive about giving them "too much freedom." Serfs themselves, as mainly illiterate, were not consulted at all.[1]

The cornerstone of the Great Reforms was the emancipation of the serfs. This measure – really a number of separate statutes – was immensely complex, filling a volume of over 300 pages. The act was announced in churches throughout Russia on February 19, 1861. The authorities' fear of peasant unrest can be seen both in the choice of this date (at the beginning of Lent, when Russians would refrain from drinking alcohol) and the mobilization of troops throughout the Russian provinces. As it turned out, despite eventual peasant disillusionment when the specific terms of emancipation came to be known, few significant clashes with government authorities or landlords occurred. The manifesto of February 19 abolished serfdom officially, making the sale of serfs with land impossible and ending the landlord's right to mete out corporal punishment on his serfs. On a practical level, however, little changed immediately: the manifesto admonished the peasants to continue to pay rents and other obligations to their landlords for the next two years.

The basic aim of emancipation was to sever the direct dependence of the peasantry on their former landlords, provide peasants with enough land so that they would not become an impoverished and dangerous rural proletariat, and leave the landlords with sufficient land to continue to serve the state as bureaucrats and army officers. Peasants were shocked to learn that they would not be granted all the land they tilled but only a part of it, and furthermore they would be obligated to pay for this land (few accepted the so-called pauper's allotment, which would give peasants a much smaller plot but without having to pay for it). Officially landlords were to receive compensation from the peasants only for the land's fair price, not for the loss of serf labor. In fact the rate at which land prices were figured was often inflated to their landlord's advantage. The former serfs were to make "redemption payments" for 49 years to compensate the government, which was to pay off the landlords. They did not, however, receive payment in cash but in government bonds that were to be cashed in over the following decades. In any case over half of the redemption payments from serfs to landowners went to paying the latter's accumulated debts to the state. Thus the emancipation statutes burdened peasants with long-term payments but did not provide landowners with capital that might have been used to modernize agriculture. In part a major banking crisis further undermined the government's ability to help finance emancipation, an indication of the weak financial position of the Russian state.[2]

Another important aspect of emancipation was that peasants did not gain private ownership of the land they "redeemed" from their former landlords. Instead the peasant commune (*obshchina*) owned the land and was responsible for redemption payments and other state obligations such as the providing of draftees for the army. In certain respects the serf's former dependence on the landlord was replaced by the peasant's dependence on the commune. Now the individual peasant had to ask the commune's permission to leave (e.g., to seek work in the city), paid taxes and redemption payments to the commune, and was called to serve in the army through the commune. There were many reasons why the government decided to entrust the commune with these responsibilities, ranging from a Slavophile belief in the intrinsic moral value of that institution to practical considerations of administration and social control. The Russian state wished to "fix" the newly liberated peasants in some kind of institution: the idea of millions of "loose" peasants freely roaming the empire was terrifying. By entrusting the land to the commune, the government gave this institution considerable power, in particular as land would be periodically redistributed among peasant households according to their growing or declining size. With the tiny numbers of provincial and rural police, the Russian state needed to count on the commune to maintain order on the countryside.

The actual implementation of the emancipation provisions took years and in some cases even decades. When peasants realized that the landlords were to retain much land – and often the best quality fields – while former serfs would be saddled with payments over two generations, they were appalled. Peasants often refused to believe that this could be the long-awaited liberation; rumors persisted of a far more favorable "Golden Charter," supposedly issued by the benevolent tsar but hidden by evil nobles. The worst case of peasant unrest after the February 19 manifesto came in the village of Bezdna in Kazan province. Here in April 1861 the semiliterate peasant Anton Sidorov, after urgently consulting the extremely complex legal language of the statutes, announced that the tsar had granted the land to the peasants and had ended payments and labor duties to landlords. As thousands of peasants flocked to the village to hear Sidorov's interpretation, the local governor sent troops to arrest him. In the ensuing clashes over 50 peasants were killed and hundreds wounded. While Bezdna was the most significant incident of peasant unrest in the wake of emancipation, the general reaction of serfs to the terms of emancipation was stunned surprise, followed by deep disappointment and resentment.[3]

Several other significant reforms were also carried out, most remarkable among them reforms of local government, education, the justice system, the military, and censorship. Local government reform was undertaken at two different levels: on the countryside and in urban areas. On the countryside an entirely new institution was set up in 1864, called the *zemstvo* (pl. *zemstva*), a word that evoked the noble land assemblies of centuries earlier (*zemlia* is the Russian word for "land"). The *zemstva* were elected in rural districts as well as for the entire province. At both levels the nobility was over-represented, but this was probably inevitable given the greater literacy and wealth enjoyed by this privileged group. More important was the fact that peasants were represented in all *zemstva* where they voted on an equal basis with representatives of the landowning nobles and clergy. The *zemstvo* was allowed to levy taxes to pay for important practical measures: building roads and schools, encouraging the local economy, setting up clinics and hiring agronomists to help modernize local agriculture. Besides these practical benefits for the local economy, the *zemstvo* influenced the development of civil society in Russia. The *zemstva* demonstrated that the Russian public (not government) could elect its own representatives – at least at the local level – who then capably carried out measures for the public good. *Zemstvo* members came to see themselves as representatives of the local people and not infrequently clashed with government administrators carrying out the orders of the central government. Participation in these bodies thus became a kind of "school for democracy." But not every region of the Russian Empire had *zemstva*: in the western and Polish provinces, for example, the government mistrusted the largely Polish nobility and refused to allow the establishment of *zemstva* there. There were also no *zemstva* in Siberia or the north of Russia because the nobility was too weak there, the government felt, to assure their proper and loyal functioning.[4]

The pre-reform administration of towns was generally agreed to have been inadequate, inefficient, corrupt, and unable to cope with basic economic and sanitary needs. The city reform law of 1870 introduced elected city governments, though the vote was slanted toward those holding considerable urban property. The elected city council (*duma*) selected from among its members an executive board (*uprava*) and a mayor (*golova*), who had to be approved by the minister of internal affairs. The elected city governments, introduced first in central Russia and later elsewhere (though not in many non-Russian regions), allowed local citizenry to play a significant part in the economic development of their town and carried out improvements such as the construction of sewers, roads, public transport systems, and the like.

Reforms attacked the educational system from both ends, so to speak. The Elementary School Statute of 1864 allowed and encouraged the creation of schools at the local level, but did not provide money. Funding had to be sought from three sources: *zemstva*, the Orthodox Church, or the Ministry of Education. University reform was particularly significant: a reform statute of 1863 abolished previous restrictions, opened universities up to members of all estates from peasant to noble, and granted universities a significant measure of self-government. Conservatives would soon complain that the university statute opened up a dangerous "free zone" where radical ideas could be discussed and advocated with impunity. Liberals saw matters differently, considering that the free exchange of ideas was crucial for the training of self-sufficient, enlightened, and professionally competent citizens.

Perhaps the single most successful reform of all was the judicial reform of 1864, which swept away a justice system universally acknowledged to have been corrupt, inefficient, and cumbersome. This reform set up a legal system independent of government administrators. Court trials were to be open to the public with both oral and documentary evidence accepted; juries decided on the guilt or innocence of the accused. With judges appointed according to their professional capabilities and enjoying lifetime tenure, it became more difficult for officials to intimidate or silence court trials. The need for competent judges and lawyers required the creation of a Russian Bar, a professional class of lawyers. Legal education was much improved and lawyers came to see themselves not just as advocates for a specific client but as the champions of justice. Many trained in the law helped create the first Russian political parties after 1905, and it is perhaps not without significance that V. I. Ulianov (Lenin) received a legal education. Parallel to and separate from the main legal system described here was a system of peasant courts generally presided over by a justice of the peace who dispensed quick, if not always legally sophisticated, justice.

Although not abolished, censorship was significantly mitigated during the Great Reforms. New regulations of 1865 abolished most "preliminary censorship" but allowed the government to confiscate, punish, or even shut down publishers responsible for material deemed in violence of the censorship law. For periodicals, a government license was required for publication and some periodicals received the privilege of not undergoing preliminary censorship. As writers and editors quickly grew accustomed to pushing the limits of censorship, a great variety of books, journals, and newspapers appeared, catering to growing literacy rates.

As we have seen, the primary impulse toward the Great Reforms was provided by Russia's defeat in the Crimean War. The complexities of the military reform meant that it was the last major reform, going into effect on January 1, 1874. The urgent need for sweeping reform of the Russian army was provided by the outstanding performance of the Prussian army in the Franco-Prussian war and the subsequent unification of Germany in 1871. With a newly united, economically vibrant, and militarily strong neighbor on its western border, the Russian Empire could not delay in improving its own military institutions.

This new conscription law obliged every male Russian (in principle) to serve in the military for a period ranging from six years to only a few months. Thus an illiterate peasant lad called to arms would serve six years, but if he had attended an elementary school his service would be reduced to only four. University graduates served only six months and if they volunteered for service this term was cut in half. After this period of active service draftees were enrolled in the reserves for an additional nine years. The principle of all Russians regardless of birth or social class carrying out military service was thus established, though in practical terms peasants were far more likely to serve for six years than their middle-class or noble coevals would. Moreover budget shortfalls meant that only a fraction of young Russian men were actually called to arms.[5] Besides the conscription law, the military reform set up new officers' schools based on western models, abolished corporal punishment for soldiers, and established literacy and basic educational training for illiterate recruits. In the next half-century before World War I more young Russians learned basic literacy in the army than in elementary schools.

The Great Reforms radically changed the political structure of Russia, transforming serfs into free peasants, creating an open and independent judiciary, allowing the public to contribute to local economic development through the elected city governments and *zemstva*. But the fundamental political reality of Russia – autocracy, the unlimited rule of the tsar – remained untouched. Alexander II refused even to allow the creation of any kind of advisory body elected from among his subjects. Moreover the government expressly forbade provincial *zemstva* to cooperate or even meet with *zemstva* in neighboring provinces, fearing that such cooperation would infringe on the administrative prerogatives of tsarist officials. In effect the tsar refused to recognize the population of Russia as citizens to whom the welfare of the country could be entrusted. Rather they remained the tsar's subjects, subject to his will and without any right or possibility to influence further political reform. This, combined with specific disappointments in the terms of serf emancipation, the limited scope of local government, and continued censorship, meant that in the next few decades a significant number of the tsar's subjects began to seek more radical – even revolutionary – solutions to Russia's economic, social, and political ills.[6]

Government under Siege: 1876–1904

On April 4, 1866, a young former student, Dmitrii Karakozov, approached Tsar Alexander II in a garden near the Winter Palace in St Petersburg, aimed a gun at him, and pulled the trigger. The gun failed to go off and the tsar was unhurt; Karakozov was instantly set upon by bystanders, arrested and eventually hanged. Alexander's first words to Karakozov were "Are you a Pole?", reflecting the tsar's knowledge of the great bitterness Poles felt toward him after his crushing of their November Insurrection in 1863–4 (see chapter 3, "Nations," pp. 97–8). In fact not just Poles but many Russians – Karakozov replied to Alexander that he was a "pure Russian" – were dissatisfied with tsarist rule, the failure to grant peasants more land, and the lack of political reform. Karakozov's shot was the work of an unstable individual, but it reflected broad dissatisfaction that would only grow in the next decades. The gap between the Russian people, whether peasants, educated professionals, or even privileged noble landowners, and the tsar's government grew steadily, as Russians sometimes expressed themselves openly but were sometimes forced underground. The unwillingness or inability of the tsarist regime to compromise on political issues or at least to coopt some segments of the population meant that when revolution finally broke out in 1905 the regime barely survived, only to be entirely broken and swept away by the stresses of World War I.

Alexis de Tocqueville once remarked that the most dangerous moment for a government was when it embarked on major reforms. Certainly this appeared to be the case in Russia in the 1860s. Following his brother Nicholas I's repressive rule, Alexander II's apparent liberalism gave rise to hopes for concessions and reforms that far exceeded anything the tsar would or could advocate. We have already seen the delicate balancing act that serf emancipation entailed in order at least partially to satisfy the demands of the liberal public, the landowners, and the peasantry. Similarly Alexander wanted to ease somewhat the extremely restrictive policies followed by Nicholas I toward Poles, but his desire to allow more free play for Polish language and culture (including the opening of a university in Warsaw) backfired in the November 1863 Polish insurrection against Russian rule. The Polish uprising and Karakozov's attempt on Alexander's life convinced conservatives, and to some extent the tsar himself, that reform needed to be scaled back to prevent further unrest – or worse. Thus from around 1870 at the latest we see the paradoxical situation in which the government grew more and more suspicious of reform even as the Russian public showed increasing enthusiasm for liberal and even radical changes.

The alienation of Russian society from its government grew steadily in the 1860s and 1870s.[7] The *intelligentsia* defined itself in opposition to a Russian state that allowed it no direct political role. The government's unwillingness to introduce even a conservative constitution like that in Prussia or Austria (from 1867 Austria-Hungary) meant that many middle-class professionals and businessmen could not see the tsarist state as supporting their interests. But the more immediate threat to the status quo came from radicals, mainly young university students who concluded that reform had run its course and failed. These young radicals advocated "going to the people" (when educated Russians said, "the people," they meant the peasantry) to convince peasants of the need for revolution. During the summer of 1874, thousands of idealistic young Russians left the towns and streamed to the countryside to propagandize the peasantry. The attempt was a failure. Peasants were certainly unhappy with the terms of emancipation, but continued to have more trust in the far-away figure of the tsar than in young radicals from the city.[8]

The failure of the "crazy summer" of 1874 convinced many young radicals that the peasantry were not ready to embrace radical measures. Since peasants remained stuck in a conservative and patriarchal worldview, the radicals would have to make the revolution themselves. The most important group dedicated to carrying out this revolutionary program was Land and Liberty, which soon divided between a moderate faction that stressed education and propaganda among the peasants, and the more radical "People's Will," which advocated terrorist violence. In the years 1879–81 the People's Will carried out a number of attempts on Alexander II's life, blowing up the tsar's train and even infiltrating the Winter Palace itself and detonating explosives there, destroying a ballroom where the tsar was supposed to have been.

These repeated well-organized attacks threw Alexander and his advisors into a panic. The tsar wooed public opinion by dismissing the reactionary minister of education and appointing a more liberal minister of the interior, Loris-Melikov. Most remarkably Alexander agreed to create a new advisory body that would include some representatives from *zemstva* and elected city governments. While this body would have lacked real legislative power, it could have been the first step toward giving Russian society a more direct voice in influencing the tsar's policies. Whether this body could have defused some of the discontent among the Russian public toward its government we will never know, for on March 1, 1881, the People's Will finally succeeded in assassinating Alexander II.[9]

The new tsar, Alexander III, firmly rejected any compromise with liberal or radical demands and quickly rounded up those responsible for his father's death; the police and the Russian public were astonished at the small number of conspirators. Of course the hoped-for peasant uprising and revolution did not materialize: the peasantry viewed the tsar's assassination with horror. Rather than attacks on tsarist police or administration, the only mass-scale violence that followed Alexander's assassination was a wave of attacks on Jews – so-called pogroms – that occurred in the southwestern provinces of the empire (present-day Ukraine) during the summer of 1881 (see chapter 3, "Nations," p. 112). While Alexander III did not foment or condone attacks on Jewish property or persons, his open antisemitism certainly did little to discourage such violence. Alexander III also tried to reach back to pre-Petrine times (that is, before the westernizing reforms of Peter the Great) and present himself ceremonially as a tsar of the Muscovite era, ruling over ethnic Russians rather than a multiethnic empire. As Richard Wortman has documented, Alexander III endeavored to introduce would-be Russian elements into his public persona, from his coronation ceremony to his home life to court ceremonies. In this context it is also significant that Alexander III was the first tsar since before Peter the Great to wear a full beard, as was the tradition among male Russian Orthodox believers.[10]

The reign of Alexander III (1881–94) was one of reaction, repression, and chauvinistic Russian nationalism. For Alexander socialism, liberalism, Jews, and Poles came down to more or less the same thing: alien threats to Russian tradition and political stability. Alexander was no ideologue but, tall of stature, cut an impressive figure. His sheer physical bulk seemed to symbolize stability, conservatism, and the unchanging nature of the Russian Empire. His policies aimed to arrest the spread of liberal and socialist ideas, to stymie the development of non-Russian cultures, strengthen the Russian center over the non-Russian peripheries (see "Russification," chapter 3, "Nations," pp. 97–8), and to restrict – though not eliminate entirely – many of his father's reforms. At the same time economic growth during his reign was impressive: industry, the railroad network, the middle and working classes all grew. But the apparent stability of Alexander III's reign masked a more disturbing truth: the growing gap between Russians and their government. While discontent was forced underground, it did not disappear.

Alexander III's son, Nicholas II, both admired and feared his father. He had not expected to become tsar (his elder brother died unexpectedly) and did not welcome the enormous power and responsibility thrust upon him by his father's death in 1894. Many hoped that the new tsar would revert to his grandfather's more liberal policies or at least mitigate his father's repressive policies. But when the Tver' province *zemstvo* dared to refer to such liberal hopes in a letter to the new tsar, Nicholas reacted harshly, dismissing these suggestions for reform as "senseless dreams" and promising to continue his father's policies.[11]

By the late nineteenth century, the reactionary policies of Alexander III and Nicholas II could not assure stability. Strikes in 1895 and 1896 demonstrated the growth of working-class discontent and showed that socialist ideas were spreading among Russian workers. An even more direct challenge to the existing political order was the formation of the Socialist Revolutionary (SR) party in late 1901. The SRs were the heirs of the 1870s radicals in at least two important ways: first, in their vision of a peasant-based revolution, and second in their embracing of terrorism as a political tactic. In 1902 the minister of the interior, D. S. Sipiagin, fell to an SR attack; his successor, V. K. Pleve, would be blown up by another SR terrorist in 1904.[12] Mere months after the forming of the Socialist Revolutionary party, a young Marxist, Vladimir Ilyich Ulianov (better known by his pen name, Lenin), published a pamphlet abroad calling for a small but dedicated party of activists who would dedicate their lives to the revolutionary cause. Lenin's 1902 pamphlet, *What Is to Be Done?*, may be seen as the founding document of what would become the Bolshevik faction of the Russian Social-Democratic party. Of course all of these radical parties could function openly only outside Russia, but the growth of their underground organizations within Russia was noted with concern by the tsarist police.

--------------------   The Beginning of the End: 1904–1914   --------------------

For almost two decades after the assassination of Alexander II, the Russian Empire may have seemed economically backward and politically reactionary, but its stability did not appear under threat. The revolutionary movement that had killed Alexander II in 1881 was driven abroad or underground. Still, the resentment felt by members of educated society and the growing working class toward a government that seemed oblivious of their interests continued to grow. This, combined with continued peasant poverty, meant that in case of crisis the government lacked a broad base of social support. Precisely such a crisis was caused by the poor performance of the Russian army and navy against Japan in 1904–5, a crisis that developed into the revolution of 1905.

The origins of the Russo-Japanese War may be traced to at least two fundamental causes: the weakness of China and Russia's expansion toward the Pacific Ocean. To be sure, Russia had claimed territory along the Pacific coast for centuries, but it was only with the construction of the Trans-Siberian Railroad in the 1890s that sizeable numbers of Russians came to settle in the Far East, in particular in the railroad's terminus at Vladivostok, a city founded only in 1860. In order to reduce the length of the railroad's eastern portion the Russian government reached an agreement with China in 1896 allowing the construction of a line across Chinese Manchuria, founding the Chinese Eastern Railway and creating a major new Russian city in the middle of that railroad at Kharbin. The completion of this line in 1901 caused the Japanese government – itself recently industrialized and extending its influence over Korea after a war with China in 1895 – to fear further Russian incursions into China and Korea.[13] In frustration at what they saw as Russian foot-dragging over evacuating their troops from Manchuria the Japanese decided to launch a preemptive strike, attacking the Russian navy at Port Arthur on the Liaotung Peninsula without a formal declaration of war on February 8, 1904.

The Russo-Japanese War began badly for Russia, with the almost total destruction of the Pacific Fleet at Port Arthur, and went downhill from there. A second fleet was dispatched around the world only to be met by the Japanese in late May 1905 at Tsushima and promptly sunk. The Russian army's performance on land in Manchuria was less abysmal, but the major battle of Mukden (March 1905) could at best be called a draw. By summer 1905 the financial strain of war combined with unrest at home made the Russian government desperate to find a way to end the war. The Peace of Portsmouth was negotiated with the help of US President Theodore Roosevelt and signed on September 5, 1905.[14]

For Russian and world history, more important than the Russo-Japanese War itself was the unrest it generated within the Russian Empire. From the start, the Russian military seemed unable to hold its own against Japan – an enormous humiliation for a major European power fighting non-Europeans. The incompetency of the military leadership seemed to epitomize the inability of the government to accommodate and further the economic and political needs of the tsar's subjects. And, with the military tied up in Manchuria, the government was helpless to put down large-scale unrest in the European part of the empire. Demonstrations, strikes, peasant attacks on manor houses, and the killing of government officials forced Nicholas II to make major concessions, but the disturbances were crushed by the use of military force only in late 1905 and early 1906.

The revolution of 1905 has a specific beginning date: January 9 (o.s.), "Bloody Sunday." On this date a mass demonstration was planned, with thousands of marchers convening on the Winter Palace in central St Petersburg. Carrying icons and portraits of the tsar, the demonstrators planned to present a petition to their sovereign who, unbeknownst to them, was not in residence. The demonstration had been planned in advance but most of the participants were unaware that permission for their march had been denied by the imperial authorities. Worse yet, the incompetent tsarist police panicked at the size of the crowd streaming into palace square and opened fire, leaving over 100 dead and many more wounded. The shock of this unprovoked attack on unarmed petitioners rapidly turned to anger and, within days, further protests and strikes. In the Baltic and Polish provinces the government essentially lost control of the situation, and even in Moscow and St Petersburg policemen refused to walk alone in the streets, fearing a bullet in the back.

Gradually Nicholas and his government, forced into a corner, made some concessions. In mid-February it was announced that the emperor would summon together "elected representatives of the people" as a kind of proto-legislature. But by the time this consultative legislature known as the "Bulygin Duma" (named after the Minister of the Interior) was to be elected, events had made it superfluous. Faced with anarchy in Warsaw, mass attacks on landed estates in the Baltic, and major strikes in the Russian interior, the prime minister, Sergei Witte, saw no other possibility of restoring order except by making significant concessions to liberal opinion. On Witte's urging, Nicholas II grudgingly issued the October Manifesto, promising to respect civil rights and to create a legislature elected by broad suffrage. Most importantly the October Manifesto promised that henceforth no law would take effect without the approval of this legislature, the Duma. For liberals, the October Manifesto could be seen as a significant concession and a first step toward a constitutional order. Radicals, however, rejected it as too little (vague and narrow) and too late (Nicholas's insincerity as a constitutional ruler was only too apparent). The October Manifesto did split the opposition to tsarist rule, but was unsuccessful in ending the revolution.[15]

The revolution of 1905 was brought to an end not by tsarist concessions, but by the more familiar tactic of repression. The St Petersburg Soviet (the word means "council" in Russian), set up by workers and leftist intellectuals to press for radical demands and coordinate strikes, was closed down by the authorities in November and December. As troops returned from Manchuria, they were used to suppress demonstrations, strikes, and rural unrest. In April 1906 Peter Stolypin was appointed Minister of the Interior and charged with the task of restoring order, a process bitterly described by one of his opponents as aiming to create "the quiet of the graveyard." Stolypin's energetic use of repressive measures caused his contemporaries to speak of the "Stolypin necktie," referring to the noose used to hang opponents of the regime.[16]

Stolypin is a complex character who has been called tsarist Russia's "last hope." While he did not shy away from the use of violence against the regime's opponents, Stolypin also recognized the fundamental reality that the government needed to work out a *modus vivendi* with the Duma. He was a convinced conservative and supporter of monarchy, but he could also agree to compromises with more liberal elements in Russia. The first Duma convened in May 1906 and was dominated by the left liberal Kadet (short for "Constitutional Democrat") party. The inability of the government to work with the Duma resulted in the latter's dismissal after 10 weeks and calls for a new election. The second Duma (February–June 1907) was, from the government's point of view, even worse. The socialists who won nearly 200 seats were more interested in denouncing the government and quarreling with the right-wing delegates than in creating a functioning legislature. When Stolypin, by now prime minister, claimed to have discovered evidence of an antigovernment plot among the socialist Duma members and demanded that 16 of them be stripped of their parliamentary immunity, the Duma balked. Stolypin seized the opportunity to dissolve the Duma, arrest the delegates, and issue the law of June 3, 1907, significantly changing the Duma electoral law to guarantee a more Russian and more pro-government (i.e., conservative) assembly.

Stolypin's dissolution of the Duma and issuing of a new electoral law was a flagrant violation of the principle that all new laws must be approved by the parliament. In a sense, however, he had no choice: to quote one of his most famous speeches (uttered to radicals in the Duma): "You want great upheavals. I want a great Russia." A Duma dominated by socialists and left liberals would have little interest in cooperating with the tsarist government. Stolypin's electoral law helped create a much more conservative assembly dominated by the Octobrist party (the name refers to their belief that the October Manifesto was a reasonable concession upon which to base a new government) with rightist and nationalist parties. Even with this much more moderate Duma, however, Stolypin and the government could not always have their way. Stolypin discovered that parliaments have a way of developing their own ethos and pride, which does not always correspond to the government's immediate wishes.[17]

While the Third Duma managed to "live out" its entire five-year term (1907–12) – the only pre-revolutionary Duma to do so, Stolypin did not survive. Despite his devotion to preserving and strengthening tsarist rule in Russia, Nicholas II, and even more his wife, Alexandra, strongly disliked their faithful servant. Incapable of decisive action himself, Nicholas deeply resented strong men like Stolypin. Probably the prime minister would have been dismissed had he not been assassinated by a former police informer under murky circumstances at the Kiev opera house (in Nicholas's presence) on September 1, 1911. Stolypin was the last capable and memorable prime minister of imperial Russia.

This is not to say that imperial Russia was doomed as early as autumn of 1911. But neither liberal society, on the whole, nor the industrial proletariat, nor the peasantry could firmly support the status quo. Stolypin had recognized this and pushed through a major reform aimed at creating a class of individual peasant landowners (see chapter 4, "Modernization," pp. 127–8). Whether this reform could have fulfilled Stolypin's hopes is impossible to gauge, as World War I intervened before the reform could make a broad impression on the Russian countryside. From 1912 major strikes broke out at the Lena goldfields in Siberia and in industrial cities throughout the empire. Revolutionary agitation spread in factories and the countryside. Then in summer 1914, faced with the prospect of its Balkan "little brother," Serbia, being overrun by Austria-Hungary, and fearful over the growing military strength in Germany, Russia was drawn into World War I.

-------------------- War and Revolution: 1914–1917 --------------------

Less than a decade after defeat against Japan, the Russian Empire did not want a new war. Although enormous efforts had been made to strengthen the army, many suspected that the German army was both better trained and better equipped. The events of August 1914 were to prove the pessimists correct. The German war plan focused on avoiding a two-front war by knocking out France with a massive assault in the first weeks of the war, and then turning on Russia. The Schlieffen Plan assumed that with its greater distances and weaker railroad network, Russian mobilization would require several weeks before the Russian army could pose a serious threat to Germany. The Germans thus concentrated the vast majority of their attack on the western front, with only a dozen or so divisions guarding the border between East Prussia and the Russian Empire.[18]

The Russian attack across that border in August 1914 deeply shocked German public opinion and forced the military to transfer troops from the western front, which may have been decisive in preventing French defeat. Once reinforcements for the German units in East Prussia arrived, however, the counterattack was devastating to the Russians. The Battle of the Masurian Lakes of August and September 1914 was a huge defeat that revealed both the superior training and equipment of the Germans and the incompetence of the Russian generals. After this battle Russian troops would never again threaten German territory.

The Russian army fared somewhat better against the Austrians. The Galician city of Lwów (now L'viv in Ukraine) was taken in early September, and Galicia was to remain under Russian occupation for nearly a year. But from spring 1915 on, the Russian army suffered a number of losses, pulling out of Galicia, losing Warsaw in summer 1915, and abandoning Vilna (today Vilnius in Lithuania) in autumn 1915.[19] In the war's first year Russia suffered four million casualties. While the initial crises in supply and ammunition were to some extent corrected by 1915, it seems clear that the only reason Russia survived militarily was Germany's choice to expend the bulk of its men and materiel on the western front.

The outbreak of war was accompanied in Russia – as elsewhere throughout Europe – by a wave of patriotism. Suddenly it became risky to be heard speaking German, and a mob sacked and torched the German embassy in St Petersburg. On the front, entire civilian populations were rounded up as "suspect," and predictably Jews were among the worst hit by these mass deportations to the Russian interior.[20] In May 1915 a riot aimed at foreign stores and merchants broke out in Moscow and ended with the destruction of many foreign-owned (or simply suspected of being foreign-owned) businesses. On a popular level there is much evidence to show a marked increase in nationalist rhetoric and action, but the government too adopted policies to strip foreign residents of their businesses and land. Thus the war years helped spur Russian national consciousness and, conversely, antiforeign sentiment aimed both at foreign citizens and at the diverse ethnic groups living within the Russian Empire (see chapter 3, "Nations").[21]

Part of the reason why Russians sought a scapegoat in foreigner residents and non-Russians was the almost unremittingly bad news from the front. From spring 1915 onward the Russian army was in nearly constant retreat, and politically matters stood no better. At the beginning of the war, the Duma had overwhelmingly embraced the war effort, with only a few left-wing delegates (including six Bolsheviks) refusing to approve war credits (they were promptly arrested). But the government squandered the possibility of better relations with the Duma and educated society by continuing to treat the Duma as an enemy or rival rather than a partner. Committees set up by *zemstva* and city Dumas to help the war effort, refugees, and the wounded, often found their efforts stymied by government officials.[22]

After some initial enthusiasm for the war, particularly among the educated middle class, war weariness set in. The peasantry, who made up the bulk of the Russian army, had never welcomed the war and, with continued defeats and withdrawals, voices calling for an end to the war grew ever stronger. The fact that the empress was by birth German (though raised in Britain) and the presence in the palace of the unsavory peasant adventurer Grigorii Rasputin did not help matters.[23] With his unfailing instinct for doing the wrong thing, Nicholas II decided in late 1915 to leave Petrograd for the army general headquarters or *stavka* (near the front lines in what is now Belarus) and assume direct control of the military. Despite the impassioned efforts of his advisors to dissuade him, arguing that he was needed in Petrograd and his presence at headquarters would associate him with military setbacks, Nicholas insisted that his place was at the head of his troops. In fact the tsar's ministers' worst predictions came true: Nicholas's presence at the *stavka* injected an unhealthy dose of court politics into military decisions, while his absence from St Petersburg gave credence to wild rumors that his "German" wife and her lascivious peasant lover Rasputin were running Russia.

The desperation of educated Russians at the military and political state of affairs is shown by two events of late 1916. On November 1, 1916, the leader of the left-liberal Kadet party, historian Pavel N. Miliukov, gave an extraordinary speech in the State Duma. Setting down a litany of government failures, Miliukov punctuated each with the question "Is this stupidity or treason?" Taking advantage of the fact that the Duma president could not understand German, Miliukov also read aloud from German newspapers, including a line accusing the empress of interfering in politics. For a liberal in a time of war to openly accuse his own government of complete incompetence or even treason is more than unusual; it is practically unprecedented and deeply shocking. Miliukov himself later wrote that his speech was interpreted as "an attack signal for the revolution," though he denied any such radical purpose, arguing that he merely wanted to clean up the corruption and incompetency that were hindering the war effort.[24]

The second event of late 1916 was in its own way even more shocking. On December 17 a group of conspirators led by Prince Felix Yusupov and a cousin of the tsar invited Rasputin to Yusupov's palace where they poisoned, beat, and shot the Siberian holy man. By murdering Rasputin, these arch-conservatives hoped to end his influence over the empress and to bring the tsar back to St Petersburg. In fact Rasputin's influence on policy was minimal – he had always opposed the war – and his death solved nothing.

In early 1917 Russians were cold, hungry, and thoroughly sick of the war. Supply problems exacerbated food and fuel shortages in Petrograd. Inflation had sparked a number of strikes and rural unrest in 1916; no improvement of living conditions could be expected before war's end. In this atmosphere demonstrations for international women's day (March 9, n.s.) came together with unhappy women, who had waited hours in line only to be told that basic foodstuffs had not been delivered, to cause serious street disturbances in Petrograd. Away at the *stavka* (military headquarters), Nicholas ordered the street demonstrations repressed, but local police and military were incapable of restoring order – indeed, many went over to the side of the demonstrators. Within days a Provisional Government was set up, drawing mainly from liberal Duma politicians. Finally realizing the gravity of the moment, Nicholas attempted to return to Petrograd, but railroad workers prevented his train from reaching its destination. Stranded in his train car outside the capital, the tsar was met by a delegation of conservative Duma politicians who begged for and finally received his abdication. The Romanov dynasty and imperial Russia was no more.[25]

Nicholas's abdication ended autocracy in Russia, and Duma politicians stepped in to prevent a power vacuum, setting up the Provisional Government that was to rule only until proper elections could be held. After an initial short period of euphoria, however, the Provisional Government was faced with the same problems as its imperial predecessor. In particular the decision to continue the war effort, we can see in retrospect, was a mistake. Similarly the blanket amnesty of political prisoners declared by the Provisional Government in its first days undermined the liberal regime's shaky stability by allowing more radical elements to stream back to Russia and St Petersburg. However, the Provisional Government was not acting on its own: its power was held in check by the more radical Petrograd Soviet, elected by factory workers and military units, which could threaten strikes or demonstrations if challenged. The weakness of the Provisional Government is revealed by its acceptance of the Petrograd Soviet's "Order No. 1," which fatally undermined military discipline by allowing soldiers to challenge orders (except on the actual front line). The period between February and October 1917 (o.s.) is characterized by this "dual power" (*dvoevlastie*), in which the Provisional Government bore the responsibility for unpopular decisions while under pressure from the Petrograd Soviet to accept quite radical policies. The blanket amnesty of political prisoners was followed by the abolition of the death penalty and the annulment of all laws restricting the rights of religious and ethnic minorities. In July suffrage was extended to all citizens 20 or over, making Russia the first major European power to grant the vote to women.

The Provisional Government, as its name implied, saw itself merely as a caretaker until a Constituent Assembly could be elected, a constitution agreed upon, and democratic elections for a proper government held. The transition to democracy is difficult under any circumstances, and in a poor country like Russia in the midst of war, it took months even to set up elections for the Constituent Assembly. In the scant eight months of its existence the Provisional Government lurched from crisis to crisis. An attempt to rally the military in a summer offensive ended in a near complete collapse of the Russian army. The leftist parties (including, though reluctantly, the Bolsheviks) attempted to grab power in July, but this ill-planned coup attempt failed. From July the prime minister was the moderate socialist Alexander Kerensky, the only member of both the Petrograd Soviet and the Provisional Government.[26] Kerensky first attempted to protect the Provisional

Government from a right-wing coup (the so-called Kornilov affair) in August and then from a left-wing power grab in October. While he succeeded in defeating General Kornilov's attempted coup, his government crumbled before the Bolshevik seizure of power. The Provisional Government disappeared not with a bang and barely with a whimper. To quote Lenin, "Power was lying on the street – we merely stooped down to pick it up." Russia had become the world's first socialist state – but few thought that the Bolsheviks would be capable of holding power for long.[27]

–––––––––– The Revolution's First Decade: 1917–1927 ––––––––––

The Bolsheviks, as good Marxists, did not imagine that Russia would long remain the only socialist country. They hoped that their example would be the spark that would set off the worldwide revolution long awaited by socialists. But initially they had more immediate concerns than spreading world revolution. Afraid that their hold on power would not last long, they aimed to make the strongest possible impression on history by passing a series of radical acts. Within days the Bolsheviks called for negotiations with the Germans to end the war, gave their approval to peasant seizure of landlords' estates, and even abolished the word "minister," adopting instead Trotsky's suggestion of the far more revolutionary-sounding "people's commissar." Thus the Bolshevik government was known as the "Council of People's Commissars" or Sovnarkom. Trotsky took over foreign affairs, where one of his first actions was to publish secret agreements between Russia and the western allies, which promised, among other things, Russian control over the Bosporus and Dardanelles. These revelations were extremely embarrassing to western leaders, as they had steadfastly denied the existence of any agreement that might prolong the war and were now shown to be liars. The Bolsheviks also publicly repudiated the tsarist debt, meaning that thousands of middle-class investors, especially in France and Belgium, found that their gilt-edged Russian securities were now worthless.

A month after the Bolsheviks came to power elections to the long-awaited Constituent Assembly took place. While the Bolsheviks gained nearly 10 million votes (almost a quarter of all votes cast), the largest vote getter was the Socialist Revolutionary party with over 17 million votes (41 percent). The Bolsheviks did best in urban areas, while the SRs, as expected, were overwhelmingly supported by the peasantry. The liberal Kadets now found themselves on the right wing of the political spectrum and gained a mere two million votes (4.8 percent). The Bolsheviks allowed the Constituent Assembly to gather in Petrograd on January 5, 1918, but when the delegates refused demands to recognize the Bolsheviks as the legitimate government, Lenin decided to shut it down. Fearful that once

Тов. Ленин ОЧИЩАЕТ
землю от нечисти.

FIGURE 1.1　Mikhail Cheremnykh and Victor Deni, "Comrade Lenin Cleanses the Earth of Scum." 1920.
Source: Photos 12 Collection/Alamy.

disbanded, even for the evening, they would not be allowed to reconvene, delegates continued their discussions until early the next morning. At 4 a.m. they were
told, memorably, *karaul ustal* – "The guard is tired." The assembly was dissolved
and, just as feared, not allowed to meet again. The Bolshevik party, not popular
congresses, would decide Russia's future.

　　The most immediate problem facing the Bolsheviks was the war. The German
government had aided Lenin's return to Russia and their investment appeared to
have paid off magnificently.[28] But Lenin could not dictate policy on his own, as
subsequent events would show. Negotiations began at Brest-Litovsk (now on the

Polish-Belarusian border) where the Bolshevik representatives were shocked at the draconian demands of the Germans. The Germans called for "national self-determination" for Poland, Ukraine, Finland, the Baltic provinces, and other territories that in 1914 had formed part of the Russian Empire. While Lenin and the Bolsheviks agreed to the principle of national self-determination, they hoped that most non-Russians would remain in some kind of federated state with the Russians. In any case the German demands were seen as too onerous and the Bolshevik party leadership rejected them in January 1918, much to the realist Lenin's fury. After further fruitless negotiations Trotsky announced to the astonished German delegation a policy of "no peace, no war" in mid-February, shortly after which the German army simply began marching into Russia. Lenin furiously demanded that any German conditions be accepted, and after several attempts succeeded in convincing the Central Committee that peace at any cost was necessary. The Treaty of Brest-Litovsk was signed on March 3, 1918. Compared with 1914 borders, the treaty deprived Soviet Russia of some 1.3 million miles of territory, including major industrial regions, and 62 million citizens, few of whom were ethnic Russians.

A week after signing the treaty, the Soviet capital was transferred from Petrograd (now some 20 miles from the Finnish border) to the historical capital, Moscow. In the same month the Bolsheviks changed their party name to "communist" to emphasize the difference between themselves and the Social Democrats who in various European countries had initially supported the war. At the same time serious frictions arose between the Bolsheviks and their erstwhile allies, the left SRs. Angered by the shutting down of non-Bolshevik periodicals, the dissolution of the Constituent Assembly, and the ever narrowing of political expression, the SRs reverted to their old tactic: terrorism. On July 6 a member of the left SR party assassinated the German ambassador, Count Wilhelm von Mirbach. SRs led insurrections against communist power in several cities and a number of prominent Bolsheviks were likewise assassinated. SR armed resistance provided the communists with the opportunity to be done with these uncomfortable allies and, at the same time, to sweep away all manner of "class enemies." The secret police set up already in December 1917 and known as the Cheka (from the first letters in Russian of "Extraordinary Commission for Combating Counter-Revolution and Sabotage") targeted not just SRs but anyone suspected of opposing the revolution and the Communist Party. Thousands were arrested and many were summarily executed. In the midst of these repressions or "Red Terror" the SR Fanny (Fanya) Kaplan attempted to assassinate Lenin, wounding him in the arm and chest. While the communist leader recovered from his wounds, they are thought to have hastened his early death in 1924.

As Fanny Kaplan was taking aim at Lenin in Moscow, communist rule was facing a far greater threat than the SRs: the so-called Whites. Various anticommunist groups had gathered in the former borderlands of the empire: in summer 1918 General Anton I. Denikin was pushing north along the Volga while troops under Admiral Aleksandr Kolchak threatened Soviet power from the east. Britain and France, furious at the Russian withdrawal from the war, assisted the White effort with materiel and to some extent with men. But the Whites were never unified, either ideologically or militarily. White supporters ranged from liberal democrats, such as former Kadet leader and foreign minister under the Provisional Government Pavel Miliukov, to conservative monarchists and antisemitic nationalists. The White armies were strong enough to threaten the communists in 1918 and 1919, but never succeeded in unifying their efforts to deal the Leninist regime a fatal blow.[29]

The Soviet regime survived the Civil War for several reasons. First of all, it always maintained control over the central part of Russia, including Moscow and St Petersburg. The fact that Moscow was always in the hands of the "Reds" meant that troops could be shifted by railroad from east to west, north to south. The main munitions factories also remained in Bolshevik hands. The communists also benefited from excellent leadership and a strictly organized party. The Whites had no leaders comparable to Lenin or Trotsky, creator of the Red Army. It is remarkable that this entirely unmilitary man Trotsky, who had spent his life in libraries, cafés, and editorial offices, suddenly proved himself an effective – and ruthless – leader of the Red Army. The one-party state and the Cheka's repressive apparatus allowed the Reds to introduce such unpopular measures as the military draft and grain confiscations from peasants to feed the troops. It must also be noted that the ruthlessness with which the communists deal with real or imagined enemies was also effective in stifling dissent during these critical years. Peasant support for the Bolsheviks, though never complete or unalloyed, also played a role. While peasants quickly became disillusioned with many communist policies, when push came to shove, they always supported the Reds over the Whites, whom they associated with their former landlords.[30] Finally the lack of unity among the Whites and the lackluster support for them on the part of the Allies (support that was to be much exaggerated by Soviet historiography) allowed the Reds to prevail.

The Bolsheviks had counted on a European-wide revolution when they took power in October 1917. Battles between Reds and Whites in Finland and the Baltic region, radical uprisings in some parts of Germany from late 1918, and the creation of the "Soviet" governments in Munich and Budapest in 1919 made it seem that world revolution might really be on the horizon. In fact by the end of the year the radicals had been defeated in all of these places. As the Civil War wound down in late 1919, Soviet Russia was drawn into a war with Poland over Belarusian and Ukrainian territory. Polish troops took Kiev in early May 1920, but the Red Army's counterattack was so successful that it was decided – against

Trotsky's advice – to pursue the war onto Polish territory. By taking Warsaw, the communists hoped, direct contact with the German working classes could be established to spark revolution there and throughout western Europe. It was not to be. In August 1920 Polish troops led by Marshall Józef Piłsudski defeated the Red Army on the Vistula River north of Warsaw, an event celebrated in Poland as the "Miracle on the Vistula." Exhausted by war, Soviet Russia and the Republic of Poland signed the Peace of Riga on March 18, 1921, ending hostilities and setting the Polish–Soviet border that would be in place until 1939.[31]

The phrase "War Communism" is traditionally used to describe communist policy in 1918–20, that is, during the Civil War. The Bolsheviks came to power without any real experience in administration, running enterprises, or supervising an economy. While Lenin and his colleagues did not set out to nationalize all aspects of the economy, within months this process was already far advanced. Factory and enterprise owners, not surprisingly, seldom welcomed communist rule. They were thus pushed aside (or worse); their place was taken by workers' councils or appointed administrators. Lack of managerial experience and simple incompetence devastated the already weak Russian economy. Basic infrastructure from railroads to electricity functioned fitfully if at all; citizens went hungry and cities remained cold and dimly lit. It became common to see a formerly well-to-do woman at the market trying to convince a peasant to give her a few kilograms of potatoes for a silk shawl, a silver spoon, or some piece of jewelry.

By late 1920 the Civil War was over. The country lay in ruins, factories and mines lay abandoned, millions were hungry and without shelter. The currency was ruined (in late 1920 a ruble was worth less than 1 percent of its 1914 value), basic foodstuffs and heating material were expensive and hard to find. The utter misery of everyday life led to strikes and demonstrations, despite severe repressions. Most shocking of all for the communist leadership was the Kronstadt rebellion of February–March 1921. Baltic sailors had been among the most fervent supporters of the Bolshevik cause, so this uprising at the island naval base near Petrograd showed just how far popular support for Soviet rule had eroded. The sailors' demands ranged from the practical (such as the right to bring food from the countryside to the cities, abolition of special "privileged" rations) to the political (return to secret ballot, reestablishment of press freedom for the left). The Communist Party, meeting at its Tenth Congress in Moscow, rightly viewed the uprising as a direct challenge to Soviet rule. After negotiations failed, communist troops stormed the island and crushed the rebellion in blood.[32]

Lenin remarked that the Kronstadt rebellion "illuminated reality like a flash of lightning." Presumably he meant that the fury expressed by the sailors revealed that the continued existence of Soviet rule in Russia required rethinking. While the communists resolutely rejected the sailors' call for more democracy and freedom of expression, their practical economic demands were to some extent

met by the New Economic Policy (NEP). Faced with almost total economic collapse in early 1921, the Tenth Party Congress decided to make concessions to the
market, small business, and in particular to the peasantry: these became the main
NEP reforms. NEP left much of the economy unchanged in state hands: all big
business, international trade, banks, and a state-run (and much reviled) system
of retail stores remained under government control. NEP did, however, open up
a certain space for the individual entrepreneur, trader, and farmer. Peasants had
to pay a tax on the foodstuffs they produced but could freely market their produce.
Butchers and bakers could set up small stores with a limited number of employees.
Overnight the retail trade was back in private hands. Artisans like shoemakers,
tailors, and seamstresses could also legally produce and sell wares. Cafés, restaurants, music halls, and other such entertainment establishments could open again.
Politically, however, the NEP did not bring any change. The Communist Party
remained the only tolerated political grouping and even factions within the party
were banned at the Tenth Party Congress.

As the terrible famine of 1921–2 (especially in the Volga region) showed, the
NEP did not instantly solve Soviet Russia's economic problems. This tragedy in
which millions starved (and many others were saved by the foreign assistance
reluctantly allowed into the region by the communist leaders) was itself a bitter
legacy of the Civil War period. Only a year or two later, however, the economy
showed distinct signs of improvement. (On the economic effects of NEP, see
chapter 4, "Modernization," pp. 130–2.) By 1926 existing factories had been
repaired, railroads put back in operation, mines pumped out and returned to
production, but, for impatient communists, this was all too little. They longed
for crash industrialization and a leap from a mainly agrarian country to a modern,
industrialized Soviet Union.

Unhappiness among communists with the slow pace of economic growth and
with the toleration – at least at the retail level – of a market economy was exacerbated by the strikingly negative social aspects of NEP. In an effort to prevent
runaway inflation, government expenditures were severely limited. Many orphan-
ages were shut down for lack of funding, and city streets filled with abandoned
or orphaned children who engaged in petty crime, sold their bodies, and threatened law-abiding citizens. This phenomenon was so widespread that the Russian
language acquired a new word for such children – *bezprizornye*, those without
anyone to look after them. At the opposite end of the income scale were the so-
called *nepmen*, profiteers who made large profits and spent it ostentatiously (while
honest communists had to scrimp). The revolution was to have brought about a
fairer, more egalitarian Russia, but during the NEP years social injustice and
inequalities continued to exist. The dissatisfaction – disgust even – felt by many
at the social injustice and vulgarity of NEP society encouraged many communists
to support an end to NEP and a more radical line. Many of those disgusted

with NEP would thus support Stalin's agrarian collectivization and crash industrialization of the late 1920s.[33]

NEP did not bring about any significant political liberalization. Institutionally the USSR was proclaimed on the last day of 1922, which further cemented the position of the Communist Party and its leadership. Since 1917 the undisputed leader – though not dictator – of the communists had been Lenin. But the "old man" (as he had been called since his thirties) suffered a stroke in May 1922 that left him partially paralyzed. Against doctors' orders he tried to continue work while bedridden by dictating texts to his faithful wife, Nadezhda Krupskaia, but Lenin would never be the same. Among the texts set down by Krupskaia was one that has come to be known as "Lenin's Last Testament" in which he angrily called Stalin "too rude" and recommended that other members of the Central Committee "think about a way to remove Stalin from [his] post [as General Secretary of the party]." At the same time Lenin critically evaluated members of the Central Committee, praised Trotsky's "outstanding ability" but also noted his (and everyone else's) weaknesses. When the great man finally passed on in January 1924, the Politburo read aloud the "testament," Stalin offered his resignation (which was not accepted), and it was decided to keep the text secret and to govern as a body.[34]

While the Politburo (Stalin, Trotsky, Grigory Zinoviev, Lev Kamenev, Alexei Rykov) publicly minimized differences between themselves, behind the scenes battle lines were being drawn. At first Stalin allied with Zinoviev and Kamenev, who feared and resented Trotsky's arrogance, charisma, and popularity with much of the rank and file. Trotsky's Menshevik past and pre-1917 statements critical of Lenin were brought up against him in party circles. But soon Zinoviev and Kamenev began to mistrust Stalin's motives and switched their support to Trotsky after the Fourteenth Party Congress in 1925. This ill-advised move allowed Stalin to play on the resentment against internationalist Jews (the three were born Ovsei-Gershon Radomyslsky [Zinoviev], David Bronshtein [Trotsky], and Lev Rozenfeld [Kamenev]) felt by many rank and file communists. Cooperating with Rykov and the new Politburo member Nikolai Bukharin, Stalin had Trotsky expelled from the party in 1927 and exiled from the USSR in 1929. Once Trotsky was out of the way, Stalin went ahead in 1928 with a program of crash industrialization (the First Five-Year Plan) and the brutal collectivization of agriculture. When Bukharin, Rykov, and Mikhail Tomsky (the head of the labor unions) opposed Stalin's policy (in particular the violence used against the peasantry), they lost their influential positions and their places on the Central Committee. By 1930 Stalin was by far the most powerful man in the USSR.

Why did Stalin prevail over Trotsky, an opponent undoubtedly more intelligent, charismatic, and with a far better understanding of Marxist thought? In part Trotsky's own strengths worked against him: he was brilliant, no one denied, but

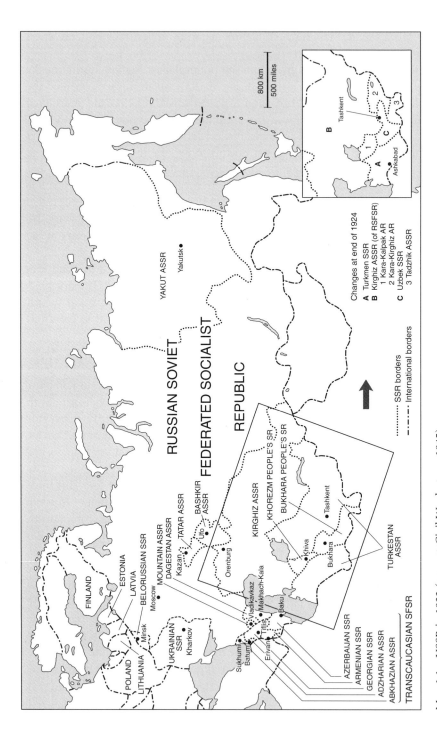

MAP 1.1   USSR in 1922 (or post-Civil War but pre-1945).

Source: based on Donald Treadgold, *Twentieth Century Russia*, 8th edn., Westview Press, 1995, p. 152.

could also be brutally intolerant of incompetence and stupidity among his subordinates. Like many intelligent men, Trotsky underestimated his opponent: Stalin did not possess a scintillating intellect, but he did grasp human psychology and probably understood the ill-educated communist rank and file better than his more intellectual fellows at the party's top levels. Stalin's acceptance of the job of general secretary when this position was first created in April 1922 also helped him in his struggle for power. The majority of members of the Politburo, including Trotsky, were only too happy to let Stalin assume the bureaucratic drudgery that this administrative position represented. Stalin, however, saw clearly that the general secretary, who had control over all party files, could easily use that information for his own benefit. While recent archival research has called into question the thesis that Stalin was able to "stack the party ranks" with his own men, it is clear that Stalin's position as general secretary gave him unfettered access to information that helped him win power.[35]

Trotsky's brilliant public speaking and charisma earned him a wide following among communists, but his dynamism and arrogance also offended – and frightened – at least as many. For many communists, Trotsky, more interested in his own brilliance than in party unity, seemed a much greater danger than Stalin. Stalin might well have been, in the communist David Riasanov's famous words, "a gray blur," but he was a far better politician than Trotsky. Stalin's careful use of fears and resentment toward Trotsky, as well as his utter lack of scruples in switching positions and misrepresenting his own and others' positions, helped bring about Trotsky's downfall. It should also be remembered that Stalin was skillful at subtly playing on antisemitic and anticosmopolitan resentments within the party. In his suspicion of Jewish intellectuals, even those with impeccable communist credentials, Stalin was also closer to the average party member than his opponents. For many, supporting Stalin made sense from the viewpoint of party unity as well as personal ambition.

Building Socialism: 1928–1939

NEP was never formally ended but, for practical purposes, the expulsion of Trotsky from the party and the adoption of the First Five-Year Plan on October 1, 1928, spelled its abandonment. The next decade would be one of immense human suffering but also impressive economic transformation. As we have seen, many communists saw NEP as a compromise with market forces unworthy of a workers' state. Controversies raged within the Communist Party, however, on just what steps should be taken to replace the NEP with a more socialist economic order. For the communists, as for Marxists in general, the "free market" was nothing more than a fiction that allowed capitalists to exploit workers. While the *nepmen* of the 1920s were hardly "capitalists" on a grand scale, they certainly used market forces to make profits, and spent their money nearly as rapidly as they made it. The adoption of the First Five-Year Plan meant a transition to a planned and supposedly more rational economy. The plan set down production targets not only for entire industries (coal mining, steel making, machine building, etc.), but for individual factories and enterprises. The advantage of the plan was that it allowed the government to coordinate resources and inject capital and manpower where needed in the economy. In reality, however, this supposed advantage was often reduced or eliminated by the disadvantages of bureaucracy and unrealistic targets.

The most serious potential obstacle to crash industrialization was the attitude of the peasantry. In order for quick industrialization to go forward it would have to be financed by the payment of low prices for agricultural goods (produced by peasants) and charging high prices for consumer goods (consumed by peasants). Would the peasants simply stockpile their grain rather than sell it? Would they even rebel against Soviet power? These were the fears that propelled the communist leadership to embark on a mass campaign to collectivize agriculture. The harvest of 1928 had not been terrible, but the amount of grain actually put up for sale (at relatively low prices) was inadequate to feed the growing cities and to export grain to pay for needed western technology. It seemed clear that the only way to force peasants to give up their grain at state-controlled prices was to use pressure – or force. In the long run the only way for the Communist Party to maintain this pressure on the peasantry, Stalin concluded around 1928, was to set up collective farms. The collective farms would serve at least three purposes. First, they would allow large-scale production that would be more productive than existing small peasant farmsteads. Second, the collective farms would be headed by managers – preferably Communist Party members – who would be responsible to see that sufficient grain was sold to the state. Finally the collective farm would destroy old rural elites (the so-called kulaks, or wealthy peasants) whom the communists suspected of hindering recruitment of peasants into the party (less than one rural dweller in 300 was a party member).[36]

After the grain procurement crisis of 1927–8, when the peasants' refusal to sell grain at low prices led to bread shortages, Stalin decided to proceed with a crash collectivization program. Initial application of violence in certain regions – the so-called Urals-Siberian Method – had brought in significant amounts of grain without setting off the feared peasant rebellion. But in 1928 still only around 3 percent of farms had been collectivized. In November 1929 Stalin announced the push for mass collectivization and the following month declared that kulaks had to be "liquidated as a class." In the next three months any relatively wealthy peasant – which could mean a farmer who merely owned a cow or horse – was labeled a kulak, singled out for arrest, confiscation of property, physical violence, and worse. Not only individuals but their entire families were targeted, often forced to leave the village (arrested or not) with barely the clothes on their back. Anyone who openly opposed collectivization or tried to organize resistance was also denounced as a kulak and shared a similar fate.

In the next three months intimidation, arrest, and violence forced many peasants to sign on to the collective farms. The communist authorities also tried to woo poor peasants by offering personal property (clothing, implements) confiscated from kulaks and painting a picture of a promising future of mechanized, prosperous agriculture. Most peasants remained skeptical, but faced with the threat of arrest or violence, gave in. Others simply fled to the cities where labor shortages meant that work was easy to find. Historians have estimated that at least six million peasants were forced to leave their homes in this short period.

On March 2, 1930, Stalin published a key article entitled "Dizzy with Success" in *Pravda*. Noting that over one-half of peasant households had been collectivized, Stalin approvingly wrote, "a radical turn of the countryside towards socialism may be considered as already achieved." Most of the article, however, took a far more negative tone, criticizing the use of violence and coercion in Turkestan (and by implication, other isolated areas) as "distortions," "bureaucratic," and "unworthy threats." The article stressed that the goal of collectivization was admirable and well within grasp, but the "voluntary principle" should be followed and "excesses" avoided. To be sure, this was all breathtaking hypocrisy coming from the man who had pressed for rapid "dekulakization," but it allowed Stalin to blame problems and violence on overzealous underlings. The timing of the article should also be noted: the communists feared that the huge disruptions on the countryside would prevent spring sowing from taking place, causing mass famine. "Dizzy with Success" aimed to reassure peasants so that they would return to agricultural work. It worked. Peasants returned to the fields, but many also dropped out of the collective farm: the collectivized rate by June 1930 was only 24 percent. Now the party turned to more gradual and methodical means of persuasion, with the result that by 1941 98 percent of agricultural land had been collectivized.

Despite promises, collectivization did not improve life for peasants. In 1932–3 a famine swept the grain-producing regions in the south of the USSR, mainly but not exclusively in the Ukrainian Soviet Socialist Republic (SSR), as well as Kazakhstan. This famine was specifically exacerbated by the unrelenting demands on local collective farms to provide grain for the cities and Russian center. Ukrainian historians refer to this famine in which millions starved as the *Holodomor*, seeing it as a cynical attempt at genocide against the Ukrainian people. Other historians have questioned the specifically Ukrainian nature of the tragedy, noting that other regions such southern Russia and the Urals also suffered severely and that a higher percentage of Kazakhs than Ukrainians perished (see chapter 3, "Nations," pp. 104–5). No one disputes, however, that Soviet grain procurement policy forced local collective farms to give up their grain for the cities even while locals were starving.[37]

The first Five-Year Plans (for more detail, see chapter 4, "Modernization," pp. 132–5) set unrealistic and unattainable goals, but the actual achievements were nonetheless impressive. The production of energy (from coal to electricity) increased, as did mining in nearly all sectors, steel production, and (particularly from 1934 to 1936) the construction of new industrial plant and even entire new cities (of which the steel-producing city Magnitogorsk is only the most famous). Certain sectors of the economy lagged behind or even declined, in particular consumer goods. By the mid-1930s the Soviet economy was humming, but most Soviet workers lived in crowded, unhygienic, depressing dwellings. The rationing of basic foodstuffs such as bread (begun in 1928) was ended in the mid-1930s, prices were high and many goods were simply unavailable. Clothing was expensive and of poor quality. In general the entire economy was geared toward the production of capital goods (i.e., more factories, more heavy industry, and by the late 1930s more weaponry) rather than making life more pleasant for Soviet citizens. However, unemployment disappeared, cities grew, industry developed, and production figures expanded throughout the 1930s.

The fevered pace of industrial expansion in the 1930s was matched by a feverish level of political discourse. Newspapers warned of constant threats on the international scene (and, to be sure, the rise of Adolf Hitler to power might well worry any Soviet citizen, communist or otherwise). Soviet citizens were admonished to be constantly wary and on the outlook for "enemies," "wreckers," "spies," and the like. The young American John Scott, who worked in the USSR in the mid-1930s, recalled seeing a play about a school training spies and terrorists to be used against Soviet interests. The climax of the piece was the revelation that "number 1," an actor made up to look like Hitler, had a Russian passport with the name Ivan Ivanovich Ivanov (i.e., "John Jones," the Russian everyman). In such an atmosphere of distrust and fear, mistakes or laziness could easily be labeled "wrecking" or sabotage and severely punished.

The first "show trial" used for propaganda purposes was the Shakhty trial of 1928 in which engineers were accused of plotting with the bourgeoisie and foreign governments to wreck Soviet development. Meanwhile, real or imagined opponents of Stalin were arrested or exiled – such as Trotsky in 1929. In the 1930s the charge of "wrecking," implying sabotage and malicious destruction of state property, came to be routinely leveled at workers whose incompetence or mistakes caused production breakdowns or wastage. But while arrests for "wrecking" were by no means rare, mass political arrests began later with the show trial of old Bolsheviks Zinoviev and Kamenev (with 14 others) in 1936 and lasted until the outbreak of World War II in 1939. Explaining the background of her own arrest in 1937, Evgeniia Ginzburg wrote, "The year 1937 began, to all intents and purposes, at the end of 1934 – to be exact, on the first of December." On that day the popular head of the Leningrad party committee, Sergei Kirov, was assassinated – possibly by Stalin's order – in his office. At the time, Stalin expressed grief and outrage at the murder of an upright communist and friend, and would later accuse his enemies of planning the murder.

Historians have long argued over the supposed link between the assassination of Kirov in December 1934 and the Great Terror that picked up speed some two years later. For one thing, did Stalin order Kirov's killing? Robert Conquest argued that Stalin had Kirov rubbed out as a feared competitor for the party's loyalty, but more recently historians have shown that no hard evidence backs up such a view (though many continue to hold it).[38] But why the lag of two years between Kirov's death and the major show trials and mass arrests? One theory is that the purges began in an attempt to root out corruption and inefficiency but in the feverish atmosphere of the 1930s snowballed into mass repressions.[39] More recently Paul Hagenloh has argued that the mass repressions of the later 1930s derived from the frustration felt by communists at the continuing existence of "alien elements" (whether slack workers, Trotskyites, or speculators) "endangering" Soviet society.[40] Recent studies do not deny the importance of Stalin in the terror, but emphasize also the thousands of "little Stalins" who eagerly participated in repressions out of fervor, to gain professional advancement, or to exact personal revenge.

The accusations levied against old Bolsheviks like Zinoviev, Kamenev, Bukharin, and Trotsky were patently absurd. These were, after all, men who had dedicated their entire lives to the revolutionary cause. How could anyone believe accusations that they had turned into agents of British imperialism, the international bourgeoisie, or (a specific charge against Trotsky) Nazi Germany? It also seems bizarre for Stalin to have mounted such a campaign when his own power was already virtually unchallenged. Historians speculate that he was possibly motivated by a combination of paranoia and thirst for revenge against party members who had once slighted him. In an atmosphere of generalized paranoia the widely publicized trials against these formerly influential party leaders snowballed into a mass purge of party members. Stalin's repeated calls for "vigilance" were then repeated endlessly by anyone in a position of power – better to arrest ten than to leave any possible "enemy" at large.

High party officials, who were more likely to have had contact with those arrested and were also perhaps more threatening to Stalin, were especially likely be arrested. Of the 1966 delegates to the Seventeenth Party Congress in 1934, over half (1,108) were arrested. Among Central Party committee members, two-thirds were arrested (98 of 139). Similarly a purge of the officer corps led to the arrest of three of five field marshals (a rank only recently revived), 90 percent of Soviet generals, 80 percent of colonels, and thousands of lower-ranking officers.[41]

During these terrible years millions were arrested and disappeared into the Gulag (forced-labor camp) system, many never to return. Hundreds of thousands were shot as spies, wreckers, and Trotskyites. An anonymous denunciation would frequently lead to arrest, even without any concrete proof – causing thousands of unscrupulous individuals to settle personal scores, denounce neighbors with attractive apartments, accuse their boss (to rise professionally), and the like. There is perhaps some poetic justice in the fact that 20,000 NKVD (secret police) operatives were also swallowed up in the arrest wave, including the head secret policeman in 1936, Genrykh Yagoda (executed in 1938). The arrest and disappearance

О каждом из нас заботится Сталин в Кремле

Figure 1.2   Viktor Govorkov, "Stalin in the Kremlin Cares about Each One of Us." 1940. *Source*: Novosti Collection/Topfoto.

of millions of Soviet citizens, it has been argued, helped create a fearful and paranoid atmosphere that in certain ways persisted in the USSR even after Stalin's death in 1953.[42]

While the arrest wave was peaking in 1937–9, the international situation appeared ever more ominous. Moscow watched uneasily as Japanese troops continued to conquer Chinese territory, and in August 1939 Soviet and Japanese troops engaged in a massive tank battle on the Mongolian border. Since 1933 Germany had been ruled by Adolf Hitler, whose maniacal antisemitism was paralleled by his fanatical hatred for communism. In 1938 Hitler had extended German rule to Austria and destroyed Czechoslovakia the following year – all without having to resort to arms. The next victim was obvious: Poland. Britain and France warned Hitler against any hostile action, while the world hoped that the fear of a two-front war would deter Nazi aggression. Thus the news of the Molotov–Ribbentrop Pact (named after the Soviet and German ministers of foreign affairs who negotiated it) on August 23, 1939, came as a massive shock to the world and most of all to Poland. And indeed, barely a week later, on September 1, 1939, Nazi troops invaded Poland. World War II had begun.

World War II: 1939–1945

When the Wehrmacht poured across the Polish border on September 1, 1939, the USSR initially took no military action, as dictated by its nonaggression pact with Nazi Germany. Then on September 17 Soviet troops crossed the border set by the Peace of Riga and occupied the eastern half of Poland, following a secret clause of the Molotov–Ribbentrop Pact dividing Poland and the Baltic States into "German" and "Soviet" spheres of influence.[43] By the end of September the Polish army was no longer capable of open resistance and went underground, while the Polish government went into exile. Following further negotiations with Nazi Germany, the USSR began to put pressure on the Baltic states (Estonia, Latvia, Lithuania) to allow Soviet bases there, legalize the Communist Party, and align their foreign policy with the USSR. This process culminated with the absorption of the three Baltic states into the USSR in July–August 1940. The former eastern territories of Poland were absorbed into the Belarusian and Ukrainian SSRs, with the city of Wilno (now Vilnius) given to Lithuania.

The USSR applied similar pressure on Finland by trying to persuade the Finns to accept a large portion of Soviet territory to the north in exchange for shifting the Soviet–Finnish border near Leningrad some 20 miles further west. The Finns assured the Soviet negotiators that neither Finnish nor foreign troops would threaten the security of the USSR, but with the important arms-producing city Leningrad so close to the Finnish border, Moscow was not reassured. The Finns, on the other hand, had every reason to mistrust Soviet intentions; furthermore, the shift of the border in the south (away from Leningrad and toward Helsinki) would have rendered useless their carefully built defenses (the so-called Mannerheim Line). In November 1939 the Red Army attacked Finland and suffered major losses. For two months the small, but nimble and well-trained Finnish troops held back the Soviet aggressors. Meanwhile, the unprovoked attack caused the USSR to be expelled from the League of Nations. But eventually the military and economic strain was too great for the Finns who were obliged to sign an armistice with the USSR in March 1940, giving up nearly 10 percent of Finnish territory and twice that of Finnish industry. Almost a million refugees fled their homes rather than remain under Soviet rule.

The Soviet–Finnish "Winter War" (Finnish: Talvisota) was a military and public relations disaster for the USSR. Soviet casualties have been estimated as at least 270,000 men – fighting an army that could mobilize only 180,000 men. While Red Army troops and commanders quickly learned from the first disastrous weeks of fighting, the overall impression remained that the Red Army was disorganized and weak. Foreign commentators argued that the purges in the officer corps had destroyed morale, placing inexperienced and incompetent men in key leadership positions. The military losses against Finland sent a shock wave through the Communist Party and Red Army leadership. Major reforms and improvements would be rushed through in the following year. Adolf Hitler and his military advisors were careful observers of the Red Army against the Finns, but underestimated the extent to which the communists learned from their mistakes.[44]

The western border of the USSR changed significantly in 1940: besides acquiring land in Finnish Karelia, the three Baltic republics of Estonia, Latvia, and Lithuania were absorbed into the USSR after fraudulent plebiscites in summer 1940. Formerly Polish territory was incorporated into the Belarusian and Ukrainian SSRs. To the south, Moscow handed the Romanian government an ultimatum in June 1940 demanding the return of formerly tsarist lands then known as Bessarabia. This territory was absorbed into the Moldovan SSR in August 1940. In all of these regions the year between incorporation into the USSR and the Nazi attack of June 1941 is remembered as a period of mass arrests, deportations, nationalization of property, and crude Stalinist propaganda.

The Molotov–Ribbentrop Pact had never been seen as permanent; Nazi Germany and the Soviet Union differed far too much in ideology for that. From September 1939 onward, especially after the disastrous Winter War with Finland, the USSR was desperately rearming and reforming its armed forces in preparation for war. At the same time Stalin went out of his way to avoid giving the Germans any excuse for a premature attack. In 1941 Stalin was convinced that the Red Army could not yet withstand the Wehrmacht; he had also persuaded himself that Hitler would wait at least another year before attacking. Despite a great deal of evidence from a number of sources that an attack was indeed planned, Stalin continued to believe that rumors of an impending invasion were spread by the British in order to pull the USSR into the war. Thus when Operation Barbarossa exploded across the Soviet frontier in the early morning hours of June 22, 1941, Red Army commanders were caught off guard. The Wehrmacht threw over three million soldiers – both Germans and allies such as the Hungarians and Romanians – against the weak Soviet defenses. At first commanders on the front lines frantically asked whether they were allowed to shoot back. In the first months of the war over a million Red Army soldiers were taken prisoner; most would die under the brutal conditions of German captivity. By autumn as the cold winds of winter began to blow, the Wehrmacht had reached the outskirts of Moscow and Leningrad.[45]

Stalin apparently suffered a nervous breakdown upon receiving word of the German invasion. He was unable to make a radio address calling on Soviet citizens to resist the invaders; ironically, that task fell to Patriarch Sergius of the Russian Orthodox Church who urged Russians to destroy and expel the invaders just as the Napoleonic troops had been destroyed in 1812. Nearly two weeks after the invasion, on July 3, Stalin took to the radio waves with a patriotic speech, but privately was pessimistic. As the Germans neared Moscow, panic broke out with citizens storming the railroad stations to get out. With a combination of violence and persuasion, Stalin ended the panic, promising that he and the government would remain in Moscow (though he sent Lenin's embalmed corpse eastward just in case).

Cut off by German troops in early September 1941, Leningrad came to symbolize the heroism and tragedy of the Soviet people in this war. Under siege for 100 days, with only a small route across the ice of Lake Ladoga to bring in supplies, some 1.5 million died of cold and starvation, with another 1.4 million being evacuated. The siege of Leningrad would be broken only in January 1944.[46]

By late 1941 it was apparent that Hitler's risky strategy to deal the USSR a knockout blow had not succeeded. Assuming that the campaign would be over before winter set in, Wehrmacht planners had not provided their troops with adequate winter clothing. By year's end, the Wehrmacht had suffered over 600,000 casualties; possibly only Hitler's fanatical refusal to allow withdrawals prevented military collapse, though at a high human cost. In 1942 the German armies failed to take either Moscow or Leningrad, but surged to the south, capturing oil fields in Azerbaijan and, fatefully, taking the city of Stalingrad on the Volga river. The Wehrmacht conquered the city with large losses in building-by-building street fighting, but the Red Army evacuated its troops and artillery across the Volga in good order. From the eastern bank of the river Soviet artillery pounded the Germans who found themselves dangerously overextended. Despite pleas from German general Friedrich Paulus to allow a withdrawal, Hitler adamantly refused to budge. As Paulus had feared, he and his army was cut off. He surrendered with 91,000 troops and 22 generals on January 31, only a day after Hitler had promoted Paulus to the rank of *Generalfeldmarshall*. Only about 5,000 of the soldiers who surrendered would survive captivity and return to Germany, some a decade or more later.[47]

Whether one considers Stalingrad in early 1943 or the Battle of Kursk six months later as the true "turning point" of World War II, by late 1943 it was clear that the Red Army had Hitler's troops on the run.[48] To be sure, it would take hundreds of battles and many thousands of casualties before the last German soldier was expelled from Soviet soil. In summer1944 the Red Army occupied the Baltic states and entered eastern Poland, setting up a communist-friendly Polish government in the city of Lublin. By early 1945 the Red Army was in East Prussia, where commanders tacitly allowed their troops to pillage, attack, and rape whatever German civilians remained. As the Red Army marched westward, millions of Germans fled toward the German heartland.

World War II in Europe – dubbed the "Great Patriotic War" like that of 1812 against Napoleon – ended for the USSR on May 9, 1945, with an unconditional German surrender. The dropping of atomic bombs on Hiroshima and Nagasaki in August 1945 brought the Asian war to an end without significant Soviet participation, but the USSR gained back from Japan the southern half of Sakhalin Island and several nearby small islands. In 1945, with its army firmly in control of eastern Europe and a goodly part of Germany, the USSR was indisputably one of the two world superpowers. At home, however, Soviet citizens were cold and hungry, Soviet cities – and enormous parts of the countryside as well – were in ruins, and tens of millions of Soviet citizens had perished in the struggle. Still, the news of the war's end was received with great joy. Many hoped that the USSR's victory against fascism and its secure place as a world power would translate into a more prosperous and less repressive Soviet Union in the postwar period.

Chapter 2
Society

Over the roughly four generations covered in this text, Russian society changed enormously. In 1861 most Russians (and non-Russians within the empire) could not read, lived on the countryside, followed patterns of everyday life that would not have differed greatly from those of a century earlier, and identified themselves mainly by religion, social class (*soslovie*), and local village. Relations between the sexes also followed traditional patterns, with one Russian proverb even declaring that "A chicken is not a bird and a woman is not a human being." Civil society was relatively weak, restrained by a suspicious and paternalist state. By 1945 much of this had changed: women held important posts in the Communist Party and worked as doctors and other professionals, many (though still not most) Soviet citizens lived in cities, illiteracy had nearly been abolished, and identity was increasingly based on professional training and the nation – as Russians or even as Soviet citizens. Everyday life depended less on natural rhythms (sunrise and sunset, seasons, and the like) than on schedules, clocks, and machines. While economically the USSR lagged behind western countries, by 1945 Soviet citizens – in particular those living in towns – were unquestionably modern citizens of an industrialized society.

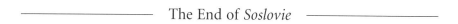

The End of *Soslovie*

Tsarist society was a paternalistic, hierarchical society. At the apex of society, as at the top of the government, stood the figure of the stern but paternal tsar, placed there by God. The paternal nature of the tsar is reflected in a common Russian phrase, *tsar'-batiushka*, or roughly "tsar-papa." Since the tsar held his position from God, a challenge to him amounted to a rejection of God's wisdom and

power. Obviously by this period not all Russians held such views, but this traditional view had not vanished, in particular on the countryside. Just as the tsar's
lofty position over Russian society was justified by divine order, so too was the
existing social hierarchy legitimate. This hierarchy was reflected, indeed codified,
in the *soslovie* system.

Soslovie may be compared to legal estates in western and central Europe
(traditionally: Church, Nobility, Bourgeoisie, and sometimes Peasantry). The
categories did not entirely overlap, however, nor did they always have the same
significance. To generalize and simplify somewhat, the main *sosloviia* (pl. of
soslovie) were nobleman, churchman, townsman, peasant. As Gregory Freeze has
pointed out, the word *soslovie* was rarely used before the nineteenth century, and
until the 1870s the main social distinction in Russian society remained the divide
between those subject to the poll tax (peasants and some townspeople) and those
who were not.[1] Still, *soslovie* and its categories remained an important marker
and indication of individual rights. As in most hierarchical societies, in the
Russian Empire one's personal rights, taxes, and access to education were determined in large part by social standing. Thus up until 1861 peasants paid poll tax,
were subject to corporal punishment, and were drafted into the army while
nobles were not. The "great divide" in Russian society was thus between nobles
and peasants – the middling groups, which made up a relatively small percentage
of the total population, were vastly less important for Russian rulers. The term
raznochinets (pl. *raznochintsy*), "people of various ranks," came to be used to
describe individuals who did not easily fit into the *soslovie* system, uneasily occupying the social space between peasant and noble. Recent research has shown
that this common understanding of the term was not always quite accurate, but
it is clear that the term *raznochinets* was used rather imprecisely to refer to
people who did not quite "fit" in the established categories.[2] In any case the
figure of the *raznochinets* who uneasily occupied the social "middle" is one
indication of the weak development of the professions, merchants, and self-
made-men in Russian society. In other words even after 1861 Russians tended
to identify more with the category of their birth than with their education
and occupation.

The Great Reforms intended to transform Russia into a modern state and, as
one part of this modernization, aimed to make Russian society less rigid. To be
sure, already in the early eighteenth century Peter the Great had attempted to
make Russian society more open to talent through the Table of Ranks, which
granted noble status to those reaching a certain rank in the military or civilian
hierarchy. On the whole, however, social mobility was the exception rather than
the rule in Russian society. The Great Reforms sought to encourage social mobility (as well as physical mobility) by limiting legal restrictions on the "lower
orders." Thus, as we have seen, both peasants and noblemen participated in the

zemstva, military service was expected from all, regardless of social standing, and the discriminatory poll tax was abolished.

Nonetheless, many vestiges of the *soslovie* system remained long after the Great Reforms and even to 1917. In part this was due to the government's uneasiness with a truly modern and mobile populace. On one level, this reflected a fear of social disorder, but it also concerned the practical issue of filling bureaucratic and military posts with qualified candidates. Even in 1914 few university graduates – or even secondary school students – came from a peasant background. The government also had to deal with existing realities, even when they clashed with principles of the Great Reforms. For example, even after the legal reform there existed a parallel legal system for the peasantry, the so-called *volost'* courts. The reason was simple: peasants could rarely afford a lawyer and preferred to have their cases on the local level settled quickly, cheaply, and with a minimum of legalese. If a peasant remained dissatisfied with the *volost'* court's decision, he or she could appeal the case to the regular courts.[3] Strictly speaking the existence of *volost'* courts violated the principle of a unified justice system, but for practical reasons this parallel court system was retained to the end of the tsarist regime.[4]

After the Great Reforms social identity continued to be largely based on *soslovie* categories. English-speaking readers of *Crime and Punishment* are sometimes puzzled by mentions of Raskolnikov's former student status. A modern reader would probably stress "former" mentally and think that Raskolnikov had likely flunked out of university ("student" in Russian only refers to those studying at institutions of higher learning). But Raskolnikov's contemporaries (the novel was first published in 1866, in the midst of the Great Reforms) would have noted instead that at one time Raskolnikov had studied at a university level; that is, he must be from the middle or upper class. Similarly visiting cards often mentioned not only the bearer's name, but "nobleman" or "merchant of the second guild" (a quite wealthy man) or simply a profession such as physician, lawyer, or professor. Among civil servants, one's rank (from the extremely distinguished first rank – never used in the late nineteenth century – to the lowly rank 14, "Collegiate Registrar," a very modest clerk) determined respect and even the form of address used. Similarly a member of the privileged classes would use the informal "you" (*ty*, like *du* in German or *tú* in Spanish) with a peasant or house watchman, but the latter would be expected to respond with the respectful *vy*.

One key sociological change between peasant emancipation (1861) and the revolution (1917) was the development of the Russian industrial working class. There had, of course, been industrial workers in Russia in the first half of the nineteenth century, but their numbers were very small. Only with industrial "take off" – around the last decade of the century – did the industrial working class really grow in Russia. Compared with western Europe, the development of the Russian working class was more rapid, more concentrated, and more directly connected with the peasantry. Russian factories tended to be large and located in a few industrialized regions, in particular around St Petersburg, Moscow, the textile-dominated "Central Industrial Region," and in Russian Poland (Warsaw and Łódź in particular). Factories were often very large: the Putilov works in St Petersburg employed tens of thousands (30,000 workers as early as 1870). The fact that large factories were concentrated in a few key regions meant that organizing labor or spreading socialist ideas was that much easier: it is far simpler to spread leaflets among 500 workers in a single factory than at 10 separate factories with 50 workers apiece.

The development of "class consciousness" among workers was not always high. Marxist commentators often blamed this on the close connections between the industrial worker and his peasant background. After all, even in 1917 few industrial workers were without direct connections (parents, siblings) in the village. On the one hand this afforded Russian workers a measure of social security: in an industrial downturn, they could usually return to their village until more work was available. On the other hand, it has been argued, the fact that the workers were so close to the village may have mitigated their demands for higher wages and better treatment. But one can equally argue that the "amphibious" nature of the Russian industrial working class and peasantry may have contributed to the spread of radical ideas in the village.[5]

The continued influence of peasant norms and values among urban workers did not prevent the development of a conscious industrial working-class identity. Coming from the village to work in St Petersburg as a young man, Semyon Kanatchikov recalled that he quickly adopted the mannerisms, speech, and clothing of a skilled worker. Workers often laid special importance on their outward appearance, not wanting to stick out as a "hick" among more sophisticated city dwellers. Despite long working hours, many workers also sought to gain or improve their knowledge of the world. An illiterate peasant would not be unusual or particularly shameful, but an uneducated worker was both easier to cheat and open to mockery from his fellows. By the eve of the revolution, a distinct workers' culture and identity had developed in Russia's industrial cities.[6]

Among the most conscious workers were skilled workers in metal-working industries and printers. In part their self-definition as workers and urban people was based on the specific needs of their jobs, which required a considerable amount of training and made them difficult to replace.[7] And, it must be noted, nearly all of these skilled workers were men: women rarely worked in printing plants or machine building plants; female workers predominated in less skilled and more poorly paid textile plants.[8] No unions were permitted in the Russian Empire before 1905 and strikes were also illegal. But workers began to organize in practical ways, such as collecting sums among themselves to insure any members against injuries on the job. Such collections were illegal but generally went unnoticed by the authorities. It was out of such groups that strike commit-tees developed, in particular in the Moscow printers' strike of 1903. The strikers' demands reflected various "sore spots" of labor-management relations: low pay, unpleasant and dangerous working conditions, but also the lack of respect paid by foremen and bosses to workers. A typical demand was that management use "polite address" (in particular, the polite *vy* rather than the informal *ty*) in addressing workers. Strikes played a major role in forcing government conces-sions during the revolution of 1905; Russia was swept with another major strike wave in 1912–14, sparked by the Lena Goldfields strike. On the eve of World War I, Russian workers were flexing their muscles. Although industrial workers made up only a small percentage of the total population, they were increasingly organ-ized, willing to take on management or even the government, and located in crucial cities like St Petersburg and Moscow.[9]

Peasants into Kolkhozniks

Imperial Russia was a rural and peasant country. Even in 1913 only 18 percent of the population of Russia lived in cities, in the 1860s that percentage probably reached barely 10 percent.[10] The overwhelming majority of nonurban dwellers were peasants. For all the huge advances in industrialization in the 1930s and 1940s, even in 1950 only 39 percent of Soviet citizens were urban dwellers. At the same time the actual lives of those living in villages changed enormously, though not always for the better. Mechanization of the countryside (the use of tractors, harvesters, etc.) and the consumption by rural people of industrial goods (tools, manufactured clothing, books) rose significantly, but in 1945, as in 1861, the Russians who worked the soil remained among the poorest Soviet citizens who did not even have the right to leave their farm – now a collective farm (*kolkhoz*) – at will.

The transformation of serfs into prosperous farmers was one of the central objectives of the Great Reforms. For most peasants, however, not much changed after 1861. True, they were no longer subject to the whim of the landlord. But on the other hand peasants could not freely leave the countryside for the city – that required permission from the peasant commune (*mir*). The continuing existence of the peasant commune provided a safety net for peasants but also stymied individual initiative. The commune – not individual peasants – was the legal owner of all land gained from the landlord after emancipation, the land was worked in common, and power resided firmly in the hands of adult male heads of households. Since the land was held in common, it was practically impossible for an individual peasant to try new crops or agricultural methods. Furthermore, peasants who did manage to purchase land on their own (outside the commune)

FIGURE 2.1   Russian Peasantry before the Revolution: A Village Council ca.1902–10.
Source: Netta Peacock/V&A Images/Victoria and Albert Museum, London.

and became wealthy enough to hire other peasants or perhaps lend money to them (other opportunities for credit were nearly nonexistent for peasants) were often ostracized by peasant society as kulaks, or "fists," stressing their antisocial and tight-fisted mentality.

When one speaks of the "Russian peasant," one necessarily simplifies a much more diverse and complicated picture. Most of the generalizations hazarded here fit best for Russian peasants who lived in the central black-earth region. At the same time many aspects of this "typical" Russian peasant's life also fit the situation in the north, west (where Russian peasantry gave way to Belarusian and Ukrainian), and south. The situation in Siberia, due to the harsh climate and large influx of peasant migrants only in the last decades of the nineteenth century, needs to be considered separately.[11]

Peasant society, like the tsarist state, was patriarchal, with women and men responsible for different jobs. The authority of the adult male in any household (which typically included his sons and their wives, at least initially) was nearly unchallenged. Women were expected to submit to their husbands, produce sons to carry on the family line, and to work in and around the house as well as in the fields. Premarital sex was generally condoned but in the case of pregnancy the father was expected to marry the expectant mother. Positive traits for potential brides included a docile temperament (important for living under the rule of her husband's parents), the ability to work hard, and a sturdy healthy body. A commentator from the Russian intelligentsia describing peasant tastes noted that while "we" (educated middle-class Russians) consider a slim figure beautiful in women, peasants favored more solidly built women. Wife-beating was common, but when a wife defended herself successfully by fighting back, the "henpecked" peasant husband could count on public ridicule and mockery. Children were often looked after by older siblings to free mother up for other duties and seldom visited a school of any kind, though this was beginning to change by the early twentieth century. Even in the early twentieth century over half of Russian babies did not survive their first few years, in great part because of unsanitary practices and the very early introduction of babies to solid food. Improvements in child mortality during the Soviet years helped to extend life expectancy: only 32 years in 1897 and over double that figure in 1955.

Russian peasants lived very simple, not to say primitive, lives. With rare exceptions they lived in one-room huts (*izby*); often small domestic animals shared this space in cold weather. Male peasants typically wore trousers and a long shirt pulled over the head and belted around the waist. Women wore full skirts, a blouse and often a vest or bodice over it. The blouses and skirts could be decorated elaborately with embroidery but far more common were simple cotton garments. By the later nineteenth century most peasants wore clothes made of manufactured cloth, not homespun. Men and women alike seldom ventured outdoors without some kind of headgear; for women this was typically a scarf covering the hair. Except in the coldest time of year, peasant feet were nearly always bare.

Peasant food was also simple. The Russian proverb rhymes: *Shchi i kasha – pishcha nasha*: "Cabbage soup and buckwheat – that's our food." Bread, potatoes, porridge (often of millet or buckwheat grains), and root vegetables were typical menu items with the typical black, dense Russian bread providing a very high percentage of calories well into the twentieth century. Meat was consumed mainly on holidays, fish was not a typical meal, and dairy products were also not commonly consumed because of the dearth of milch cows (though sour cream – *smetana* – could be added to soups and porridge). One new addition to common peasant fare in the course of the nineteenth century was tea, drunk weak and hot, typically filtered though a piece of sugar (granulated sugar was not yet available) held in one's front teeth. The habit of drinking sweet tea also led to widespread tooth decay among Russians, and not just in the peasant class. Alcohol consumption was not particularly high among Russian peasants; they could not afford regular imbibing. Typically, however, any kind of celebration (wedding, christening, holidays) involved men (but not usually women) drinking vodka.[12] It should not be forgotten that hunger – especially in the spring when reserves had been eaten but new crops not yet harvested – was common, and famines swept large parts of Russia and the USSR in 1891, in the early 1920s, and 1932–3.

From the peasant emancipation to the end of the old regime, a constant problem for the Russian peasantry was so-called land hunger. That is, given the low level of agricultural technology and the relatively high level of population increase, there was simply too little land to support Russian peasants adequately. Unlike Polish, Ukrainian, and Lithuanian peasants (or their German, Norwegian, and Italian counterparts), Russians hardly emigrated overseas and the large migration to the industrializing cities and, to a lesser extent, to Siberia was not enough to "soak up" the excess population. For peasants the solution was simple: land should be taken from the landlords, who did not work it personally anyway, and given to needy peasants. Peasants tried to achieve this "solution" in 1905 and to a great extent did accomplish the takeover and dividing up among peasants of the landlord's fields in 1917 and ensuing years.

Peasants suffered disproportionately during World War I (most Russian soldiers came from peasant families, after all) and the Civil War period, though the ability to grow their own food mitigated some of this suffering. The dissatisfaction of peasant soldiers with military life was one reason for the dissolution of the Russian army in the course of 1917. After the February 1917 revolution, rumors spread that peasants would be awarded allotments of land and many peasant soldiers deserted and returned to their villages in order not to be absent when the land was doled out. Lenin said famously that the peasant soldiers "voted with their feet" by leaving the front and returning home.

One of the Bolshevik slogans popular with peasants was "Land and Peace." With few exceptions, neither peasants nor industrial workers understood why the war was being fought, and even fewer wished to continue the bloodshed after the initial wave of patriotism in 1914–15. After the October 1917 revolution, peasants seized landowners' property with the approval of the Bolsheviks, who passed a land decree on October 26 confiscating noble estates and lands owned by the Church and imperial family. Contrary to their pre-1917 ideology, the Bolsheviks did not nationalize this land (which, given the chaos at the moment, would have been impossible to carry through) but instead let peasant communes divide it up among their members. Thus initially the peasantry gained from the October revolution.

Rapidly, however, the peasants' positive attitude toward the new rulers of Russia soured. In order to feed the cities – which had shrunk considerably during the war – the Bolsheviks forbade free trade of any kind, confiscated grain from peasants, and even shot peasants caught hiding their produce. Already in mid-1918 peasants expressed their hatred for the "communists" while retaining a favorable opinion of the "Bolsheviks" – of course this was the same party, having only changed its name in March 1918 (a few months before grain confiscation began to hit hard).

Caught between Red and White armies during the Civil War, the peasantry suffered at the hands of both. Cooperating with troops from either side would often bring brutal reprisals if a town changed hands. Some peasants attempted to defend themselves against Reds and Whites by forming their own so-called Green units (the most famous of which was led by the peasant anarchist Nestor Makhno) and, in 1920 and 1921, rising up against Soviet authorities, refusing to hand over grain, and killing local communists. Historian Orlando Figes makes a persuasive case for the Russian Civil War as a series of local peasant wars.[13] The collapse of the economy in the Civil War period also brought a flood of unemployed workers of peasant origin back to their native villages. The arrival of thousands of hungry mouths in a time of dire scarcity brutalized attitudes and made survival that much more difficult. The combination of peasant unrest and the widespread famine of the early 1920s helped convince the communists to adopt more pro-peasant policies, in particular the New Economic Policy (NEP).

As we have seen, the NEP created a legal market for grain and other foodstuffs, allowing peasants to sell their produce freely after having paid a fairly small tax in grain. Many Soviet peasants lived better in the NEP years than any time before or after. Not rarely peasants were able to barter with hungry town dwellers and acquire consumer goods such as shawls, furniture, even pianos. But mainly peasants simply ate better – which became a problem for the Soviet leadership, who wanted grain to sell abroad or to feed city populations. Peasants continued to cultivate their lands using primitive methods, nearly all work being carried out by human or animal labor. Few peasant households owned more than one or two horses, and it was a rare village indeed that had ever seen a tractor. The destruction of large estates and even of the private farms that had been set up by the Stolypin agricultural reforms since 1907 meant that overwhelmingly the Russian countryside was divided up into small plots. For individual peasants, these small plots might provide a decent income in the 1920s, but for the USSR as a whole and the Communist Party they represented a major obstacle for the modernization of the countryside, both economically and politically.

Many customs and other aspects of peasant everyday life survived well into the Soviet period. In many ways Soviet power barely touched the villages in the 1920s. Most peasants continued to attend church, celebrate weddings and traditional religious holidays, engage in manual labor, and raise their children as before 1917. Even in 1925, three-quarters of peasant marriages took place in church.[14] But change was coming, also to the village. Even before the great break of 1928, schools and "literacy huts" were set up also in the countryside to help both young and adult peasants to learn to read. The party made special efforts to recruit peasants, though without spectacular results. Communist propaganda touted the union of industrial workers and peasantry in word and image, speaking of a *smychka* – or "alliance" between these two laboring classes. The communists also tried to drive a wedge between wealthier and poorer peasants, describing the former as kulaks. As mentioned earlier, the negative phrase, meaning "fists," had been used to describe peasant exploiters and moneylenders already before 1917. While condemning the kulaks, the Soviet authorities tried to woo less prosperous peasants, setting up "committees of the poor [peasants]" called *kombedy*. In the end, however, few peasants trusted the communists or felt attracted to or interested in communist ideology, viewing most communists as urban outsiders.[15]

Collectivization ended this period of relative peasant prosperity. Despite the image of the hammer and sickle symbolizing the union of industrial workers ("hammer" – nearly always a man in Soviet iconography) and the peasantry ("sickle," a harvesting implement typically used by women), the peasants never really fitted in communist ideology. After all, Marx himself had denounced the "idiocy of rural life" and sneered that peasants could never form class consciousness, remaining forever – in his classic phrase – a "sack of potatoes," each peasant-potato living contentedly on his own small plot. Nor did peasants trust the communists, whom they saw as urban dwellers and those who had carried out brutal confiscations of peasant grain just a few years earlier during the Civil War period. But the brutalities of the Civil War paled at what amounted to class warfare on the countryside in 1929–31 during collectivization. Rather than give up their livestock to the collective farms, many peasants slaughtered and ate the animals. Widespread resistance to collectivization was only suppressed by violence. Over two million peasants, in particular wealthier ones – "kulaks" – and anyone opposing the collective farms, were beaten, arrested, thrown out of their homes, or simply shot.

The collective farms (*kolkhozy*) set up during collectivization initially resembled simple peasant villages – which they had been only a year or two earlier. All livestock and tools were held in common (though many peasants had slaughtered and eaten their livestock rather than give it up to the *kolkhoz*) but peasants continued to live in their own huts. A collective farm chairman oversaw operations and "Machine Tractor Stations" (MTS) were set up on the countryside to lend out tractors, harvesters, and other farm machinery to individual collective farms. The MTS also had party representatives who kept an eye on local peasants or, to use the Soviet term, *kolkhozniky* – "collective farmers." No longer was the word *krestianin* ("peasant," with overtones of "cross" – *krest*, and "Christian" *khristianin*) to be used. Traditional peasant garb, festivals (often of religious nature), songs, and stories were now to be replaced by modern Soviet culture. The effort to transform "backward, illiterate peasants" into modern Soviet citizens had some positive aspects, aiming to introduce forms of modern technology to the

Figure 2.2   Nikolai Mikhailov, "There Is No Room in Our Collective Farm for Priests and Kulaks." 1930.
Source: Hoover Institution Archives.

countryside, to bridge the gap between city and countryside in culture, in short, to better incorporate peasants into Soviet society. But the destruction of peasant traditions also impoverished Soviet culture while often failing to replace traditional culture with modern practices. Even in 1945 many collective farms lacked electricity, sewers, running water, and other basic elements of modern life. At the same time collective farmers did not have the right to move away from the *kolkhoz* – their internal passports (required to register for lodging or work) were held by the collective farm chairman.[16]

─────────────── "Civil Society" and Intelligentsia ───────────────

In the Russian language the word *obshchestvo* – "society" – typically excludes peasants. That is, "society" referred to educated, upper- or middle-class people. It also excluded the *meshchanstvo*, a term that officially referred to poor towns-people but that in Russian carries very negative connotations of ignorance and vulgarity. Only with widespread education, it was thought, would peasants and ill-educated townspeople gradually join "society." Because of the extreme poverty and high illiteracy among the peasant masses, developing "civil society" rarely included them. The term "civil society" suggests and presupposes the free exchange of ideas and the creation of a civil sphere separate from the state. In Russia the state was far more present in middle-class lives than, say, in Britain or Germany. Censorship was considerably more strict; German and English literatures have no parallels to famous Russian authors like Dostoevsky and Chernyshevsky who were arrested for political crimes and sent to Siberia. Also unlike western and central Europe, in the Russian Empire associations (even charities and the like) were strictly regulated and monitored by the state; no political parties (even arch-conservative monarchist ones) were permitted until 1905. And yet a kind of "civil society" did nonetheless develop in Russia despite these restrictive conditions.[17]

One word that Russian has given to world languages – aside from "vodka" – is *intelligentsia*. In its original nineteenth-century meaning the word not only implied a certain degree of education (though this might not be from formal training) but also a critical political stance. Members of the intelligentsia – *inteligenty* (the "g" is hard, as in German) – aimed to use their education and talents to help Russia and the less-fortunate masses, but seldom in tandem with the Russian state. On the contrary, the intelligentsia generally regarded the autocratic Russian state and the tsar's bureaucracy as hindering the proper development of the country. In great part the Russian state had itself to blame for the alienation between this important class and itself. The state seldom valued individual initiative positively, as the frequent strife between elected *zemstva* and the bureaucracy showed. Rather than attempting to harness this social force, the tsarist state harassed and persecuted it. When at long last in 1905 the government began to make cautious concessions to the intelligentsia, generations of suspicion made cooperation between "society" and "state" (e.g., the Duma and Stolypin) very difficult.

In many ways the intelligentsia may be regarded as the quintessence of the "middle class," a term that deserves some discussion here. The original meaning of this none-too-precise term was to designate all those falling somewhere between the upper (noble, landowning) and lower (peasants, manual labors) classes. In the modern world middle-class people define themselves by their education and occupation, not by their birth or ancestry. But the middle class also includes merchants, traders, and to some extent artisans. In Russia the middle class was relatively weak but grew significantly in the generations after 1861. Not all members of the middle class belonged to the intelligentsia, but all *inteligenty* were middle-class people in the sense of defining themselves by their profession or role within society. Thus even the many members of the intelligentsia of noble birth, like novelist Lev Tolstoy, can be seen as upholding middle-class ideals of social utility. The intelligentsia did not, however, regard itself as representing middle-class values alone: it felt that it represented the conscience of the nation, responsible for improving the lives of all classes of Russians, including industrial workers and peasants.[18]

Both before 1917 and later, some (mainly conservative) commentators accused the intelligentsia of being overly theoretical and doctrinaire. Because *inteligenty* were not allowed any part in governing Russia, it has been argued, they tended to support extreme positions, even refusing to condemn the use of terrorist methods by far left parties.[19] In the context of late nineteenth-century Russia, however, such criticism is unhistorical and misses the point. While the intelligentsia was generally liberal or mildly socialist in its political stance, the government tended to lump these moderate views together with those of the extreme left. For that reason, it made sense for the liberal intelligentsia to support the left – at least until the government started to differentiate between liberals and radical socialists, which was beginning to happen only after 1905.

Who belonged to the intelligentsia? No adequate sociological answer may be given because this "class" was as much a state of mind as a concrete grouping of people with similar incomes, education, or politics. Still, some generalizations can be made. Most *inteligenty* were educated, "self-made" men and women. Typical for middle-class people, they derived their identity less from the situation of their birth (as a prince or baron might) than from what they did. But belonging to the intelligentsia also implied a sincere desire to work for the good of the nation, to use one's training less for self-enrichment than for the common good. Doctors, lawyers, engineers, teachers, journalists, and agronomists each in their own ways represented typical intelligentsia professions.[20]

In carrying out their professions, these men (and also, though less frequently, women) also helped develop civil society in Russia. For example, *zemstva* delegates and workers, despite the prohibition on communicating with other *zemstva*, did secretly consult with their colleagues on practical matters. As in other countries, Russian professionals attempted to form their own associations to spread scientific knowledge. The Russian Bar Association was formed in the midst of the legal reform of the 1860s, and the government grudgingly allowed medical doctors, engineers, and others to meet to discuss professional matters. Inevitably the "professional" became mixed with the political; in particular as many professionals felt – as good members of the intelligentsia – that one of their highest professional goals was to improve life and culture in Russia.[21]

Another aspect of civil society is the press. Censorship complicated but did not prevent the development of a lively, informative, and at times even cautiously liberal press in Russia. In this development the so-called fat journals played a certain role (journals of a certain thickness were not subject to preliminary censorship). In such journals as *Vestnik Evropy* (European Messenger), *Otechestvennye zapiski* (Fatherland Notes), and *Russkoe bogatstvo* (Russian Wealth) one could learn about recent elections in the United States, read serialized novels by Russian and foreign authors, catch up on events throughout Russia and around the world, and even take in discussions and analysis of burning topical questions such as antisemitism, different forms of parliamentary democracy, and socialism. Russian writers became adept at "Aesopian language" to get around censorship, for example, by criticizing policies or events in foreign countries that had clear parallels in Russia, such as antisemitism in Germany or Austria. By the early twentieth century, and especially after censorship was made less severe after 1905, inhabitants of Russia's cities could choose from a number of daily newspapers, often in a variety of languages and representing a diversity of views. Some of these papers specialized in scandalous stories and recounting crimes, while others concentrated on more highbrow matters of international politics and high culture.[22]

For all its positive aspects, the Russian intelligentsia also exhibited various negative traits. Typically for nineteenth-century liberalism, it was an elitist ideology that was only potentially and "in the long run" democratic. In his memoirs, the metal worker Semyon Kanatchikov wrote slightingly of the upper-class (for him) *inteligenty* who invited workers to their gatherings but then treated them like curiosities. While *inteligenty* supported universal suffrage, they were shocked when workers and peasants did not always support "progressive" parties like the Kadets. On the other hand, when the intelligentsia came to power in February 1917, its sincere commitment to free speech and open political debate (by amnestying all political prisoners and ending censorship) certainly made it easier for a nonliberal and antidemocratic party like the Bolsheviks to gain power.

The classic Russian intelligentsia was shaken up and in many cases swept away by the October 1917 revolution.[23] But Lenin himself displayed many qualities of the *inteligenty*: selfless, a bit humorless, dogmatic, dedicated to the cause and heedless of his own professional or economic advancement. Like many members of the intelligentsia (indeed, more than most), Lenin was quite cut off from everyday life and troubles in Russia – after all, he had spent nearly his entire adult life in western Europe. Lenin's concept of an elite and totally dedicated party (as opposed to a broader mass organization) can also be seen as an extreme development of intelligentsia elitism. Lenin's concept of revolution was always *for* the common man, but seldom *through* him. Many *inteligenty* rejected the Bolshevik revolution as a betrayal of their liberal traditions, but others supported the communists as a group dedicated to transforming Russia into an egalitarian, just, and modern state.

Members of the intelligentsia were among the thousands of Russians who emigrated in the years after 1917. Among them were historian Pavel Miliukov, Nobel-prize winning author Ivan Bunin, and composer Igor Stravinsky. Russian daily newspapers, journals, and books were published in dozens of cities from Berlin and Paris to San Francisco and Shanghai (see chapter 6, "World," pp. 194–6). The emigration of thousands of educated specialists who allowed this spreading of Russian culture around the globe presented a huge problem for Lenin and the communists who needed to create a new educated class within Soviet Russia.

For the communists, creating a new educated class was both a challenge and an opportunity. The old liberal ideas of the nineteenth-century intelligentsia had, after all, little place in the brash young socialist state. On a practical level, however, the communists needed the specialist knowledge of the pre-revolutionary educated class in order to train a new Soviet intelligentsia. Universities were opened to (generally less-qualified) working-class students, much to the disgust of more traditional professors. Special workers' universities were opened up along with night courses so that working people could get more specialized training. A new group began to emerge, the "technical intelligentsia," often more narrowly educated (typically as industrial managers or engineers) than the pre-revolutionary intelligentsia and far more devoted to the Soviet status quo.[24] At the same time, as Daniel Beer has recently shown, the pre-revolutionary discourses of "degeneracy" could in many cases be harnessed to the communist project of reforming Soviet society by purging it of retrograde and reactionary elements.[25]

Inevitably the Soviet intelligentsia differed very significantly from its pre-revolutionary counterpart. The critical attitude toward the state was replaced by *partiinost'*, or party spirit – almost a complete reversal in attitude. Since the Soviet state defined itself as the protector of worker and peasant interests, the intelligentsia no longer had to fill that role. Instead the educated middle class was urged to use its professional training to strengthen the Soviet state. At the same time the skepticism of the old-fashioned intelligentsia did not entirely die out but disappeared from public view. Under Soviet power any overt attempt to carve out a "civil society" detached from the state was tantamount to political crime. All organizations from soccer teams to gardening associations were integrated into the Soviet state, censorship was considerably harsher than in tsarist times, and the penalty for appearing to challenge state norms became far more serious. For all of these reasons, the Soviet middle class was better integrated into state structures but also largely deprived of the autonomy that liberal theorists usually ascribe to civil society.

The ideal of the Soviet middle class changed significantly from the 1920s to 1945. As literary scholar Vera Dunham pointed out, by the 1940s middle-class values such as a cozy home, traditional gender roles, attractive clothing, and the like began to make their appearance in Soviet novels.[26] The proper female communist of the 1920s might resemble Dasha of Fyodor Gladkov's *Cement*, whose dedication to the revolution precluded family life (even leading indirectly to her daughter's death). A generation later heroines did not abandon their communist (public) duties but also created a soft, warm, protective "nest" for their husbands and families. Women also continued to be expected to work outside the home and contribute to the family's budget while carrying out nearly all household chores, including the raising of children. Dunham argues that the pre-revolutionary petit-bourgeois attitude of the *meshchanstvo* had by the 1940s been transformed into a no less vulgar and materialistic Soviet counterpart.

The "Woman Question"

It is not by chance that most of Dunham's examples involve Soviet women rather than men. The Bolsheviks aimed to revolutionize social relations not only in the economic sphere but also at home. Gender roles were to be completely reexamined, family life reconstructed, women and men were to work together as partners to build communism. While no communist leader disagreed on the principle of equality between the sexes, very serious controversy raged over practical application of this principle to life. The communists knew very well how little support they enjoyed among the socially conservative peasantry and were loath to exacerbate relations further over gender issues. In any case the Bolshevik leaders themselves considered the heterosexual family a norm upon which to build socialism and shied away from utopian projects that foresaw the communal raising of children. Transforming a patriarchal peasant society into a socialist community where gender roles would not determine profession or dignity would be an uphill battle.

For Russian peasants, as in many traditional cultures, nature dictated that women take a subordinate role to men. The peasant commune was made up of households headed by an adult male, and in the pre-reform period taxes were levied according to "souls," that is, male serfs. Girl babies were often considered a disappointment by their father (though welcomed as a helpmate by their mother); women were nearly always valued for their labor potential rather than intelligence or even beauty. The most important virtues for a peasant woman were docility and obedience. A young wife needed such characteristics especially during the first years of marriage when she resided with her husband's parents. The figure of the overbearing mother-in-law and the lascivious father-in-law were unfortunately not simply stereotypes. On the other hand, peasant women were not entirely without rights. They retained control over their dowry and in extreme cases could return to their parents' home. Single women, however, had no place in peasant society and were regarded with pity or suspicion. One way out for these women was to join a convent: in the later nineteenth century, the number of women of peasant origin to take the cloth increased significantly.[27]

In the half-century between serf emancipation and World War I many thousands of young Russians – both men and women – flocked to the cities. Women worked as servants, in the textile industry, and, inevitably, as prostitutes. As in all European countries, the greatest number of peasant girls coming to the city obtained employment as servants, cleaning and cooking for middle-class and wealthier Russians. Domestic work had the advantage of providing room and board (though often little more in the way of renumeration), while appearing respectable. But the hard work, constant surveillance, and pitiful pay of domestic service meant that after a few years in the city many young women looked for factory work. In particular textile factories employed young women and, while pay was low and working conditions dangerous, such jobs gave women a degree of freedom unmatched either on the countryside or in domestic service. Whether as a servant or as a factory worker, employment was nearly always terminated when a woman married or at latest upon signs of pregnancy.

In Russia prostitution was a legal, though hardly respectable, profession. Women wishing to carry on this trade were required to register with the police, undergo a medical examination, and carry the notorious "yellow ticket" marking them as prostitutes. Besides "official" prostitution – some 34,000 women were registered in 1900 – many thousands more plied the trade illegally. For middle-class reformers (and writers like Dostoevsky and Chernyshevsky) the figure of the prostitute became metaphorical for the ills of late imperial Russia.[28] In a society where paid employment for single women was limited (and even less available after marriage), prostitution was a logical if unsavory social phenomenon.

The expanding middle class did offer new opportunities for women. While no Russian university officially admitted women, in some cities parallel courses existed for female auditors. Of these the Bestuzhev courses in St Petersburg and the Guerrier courses in Moscow (both set up in the 1870s) were the most famous. In this way young women could obtain training to be teachers, doctors, engineers, pharmacists, lawyers, and dentists.[29] Many other young women from the Russian Empire went abroad (especially to Switzerland) to obtain a university education. Among them perhaps the most famous is the Polish scientist Maria Skłodowska, better known as "Mme. Curie" and the first women to be awarded the Nobel prize in Physics (1903) and the first person to obtain a second Nobel prize (this time in chemistry, 1911). Born in Warsaw four years after the Polish January Uprising of 1863, Maria had no chance of obtaining an education in her native tongue.

Like many other young women from the Russian Empire, she sought to advance her education in western Europe. Her desire for a higher education was far from unique; Curie's genius and spectacular achievements in science would later make her stand out. The figure of the earnest and dedicated young woman seeking education became common in late-nineteenth century Russian journalism and literature, partly as a figure of fun but also with respect for her sincere wish to improve herself and to help her fellow (wo)men.

Gender equality formed an element of intelligentsia faith, all the more so on the left reaches of that group. Indeed the most famous description of radical "new people" (to quote the book's subtitle) of the late imperial period, in Nikolai Chernyshevsky's 1863 novel *What Is to Be Done?*, portrayed as its main protagonist an energetic and unconventional young woman. Vera Pavlovna escapes from her oppressive petit-bourgeois family with the help of a fellow (male) radical, enters into a fictitious marriage with him (even radicals had to consider respectability), and sets up a sewing cooperative to rescue prostitutes. Vera is sincere, tough, and hard working – though in the end she falls for the ultimate radical, Rakhmetov.[30]

Real women played important roles in illegal organizations, including in the assassination of Alexander II, for which Gesia Gelfman and Sofiia Perovskaia were condemned to death. The attempted murder by Vera Zasulich of the commander of the Peter and Paul Fortress in 1877 led to a public trial at which Zasulich was acquitted by the sympathetic jury despite Zasulich's open confession. While female participation in the radical movement probably did not exceed 15–20 percent (judging from arrest records), names like Vera Figner, Ekaterina Breshkovskaia, Maria Spiridonova, Elena Stasova, and of course Lenin's wife Nadezhda Krupskaia, all played visible and important roles. Thousands of less famous women also joined the ranks of the radicals and dedicated their lives to ending oppression and tsarist authority in Russia.[31]

While few members of the middle-class intelligentsia would have denied equal rights to women, radicals often dismissed the women's emancipation movement as bourgeois and detracting from the more important revolutionary movement. There was also the tactical issue of whether to press for specific women's rights when all subjects of the tsar lacked basic civil and political rights. Radicals and liberals agreed that divorce had to be made simpler (before 1917, it was very difficult to get a legal divorce in Russia) and women's rights in the family (especially for legal separation) needed to be strengthened. But in the Duma period (1906–17) even Pavel Miliukov, head of the left liberal Kadet party, in order not to alienate more traditionally minded voters refused to endorse the vote for women (despite his wife's public urging).[32]

During World War I, women played an important role in the war effort. Aristocratic and middle-class women were prominent in charitable organizations, raising funds to help soldiers and their often impoverished families, and in nursing. Both Tsarina Alexandra and Lenin's sister, Maria Ulianova, worked as nurses during the conflict. Probably the most remarkable contribution to the war effort from Russia's women, however, was their active engagement as soldiers. At first, as in all European countries, women were banned from active combat units. This did not, however, stop dedicated women like Maria Bochkareva from dressing up like men and enlisting. Bochkareva was given special permission by the tsar to enlist and after being twice wounded and three times decorated won the respect of her fellow soldiers. In 1917 the Provisional Government, desperate to stem desertions and prop up morale, called on Bochkareva to form the Women's Battalion of Death. The main government motivation was to shame male soldiers through the example of fighting women, but the several female units formed in the Russian army in 1917 performed quite well in battle. Unfortunately for both the women soldiers and the Provisional Government, most male soldiers were angered and outraged rather than shamed at the prospect of being "out-soldiered" by mere women. Despite the bravery of these female warriors, the Provisional Government was swept away by the Bolsheviks and the Red Army never created similar female fighting units. The unfortunate Bochkareva was executed by a Cheka firing squad (for supporting the white military leader, Admiral Kolchak) in May 1920.[33]

Once the Bolsheviks came to power, the "woman question" did not top their agenda. After all, Russia was in the middle of a war, basic necessities of life were in short supply, and the revolution itself appeared under threat. None of the most important Bolshevik leaders was a woman, though Lenin's wife had published a work entitled *The Woman Worker* in 1899. The "woman's section" or *Zhenotdel* of the Communist Party was only set up in 1919 and throughout its short history (it was closed down in 1930) was never entirely taken seriously by party higher-ups, who even mocked it by calling it the *Babotdel* ("baba" being a somewhat derogatory term for a peasant woman). Certain aspects of the "woman question" were "solved" already in 1917: women received the vote, divorce was made much easier to obtain, and the principle of equality of sexes was embraced. But old practices die hard and Bolshevik feminists (they would have rejected the word as "bourgeois") like Alexandra Kollontai and Inessa Armand suffered from the sexism of their communist colleagues, the suspicion being that pushing for specific women's issue was "separatism" that detracted from larger revolutionary issues, and the correlation in most Russian radicals' minds of "women's matters" with the arch-traditional, religious peasant *baba*.[34]

Still, in the 1920s radicals like Kollontai were active in propagandizing the ideal of breaking down old gender and sexual restrictions. Kollontai's "Winged Eros" advocated a free and romantic sexuality that shocked such party fathers as Lenin. In general, like most other intelligentsia males, communists found discussions of sexuality uncomfortable and preferred to stress the need for healthy families in a socialist state. For all the communist rhetoric about gender equality (not a term they would have used), women continued to be regarded as mothers and help-mates to their husbands. There were even special congresses of the wives of shock workers where these dynamic women spoke not so much about their own produc-tion but how they spurred their husbands on to overfulfill their plan and become Stakhanovites. And at the apex of the Communist Party, the Politburo, one saw only male faces.[35]

Activists like Kollontai tried to bring more women into the party (membership was overwhelmingly urban and male) but found that even Communist Party members – in particular in rural and non-Russian regions – did not always look fondly upon the prospect of their wives as communist activists. Male opposition to communist "feminism" in rural areas was buttressed by working-class women's dislike for new family law that by making divorce easier had the practical effect of leaving them to raise the offspring of such broken unions unaided by the father. In Muslim regions like Azerbaijan and central Asia, communist efforts to give women a more public role (in central Asia this often involved campaigns against wearing the veil and other traditional female garb) led not infrequently to vio-lence, even murder.[36]

In the 1930s, as we have seen, more traditional models of family life were embraced. At the same time women played a growing role in public life. By the 1930s the idea of women working outside the home and holding responsible positions as teachers, doctors, and (less frequently) engineers or plant directors was gaining acceptance. The labor shortages of the first Five-Year Plans brought increasing numbers of women into the paid workforce. Educational opportunities for young women also expanded and already in 1927 nearly one-third (28 percent) of students in higher education were women. On the other hand, while women increasingly worked outside the home, men rarely helped with "women's work": housework, shopping, and raising children. Thus the "double burden" of working a full shift in office or factory, then returning home to cook, clean, and care for children, became a typical aspect of Soviet reality for women.

Like other European states, the USSR was vitally concerned with birthrates and offered substantial bonuses and other benefits to encourage families to have chil-dren. Healthy families were important not just to produce a new generation of soldiers and workers (though of course this was one consideration), but also as the fundamental basis of the socialist state. Soviet posters encouraged mothers to keep a clean house, breast-feed their babies, and wash the infants frequently. One slogan proclaimed, "Cleanliness – guarantor of health!" Since it was assumed that women would spend much more time with children than men would, special efforts were made to instruct young women in the basic ideas of Marxism-Leninism and to show motherhood itself as a vital contribution to building the

Soviet state. But the difficulty of life in the USSR in the 1920s and early 1930s, especially in cities, made many young women opt for having fewer children or none at all. In large cities abortions outnumbered live births in the early 1930s, to the great consternation of Soviet leaders. A decree of June 1936 banned abortions except for medical reasons. Despite the lack of other forms of birth control, Soviet birth rates did not increase dramatically, indicating that citizens found other ways of avoiding or terminating unwanted pregnancies.[37]

During World War II, Soviet women were not drafted into combat units like men, but nonetheless played a vital role in the defense of the motherland. The most famous poster of the conflict showed a maternal woman holding a copy of the oath taken by soldiers and gesturing toward the caption "The Motherland Calls." Women worked as truck drivers, physicians, and nurses. They were also active in partisan units as well as in more traditional roles as nurses and drivers. At home, women had to work longer shifts and, on the countryside, essentially take over all jobs to make up for the absent male kolkhozniks. And some exceptional women did play a role in combat operations. Though only revealed much later, hundreds of exceptional women also flew combat missions during the war, including Marina Raskova who died when forced to make a crash landing in early 1943. Before her death at the age of 30 Rakova had flown hundreds of missions.[38]

Bureaucrats and Society, Tsarist and Soviet

The intelligentsia defined itself in opposition to the tsarist state and in particular against "the bureaucracy." The traditional opposition of "society" (enlightened, selfless, progressive) and "bureaucracy" (rigid, authoritarian, corrupt, reactionary) was a cherished myth of pre-revolutionary Russia and, like most myths, not entirely without justification. As any reader of Russian literature of the nineteenth century (especially Gogol and Dostoevsky) will recall, corruption was a common enough phenomenon, as were mindless paperwork and a petty-authoritarian slavishness to rank. Still, while no one would deny that corruption was a problem in the Russian bureaucracy, many tsarist bureaucrats, or *chinovniki*, saw themselves as patriotic and even progressive Russians wanting to reform the system "from inside." To take just a few famous examples, there were the Miliutin brothers (Nikolai and Dmitry) active during the 1860s and in particular important in shaping the military reform; and Sergei Witte, who gained a degree in mathematics, worked as a railroad administrator and eventually became Finance Minister and Prime Minister during the upheavals of 1905. Furthermore as engineers, physicians, and economists were called into government service, the boundary between "society" and "bureaucracy" became more difficult to determine.

Soviet historian Petr Zaionchkovsky and his American colleague Daniel Orlovsky pointed out some time ago that the image of the corrupt bureaucrat is a stereotype needing revision.[39] By the final decades of the nineteenth century it became increasingly common for *chinovniki* – in particular at the higher ranks – to have university degrees. Most bureaucrats of the higher ranks were of noble origin but increasingly did not come from wealthy families. Indeed even among men (all *chinovniki* were by definition male) of the higher ranks, by the late nineteenth century a majority owned no landed estates. At the lower reaches of the bureaucracy it was almost impossible to raise a family on the salaries paid for clerks and other lowly office workers. Still, working in an office gave one social prestige and respectability, even if it often meant penury. Finally there was always the possibility of advancement – and of supplementing one's pay with bribes.[40]

The state employed an increasingly large number of people who, while not traditionally thought of as "bureaucrats," also derived their income from public sources. Among such positions were engineers for building roads and railways, telegraph clerks and delivery boys, typists (typewriters began to be widely used around the 1880s), teachers, university professors, and all sorts of jobs connected with the expanding railroads. Aside from state employment, there were also new jobs offered by the *zemstva* on the countryside and by the city governments. The frictions between *zemstva* employees (the so-called Third Element) and tsarist bureaucracy should not blind us to the fact that in many cases employees of the *zemstva*, such as teachers and physicians, lived very similar lives and held similar views to individuals in similar professions employed directly by the tsarist state. After all, obtaining one's income from the state does not necessarily make an individual support the existing government.

The increasing fluidity between educated society and the tsarist bureaucracy is shown by the career of Sergei Witte. Born to a noble but not wealthy family, Witte studied at the newly founded (1865) Novorossiiskii University in Odessa. He then made a very successful career as a railroad entrepreneur and administrator in the southwestern region of the Russian Empire (now in Ukraine). Witte was a practical man, but in no way a reactionary. His business dealings in the ethnically mixed southwestern provinces had brought him into contact with numerous national groups, especially Jews and Poles, and while he was not free of his age's prejudices, he despised "zoological" nationalism and even married a woman of Jewish background.

It was probably inevitable that the successful director of a private railroad line would be asked to participate in government decisions about encouraging economic development, but Witte came to the tsar's attention in a unique way. Both Tsar Alexander III and Witte were blunt men, and Alexander was impressed that the railroad director dared to point out to him the dangers of running the imperial train at high speeds (as the tsar loved to do) towards the imperial vacation palace on the Crimea. In 1888 Witte's prediction came true when Alexander III's train was involved in a serious wreck, and the tsar had occasion to recall the blunt administrator's words that it was preferable to sacrifice speed than the life of the tsar. While Alexander had not heeded Witte's original warning, the tsar did respect the man who had dared to challenge him – and turned out to be correct. Witte came to head the state railroad agency, then the Ministry of Finance, and finally Ministry of Finances, where he presided over Russia's industrializing boom of the 1890s and first years of the twentieth century. Under Nicholas II, as we have seen, Witte even achieved the status of prime minister before being dismissed by that tsar. Witte's career demonstrates both the possibilities and limitations for educated professions in the tsarist bureaucracy. While professional competence and energy could propel a talented individual to a top position, ultimately one's fate depended upon the tsar's whim.[41]

Another case of the connections between "society" and "bureaucracy" involves a far more famous individual than Witte, namely Vladimir Ilyich Ulianov, better known as Lenin. Lenin's father, Ilya Nikolaevich Ulianov, served as a teacher and ultimately school inspector in the southeastern province of Simbirsk, on the Volga river. Ilya Nikolaevich was a successful provincial educational bureaucrat but simultaneously a progressive member of the intelligentsia. Lenin's father was so successful in his position that he rose to a rank giving him the status of hereditary nobleman. It is a historical irony that this progressive state employee was father to two sons whose lives were intimately connected with the revolutionary movement. Alexander, his eldest son, was executed in 1887 for involvement in a conspiracy to assassinate Alexander III; the historical role of V. Lenin is only too well known. Just as the career of Sergei Witte demonstrates the possibility of "crossing the line" from the private business world to government bureaucracy, the Ulianov family shows that progressive bureaucrats, intelligentsia ideals, and revolution could coexist within a single family.

Revolutionaries like Lenin always defined themselves in opposition to the tsarist bureaucracy. Upon coming to power, however, the Bolsheviks quickly discovered that a modern state needs a bureaucracy to function. While the highest officials were sacked after the October 1917 revolution, nearly all other functionaries kept their jobs. Recent studies have shown that more than half of officials in the Soviet Commissariats of Agriculture and Food Supply had been serving in the same or similar posts before 1917. Even in the army, though most officers had sided with the Whites, "repentant" officers were generally welcomed into the new Red Army (though kept under close watch). Among the most famous officers to be absorbed into the Red Army leadership were General Aleksei Brusilov and Mikhail Tukhachevsky who served as a young lieutenant in World War I, was captured by the Germans, escaped to Russia just before the Bolshevik revolution, and rose rapidly in the Red Army, being promoted to the highest rank of Marshall of the Soviet Union in 1935 at the age of 42. Many tsarist bureaucrats remained at their posts – usually with slightly different job titles – well into the 1920s and even longer. At the same time the Communist Party's own membership – and bureaucracy – expanded greatly even during the chaotic Civil War years.

The word "bureaucracy" was a highly negative one for the new communist leadership, denoting inefficiency, petty power struggles, and even counterrevolution. But any modern state needs its army of civil servants to carry out orders, and the Soviet state was no different. Indeed the very fact that the communists took on cultural, social, and economic tasks that most modern states would leave to the private sector meant that the Soviet bureaucracy inevitably became enormous. Even during the NEP years, when government expenditures had to be slashed, despite numerous campaigns to reduce the bureaucracy, it actually grew in size. While the party demanded a slimmer bureaucracy, at the same time it required constant surveillance and allowed little room for personal initiative. The result was ever-increasing demands for documentation, reports, passes, testimonies – all the mind-numbing paperwork that would be familiar to any resident or visitor to the USSR to the very end and that in many ways continues in twenty-first-century Russia. On the other hand all these bits of paper – *bumazhki*, in Russian – that had to be filled out, stamped, and examined, provided employment for millions and, in many cases, the ability to exert petty-bureaucratic power over the hapless applicants. After he had been forced out of the USSR Trotsky would repeatedly criticize the Stalinist regime's massive bureaucracy, but in the Civil War period and early 1920s he too had been instrumental in creating this system.

Initially, large differentials in the salaries of government employees and especially party bureaucrats were to be avoided. The "party norm" set down that the salary of a communist official, no matter what position she or he held, should not exceed that of a qualified worker. After all, Lenin had recently written (in *State and Revolution*, 1918) that under communism even cooks (i.e., nonskilled citizens) would have to participate in the running of the state. By setting down the rule that even high officials in the communist government would not be paid more than ordinary workers, the Bolsheviks wanted to emphasize their solidarity with the working class. But very quickly this rule was ignored or side-stepped. In any case during the time of the War Communism and Civil War, payment in food and other goods was far more important than salaries in a depreciating and even worthless currency. Rather than higher wages, party workers often received specific rations or access to goods not generally available. One of the demands of the Kronstadt Rebels in early 1921, after all, was the elimination of such privileges. In the NEP period, efforts were made to reduce the number of administrative employees (in particular to cut budgets), though with indifferent results.

In the 1930s pay differentials among workers and high officials grew wider and the very idea of egalitarianism was denounced by Stalin, who explicitly defended higher wages for more qualified workers. While Stalin did not openly call for higher wages for high party officials, in fact by the late 1920s (and in many cases much earlier) members of the party elite were living far better than average Soviet workers. Even in the 1920s, middle-level administrators were being paid more than workers – which encouraged the latter to abandon the workbench in favor of the less dangerous, more prestigious, and better paying office.

Already in the 1920s one can see the beginnings of what the Yugoslav dissident Milovan Djilas later called "the new class."[42] This new "Soviet bourgeoisie" was made up of specialists, high administrators, and upper party officials. The term *nomenklatura*, popularized only much later, after World War II, describes this group that clearly already existed in embryonic form from the later 1920s. *Nomenklatura* refers to two separate phenomena: on the one hand to the practice of appointing only Communist Party members to certain positions (from ambassadorships to heads of research institutes to directors of factories), and on the other to the actual holders of such privileged positions. The *nomenklatura* (used in the second, sociological, sense) became the privileged elite of the USSR. They enjoyed high salaries (by Soviet standards) and, more importantly, access to specific stores and other privileges (foreign travel, exclusive vacation resorts on the Black Sea, goods and services available without long waits in line) not available to the average Soviet citizen.[43] The construction (1928–31) of an enormous and quite opulent apartment building on the banks of the Moscow river – later made famous in Yuri Trifonov's novel *The House on the Embankment* – symbolized the increasing divorce between the Soviet elite and everyday people. While members of this elite were hit hard by the purges of the late 1930s, the privileges themselves continued until the very end of the USSR.

In the USSR, where everyone worked for the state, it makes little sense to speak of "government employees." But a new kind of bureaucracy did develop under Soviet rule, the so-called *apparat*, or Communist Party apparatus, whose employees came to be known as *apparatchiki*. Being an *apparatchik* meant full-time employment as a party bureaucrat, perhaps overseeing party propaganda, or the young communists (Komsomol), or any number of diverse party offices. *Apparatchiki* were by definition party members, but most party members held jobs outside the *apparat*. Not all *apparatchiki* were members of the *nomenklatura*, though the most important positions would fall into that category. The growth of the *apparat* was important not just as a drain on government resources but also because it created a kind of state within a state, sheltering party *apparatchiki* from new ideas or criticism. Indeed one may interpret the purges of the late 1930s as Stalin's attempt to shake up this group. At the same time it needs to be noted that the most radical reformer in Soviet history, Mikhail Gorbachev, was the epitome of an *apparatchik*, having spent his entire professional life working in

Communist Party offices. His reform's failure may be attributed to the shelter – and blinders – that this kind of professional life provided.

Edges of Society: Criminality, Social and Sexual "Deviance"

Like all societies, the Russian Empire and USSR had their "deviant" members. It should be stressed that as used here, "deviance" is not a moral category but a sociological label applied to individuals falling outside the acceptable norms of a given society. For example, in the twenty-first century few would categorize homosexuals as "deviant," much less criminal, but in both the Russian Empire and (after 1934) USSR homosexual behavior (between males, in any case) was a criminal offense. In general both before and after 1917, societal norms in Russia-USSR were considerably less permissive than most twenty-first-century European or North American societies. Young people were expected to respect elders, women needed to defer to men, state and police authority could seldom be challenged by citizens.

Throughout this period, it was expected that practically everyone would marry and, if possible, bear children. The few exceptions to this rule were usually religiously sanctioned; that is, Catholic priests or Orthodox monk and nuns. But Orthodox parish clergy, rabbis, and Muslim clerics all married and had families. Thus the heterosexual family was considered the norm and any other form of sexuality a deviation. Sexual relations before marriage were not, however, unusual nor particularly condemned. If a pregnancy resulted, however, the couple was expected to marry. Failure to do so brought dishonor to both individuals though, of course, the young man could deny his involvement. The frequency of extramarital affairs is impossible to gauge with any precision, but it is clear that they were far from rare, though rates of illegitimacy were lower in Russia than in western Europe (the rates reflect, of course, babies *born* to unwed mothers, not *conceived* by unmarried women). A sexual double standard predominated by which men were expected to have occasional "flings" outside marriage, but the same behavior for women was severely condemned. Two literary sources reflect this attitude: Anna Karenina's life is destroyed by her love for Count Vronsky. On a less dramatic note, in Chekhov's exquisite short story "The Lady with the Little Dog" Dmitry Dmitrich has clearly engaged in numerous extramarital affairs before meeting Anna Sergeevna ,who equally clearly has never before cheated on her husband.

Prostitution, though disdained and censured by religious and civil authorities, was both legal and common in the pre-revolutionary era. Even on the countryside the practice of granting sexual favors in return for payment was not unheard-of, though of course the young lady in question would often have a difficult time finding a husband in her community. In the cities there were brothels, licensed prostitutes (registered with the police and carrying a "yellow ticket"), and illegal streetwalkers. As in many other European countries, frequenting prostitutes was widely tolerated as a necessary outlet for excess male sexual drive, even for married men (another form of the prevalent sexual double standard). And in the cities many young male workers came from the countryside without family (or before marrying) and had no other sexual outlets.

With the revolution, prostitution was outlawed in Russia but continued to exist on the margins of society. During the NEP (the 1920s), the disparity of income between most workers and the free-spending *nepmen* meant that many women and girls were forced to supplement their incomes through different forms of prostitution. The authorities did not extend a great deal of energy in the 1920s in eradicating prostitution, placing their emphasis instead on educating the populace on healthy sexuality, including avoiding venereal diseases. The 1920s were a period of unprecedented sexual freedom for many but with the usual unintended consequences – unwanted pregnancies, spread of disease, and the disruption of traditional family structures. While contraceptive devices and abortions had been completely banned in pre-revolutionary Russia, after 1917 both were – in principle – available, though in fact Soviet industry was not capable of producing much in the way of contraceptives either in the 1920s or later. Abortions were a different matter. While broadly condemned (more as a health than moral issue), without practical alternatives the number of abortions carried out annually rose in the 1920s, already exceeding the number of live births by 1922 and with over 12 times as many abortions as live births in 1929. With the turn to more traditional values after Stalin had consolidated power, abortions were outlawed in 1936 (this prohibition would only be lifted after Stalin's death, in 1955).[44]

In the Russian Empire, homosexuality was seen as a sinful act that deserved punishment. Few were ready to address the issue openly or even to admit that it existed. Despite this widespread silence, however, there is evidence that a man who sought homosexual sex in St Petersburg and Moscow (at least) could find it in bathhouses and other specific spots, known to homosexuals, young males wishing to earn money, and the police. In the memoirs of Russian homosexuals, nearly all of middle-class or wealthy backgrounds, bathhouse attendants, young soldiers, and carriage drivers figure among prospective partners. But homosexual behavior was generally considered a mainly upper-class perversion and finds next to no mention in the (admittedly scanty) sources we have on Russian peasants. Mikhail Artsybashov's novel *Sanin* (published 1907) dealt frankly with the topic of homosexuality (and other "deviant" behaviors), making the book a *succès de scandale*. Ironically one of the best-known homosexuals of the post-reform period was the arch-reactionary Prince Vladimir Petrovich Meshchersky whose sexual proclivities did not prevent him from being a visitor to the imperial palace under

Alexander III. Because women had less access to the public sphere – a respectable woman could hardly go alone to a restaurant, much less to a bathhouse – we have far less evidence of female homosexuality (the word "lesbianism" was almost never used at the time).

After the revolution homosexuality ceased, at least for a time, to be a crime but continued to be considered deviant behavior that could be treated by psychological and other methods. However, homosexuals continued to be persecuted both on a social level and by actual statute in different parts of the USSR. Even this limited toleration came to an end in the mid-1930s with sodomy being recriminalized in 1933–4, subject to a five-year prison sentence. But once again the recriminalization of homosexual behavior applied, strictly speaking, to men alone. Apparently the Stalinist rulers of the USSR did not consider female homosexuality to be a threat to the social and political order – or simply could not conceive of such a thing.[45]

If homosexuals were relegated to the "edges" of both Russian and Soviet society, criminals were quite literally a society apart. Russia was only beginning to develop a modern penitentiary system in the post-reform period; before that time, minor misdemeanors were dealt with by flogging, while more serious crimes were punished by exile to Siberia. Compared with other European countries, the death penalty was rarely carried out in Russia, with the exception of very serious political crimes. Instead exile in Siberia removed convicts from European Russia, where they would often found families and live out the rest of their lives. The Great Reforms also brought an abolition of the "barbaric" (from a liberal European point of view) practice of flogging, though it appears that for many poor Russians, physical chastisement was preferable to a prison term, which often left the convict's family destitute.[46]

With the large influx of peasants to cities in the final decades of the nineteenth century and into the early twentieth century, crime rates rose in Russian cities. Respectable people increasingly complained about "hooligans" (the English word became part of the Russian language) who preyed on middle-class people. After the revolution of 1905 both the "public" and government were convinced that the public order was threatened by street crime. In many official reports the connection between revolutionary activities and banditry was made directly. The usual solutions proposed were more surveillance and stricter punishment, but the Russian Empire's chronic lack of funds frustrated any significant reform.[47]

The attitude toward "criminality" changed significantly after the revolution. Now the criminal, rather than being a wayward sinner who merited punishment for transgressing divine and earthly law, was seen as a mirror of abnormal social relations. This did not mean, of course, that criminals no longer faced punishment but that – in theory, at least – the purpose of prison was to rehabilitate the criminal rather than to expiate crimes. During the 1920s, disagreements over just

FIGURE 2.3   *Bezprizornye* (street orphans).
Source: David King Collection, London.

what constituted a crime and how criminals should be punished/rehabilitated combined with the building of a court system and overall social (not political) laxity, with the effect that many petty-criminal acts were not prosecuted. Indeed the decade was characterized by the seldom-legal activities of bands of unsupervised children – the so-called *bezprizornye* – who lived on the streets and engaged in prostitution, thievery, and other deviant behaviors. The *bezprizornye*, often orphans or displaced children whose parents had left Russia, died, had been arrested, or otherwise disappeared, formed a juvenile criminal class that the Soviet authorities was quite incapable of dealing with throughout the NEP period.[48]

With the industrial push of the Five-Year Plans in the 1930s and the mass arrests and dislocations of collectivization on the countryside, millions of Soviet citizens found themselves uprooted. American historian Moshe Lewin speaks of a "quicksand society" at this time, where previously accepted norms and social structures had disappeared but new standards of everyday life were still being worked out.[49] Archival research has shown that communist authorities in the 1930s were very worried about the potential for social unrest posed by millions of people on the move from countryside to city. The 1932 law introducing internal passports, required of all Soviet citizens, was one attempt to keep tabs on the potentially troublesome populace. In order to live or reside in any part of the USSR, citizens had to present this vital document. Residence in large cities such as Moscow and Leningrad required additional special permission.

In the early 1930s harsh laws were passed to punish, among other things, theft of state property, speculation (often selling that property), banditry, and hooliganism (a catch-all term that could range from vandalism to vagrancy to public drunkenness). The repressive apparatus put in place to fight such criminality would be used in the second half of the 1930s against those accused of political crimes during the Great Terror. The label of "socially harmful elements" and "enemies of the people," thus shifted from everyday criminals to real or imagined political opponents like "Trotskyites" or "Zinovievists." We should not, however, lose sight of the fact that under Stalin, the distinction between "ordinary" and "political" crime was fuzzy or even nonexistent. A peasant who "expropriated state property" (by taking home grain to her family) or a worker who "sabotaged production" (by showing up for work drunk and damaging a machine) was regarded as just as great a threat to the stability of Soviet society as were followers of Trotsky.[50]

The mass arrests of the late 1930s sent millions to Siberian labor camps, and these individuals, even after they had served their sentences, would for decades afterwards bear the stigma of having been arrested as an "enemy of the people." In many ways their experiences paralleled those of Siberian exiles of the nineteenth century who were also often forbidden to return to European Russia even after serving their sentences. The mass arrests not only stigmatized the millions who spent time in the Gulag but left its mark on their parents, spouses, and children who were often treated with fear and mistrust back at home.[51]

Amusements, Free Time, Leisure

Since Adam bit into the fruit, if we accept the biblical account, human beings have been condemned to earn their living "by the sweat of their brow." But life is more than just work: festivals, amusements, and games have always provided relief from the workday grind. Still, the concept of mass "leisure" and "free time" is a quite recent one, dating from the spread of industrialization in the nineteenth century. By the late nineteenth century, as middle-class people and skilled workers began to enjoy somewhat more time away from the job as well as having a little more money to spend on pleasure, a new "leisure industry" began to take shape in Russia, as in western Europe.

When one speaks of amusements in the Russian context, it makes sense to start with vodka. In Russian culture vodka is inextricably linked with celebrations, conviviality, and social gatherings. Drinking – at least in its socially acceptable

Society   83

form – is never done alone, but always with companions, usually male. True, in the family sphere one might celebrate a birth or wedding, or mourn a death at a funeral, by drinking vodka. Special guests were usually welcomed with a glass and, as even present-day visitors to Russia can attest, refusing such a welcoming drink can be very awkward indeed. At the workplace, newcomers were often expected to pay for a round of drinks for co-workers; refusing to drink would gain one a poor reputation as antisocial. Vodka also played a role in masculine rites of passage, as when apprentices or younger workers treated older workers to vodka upon finishing training or being advanced to a more skilled job. Bosses too were expected to provide libations for special occasions – for example a name day or birth of a child.

Most drinking in pre-revolutionary Russia, however, took place in the tavern, often the only place where men could gather outside church, work, or the home. Women were not welcome in taverns; indeed a respectable woman, even if seeking her husband inside, would not cross the tavern threshold. Because taverns rarely served very much aside from vodka, their social function inevitably involved imbibing. In this way conviviality, relaxation, and getting away from the worries or irritations of home life generally involved drinking. To be sure, lack of funds and long working hours prevented most workers or peasants from visiting taverns frequently, but Sundays generally found drinking establishments full – and employers complained of increased absenteeism on Mondays. By the early twentieth century one could visit a number of different "classes" of taverns in Russian cities, from modest establishments offering little more than vodka and billiards to more refined places where one could listen to music, play cards, and perhaps even have dinner with a lady. In this way the boundary between lower-class taverns and respectable restaurants and cafés was becoming hazy.[52]

The prohibition on sales of vodka proclaimed upon the declaration of war with Germany dealt traditional taverns a mortal blow. While wine and beer continued to be legal in most parts of Russia, even these could not be sold in St Petersburg. These prohibitions on hard liquor continued well into the Soviet period before being completely abolished in the mid-1920s. Allowing the sale and consumption of vodka did not, however, mean that the communists accepted this form of pre-revolutionary conviviality. Drunkenness was termed socially harmful and possibly even counterrevolutionary. Propaganda efforts showed the bad effects of excessive alcohol consumption on the human body as well as on family and society as a whole. One poster of the 1920s even connected public drunkenness with another "backward practice," religion, showing drunken men lying unconscious on the ground, with the caption "Drunkenness: a survival of religious festivals." The proper communist could drink vodka but must never become drunk: drunkenness was one of the most common reasons for individuals to be kicked out of the party in the 1920s.[53]

Of course the tavern was not the only place of amusement for Russians. Already by the later nineteenth century church, state, and societal organizations had recognized that alternatives to drinking as a pastime had to be offered. But the most frequent "solution" – setting up tearooms where workers could sit and read in a "cultured" manner – did not find wide appeal. In the end not charities but private enterprise offered more popular alternatives to the tavern. By the early twentieth century, a Russian city dweller of relatively modest means had a number of choices on how to spend an evening: at a music hall or cabaret, in a crowd cheering on athletes at the bicycle races or a prizefight, at the circus (unlike in the west, Russian circuses are permanent, not traveling, institutions), at a movie, or simply at home, reading one of the action-packed books written specifically for a semiliterate public. While the intelligentsia bemoaned or mocked such new manifestations of culture, we need not accept their elitism. After all, the main purpose of leisure was enjoyment, not necessarily edification. It should be noticed, however, that nearly all of these new forms of leisure activity involved an urban population, not the peasant majority.[54]

The middle class, too, enjoyed new forms of leisure. One was simple consumerism, though the word did not exist yet. But Russian cities did have growing numbers of department stores where middle-class people – in particular women – could spend time looking at, trying on, or even purchasing fashionable clothing or other items. The department store gave middle-class women a respectable place to spend time in public, another innovation. While men of this class were expected to spend their times at work earning money, one important task for bourgeois women was to spend that money in a wise and economical manner, while also creating a respectable home. The quest for respectability extended to all spheres of life, as numerous very popular books on good manners and proper public behavior attest. Clearly many Russians both desired to be seen as respectable and were unsure of exactly what respectability entailed. The mass-produced instruction book helped someone without an elite upbringing to fit in with "polite society."

The railroad enabled more and more people to leave their native place, whether for a short visit, to work in the city for a longer period, or to change one's residence permanently by emigration abroad or to Siberia. While most Russians could not afford to be "tourists" (a word that came to Russian from English in the early twentieth century) in this period, the number of excursions and resorts – especially on the Black Sea – was growing. And, of course, wealthier Russians spent their summers in German spas or the French Riviera in greater numbers than ever before. After the revolution, and in particular from the late 1920s onward, it became difficult for Soviet citizens to travel abroad, but they did to some extent pursue *turizm* within their vast country. Only after World War II, though, indeed not until the 1960s or 1970s, did it become fairly common for Soviet citizens to spend a summer vacation away from home.[55]

In the years immediately after 1917 most Russians were more interested in simple survival to be much concerned with leisure. During the NEP, dance halls and restaurants catered mainly to the sordid tastes of the *nepmen* but were far too expensive for most honest Soviet citizens. The communists were concerned, however, with creating wholesome and enjoyable leisure activities. Like pre-revolutionary middle-class reformers, communists deplored the tavern and advocated new ways of spending free time. One alternative was "physical culture" – *fizkultura* – that is, sport, body-building, gymnastics, and the like. *Fizkultura* combined public ceremonies, enthusiastic poems, and physical activity – with a certain amount of military training thrown in for good measure. Physical activity was seen as a way of promoting health, keeping young (and not-so-young) people away from vices, and building class consciousness. Large-scale marches became a traditional way to celebrate International Worker's Day (May 1) and the anniversary of the Great Socialist Revolution of 1917 in November. The USSR also sponsored a number of professional sports teams, in particular for football ("soccer"), such as the Moscow Dinamo team whose stadium, constructed in 1935, could hold 35,000 fans. Other Soviet *sportsmeny* excelled in hockey, track, and basketball (the incorporation of Lithuania in 1941 would help there) but the USSR did not participate in the Olympic Games until 1952.[56]

Conclusion

Taking the span 1861–1945 on a macro level, many constants are apparent throughout these roughly four generations. While the USSR in 1945 was vastly more industrialized than the pre-reform Russian Empire, even at the latter date most Soviet citizens still lived on the countryside. While no longer serfs, *kolkhozniki* in 1945 lacked basic civil rights (such as the right to move away from the collective farm) that other Soviet citizens possessed. Women, though enjoying many more rights than in 1861, continued to be employed disproportionately in low-status, low-paying jobs and remained under-represented in the Communist Party, especially at its higher reaches. Sexual "deviants" like homosexuals continued to live their lives on the edges of society, subject to both personal scandal and even to criminal penalties. Those who broke the law continued to be subject to severe punishments; indeed it was more likely that a convicted felon would receive the death sentence.

For all that, society as a whole had changed immensely. Serfs became free peasants, and from the 1890s streamed to the cities to become industrial workers. The nascent industrial working class of 1917 grew enormously during the Five-Year Plans of the 1930s, bringing millions of peasants (often unwillingly) to growing industrial cities. Everyday life also changed as electricity spread across cities, towns, and even to the countryside. Women increasingly took on paying work outside the home and were encouraged by communist ideology to join the party and play a public role in spreading communist ideals. While traditional gender roles and even symbols of middle-class comfort began to run in the second half of the 1930s, the new middle class had shed the antigovernment, critical stance of the pre-revolutionary intelligentsia. Instead the "New Class" of privileged Soviet intellectuals and functionaries were relentlessly positive about the achievements and progressive trends in the Soviet state.

Chapter 3

Nations

Neither the Russian Empire nor the Soviet Union was a nation state. That is to say, both before and after 1917 the legitimacy of the polity ("state") was derived not from the consent of its citizens ("nation"); nor did any one ethnic-linguistic group ("nation") make up the overwhelming majority (or, depending on definition, even a simple majority) in the country. Before 1917 the tsar considered himself a legitimate ruler not because he belonged to the Russian nation but more simply because God had placed him in his role as head of the Russian Empire. After 1917 the communist leadership replaced "God" with the legitimacy of history, as interpreted by Karl Marx. Thus Stalin, born a Georgian and speaking Russian with an accent, could see himself as no less legitimate a ruler than Tsar Nicholas II, who spoke English with his wife and children at home. In short, when considering "Russian" history in this period, we must be careful not to fall into the trap of imposing categories more appropriate to western European nation states.

At the same time it would be inaccurate and foolish to deny the overwhelming importance of the Russian nation, Russian language, and the Russian Orthodox religion. While the tsars after Catherine the Great certainly had more German than Russian blood in their veins, they spoke Russian and were required to follow the Russian Orthodox religion. While all tsars in the nineteenth century married foreigners (all German except for Alexander III's wife, Dagmar of Denmark), before these foreign princesses could wed the tsar they were obliged to convert to Orthodoxy. All of the tsar's children, it goes without saying, were also brought up in that religion. Similarly, while both tsars and – at least initially – many Bolshevik leaders spoke several European languages and felt at home in European culture as a whole, the language used in official discourse was always Russian. It was taken for granted that all of the tsar's subjects, no matter what their native

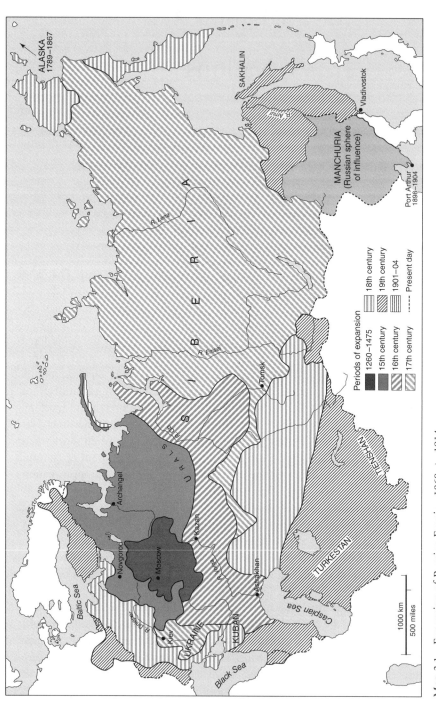

MAP 3.1   Expansion of Russian Empire, 1860s to 1914.
Source: based on Gregory Freeze, ed., *Russia: A History*, Oxford University Press, 1997, p. 423.

tongue was, would learn some Russian, in particular if they wished to rise in the world. Under the Soviet system, much more importance and respect was afforded "minority languages," but after the 1920s the predominance of Russian returned, and showing too much interest, for example, in using Ukrainian in schools and official places could land a Soviet citizen in trouble.

In Russian it is possible to distinguish between *russkii* and *rossiiskii*, words that in English must both be translated as "Russian." *Russkii* is the more common adjective, referring to language and ethnic group. *Rossiiskii* has a much more narrow usage, referring to the Russian state as a whole (geographically, not ethno-linguistically) and being used mainly in such official turns of phrase as "Russian Empire" and (today) "Russian Federation." The problem is, when Russian officials in the pre-1917 period spoke of their "broad homeland" (to use a Soviet phrase), they nearly always used the adjective *russkii*, even where *rossiiskii* would have been more accurate. Thus the Russifying Turkestan governor general, Konstantin Kaufman (despite his German surname, he certainly considered himself *russkii*), asked to be buried in the *russkaia* soil … of Tashkent, in central Asia! In this way the Russian Empire (and, to a lesser extent, USSR) at times was regarded by Russians as a kind of nation state in the making. This tension is reflected also in the tendency outside Russia to speak of Stalin (to take only the most obvious example) as a "Russian" statesman or to speak of "Russian" foreign policy in the 1920s and 1930s.

Comparing the "nationality policy" (a term referring to the totality of laws and administrative practices the Russian/Soviet state adopted toward non-Russians) of the Russian Empire and the USSR, the first obvious difference is the far more overt and activist nature of Soviet nationality policy. The Russian Empire lacked any specific legal definition of "nationality," while the USSR already by the early 1930s demanded that each citizen possess a single nationality (e.g., Uzbek, Jewish, Russian, Ukrainian, Georgian, etc.) that would be inscribed in his or her passport. For the pre-1917 period, religion was much more important for people's identity than nationality was. In the Soviet period, religion was regarded officially as a "survival of the past" doomed to disappear, while nationality was seen as a necessary part of a modern identity. More than that, the USSR went out of its way to use ethnicity as an organizing principle for education, party structure, and administrative boundaries. Thus, at least in principle, the Soviet leaders saw absolutely no conflict between being Russian (or Latvian, Armenian, Uzbek) *and* Soviet. One's "broader fatherland" was the USSR, to be sure, but this did not necessarily mean that one spoke Russian at home. Of course, as we will see, the realities were more complex.

Especially in the 1920s and early 1930s, the Soviet authorities expended significant resources to promote national cultures, setting up schools, periodicals, and publishing houses. Unlike the Russian Empire, the USSR always officially proclaimed itself to be a multinational state with equal rights for all cultures. While the USSR officially repudiated Russification as a policy, in fact it was far more successful at spreading the Russian language than the Russian Empire had been. While in principle Soviet citizens could have their children educated in, say, Belarusian, Kazakh, or Tatar, everyone was expected to learn at least some Russian (which was the language of command in the Red Army), and to "get ahead" in Soviet society good Russian skills were a prerequisite. Throughout the Soviet period, one can observe a tension in nationality policy between the ideology of "friendship of nations" and the reality of one dominant language and culture.

Nationalities in the Russian Empire

The first and only modern census carried out in the Russian Empire in 1897 demonstrated the ethnic diversity of the empire's population. The tsar's subjects belonged to dozens of ethno-linguistic groups and a variety of religions from pagan (nature-worshiping) tribes to Sunni and Shi'ite Muslims, a variety of Christian denominations, Jews, and even Buddhists. Among languages, native speakers of East Slavic tongues (Russian, Belarusian, Ukrainian) made up around two-thirds of the total population, with Russian speakers representing 44.31 percent of the total population. Besides these three groups, ten others represented more than 1 percent of the empire's total population (or, in absolute numbers 1.2 million individuals): Poles, Jews, Kazakhs, Tatars, Germans, Lithuanians, Bashkirs, Latvians, Georgians, and Armenians (in descending order according to size).[1] "Moldavians," Mordvin, Estonians, Uzbeks, and Tajiks made up between 0.9 percent and 0.3 percent (1.1 million to 0.4 million). Looking over these ethnic groups we get some idea of the diversity of the empire's population. Among them we find Muslims (Kazakhs, Tajiks, Uzbeks, "Tatars" – the latter group including both Sunni Volga and Crimean Tatars as well as mainly Shi'ite Azeris), Catholics, Protestants, Jews, and nominally Orthodox but retaining some pagan practices (Mordvin). Linguistically we find, besides Slavs, a number of groups ranging from Indo-European Armenian and Tajik (related to Persian), to Turkic Uzbek and Kazakh, to Finnic Mordvin.

Official statistics give only one, quite simplified, side of the story. To begin with, there was the problem of bias. Even at the time it was thought that the numbers for Russians ("Great Russians") were exaggerated and those for certain ethnic groups (e.g., Jews, Poles, Armenians) under-reported. Even more difficult was the question of defining the nation and, more specifically, setting down criteria determining where one nation (or language) ended and another began. For example, the people we now know as "Kazakhs" were called "Kirgiz" by official Russia in this census (the group we term "Kyrgyz" were called "Kara-Kirgiz" or

"Black" Kirgiz). While statisticians did record Ukrainian ("Little Russian") and Belarusian ("White Russian") as native tongues, officially both of these (and "Great Russian") were considered dialects of a unitary Russian language (and nation).

And what to do with the Jews? In western (and even central) Europe Jews were generally considered English, French, or German, differing from their fellow citizens only in religion. This kind of definition did not fit pre-1917 Russia. Besides their religious differences, Jews spoke a different language (more than 90 percent were native speakers of Yiddish), tended to live apart from their Christian neighbors, and even when acculturated – an unusual case before the twentieth century – were generally regarded as Jews rather than Russians (or Poles) by their Gentile neighbors. In a later section the thorny issue of the Jewish nationality will be considered in more detail; at this point it suffices to keep in mind that Jews were nearly universally (and not just by antisemites) seen as a nation apart.

The example of the Jews should alert us to the frequent connection between nation and religion. Again this phenomenon in Eastern Europe (and, it must be said, in most of the rest of the world) runs counter to the ideal type of the secular nation as developed in and after the French Revolution. In the Russian Empire there was no legal definition of "nation" – but every individual had a religion (the possibility of being atheist or *konfessionslos* ["without religious denomination" – a legal category used in France and central Europe] did not exist). Later the USSR would make nationality a required category in official documents, such as in internal passports. Before 1917, however, while certain nationalities suffered legal disabilities (e.g., Poles could seldom get state jobs in the western part of the empire), factors like religion, culture, and language used at home had to be used to determine nationality. In the end, language and religion were the most significant criteria. Some national groups (e.g., Estonians, Lithuanians, Armenians) spoke a unique language that set them apart from others. But the dividing line between peasants speaking a version of Belarusian and others speaking a version of Polish would not be so clear because of the similarity of these Slavic languages. By equating Catholic and Polish, the government inadvertently pushed Catholic Belarusians toward the Polish nation (even while some officials, particularly from the turn of the century onward, realized this and spoke out against the Catholic = Polish equation).[2] In central Asia matters were even more complicated, with a number of groups (Kyrgyz, Turkmen, Kazakhs, Uzbeks) speaking similar Turkic languages and all belonging to the Muslim religion, though often following very diverse religious rituals and practices. It was only during the Soviet period that strict differentiation between these nations was achieved, in part by using nomadic versus settled urban lifestyles as markers of national difference (depending on location, town dwellers were often termed Uzbek) and codifying languages to enhance differences between them.

Like most Europeans and North Americans of the time, the Russian state did not regard all ethnic groups as equal. An implicit hierarchy of ethnicity and religion existed and informed policy. At the top stood Christians and settled agriculturalists or town dwellers; at the bottom were pagans and nomads.[3] (A similar hierarchy in North America led to policies intended to destroy native cultures and languages, replacing them with English-speaking Christian culture.) In general, however, the Russian Empire did not go in for ambitious projects of social engineering. Rather national groups were generally tolerated, as were diverse religions, as long as the groups remained loyal to tsarist rule (which meant practically that taxes were paid and public order was preserved). Thus for the most part pagan tribes in Siberia were left to follow their own way or life, and the ardent Russian nationalist Konstantin Kaufman (mentioned above) as governor general of Turkestan specifically forbade active Orthodox proselytizing among Muslims, fearing that such activity would lead to public unrest.

Thus, perhaps ironically, the most problematic national groups from the point of view of St Petersburg were not Muslim Kazakhs or Buddhist Kalmyks but Jews and Catholic Poles, and to a lesser extent Protestant Germans. In part the hostility of Russian officialdom toward these groups may be explained by their residence along the western borderlands of the empire, where the growing menace of the German Empire was felt. The fact that all three groups lived on both sides of the Russian–German and Russian–Austrian border must have contributed to the unease felt by tsarist officials toward them. As for the Poles, the complicated relations between this Slavic nation and the Russians goes back at least to the early seventeenth century when a Pole – briefly – occupied the Muscovite throne. Russians mistrusted Poles as followers of Roman Catholicism who wished to spread that religion to the east; Poles regarded Russians as culturally inferior adherents to a schismatic version of Christianity.[4] Poles did not forget the participation of Russia in the Partitions of Poland (1772–95) that destroyed Polish independence for over a century; Russians remembered the Polish uprisings of 1830 and 1863, which had aimed to destroy Russian rule over them (and had in both cases failed, bringing further Russian repression). Poles considered the partitions a historical crime; St Petersburg looked on its Polish subjects as potential rebels who required constant surveillance.[5]

As for Jews, Russian officials were less motivated by age-old Christian prejudices against "Christ killers" – though such prejudices certainly continued to exist – than by more modern considerations of Jews as economically exploitative of "Russian" (for us, Ukrainian and Belarusian) peasants and by fears of a younger generation of Jews influenced by western ideas of socialism. Tsarist officialdom certainly regarded Jews as the single most problematic national group in the empire, and worst of all were young, Russian-speaking and nonreligious Jews such as Leon Trotsky, born Lev Davidovich Bronshtein in 1879. While St Petersburg was prepared to tolerate and even to some extent respect traditional Jewish religion, modern Russian-speaking Jews, whether radicals like Trotsky, liberals like the lawyer Genrykh Sliozberg, or Zionists like Vladimir Zhabotinsky were seen as inherently dangerous elements.

Germans represented a near total opposite from Jews in the Russian official mind. They lived as successful farmers along the Volga River (having been invited to settle there by Catherine the Great) and in small agricultural colonies throughout the Russian southwest (today's Ukraine). Most important from the official point of view, however, was the relatively small but wealthy German nobility that for most of the nineteenth century dominated cultural, economic, and even autonomous political life in the Baltic provinces (today's Estonia and Latvia). Allowed by the Russian tsar to retain their privileged position here after the incorporation of this region into the empire by Peter the Great, the Baltic Germans repaid the tsar's trust by serving with distinction in the tsar's army, administration, and diplomatic corps.[6]

With the unification of Germany in 1871, however, some elements among Russian officialdom feared – without a great deal of justification – that allowing continued German-dominated autonomy in this strategic region could endanger the Russian Empire in case of war with Germany. For this reason in the 1880s the privileged political situation of the Baltic Germans was essentially abolished, though, it must be said, without seriously damaging their economic and social predominance. Unlike the Poles, the Germans never showed any significant disloyalty to the tsar; it was only the largely theoretical problem of dual loyalties between Russia and Germany that disturbed Russian officialdom. Nonetheless this not-entirely rational fear of Baltic Germans supporting the Russian Empire's enemies in time of war led to policies aimed against German privileges, fomenting the very German national sympathies that Russian officials had feared.[7]

Central Asia represented a totally different region from the Baltic. Russian "Turkestan," as the region was broadly known, had been acquired in the second half of the nineteenth century and was for most Russians a completely foreign and exotic land. In the 1860s and 1870s the Russian Empire extended its rule into central Asia, capturing the cities of Tashkent, Bukhara, Samarkand, and Khiva. In 1867 the new governor-generalship of Turkestan was created, with Tashkent as its capital and General Konstantin Kaufman as its first governor general. By around 1890, Russian conquest of central Asia was complete, from the eastern shores of the Caspian to the border of China and reaching to the south to Afghanistan. This Russian expansion was aided by a number of factors, two of which are of primary importance. First the local peoples had little connection with one another aside from the Muslim religion, and even that was practiced quite differently by nomadic Turkomen or Kazakhs and settled Sarts (ancestors of present-day Uzbeks). Second no other major power had designs on this region

– once the Russians began to approach Afghanistan and British India (present-day Pakistan), British disapproval and veiled threats put an end to Russian expansion.[8]

More than any other region of the Russian Empire, central Asia resembled a true European colony. In Tashkent, for example, the "European city" built from the 1860s was both architecturally distinct and physically separate from the traditional town, as in French Algiers in northern Africa.[9] Russians in central Asia tended to regard themselves as the bearer of a superior civilization, just like the British in India or Germans in Southwest Africa (today's Namibia). And economic relations between central Asia and the Russian center were also on a colonial basis: the growing Russian textile industry required increasing amounts of raw cotton. The disruption of cotton deliveries from the US south caused by the American Civil War (1861–5) helped convince Europeans, including Russians, to seek alternative sources of the precious fiber. By the end of the century, most cotton spun into cloth in Russian textile mills came from central Asia. In turn, manufactured goods from the Russian center dominated markets in the region.

───────── Imperial Expansion and Policy: 1863–1917 ─────────

Already by the mid-sixteenth century under Ivan the Terrible Russia had become a multiethnic state by conquering Muslim Tatar lands along the Volga. Peter the Great extended Russian rule to the Baltic Sea and attempted less successfully to acquire Ottoman territory to the south. Peter was also the Russian ruler who for the first time used the title *imperator* (emperor) and called the state *Rossiiskaia Imperiia* (Russian Empire). By the end of the Napoleonic Wars (1815), Russia extended to the Black Sea to the south, eastward to the Pacific, and reigned over Finland (as an autonomous Grand Duchy), the Baltic Provinces, and the Kingdom of Poland in the west. Tsar Alexander I (reigned 1801–25) managed to gain the majority of Polish lands at the Congress of Vienna (1814–15), including the capital city Warsaw. In the first half of the nineteenth century Russian rule extended south across the Caucasus mountains to include nationalities such as Georgians, Armenians, "Tatars" (as all Muslims tended to be called at the time), and various "mountain peoples" such as Chechens and Lezgins. The Russian Empire also extended across the northern reaches of the central Asian steppe (today's northern Kazakhstan), though its expansion to the south towards Afghanistan would occur in the second half of the century.[10]

It should be remembered that at the beginning of our period, Russia extended across the Bering Strait and included Alaska. Recognizing Russia's inability to hold that territory and needing money to finance the Great Reforms, Alexander II agreed in 1867 to sell the enormous territory to the United States for $7.2

MAP 3.2 Russian Poland and the Jewish Pale of Settlement.
Source: based on Benjamin Nathans, *Beyond the Pale*, University of California Press, 2002, p. 30.

million. This lost territory was more than made up for as the Russian Empire extended south into central Asia. There was no clear plan of imperial conquest here. In fact the ambitious General Michael Cherniaev violated direct orders when he took the central Asian city of Tashkent for Russia in 1865. Because of his success, however, Cherniaev received a promotion instead of a court martial.[11] Over the next two decades the Emirate of Kokand and the Khanate of Khiva came under Russian control (though the latter officially remained a "protectorate").[12] By the end of the century the Russian Empire's southern boundaries (with Afghanistan, Iran, and the Ottoman Empire) had reached their furthest extent – to the great concern of British imperialists in India who feared (without much reason) nefarious Russian plans to interfere in British India (for more detail see chapter 6, "World," pp. 179–80).

There was never a coherent "nationality policy" in the Russian Empire; indeed as we have seen, St Petersburg was uncomfortable with the very concept of "nationality." Like it or not, however, the empire had to deal with the large number of non-Russians living within its borders. Policies toward non-Russians were always connected with other issues – religion, the economy, politics, education, administrative centralization – and were not always even perceived as mainly "national" in St Petersburg. To simplify, one may sum up these policies as belonging under four general rubrics: denial, avoidance, centralization, or reactive repression.

The best example of denial was official policy toward Ukrainians and Belarusians. Both of these ethnic groups were regarded as branches of the Russian nation and it was expected with education (in Russian, of course) both would gradually wither away. To quote the (in)famous 1863 words of the Minister of the Interior, Petr Valuev, "no separate Little Russian [Ukrainian] language has ever existed, does exist, or could exist." The vociferous tone of the statement suggests that Valuev knew very well that the Ukrainian language did exist at least as a potential vehicle of high culture and science. By denying the existence of the Ukrainian or Belarusian languages St Petersburg justified the use of Russian in schools (which in any case were few and attended by a minority of the local population) and hoped that the population – mainly peasants – using these languages, once educated, would be absorbed into the Russian nation.[13]

Avoidance of the national issue can be seen in central Asia and the Caucasus. That is, Russian administrators made no serious efforts to spread their language and culture (including the Orthodox religion) in these regions, fearing social unrest. Instead Russian farmers were encouraged to settle in central Asia, and cities like Tashkent were split between the "Russian" or "European" new town and the older, less hygienic districts dominated by non-Russians. Avoiding the national issue made future conflict almost inevitable. As thousands of Russian farmers settled in Turkestan local resentment grew and exploded into a widespread revolt against Russians and Russian power in 1916, which was crushed with great bloodshed. Thus "avoidance" could easily tip over into "reactive repression."[14]

Many measures seen by non-Russian elites as "Russification" were justified in St Petersburg as simple centralizing initiatives. Thus, by eliminating the privileges enjoyed by the German elite in the Baltic provinces (from the 1880s), Russian administrators aimed to draw these provinces closer to the rest of the empire. Similarly in the Grand Duchy of Finland (in the 1890s and into the twentieth century), the urge to centralize was interpreted by Finns as a direct challenge and violation to their autonomy, while St Petersburg regarded these measures as a justified effort to rationalize Russian rule over the province. Neither side was entirely correct: the Russian government certainly did aim to spread its language and culture (seeing it as the legitimate "reigning language" and one key factor for keeping the empire intact). On the other hand the traditional and underfunded tsarist bureaucracy had no serious plans to "assimilate" Germans or Finns into the Russian nation. In the end these centralizing policies backfired. Not only did these policies seriously antagonize Germans and Finns – both of whom had previously been among the most loyal subjects of the tsar – but they also had the unintended consequence of encouraging the development of Estonian and Latvian national-cultural identity. These national movements were directed primarily against the German privileged class, but by the early twentieth century also to some extent against the Russian administration.[15]

Policies toward non-Russians could also be brutal and repressive. The phrase "reactive repression" describes quite well policies pursued against the Poles. The Poles occupied a special place among the non-Russian subjects of the tsar because of numbers, history, geography, and Polish patriotism. Eight million Poles (by native tongue) lived in the empire at the turn of the century, mainly along the western border with Germany – the probable site of future conflict. Poles had possessed one of the largest and most important states in Europe in the early modern period; Polish history and high culture were well developed both within and without Russia. Unlike any other non-Russian nationality (except the Baltic Germans), Poles could boast of a strong noble landowning class as well as their own university, dating from 1364, just across the border in Kraków. More important still for Russian policy-makers, Poles had led two insurrections against Russian rule, the first in 1830 and the second in 1863. Both were crushed by Russian forces and followed by severe repressions. After 1864 Poles were restricted in their rights to education, to purchase land (outside the 10 ethnic Polish provinces), and even to use their native tongue in public. Education in Polish was kept within narrow limits, though "secret schools" continued to educate young people in their native tongue. The University of Warsaw was turned into a Russian institution despised by Poles, and Poles seeking government employment had to move away from the ethnically Polish "Vistula Land" (as the Kingdom of Poland was officially called after 1864), in particular if they had hopes of a successful career.

Nationality policy after 1863 is often described with the word "Russification." This term is often interpreted in greatly divergent ways, so some explanation is in order here. The Russian government rarely actively sought to "denationalize" non-Russians (with the exception of Ukrainians and Belarusians, as these peoples, who spoke dialects of the Russian language, were considered already part of the Russian nation). Rather policies aimed to punish disloyalty, prevent unrest, centralize, and spread Russian as the lingua franca for all the tsar's subjects. Ironically the one national group who by the early twentieth century began to be successfully "Russified" (in the sense of trading their original native tongue for Russian and adopting Russian culture) was the Jews (discussed in some detail below), and the tsarist bureaucracy regarded this phenomenon with great misgivings. From the point of view of non-Russians, however, restrictions on education in their own languages, strict censorship or even prohibition of publishing in certain languages (in different places and specific cases, Ukrainian, Belarusian, Lithuanian, Yiddish, to name a few) seemed like a direct attack on their culture and nation. And, it must be admitted, Russian administrators cared little about the development of non-Russian culture and, in particular, like many other educated Europeans and North Americans, regarded the dying out of peasant or nomadic cultures and tongues as neither particularly regrettable nor worthy of state attention. For a patriotic Kazakh, Ukrainian, or Lithuanian, of course, matters would seem very different.[16]

The revolution of 1905 changed much in the Russian Empire, including policies toward non-Russians. On the one hand censorship became less strict. Daily newspapers appeared for the first time in Yiddish, Ukrainian, Lithuanian, and other languages, new schools teaching in various languages opened up. On the other hand Russian policy, particularly under the energetic Prime Minister Peter Stolypin, became more specifically pro-Russian and even nationalistic. Election campaigns for the State Duma were often fought along national lines, further exacerbating relations, for example, between Poles and Jews. While separatist nationalism remained rare in the Russian Empire before 1914, more and more non-Russians were becoming "nationalized"; that is, they were coming to regard themselves not just as locals or believers in a certain religion, but as members of a larger entity: the Lithuanian, Armenian, or Tatar nation. War and revolution spared the Russian Empire from having to deal with this phenomenon.

Muslims in the Russian Empire were also feeling the effects of modernization. To be sure, the degree that "modernity" in any sense of the word touched on Muslims varied enormously. After all, speaking of "Muslims" as a group in the Russian Empire is inherently misleading, as urban Tatars differed enormously in lifestyle and identity from, say, semi-nomadic Turkmen or Kyrgyz. This was also a problem for would-be Muslim modernizers, who were never quite certain whether they were addressing all Muslims in the Russian Empire or members of their own ethnic group (especially the more literate and urbanized Tatars).

This complication is well illustrated by the modernizing movement that arose in the late nineteenth century, led by Ismail Hasbarli (better known by the Russian version of his name, Gasprinskii, 1841–1914). These reformers, known as *jadids* (from the Arabic word for "new [method]"), very much like the somewhat earlier *maskilim* (enlightened) among the Jews, argued that Muslims needed to become part of the modern world, learn modern languages, dress as Europeans, and participate as citizens together with non-Muslims. Again, like the *maskilim*, the *jadids* saw modern, secular (though not irreligious) education as the key to a healthy Muslim future. Many, like Gasprinskii, learned Russian and even published in that language, seeing in that language both a necessity for the economic betterment of Muslims living under tsarist rule and a bridge to modern European learning. But Russian was seen only as a second language, with Muslims also retaining their native tongue. Gasprinskii even tried to create a standard Turkic language that could be understood by all Turkic peoples living in the Russian Empire. Though Gasprinskii failed in his effort to unify all Turkic subjects of the tsar, his movement showed that Muslims too felt the need to find compromises with modernity.

The *jadids* were opposed by religious conservatives, who are sometimes called *kadim*, after Muslim judges. In general the Muslim clergy – like the Jewish rabbis – had little reason to compromise with the modernizing *jadids*. As Robert Crews has recently shown, the Muslim "church" (as Crews provocatively terms the religious establishment) enjoyed a stable and even privileged position under tsarist rule. The *jadids* were labeled irreligious, Russifying, and not proper Muslims. For the most part, the religious conservatives carried the day. The *jadids* had little to offer the Muslim masses, who were illiterate and deeply attached to their faith. The "enlightenment" offered by the *jadids* appealed mainly to those few Muslims who had already begun to rebel against traditional religious life. But for the great majority, Islam remained an unchanging pillar of everyday life, customs, and worldview.[17]

Before 1917 it was difficult to differentiate clearly among Muslim "nationalities." Some, like the Tatars (of which Gasprinskii was one, a Crimean Tatar to be precise), already had a written language, but others, like Turkmen and Kyrgyz, remained nomadic tribal peoples, not modern nations. The largest "national" divide among Muslims of the Russian Empire was between those speaking Turkic languages and those who did not. The former (modern Tatars, Azeris, Kazakhs, Kyrgyz, and others) made up the great majority; among the latter, the Tajiks, speaking a language related to modern Persian (Farsi) are the most important. But few of these people saw themselves as part of a larger nation; rather their loyalties were to local tribe or village. After 1905 the *jadids* formed an organization called *Ittifaq Moslemeen* (Muslim Unity), but its call appealed mainly to Tatars and failed to find broad resonance. Only in the Soviet period would Muslim nationalities be clearly delineated.

The Great Liberation: 1917 to ca. 1930

Coming to power in October 1917, the Bolsheviks promised not just political but also national liberation. Lenin had famously described the tsarist empire as the "prison house of nations" and his party, the Bolsheviks, promised to do away with all restrictions on languages and the development of non-Russian cultures. There was, however, a catch. For Lenin and the Bolsheviks, the revolution always came first and all social phenomena, including culture and language, needed to be regarded first of all from the point of view of whether it served or hindered the revolution. Thus when national organizations – including those of socialists – came in conflict with the communists' policies, these organizations were denounced as "bourgeois nationalist"; that is, to be crushed. The communists also favored centralization over federation and this political attitude inevitably favored Russians and Moscow (just as the efforts to centralize before 1917 had seemed like Russification on the periphery). On the other hand the communists did not oppose the use of local languages and indeed expended a great deal of resources developing, codifying, and spreading native languages in various parts of the Soviet Union. In the 1920s in particular many Russian-speakers were annoyed (to put it mildly) by the privileges afforded local languages and in particular by the demand that Russians learn other languages. After 1930, however, the pendulum swung back toward centralization and Russian.

One of the Bolsheviks' first official acts was the Declaration of the Rights of the Peoples of Russia, issued on 2/15 November 1917. Here Lenin and Stalin (as People's Commissar of Nationality Affairs) criticized the Provisional Government's nationality policy as hypocritical and promised to respect the rights of all peoples of Russia to effect "an honest and lasting union." There is a strange tension in this document that on the one hand specifically concedes "equality and sover-eignty" to the peoples of Russia and allows "free self-determination, even to the point of separation and the formation of an independent state," but also speaks of union and mutual trust between peoples. To be sure, when this document was issued the Bolsheviks were not at all sure that they could hold onto power, and in any case were unable to exercise any real control over peripheral regions of Russia. But it would be wrong to dismiss these promises of equality and self-determination as entirely hollow propaganda rhetoric. The Bolsheviks did believe that properly harnessed, the development of national cultures would strengthen the new socialist state and help spread its revolutionary accomplishments, first among the diverse peoples inhabiting the erstwhile Russian Empire, and then around the world.[18]

During the Civil War period (to 1921), Bolshevik control over the non-Russian peripheries was shaky at best. With the Treaty of Brest-Litovsk (March 1918) the Bolsheviks essentially relinquished – for the moment at least – pretensions to Finland, the Baltic, Poland, and Ukraine. The armistice of November 1918 and withdrawal of German troops was accompanied by the declaration from Finland to Poland of independent states, all entirely or partly carved out of territory previously belonging to the Russian Empire. The fact that White armies were active in these regions did not endear the new national governments to Moscow; these for their part tended to view the communist embrace as just window dressing for an attempt to restore Russian rule over them. In the ethnically mixed region between the Black and Caspian Seas, an early attempt to form a Transcaucasian Federation soon fell apart amid squabbling between Armenian, Azeri, and Georgian leaders and led to the intervention of English and Turkish troops. Only in 1920–21 were the communists able to reestablish control over the three Transcaucasian republics, and this was done in a particularly brutal way, causing a major riff between Stalin and Lenin. In central Asia a chaotic situation pitted local peoples against Russian settlers with the communists generally supporting the latter (there were next to no native communists among the native Turkic peoples). The so-called Basmachi (bandits), which had started as an anti-Russian movement in 1916, also opposed the communists by force of arms. The Basmachi represented a conservative strand of Islam and were only finally defeated in the mid-1920s. The Civil War years were a true catastrophe for central Asia, where hundreds of thousands died of starvation or fled over the border into neighboring China.

Unlike the tsars, Lenin did not underestimate the importance of the national question. The Narkomnats (People's Commissariat of Nationalities) had already been established in mid-1917 by the Petrograd Soviet, but Lenin appointed Stalin (one of the few non-Russians – aside from Jews – among the Bolshevik elite) as its head and worked to avoid antagonizing non-Russians. Within the Narkomnats there arose several subcommittees to deal with Jews (Evkom), Muslims (Muskom), and others. When Stalin was the head of Narkomnats (1918–22), his conception of nationality (and attitude toward national-culture rights) was different, and considerably narrower, than Lenin's. Stalin openly rejected the secession of border regions in 1920 and in his writings as head of Narkomnats stressed the "backward" nature of most non-Russian nationalities. Lenin was more willing to proceed cautiously on the national issue in order to avoid the perception that imperial Russian chauvinism was merely being replaced by Soviet Russian repression of national groups.

The end of the Civil War allowed the communist leadership to give their concept of the relationship between nationality and socialism concrete institutional form. The formal creation of the Union of Soviet Socialist Republics in December 1922 attempted to balance between a strong central power (Moscow), cultural rights for local nationalities, and economic needs of the country. The new country significantly did not bear the name "Russia" and at least technically was a union of equal, sovereign republics. The USSR was made up of two kinds of republics: "union republics" like the Russian Soviet Federated Socialist Republic (RSFSR), Ukraine, and so on, and "autonomous republics," which were located within a union republic but enjoyed significant cultural and even economic autonomy. Each union had its own capital, parliament, and, with one exception, its own Communist Party. The exception was the RSFSR: the by-far largest (72 percent of the population, 90 percent of the territory of the USSR in 1923) republic lacked its own Communist Party but, of course, central organs of the all-union Communist Party of the Soviet Union were located in Moscow. Besides union and autonomous republics there were smaller ethno-territorial units such as the autonomous region (*oblasti*) the Birobidzhan Jewish Autonomous Territory formed in 1934, and the smaller autonomous territories (*okrugi*) like that of Chukhotka in eastern Siberia. In general the USSR used language and ethnicity as an organizing and administrative principle far more frequently than the Russian Empire had.[19]

The main Soviet approach to nationality in the 1920s was the policy of *korenizatsiia*, or "indigenization." This policy had two main aims: on the one hand to bring Soviet power home to non-Russians by presenting it in their own language, and by giving them incentives to participate in the new political system; on the other to speed up the cultural, economic, and political development of non-Russian peoples. Terry Martin has described the USSR in this period as the world's first "affirmative action empire," expending considerable government resources to bring non-Russians into the socialist mainstream.[20] Another North American historian, Yuri Slezkine, has described this early decade as the creation of a "communal apartment" of nationalities, using this colorful metaphor to describe the Soviet programs to codify ethnic distinctions, create written versions of central Asian languages, set up individual administrative units along ethno-linguistic lines (the union and autonomous republics, *oblasti* and *okrugi* mentioned above).[21]

Korenizatsiia worked on several levels. On the local level it meant that native languages could (and should) be used in schools, courts, and local Communist Party units. In many cases, however, this required the writing of new textbooks, training of teachers using Ukrainian, Kazakh, or Belarusian, or even the establishment of a written form of a language. Because Russians (and Russian-speaking Jews) made up such a large percentage of communists throughout the USSR, special preference was to be given to non-Russians interested in joining the party.

These preferences extended as well to filling positions within the republican communist hierarchy, Communist Party jobs, and in general for employment, including the heads of factories, schools, and other institutions. The fact that members of the "titular nationality" (i.e., Ukrainians in the Ukrainian SSR, Kazakhs in the Kazakh SSR, etc.) were privileged necessarily meant that equally qualified Russian speakers would be passed up for promotions, employment, and the like. This fact was freely noted and acknowledged, but Russian-speaking communists were urged to accept this sacrifice for the party (and of course they had little choice). With Russians making up the majority of Communist Party members in nearly all republics, they looked perilously similar to Russian administrators in, say, central Asia, before 1917.

At the same time the policy of encouraging ethnic particularism also revealed the fundamental contradiction – or mistaken assumption – of *korenizatsiia*. The policy assumed that minority nationalities, as long as they were given considerable freedom to develop their languages, culture, and national elites, would be incorporated into the Soviet system and recognize the progress and positive nature of Soviet socialism. The idea that national-cultural development and the building of socialism could clash was either not considered at all or dismissed as a misunderstanding of "proper" cultural development. But already in 1923 the important Tatar communist M. Sultan-Galiev had been arrested for "national deviance"; that is, putting the interests of one's own national group before that of the party and USSR as a whole. In subsequent years the accusation of "Sultangalievism" was leveled at a number of non-Russian communists, usually ending their career and often their life as well. While the general party line of *korenizatsiia* and promoting national cultures remained in place for another decade, Sultan-Galiev's fate indicated that there could be, after all, a conflict of interests between Moscow and non-Russian communists.

By the end of the 1920s, especially in the context of Stalin's almost total takeover of power in the party, several cases arose showing a divergence of interests between Moscow and local elites. Stalin recognized that the encouragement of local elites and local cultures could easily provide a space for challenging central – that is, Stalin's – authority and reacted harshly against "bourgeois nationalists" in different republics of the USSR. In the 1930s non-Russian communists were among the most likely to be arrested or executed.

——— Contradictions of Soviet Nationality Policy to 1945 ———

Up to the early 1930s, Soviet Nationality Policy was much more concerned with nurturing non-Russian culture and language than with strengthening the position of Russian culture as the "glue" between all Soviet citizens. This began to change during the 1930s for a variety of reasons. In general after 1930, policy in the USSR turned away from more pluralist utopian ideals and towards unitary, authoritarian approaches, so one may argue that it is only natural that a more centralizing, unitary approach would also prevail regarding nationalities. The 1930s were also the period of economic crash industrialization, which involved an enormous mobilization of the entire population with millions of individuals moving from country to city and from one part of the USSR to another. The percentage of Russians living outside the RSFSR jumped in this period, largely because specialists, communist functionaries, and skilled workers were more likely to be Russian than, say, Kazakh or Armenian. Finally tensions on the international scene with the growing threat of Japan to the east and Nazi Germany to the west certainly fed Stalin's paranoia and desire to strike out at real or imagined enemies at home, including national elites and even entire nations (e.g., Germans, Poles, Koreans).

A number of events in the early 1930s signaled a turn away from *korenizatsiia* toward a more centralizing, Russocentric nationality policy. "National communists" like N. A. Skrypnik in Ukraine were removed from their posts and often arrested and shot. The place of Russian in education (especially higher education) was strengthened; by the late 1930s all Soviet children regardless of nationality had obligatory Russian language courses and in areas of mixed (Russian and other) nationality the number of schools and classes taught in Russian increased. Scholars were also affected: in the 1930s Russian historians reevaluated the growth of the Russian Empire, emphasizing its progressive aspects and the positive influence of Russian culture. Ukrainian historians who had previously written of the heroic struggles of political leader Ivan Mazepa and poet Taras Shevchenko against the Russian Empire were obliged now to "reinterpret" these figures and the historical relationship of Ukraine to the Russian Empire.[22] Similarly in the Tatar Autonomous Republic Evgeniia Ginzburg was arrested because of her participation in an edited volume on Tatar history that suddenly in the mid-1930s was deemed "bourgeois nationalist."[23]

A crucial event in the history of nationality in the USSR was the famine of 1932–3. For many historians like Robert Conquest, Moscow engineered (or, at least, greatly exacerbated) this natural disaster in a specifically genocidal way: to punish Ukrainians and to a lesser extent Kazakhs. Ukrainian historians almost universally accept this thesis, speaking of this famine as the *Holodomor* – death by famine. No serious historian doubts that the famine was at least in part engineered by Moscow, but many western historians emphasize that Stalin aimed to punish not specific ethnic groups but all regions where resistance to collectivization had been significant. After all, they point out, mainly ethnic Russian regions like the northern Caucasus were equally affected. Among Kazakhs, the impact of collectivization – which also amounted to "denomadization" and the destruction of their traditional way of life – was even more devastating than for the Ukrainians.

One-third of all Kazakhs in the USSR, some 1.5 million persons, died during collectivization. Whether one accepts the argument of "attempted genocide" or not, it seems clear that the millions of deaths caused by the terror famine had a chilling effect on any possible ethnic separatist movements among Ukrainians or Kazakhs.[24]

There was no official end of *korenizatsiia*, just as the NEP was never formally abolished. Rather in both cases the fundamental point of departure for policy-making in Moscow changed so radically that the previous policy line became simply irrelevant. That is to say, rather than an official declaration of a change in policy, one witnesses in the mid- and later 1930s more use of Russian in Soviet schools combined with an increased emphasis in history lessons on the benevolent and positive influence of Russian culture (and even of the Russian Empire) on non-Russian cultures. At the same time, arrests and executions of local national communists made the new, more-Russocentric party line clear. Henceforth, while local languages continued to be widely used, local educators, scholars, and communist leaders had to take pains not to appear "separatist" or "anti-Russian."

Unfortunately the exact line separating the healthy development of national culture and anti-Soviet (i.e., anti-Russian) bourgeois nationalism was never quite clear, as the mass purges of non-Russian communists showed. During the purges of the 1930s over half of party members in the Tajik, Georgian, Ukrainian, Belarusian, and Azeri republics were purged, with thousands of these being shot. National cultures also suffered. Non-Russian teachers, historians, and writers were particularly hard hit by arrests and executions; nearly an entire generation of those writing in Belarusian, Tatar, Bashkir, Yiddish, and other Soviet languages were arrested, forced into camps, or had their lives cut short.

Any foreign (i.e., from outside the USSR) influences on native cultures were strictly purged. Thus a new Soviet-standard Yiddish spelled Hebrew words taken from that language phonetically to distance "Soviet Yiddish" from the standard used elsewhere. Polish influences in Ukrainian and Belarusian culture and language were denounced and purged. Among central Asian and other Muslim cultures, Arabic and Persian phrases and words in local languages came under fire. In all of these cases, these new policies aimed to purge languages of traditional elements now associated with foreign, non-Soviet cultures. At the same time many languages that had in the 1920s been given a writing system using Latin letters, in particular in central Asia, in the 1930s abruptly switched to a Cyrillic-based writing system. Language policy of the 1930s strived to cut off Soviet cultures from foreign influences and to strengthen their links to Russian language and culture.

The predominant place of Russian throughout all institutions of the Soviet Union was repeatedly emphasized throughout the 1930s. Military service too was used to instill Soviet identity, which increasingly depended on Russian language and culture. In 1938 the Red Army was reorganized to eliminate national units; now draftees from different republics would serve together, usually far from home. The language of command was exclusively Russian; soldiers were also trained in that language and the use of native languages was discouraged. Since all young Soviet men did military service, the Red Army provided a very significant site for spreading Soviet-Russian culture – though for many non-Russians, serving in the Red Army did little to inspire love for Moscow or for Russian culture.

Some republics were more successful in defending their languages and culture. By 1938 only Armenia and Georgia retained their own languages as "official"; in the central Asian republics higher education took place mainly in Russian, alienating the educated classes from the rest of the nation. Scholars disagree on the extent to which Soviet policies really aimed at "Russification" in the sense of replacing native languages with Russian. At the very least, however, by the late 1930s loyal Soviet citizens were expected to know Russian. And not infrequently parents often preferred for practical reasons (making a successful career in Soviet society required fluency in Russian) to have their children educated in Russian. Among Jews, Ukrainians, and Belarusians, already by the later 1930s Russian was becoming a significant and even predominant native language.

More brutal measures against "suspect" nationalities could also be taken. Historian Terry Martin speaks of a program of "partial removal of stigmatized ethnic groups" already in the 1930s that escalated into mass expulsions by the end of that decade and during World War II.[25] Soviet citizens of Chinese and Korean nationality were deported from border areas in the early to mid-1930s; tens of thousands of Chechens and Ingush were arrested and deported in a mass action in summer 1937; and later that year hundreds of Armenians living in the Ukrainian SSR were resettled elsewhere. These measures had two main purposes: to prevent suspect ethnicities from making common cause with their ethnic brethren across the border, and to achieve a higher degree of ethnic homogeneity – what Martin calls "ethnic consolidation" – within union and autonomous republics of the USSR. These population transfers in the 1930s were a mere taste of far more sweeping and brutal transfers after 1939.

Two weeks after the German attack on Poland in September 1939, following a secret provision of the Molotov–Ribbentrop Pact agreed upon the previous month, the Red Army marched into what had been the eastern provinces of Poland. These territories were inhabited by a mixed population, with Belarusians and Ukrainians dominating in the countryside, and cities populated mainly by Jews and Poles. Poles were suspect both for class reasons (landowners, middle-class professionals) and simply on account of their nationality. The new Soviet authorities also distrusted middle-class Jews as class enemies. In late 1939 and 1940 thousands of former Polish citizens – mainly but not exclusively of Polish nationality – were arrested and summarily evacuated to Siberia and central Asia. Thus in the short period between the Soviet takeover in 1919 of what had been eastern Poland and the Nazi invasion in June 1941, to a very great extent the Polish cultural and economic position in this region was destroyed. Those Poles remaining here in 1944 would be "repatriated" to Poland in the immediate postwar years, ending centuries of Polish presence in these mainly Belarusian and Ukrainian regions.[26]

In the summer of 1940 the three Baltic republics of Estonia, Latvia, and Lithuania, which had achieved independence at the end of World War I, were incorporated into the USSR. Here too mass arrests of middle-class people, politicians, peasant leaders, and intellectuals took place. Post-communist Baltic historians have sometimes pointed to these deportations of tens of thousands of people as a Soviet plan for "genocide," but the word seems inappropriate. The Soviet leadership never aimed to eliminate the culture and language of Estonians, Latvians, and Lithuanians – they did, however, have no qualms about "purging" these populations of any real or potential anti-Soviet elements. Indeed in the Lithuanian SSR in 1940–41 Poles and Jews were more likely than ethnic Lithuanians to be deported. At the same time the incorporation of these three republics into the USSR in summer 1940 could be regarded by the local population only as a return to Russian rule, especially when Soviet rule was accompanied by the arrival of thousands of Russian-speaking party, military, and secret-police workers.[27]

Both before and after the German attack on the USSR in June 1941 the Soviet government undertook extensive population transfers based mainly on nationality. Tens of thousands of Kurds were removed from Azerbaijan in 1941, and their autonomous region within that republic was abolished. After the Nazi attack the Volga-German ASSR was abolished and its inhabitants – the descendants of farmers who had immigrated to Russia in the late eighteenth century – were deported to central Asia. Soviet citizens of German nationality living in other parts of the USSR shared their fate; all in all some 800,000 Germans were arrested and resettled, many of them dying along the way.[28]

Stalin's rhetoric during the war drew almost exclusively on heroes from the Russian past, generals like Mikhail Kutuzov who defeated Napoleon, leaders such as Dmitry Donskoi and Alexander Nevsky who fought the Tatars. Soviet propaganda dubbed the conflict the "Great Fatherland War," a term used previously for the defeat and expulsion of Napoleon from the Russian Empire in 1812. Even the Russian Orthodox Church was allowed to contribute its voice to the patriotic fervor, further blurring the distinction between "Russia" and "Soviet Union." The Russian nation was explicitly described as the "older brother" of other, lesser Soviet nations. At war's end, on May 24, 1945, Stalin would famously drink a toast to "the health of our Soviet people and above all the Russian people."

This Russo-centricism went far beyond words. Ethnicities suspected of collaboration with the Germans were brutally expelled from their homelands soon after the Germans left. There was no effort made to seek out actual collaborators: all members of the suspected national group were rounded up and deported. Among the nationalities subject to mass arrest and deportation were Chechens and Ingush living in the northern Caucasus, Crimean Tatars, and Meskhetians (Muslim Turkic-speakers of Georgian origin). In the Baltic republics and Ukraine,

FIGURE 3.1   V. Elkin, "Long Live the Fraternal Union and Great Friendship of the Nations of the USSR!" Soviet ethnicities in national costumes, each banner greets Stalin in the national language. 1938.
Source: Hoover Institution Archives.

where many locals had in fact collaborated with the Germans (sometimes from anti-Soviet sentiment, sometimes simply to survive), hundreds of thousands were arrested and deported. In all of these cases, a high percentage of those deported died on the way east due to the brutal conditions of deportation. While these arrests were not based exclusively on nationality, the simple fact of mass arrests of Estonians, Latvians, Lithuanians, and Ukrainians did much to terrorize the entire population and discourage any overt signs of anti-Soviet patriotic sentiment.

It is difficult to overstate the brutality of the years 1939–45 in the USSR and in particular in its western regions. To begin with, the Jewish population of this area, numbering in the hundreds of thousands, was either deported or – in the vast majority of cases – murdered by the Nazi death machinery. The much smaller but also significant German community had either been "called home" by the Nazis in late 1939 (some then returned after the Nazi invasion in 1941) or had fled before the Red Army. The western frontier of the USSR was significantly altered, extending the Soviet border around one to 200 miles to the west. The nationality mix among this region's population changed even more radically. To the north, when the border with Finland was pushed around 100 miles to the west, one million Finns fled rather than live under Soviet rule. In the Baltic countries mass emigration to the west combined with mass arrests deprived these nations of badly needed educated leadership. In western Belarus and Ukraine, newly incorporated from interwar Poland, the Polish land-holding class and intelligentsia resident there for centuries were arrested, deported, and in thousands of cases murdered by their Ukrainian neighbors. In 1944 agreements were signed by the Belarusian, Ukrainian, and Lithuanian SSRs and Poland for voluntary population exchanges. Millions of Poles left their homes in what was now the USSR; hundreds of thousands of Ukrainians had to resettle from Poland to the Ukrainian SSR. While these population transfers were ostensibly "voluntary," they were carried out in an atmosphere of fear and violence that makes it difficult to speak of truly free choice.[29]

The extension of Soviet rule westward was not received passively. The Ukrainian Insurgent Army (UPA) fought first the Germans, then the Red Army, and also attacked local Poles, wishing their departure from a pure ethnic Ukraine.[30] Despite desperate odds, Ukrainian resistence against Soviet rule continued until the early 1950s. Similarly in the Baltic republics, anti-Soviet national partisans known as the "Forest Brethren" carried out attacks on Red Army personnel and Communist Party members. This was a nearly suicidal struggle but when faced with the stark choice between arrest by the Soviet authorities and armed resistance to them, many Baltic and Ukrainian patriots took the latter course. Partisan leaders such as Stefan Bandera of Ukraine have now, in the early twenty-first century, become nationalist heroes in independent post-Soviet countries.

At the end of World War II the fusion of Russian and Soviet patriotism seemed complete. For many the continuity between the Russian Empire and the USSR seemed only too apparent. An antisemitism similar to that of pre-1917 government officials, while never openly espoused, can be detected in the almost blanket refusal to acknowledge either Jewish contributions to the war effort or the specific tragedy of the Jewish people under Nazi rule. Already in 1944 and 1945 Soviet press accounts of sites of mass murder of Jews, such as Baby Yar outside Kiev or Ponary (Paneriai) outside Vilnius, mention Jews – if at all – only as one persecuted nationality among many. Nonetheless we should not lose sight of the very significant differences between Soviet nationality policy and that of the Russian Empire. To start with, unlike tsarist officials, the communist rulers explicitly acknowledged the rights of non-Russians to develop their culture. Even while carrying out measures of breathtaking brutality (e.g., against Lithuanian nationalist partisans in the mid- to latter 1940s), Moscow was expending resources to set up journals, schools, universities, and other institutions to nurture these languages and cultures – but of course as part of the greater Soviet family of nations. The contradictions of Soviet nationality policy, both repressing and encouraging national cultures, would never be resolved, and in the 1940s reached perhaps their most brutal extremes.

Russia's "Jewish Question": 1861–1945

Jews have played a unique and striking role in European and world history, quite out of proportion to their numbers. The same can be said for Russian history, where in 1897 Jews made up just over 5 percent of the total population according to official figures. At this point more Jews lived in the Russian Empire than in any other country of the world, and their "visibility" for the Russian government and for Russian society was far higher than their percentage in the total population. After all, Muslims taken as a whole made up a larger percentage of the tsar's subjects, but one only seldom encounters discussions of the "Muslim question" in Russian journals or newspapers before 1905. Nor were Muslims ever considered a nationality, as Jews were both unofficially before 1917 and officially under Soviet rule. Jews were unique in the fact that their religion and "nationality" (defined as language, culture, everyday life) more or less coincided in the Russian Empire and much of eastern Europe up to the early twentieth century. And the unique strength of antisemitism, which was transformed from a religious prejudice to a political-racial ideology in the decades before World War I, also contributed to the identity of Jews as a nation, not just a religious group.

The "Jewish question" was something of an obsession both among liberals and conservatives. For Russian liberals, Jews were potential allies in the struggle for a democratic, secular, progressive Russia. For conservatives, Jews represented the evils of modernity (capitalism, secularism, loose morals, socialism) lumped together. In both cases, the liberal and conservative viewpoint, of course, we are dealing more with myths than with objective realities, but one should never underestimate the importance of myths in history. The "Jewish myth" – whether positive or negative – played every bit as important a role in Russian/Soviet politics and culture as did actual political, economic, and sociological realities.[31]

This is not to say that realities have no importance. One of the reasons why the image of "the Jew" was so ubiquitous was the fact that Jews lived in significant numbers in European Russia – over five million in 1897. Jews were the only large non-Christian population in the west of the empire, and lived among Slavic (Ukrainian, Belarusian, Polish) peasants. Before the late eighteenth century (the Partitions of Poland) no Jews had been allowed, at least officially, to reside within the Russian Empire. Even Peter the Great, who welcomed so many other foreigners to Russia, would allow the immigration of Jews. This situation changed abruptly with the Partitions of Poland, when suddenly the largest Jewish community on earth found itself living within the western borderlands of the Russian Empire.[32] By the mid-nineteenth century Jews lived in significant numbers only in specific provinces that a century earlier had belonged to the Polish-Lithuanian Commonwealth, the so-called Pale of Settlement stretching from present-day Lithuania to Ukraine. The Kingdom of Poland, created at the Congress of Vienna with the tsar as king, did not legally belong to the Pale, but also included a large Jewish community. Except for very wealthy merchants, Jews could not live outside these specific provinces and were subject to a number of other restrictions on livelihood and mobility in different periods.

Living among Slavic and Lithuanian (but not, with rare exception, among ethnic Russian) peasants, Jews spoke their own languages (Yiddish, and for sacred purposes, Hebrew), married within their own community, and led an everyday life (food, clothing, holidays) quite distinct from their Slavic neighbors. Jews rarely tilled the soil, earning their meager keep instead as traders, shopkeepers, and artisans. The figure of the Jewish peddler, innkeeper, or petty trader in Lithuanian, Russian, Polish, and Yiddish literature was based on this sociological reality: shops run by Christians, in most towns of the region, were unusual enough to deserve special mention. In great part this commercial tradition on the part of Jews was part of the heritage of medieval and early modern Poland, where Jews had served as the agents of landowners. Such was, in a nutshell, the general situation of Jews in Russia around 1861.[33]

The small community of educated, Russian-speaking Jews in the 1860s had high hopes for emancipation during the Great Reforms. Following the example of the "enlightened" followers of Moses Mendelssohn in Berlin – the *maskilim* – they envisaged a progressive community of Russian-speaking Jews who would be both Russian patriots and devout Jews. But Alexander II could not be persuaded to eliminate all restrictions on the Jews (in particular their forced residence within the Pale) and instead only issued specific "privileges" for certain individuals, such as artisans, students, and other groups deemed of economic importance for the Russian Empire. The relationship of the Russian government toward the Jews was always conflicting, on the one hand distrusting "backward, Asiatic" traditional Jews, while on the other highly uncomfortable with modern, Russian-speaking Jews. To be sure, one could convert to Russian Orthodoxy, at which point one ceased – legally – to be a Jew. Even here, however, the Russian government was too conservative to encourage mass conversions, seeing (correctly) that in many cases conversions were motivated less by religious conviction than by the desire to free oneself of legal restrictions. At the same time state schools for Jews were set up using Russian (and in Warsaw before 1863, Polish) as the language of instruction. Jewish parents usually avoided these institutions, fearing that their real purpose was to convert their children to Christianity.[34]

Among the terrorists who assassinated Alexander II on March 1, 1881, there was one irreligious woman of Jewish descent, Gesia Gelfman. But even the presence of this lone Jewish radical among the terrorists was used by Russian conservatives to whip up a press frenzy in the months afterwards against the Jews as disloyal revolutionaries. In part due to this press campaign a wave of attacks against Jewish homes and businesses broke out in the southwestern provinces (now Ukraine) in summer 1881.[35]

At the time it was widely believed that the Russian government planned these pogroms (the Russian word soon passed into English), but extensive research in the past few decades has shown this to be very unlikely. To be sure, Russian officials – and the new tsar Alexander III – did not harbor positive feelings about Jews, but they feared above all public disorder and would not have been likely to encourage attacks on property, even Jewish property. In any case no archival documents supporting the thesis of government planning of pogroms have been found, though the failure of local police to respond quickly to attacks on Jews may well have been motivated by anti-Jewish sentiments. Be this as it may the pogroms of 1881 came as an enormous shock and seemed to call into question the very possibility of assimilation into the Russian nation. The pogroms were followed, moreover, by further legal restrictions on Jews, the so-called May Laws, which prevented Jews from settling in rural areas of the Pale and obliged them to refrain from doing business on Christian holidays. Increasingly Jews had a difficult time earning even the most modest living and the word *luftmentsh* – someone who lives on air – was frequently used to describe the economic misery of the Jewish community in Russia. The great waves of Jewish immigration from Russia to North America and England began in the decade after the 1881 pogroms.[36]

In the final generation before the 1917 revolutions the number of Russian-speaking Jews increased significantly, as the growth of the Jewish community in St Petersburg shows.[37] But speaking a language does not necessarily mean feeling a part of a nation. By the early twentieth century a number of Jewish parties (before 1905, like all political parties in Russia, illegal) existed that exhibited all possible mixtures of socialism, liberalism, and nationalism. The two most important lines were the socialist Bund that combined socialist political ideals with a secular Jewish national identity based on the Yiddish language, and various strains of Zionism that envisaged an independent, Hebrew-speaking Jewish state. Many Jews also participated in Russian and Polish political parties, from the liberal Kadets and the Polish patriotic-socialist PPS, to the radical Mensheviks and Bolsheviks.[38]

In Russia, as throughout Europe, antisemitism grew in the decades before 1914. The reasons for this phenomenon are many: the general growth of nationalist sentiment in these years, the feeling that the Jews were "getting ahead" (i.e., successfully adapting to the conditions of modern society) too fast, and the mythic image of the Jew as the embodiment of modernity, incorporating fear of capitalism, secular society, and parliamentary democracy. In the Russian Empire antisemites could point to several well-known individuals of Jewish origin (the fact that many had converted was of no importance for antisemites) such as the sugar magnate Lev Brodskii, the railroad entrepreneur Ivan/Jan Bloch, and the banking family Kronenberg, as proof that the "Jews were taking over." The fact that young Jews were visible in illegal revolutionary activity was blown up into a general threat to stability, Christianity, and fatherland.

In fact most Jews in Russia remained poor, traditional, and religious. At the same time increasing numbers of Jews were succeeding, by dint of intelligence and hard work, in bettering their lives through education. Despite tsarist restrictions on Jews at institutions of secondary and higher learning, the figure of the Jewish doctor or lawyer, speaking fluent – if perhaps accented – Russian or Polish, become more and more common, to the rage of antisemites. These middle-class Jews often held liberal political views, were great Polish or Russian patriots, and fervently believed that it was possible to combine Jewish and Russian (or Polish) identities. Their children, however, brought up speaking only a Gentile tongue and in most ways culturally identical to their Christian neighbors, often felt keenly their alienation from both traditional, Yiddish-speaking, religious Jewry on the one hand, and from the Russian and Polish nations on the other. Some of this younger generation, like Lev Davidovich Bronshtein ("Trotsky"), would see the solution in socialist revolution; others, like the leader of Zionist revisionism, Vladimir Zhabotinskii (born 1880), would opt for Jewish nationalism.[39]

The crisis in Jewish relations with their Christian neighbors can be seen in the increasingly violent pogroms of the early twentieth century, starting with the

Kishinev (now Chişinău, Moldova) pogrom in 1903. In 1881 property damage had been high, but there were almost no mortal victims (perhaps one or two). In Kishinev, Jewish homes and businesses were destroyed and dozens of Jews were murdered during attacks. Outrage at the Kishinev massacre was expressed in public meetings across Europe, at Madison Square Garden in New York, and by condemnations of anti-Jewish policies in Russia made by the US Congress and President Theodore Roosevelt. During the 1905–6 revolutions, attacks on Jews were even bloodier, with thousands losing their lives. Violence escalated during the Civil War (1918–20), with tens of thousands of Jews killed, mainly by soldiers of the White armies.[40] Several factors came together to cause this massive out-pouring of violence. Jews found themselves branded socialist and antipatriotic (ironically often by both sides of a dispute, such as by Poles and Ukrainians alike). The Whites openly equated Jews with revolution and often allowed their soldiers to run riot in the Jewish sections of town, robbing and committing violence at will. The participation of White, Polish, and Ukrainian troops in anti-Jewish atrocities made many Jews look more favorably on Soviet power for its vociferous condemnation of antisemitism and support for Jewish equal rights.

It was not the communists, however, who had granted Russia's Jews legal equality: that was done under the Provisional Government in 1917. Even before 1917 Lenin had shown himself to be consistently contemptuous of antisemites, but equally impatient with the idea of Jewish nationality and with the Jewish Bund's pretensions to represent the Jewish working class. After the October 1917 revolution Jews were guaranteed the right to use their native tongue (Yiddish) in schools and publishing. The communists treated the Jewish religion like any other, guaranteeing its freedom in principle but in practice restricting its practice and regarding it as a survival of a less enlightened epoch and a force fundamentally hostile to Soviet power. A special section of the Communist Party ("Evsektsiia") was set up both to fight other Jewish parties (especially the Zionists and the Bund) and to help integrate Jews into party life.[41] In the 1920s Yiddish-language publish-ing flourished in the USSR (especially in the Belarusian capital Minsk) and pro-posals for an autonomous Jewish territorial unit somewhere in the USSR were hotly debated. In 1934 the Jewish Autonomous Region of Birobidzhan was estab-lished thousands of miles east of any large Jewish settlements on the border of China and far closer to Tokyo than to Jerusalem. Birobidzhan was supposed to provide the three million Jews of the USSR with a Yiddish-speaking "homeland" (to rival the one being established by Zionists in Palestine / Erets Israel) but the remote, harsh region failed to attract large numbers of Jewish settlers: in 1939 fewer than 18,000 Jews lived there, around 16 percent of the autonomous region's total population.[42]

The Jewish future in the USSR lay not in Birobidzhan, but in burgeoning cities like Kiev, Moscow, and Leningrad. In the 1920s, and even more in the next decade, hundreds of thousands of Jews left the countryside or the Jewish small town (*shtetl*) for the big, Russian-speaking city. They generally left the Yiddish language and traditional modes of Jewish life behind. Abandoning the religious and linguistic culture of their forefathers, Soviet Jews were the ideal recipients for secularized, Russian-speaking Soviet culture. The USSR seemed to hold out the promise of creating a new, progressive nation based not on the past (ancestors, native tongue, heritage) but the future. For many Jews, especially of the younger generation, the prospect of participating in the creation of this new society was intoxicating. And viewed statistically, Jews achieved great accomplishments in the first decades of the USSR. Jewish membership in the Communist Party considerably exceeded their percentage in the general population, Jews figured prominently among college graduates, and by the end of the 1930s dominated in a number of professions. Yuri Slezkine notes that in 1939 Jews made up more than half of all dentists and pharmacists, over a third of doctors and defense lawyers, and a quarter of musicians in Leningrad.[43] Before 1917, it should be remembered, only Jews of certain privileged categories had been permitted to live in the city.

While Jews gained much in the first generation of Soviet rule, they also gave up much. By the end of the 1930s it had become exceptional for Jews to raise their children in Yiddish or to keep kosher. To be sure, similar if more muted processes can be observed among American Jews. In the USSR, however, Jewish identity was increasingly rejected in favor of a broader Soviet-Russian self-image. But, as the old rabbi's words have it, "If you forget you're a Jew, don't worry: a Gentile will remind you." While many Soviet Jews had begun to shed their Jewish identity and intermarry with Russians, anti-Jewish prejudices remained strong in Soviet society and even among communists, Stalin included. The rapid advance of Jews in Soviet society was resented by those less successful, and Stalin had never forgotten the Jewish origins of Trotsky and many of his supporters. At the same time anti-Soviet propaganda in the west often portrayed communist rule as a conspiracy of Jews to exercise power over Christians, as in the Polish myth of *Żydokomuna*. After World War II a new kind of specifically Soviet antisemitism would be created, drawing on all of these resentments and prejudices.

In the late 1930s and early 1940s, of course, the immediate threat to Jews emanated from racial antisemitism as embodied in the Nazi party in Germany. While the USSR continued to condemn all forms of racism, including antisemitism, the Molotov–Ribbentrop Pact between the USSR and Nazi Germany could hardly reassure Soviet Jews. But the legal status of Jews in the Soviet Union remained unchanged. The terrible events of the period 1939–45 – mass arrests, war, the Holocaust – destroyed what remained of traditional Jewish culture in the USSR. Ironically those thousands of Jews arrested by the Soviet authorities in 1939 and 1940 often survived because they had been deported to Siberia or central Asia. With the almost total extinction of native Yiddish-speakers in Lithuania, Poland,

and Ukraine, that linguistic culture lost not only its main readership, but also the potential for future invigoration. After the Holocaust, Soviet Jews remained by far the largest Jewish community in Europe, but their knowledge of basic elements of Jewish tradition, culture, and religion remained low and their tendency to intermarry with non-Jews called into question their future as a separate community.

Conclusion

The "nationality question" was a constant challenge and irritation for Russian and Soviet leaders. The Russian Empire preferred to ignore the issue whenever possible, acting as if non-Russian nationalities were peripheral and insignificant, placing restrictions on the rights of some non-Russian nationalities (especially Poles, Jews, and Muslims), and reacting with brutal repressions when national separatism seemed a threat. The USSR took a different tack, setting up a special People's Commissariat to deal with the issue, forcing Soviet citizens to choose a single national identity, and institutionalizing nationality in territorial units such as union republics and autonomous districts, as well as in every Soviet citizen's passport.

Yet from the mid-1930s at latest the USSR also fell back on traditional forms of Russian dominance, not overtly denying other nationalities their rights but insisting on the preeminence and predominance of Russian culture within the USSR. Pushkin and other classics of Russian literature were translated into, for example, Tajik and Georgian, but rarely did the Soviet cultural authorities consider it necessary to introduce Russians to the poets and artists of non-Russian Soviet nations. It is a bitter irony of history that the one national group to become most "successfully" Russified and Sovietized (the two terms are not always easy to distinguish), the Jews, became increasingly discriminated against and alienated from Soviet Orthodoxy in the generations after 1945. In the twenty-first century, both in the Russian Federation and the other 14 countries formed after the dissolution of the USSR, nationality remains a prickly and contentious issue.

Chapter 4
Modernization

When speaking of "modernization" the break of the 1917 revolution seems of overwhelming importance. The Russian Empire, after all, can hardly be considered modern. The tsar ruled unchallenged as an autocrat unfettered by constitution or (until after 1905) parliament, most of his subjects lived from agriculture, and the rhythms of everyday life remained preindustrial, religious, and traditional. To be sure, the Great Reforms aimed to modernize Russia but, as we have seen, the tsarist government sought to limit that process to the economic sphere without allowing a parallel development of modern social and political structures.

The Bolsheviks, on the other hand, were all about modernization. They boldly demanded that nature be changed, whether it be "human nature" in the form of relations between classes, nations, or the sexes, or the physical world, which had to be exploited, dominated, and tamed for human progress. As we will see, however, the immense economic and human changes brought about under communist rule had their origins in the period before 1917. The Great Reforms, after all, aimed to set the stage for Russian modernization (even if the tsar feared some of its consequences, as was reflected in contradictory policies). And, even though the USSR had undergone immense changes between the First Five-Year plan and the end of World War II, plenty of "survivals" of earlier periods remained, in the countryside, in political culture, and even in relations between the sexes.

──────────── The What and Why of Modernization ────────────

Before we look at the successes and failures of modernizing the Russian-Soviet state, we need to answer, at least tentatively, two questions: What is modernization, and why is it important? Modern states and societies exhibit a number of characteristics, including relatively high levels of urbanization, industrialization, literacy, and social mobility. In modern states politics are based on a constitution (written or, in the case of Great Britain, unwritten), which regulates relations between rulers and ruled, while a body of laws to which all are subject (even rulers) regulates social relations. A modern state is prosperous, industrialized, and democratic; it is also sovereign and able to defend its independence, through the force of arms if necessary. Obviously these are ideal types and actual modern states differ in many significant ways from the simple sketch given here.

Neither the Russian Empire nor the USSR ever achieved a western-style constitutional democracy, but already in 1905–6 a kind of constitution (though the tsar and conservatives refused to call it that) was in place. In the economic sphere even in 1945 Soviet citizens remained far behind western levels of prosperity, but compared with their grandparents in 1861 one could certainly discern very significant economic progress. Thus we should take these ideal characteristics of a modern state not as a "norm" or reality but as a model to help us understand the changes that the Russian economy and society underwent over these three generations.[1]

Why should a state or society wish to be modern? The main motivation for Alexander II's Great Reforms indicated the most obvious reason: in order to remain a respected and sovereign state in the later nineteenth century – and all the more so in the twentieth – a modern industrial economy was necessary. Very simply a premodern state could neither produce the weapons required to defend itself, nor could it pay for them. The despised Ottoman Empire was the great negative example of what happens to states that fall behind in modernizing, and the Russian Empire certainly did not wish to follow its example. Other motivations must also be factored in. Russians, or at least Russian "society," thought of themselves as Europeans and were keenly sensitive to accusations of "backwardness" on the part of central and western Europeans. Russian national prestige was thus connected with being modern; that is, developing along the lines of Britain, France, and Germany. Obviously the visions of modernity held by the tsar and by liberal Russian society (much less Russian radicals) differed greatly, but few, not even born-again Slavophiles like the novelist Fyodor Dostoevsky, truly believed that Russia could avoid modernizing.

To not be modern was to be looked down upon, despised, and eventually conquered. Stalin summed up this attitude nicely in a celebrated speech to industrial managers in February 1931. Rhetorically answering the question whether the pace of industrialization could not be slackened, Stalin exclaimed:

> To slacken the tempo would mean falling behind. And those who fall behind get beaten. But we do not want to be beaten. No, we refuse to be beaten! One feature of the history of old Russia was the continual beatings she suffered because of her

backwardness. She was beaten by the Mongol khans. She was beaten by the Turkish beys. She was beaten by the Swedish feudal lords. She was beaten by the Polish and Lithuanian gentry. She was beaten by the British and French capitalists. She was beaten by the Japanese barons. All beat her because of her backwardness, military backwardness, cultural backwardness, political backwardness, industrial backwardness, agricultural backwardness. They beat her because to do so was profitable and could be done with impunity. … It is the jungle law of capitalism. You are backward, you are weak – therefore you are wrong; hence, you can be beaten and enslaved. You are mighty – therefore you are right; hence, we must be wary of you.[2]

In other words, to paraphrase Stalin, throughout history the Russian state had failed to modernize and had paid, time and again, for this failure. The Soviet Union, Stalin promised, would cast away this pitiable tradition and become a truly modern state, rapidly and with no consideration of how heavy the human price might be. One can dispute Stalin's interpretation of the past, but for many Russians – and especially for most communists – it seemed compelling. For them, the need to modernize and strengthen the Soviet state trumped other considerations of, say, individual rights or material prosperity.

For both tsarist and Soviet rulers, however, modernization was a two-edged sword. While all acknowledged the need to industrialize, encourage social mobility, expend greater resources to expand literacy and technical knowledge, and to create a modern civil and military bureaucracy, none of Russia's rulers wanted truly free exchange of opinions. That is to say, the creation of civil society that could challenge the ruling order – the cornerstone of traditional models of modernization based on the British or American tradition – was not part of the Russian or Soviet model of modernization. Tsars and, to a lesser extent, Soviet leaders feared overly rapid change leading to social and economic chaos. As Karl Marx had warned, with the coming of capitalism – another way of saying industrial modernization – "all that is solid melts into air, all that is holy is profaned." Neither tsarist nor Soviet leaders had any intention of "melting into air" but both recognized the danger inherent in the thoroughgoing (and continual) change that modernity demanded. Both wanted modernity on their own terms, but ultimately both regimes would be swept away by their inability to keep pace with the rapid change of the modern industrial (or, by 1991, postindustrial) world.

Tsarist Modernization to 1900

As we have seen, the miserable showing of the Russian army during the Crimean War was a primary motivation for the Great Reforms. Among the goals of reform were a reinvigorated economy, a modern conscript army, a prosperous peasantry, and a more efficient (and less corrupt) bureaucracy that could collect sufficient taxes to pay for state needs while carrying out tsarist policies on the local level. The Great Reforms aimed to create the social preconditions for modernization, including greater social mobility (especially for peasants), a modern legal system, improvements in education, and a lessening of censorship to encourage the exchange of information and ideas. But industrialization would require more: infrastructure, investment, a functioning legal system, technical education, and the creation of a modern industrial working class.

In 1861 Russia lagged far behind western and central Europe in one key element of infrastructure: railroads. In that year Russia had only 1,626 kilometers of railroad; the St Petersburg–Warsaw railroad (which then connected to western Europe) was only completed a year later. No railroads connected Moscow with the Black Sea or reached east of the Ural Mountains. By 1880 the Russian railroad net had increased more than tenfold and would double again (to over 50,000 km) by 1900.[3] The Trans-Siberian Railroad, begun in the 1890s, was the most spectacular example of railroad building, but the more modest lines connecting up the countryside with markets and ports were probably even more important economically. Of course modernization is more than economic development: the Trans-Siberian Railroad allowed thousands of peasants to migrate and settle along its length, connected up European Russia with the distant Pacific, and represented a technological achievement that all Russians could be proud of.[4]

Railroads spurred further economic growth. Only with railroads did it become economically feasible for Russia to export grain; in the last decades of the nineteenth century Black Sea ports like Odessa and Kherson boomed as depots for the export of grain and other products. Along the railroads towns and villages grew with increasing numbers of railroad workers, mechanics, and station employees; and indirectly from the new jobs economic opportunities were created by the railroad for catering to travelers, feeding them, providing them with places to stay for the night, and the like. The growth of railways allowed the development of modern tourism, and while Russia was far behind Britain or western Europe in numbers of tourists, by 1914 it was becoming increasingly common for a well-to-do doctor or professor from Moscow to spend part of the summer in the Crimea or even abroad. The railroad was also directly connected with another modern improvement of Russian communications: telegraph and later telephone lines often ran parallel with the railroad tracks. Very often for rural dwellers the closest telegraph station was at the railroad station; the numbers of these railroad telegraph stations more than doubled between 1880 and 1900. Finally the expanded railroad net and decreasing railroad fares made possible increased migration, both to cities in European Russia and for hundreds of thousands of peasants to Siberia.[5]

Industrial development requires investment. One means of financing industrialization is by taxation. Taxes on necessities of life from matches to kerosene to vodka weighed heavily on the poor but helped finance state investment. The fact that the single greatest source of income for the Russian Empire was the tax on vodka also disturbed social reformers who pointed out the high cost to society of encouraging alcohol consumption. By the end of the 1880s the poll tax – earlier one of the most important sources of state revenue – was abolished; taxes on land and business profits (from the 1890s) became more important. As Yanni Kotsonis has argued, taxation policy in this period (and especially in the final two decades before World War I) emphasized individual over collective responsibilities and in that way helped to foster a sense of modern citizenry among Russians.[6] Still, with most subjects of the tsar still rural and illiterate on the eve of World War I, modern identity as citizens was only in an embryonic state.

Throughout this period the tsarist government budget remained in chronic deficit, in great part because of high expenditures on the military – by far the largest single government expenditure. Because of its limited income and heavy obligations, the Russian state could play only a secondary role in financing industrial development. As a poor country with limited domestic capital, the Russian Empire had to attract foreign investment, which increased more than tenfold (from 97.7 to 1,037.4 million rubles) between 1880 and 1905.[7] Russian state bonds became a favorite investment for middle-class French and Belgian investors. The Russian government encouraged railroad investment by guaranteeing profits over a certain period of time; it also floated loans abroad to help finance industry. Like many developing countries Russia adopted a protectionist tariff, particularly under Finance Minister Sergei Witte in the 1890s, thereby forcing foreign investors to produce within the borders of the empire to avoid paying high levies on imports. The adoption of the gold standard in 1897 also encouraged foreign investment by assuring foreign businessmen that their profits would not be eaten up by currency fluctuations.

Parallel with increasing investment (indeed a precondition of it) was the development of an efficient banking system. The State Bank was established in 1860 and functioned as the "bank of banks," housing Russia's gold reserves and providing loans for other banks. The first joint-stock bank was chartered in 1864 in St Petersburg, allowing investors to channel their savings into investment with minimal risk. In Moscow banking was largely in the hands of Old Believers (see chapter 5, "Belief," pp. 151–2) and tended to be less connected with state enterprises. Another major banking center was Warsaw, helping to finance railroads and the textile industry in the Polish provinces. In 1883 the State Peasant Land Bank was founded, followed two years later by the State Noble Land Bank. These banks were mainly engaged in the issuing of mortgages for the purchase and modernization of agriculture. But a major weakness of the Russian financial system was the lack of small-scale credit institutions on the countryside. Peasants needing small loans were usually forced to pay exorbitant interest rates; lenders on the other hand needed to charge such high rates because of the very frequent defaults on such loans.[8]

Banks are obviously necessary for successful industrial development. No less crucial, if less obvious, is the role played by the legal system. In a modern state, relations between individuals and groups are regulated not by the personal whims of rulers, but by laws. The modern state is, or at least strives to be, a *Rechtsstaat*, a state ruled by law. Unlike premodern states (including Russia before 1861), where one's birth determined rights and privileges, in a *Rechtsstaat* all – whether ruler, millionaire, or proletarian – are equal before the law. With the judicial reforms of 1864, Russia took a great step toward the ideal of the state of law. Trials were to be public, judges not subject to dismissal, and jury trials were to assure that citizens influenced the proper outcome of justice. A Russian bar was set up in the 1860s and quickly became an important social organization. Russian legal journals like *Pravo* (The Law) published sophisticated articles concerning not just legal, but more broad, social and political questions.[9]

Yet Russia's legal modernization was far from smooth or uniform. Juries made up of peasants often resented being forced to serve and could barely comprehend the trial evidence and their role in it. The enormous gap between educated Russian society and the Russian masses came face to face in the courts. Another major problem was the lack of a unified legal code. Not only did different regions of the empire (Finland, Baltic provinces, Kingdom of Poland, etc.) follow at least in part different legal norms than the Russian center, but even in European Russia the legal code consisted of an amalgamation of laws rather than a coherent unified legal code. To be sure, in the early twentieth century efforts were made to review and unify the Russian legal code, but these efforts had not been completed by 1914. Despite these weaknesses, the reformed legal system represented a significant step forward, allowing greater transparency and more predictable justice. Not only businessmen and investors, but also everyday citizens, benefited from this more modern judicial system.[10]

A modern economy requires engineers, architects, and trained industrial workers no less than bankers and lawyers. Nineteenth-century universities throughout Europe were ill equipped for technical education: since the Middle Ages, they had been designed to produce doctors, lawyers, theologians, and bureaucrats, not chemists, engineers, and inventors. A new kind of institution of higher learning, the technological institute, was developed first in Prussia and quickly adopted in other parts of Europe. In Russia the St Petersburg Technological Institute had already been founded in 1828; similar institutions for technical education were established in Moscow, Riga, Kharkov, Ekaterinoslav, and the Siberian city Tomsk. Government policy even favored such schools over traditional universities, seeing the latter as hotbeds of revolutionary activity. Between 1898 and 1902 new "polytechnic institutes" were opened in Warsaw and Kiev.

On the eve of World War I, the Saint Petersburg Polytechnic was the second largest institution of its kind in Europe, enrolling over 5,000 students.

While technological institutes trained engineers and managers, industrial workers usually learned their craft on the job. Russian workers, especially in the first generation after 1861, were overwhelmingly peasants who came to the city seeking employment. Links between countryside and factory tended to be close, providing workers with a refuge in times of industrial downturn and unemployment. Consider Semyon Kanatchikov, who came from the village to work in a St Petersburg factory in the mid-1890s. In his later autobiography he describes himself as arriving in "Piter" as an illiterate bumpkin who however rapidly learned to read, qualified as an expert worker, traded his peasant clothing for spiffy city duds, and became interested in socialism. While most peasants turned proletarians did not write autobiographies, Kanatchikov was in other respects not so atypical. The migration of peasants to work in factories began slowly in the 1860s–1880s, turning into a flood in the final decade of the nineteenth century. Coming to the cities, the peasants-turned-workers found themselves in a new world requiring not just new skills and rhythms of everyday life, but also offering entirely new ways of looking at the world. No wonder that so many workers, like Kanatchikov, became alienated from religion and turned to science and socialism. Other workers, however, sought in Orthodox religiosity meaning and community; obviously it would be wrong mechanically to equate "modernity" with secularism.[11]

The influx of workers was one reason for the growth of Russian cities after 1861. Another reason was the overall large population growth: despite the emigration of millions of Jews, Germans, Poles, Lithuanians, and others (though few ethnic Russians), the population of the Russian Empire approximately doubled between the 1860s and 1914. The urban population increased even more rapidly. St Petersburg and Moscow more than doubled in size, each having over a million inhabitants by the early twentieth century. Interestingly the third largest ethnic Russian city was Saratov on the Volga, with a population of only 137,000 in 1897. After the capitals the next seven of the Russian Empire's largest cities were all on the periphery: Warsaw, Riga, Kiev, Odessa, Tiflis (Tbilisi), Tashkent, Kharkov. Among the empire's cities, perhaps the most striking growth of all occurred in the center of the Polish textile industry, Łódź, which grew from a mere 32,000 in 1862 to over half a million on the eve of World War I. Despite this rapid urbanization, in 1914 the great majority of the tsar's subjects still lived on the countryside and earned their living directly or indirectly from agriculture.[12]

The first wave of rapid Russian industrialization occurred during the reigns of Alexander III and Nicholas II and is associated with two men, Ivan Vyshnegradskii and Sergei Witte. Both were in their own ways "new men," unusual among tsarist ministers of the day. Vyshnegradskii had been a professor and director at the

St Petersburg Technological Institute and Witte, who had studied mathematics at university, a railroad executive in the Southwest (Ukrainian) provinces. Vyshnegradskii became minister of finance in 1887 and based his industrialization program on balancing the budget and increasing exports. It was his misfortune to have remarked, when pressed on the economic hardships suffered by peasants due to high taxes and exports, "We will starve, but we will export grain" – just before a massive famine hit large parts of Russia in 1891, killing hundreds of thousands.

Replacing Vyshnegradskii in 1892, Witte continued many aspects of his policies but also expertly used foreign investment and loans to encourage industrialization. By placing the ruble on the gold standard in August 1897, Witte was able to reassure foreign investors about the Russian Empire's economic stability and thereby obtain more favorable interest rates. Russian industrial growth rates in the 1890s were the highest the world had ever seen, though they were soon to be eclipsed by Japan's.[13] In petroleum production Russia was number one in the world in the first years of the twentieth century, though it was soon overtaken by the USA. By the early twentieth century Russia ranked among the world's major economic producers, though per capita production remained far lower than that in western Europe or North America. Industrial growth since the 1880s had been impressive, but the revolution of 1905 demonstrated that rapid economic change can have negative social and political consequences.[14]

Stresses of Modernization: 1900–1917

While the revolution was sparked by police firing on unarmed petitioners rather than strikers or labor protestors on 9/22 January 1905, it was industrial strikes and agricultural disorders after that event which nearly toppled the tsarist regime. The explosion of 1905 had been long in the making and laid bare with startling brutality the inadequacies and contradictions of tsarist modernization. While the two generations since peasant emancipation had seen great economic changes and even significant economic growth, this progress was unevenly spread and a significant percentage of the population was bitterly dissatisfied with its circumstances. This dissatisfaction was not, of course, limited to one class: peasants, industrial workers, and the middle class all had reason to want major political change by the early twentieth century.

In 1861 most Russians had been serfs or state peasants. At the beginning of the twentieth century most Russians, though no longer under the direct control of landlords, remained peasants living lives not very different from those of their grandparents. Historians disagree on the level of peasant poverty, but no one denies that millions of rural dwellers remained illiterate and poorly clothed; in the case of a bad harvest they could easily go hungry – or worse, as the famine in 1891 showed. As discussed earlier, emancipated serfs had to pay for the land they had received. In fact arrears on these "redemption payments" grew steadily in the ensuing decades until they were finally canceled amidst widespread rural violence against landlords during the 1905 revolution. While some historians have pointed to data indicating that agricultural efficiency and peasant standards of living did improve somewhat, the improvement was clearly not enough to stave off major social upheavals.[15]

Several factors hampered the improvement of rural life. To start with, Russia simply had too many peasants and the surplus in rural labor reduced the need to improve agricultural methods. David Moon estimates that between 1857 and World War I the peasant population in Russia nearly tripled, from 32 to 90 million.[16] The number of peasants far outstripped both the need for rural labor and the ability of the land to support them properly, given the low level of agricultural technology. The weak sense of private property among Russian peasants – enshrined in the periodical redistribution of land by the peasant commune (*mir*) – was a significant obstacle to development. Knowing that the land he was plowing this year might be redistributed to another peasant, an ambitious plowman had little incentive to improve his plot. The communal practice of allotting families not a single plot but numerous small strips also made agricultural rationalization (fertilizing, sowing of legumes, etc.) difficult. The very low level of peasant education (in 1897 only 26 percent of peasants were literate) also hindered agricultural innovation.[17] For all of these reasons it is impossible to speak of successful modernization among the peasants of the Russian Empire.

Nor were industrial workers satisfied with the status quo in the early twentieth century. While working conditions had improved between the 1870s and 1900 – a factory inspectorate had been established in the 1880s and an 1897 law limited the number of hours both adults and children could legally labor – factory work remained dirty, dangerous, and poorly paid. Unions were not allowed until 1906 and strikes were illegal. Despite these circumstances, already from the 1870s major strikes shut down production in some factories and workers began to organize illegally. The task of spreading socialist propaganda and organizing workers was made easier by the great concentration of industry in a few areas (Moscow, St Petersburg, Łódź) and in large factories, to take just one example, at the turn of the century over 10,000 workers labored in the Putilov plant in St Petersburg. Russian industrial workers tended to remain in quite close contact with the countryside, often returning home to the village in case of ill health or during periods of high unemployment. Thus the line between "peasant" and "urban worker" is often difficult to draw in pre-revolutionary Russia.

The Russian middle class was also unhappy with its lot. Here the grievances were less economic than political. While the middle class in Russia was considerably weaker than in, say, France or even Austria, tens of thousands of lawyers, engineers, teachers, professors, scientists, journalists, and other middle-class people lived in the empire. Unlike their counterparts in Paris, Vienna, or Milan, however, educated Russians could not organize political discussions, collect money for a cause, or influence politics. The refusal of the tsarist government to allow even a consultative legislature, combined with the frequent friction between middle-class leaders in *zemstva* and local officials, exasperated this growing class. Well aware of the political and economic power of the middle class in western Europe and North America, middle-class Russians resented their lack of say in political matters at home. Many of them would be sympathetic to the "Union of Liberation" (*Soiuz osvobozhdeniia*), founded by the liberal economist Peter Struve in 1903, and would join the liberal Kadet (Constitutional Democracy) party after 1905.

The upheavals of 1905 revealed the fundamental fragility of tsarist modernization. The Great Reforms had aimed to restore and enhance Russia's military power but in the Russo-Japanese War the Russian army was defeated by a newly industrialized Asian power. The failure at creating a contented, prosperous peasantry was shown by the widespread violence on the countryside. Nor could the Russian Empire assure order among its different peoples: among the worst-hit regions were the western borderlands: the Baltic provinces, where Estonian and Latvian peasants burnt and plundered the estates of their German landlords, and Poland, where strikes and street demonstrations combining socialist and Polish national demands essentially wrested power from the Russians for most of 1905.[18] Cities, the locus of modernization, essentially passed out of the government's control during 1905, with policemen reluctant to patrol the streets, fearing a bullet in the back from revolutionaries. The near total breakdown of order forced even a convinced conservative like Prime Minister Sergei Witte to press Tsar Nicholas II to make significant concessions to society embodied in the October Manifesto. The manifesto has to be considered a great step forward in the political modernization of Russia, promising civil rights (personal inviolability, freedom of conscience, speech, assembly and association), broader voting rights, and assuring the principle that no new laws would be passed without the consent of the legislature (the State Duma).

The events of 1905 indicated the total failure of the attempt to modernize economically while retaining an unreformed political system. Indeed the most "modern" parts of the empire – industrial cities, the more advanced agricultural regions on the western borderlands – were hardest hit by revolution. Overwhelmingly, educated middle-class people and industrial workers were joined by the peasantry and national minorities in rejecting the tsarist order. The key question after 1905 was whether Tsar Nicholas II and his administration could really turn over a new leaf and embrace a more open and democratic social and political order.

Historians disagree as to whether the tsarist regime in Russia had a serious chance of long-term survival after 1905. One thing seems certain, however: by his hesitation, unwillingness to compromise, and inability to work with competent prime ministers (much less with the Duma), Nicholas II inadvertently did all he could to minimize these chances. Perhaps the gap between society and government was simply too wide to bridge by 1905, but if the empire were to exist in any form, it would have to reform. While Nicholas refused to acknowledge this simple fact, his most famous prime minister, Peter Stolypin, knew it to be true.

Stolypin remains a fascinating figure because of his dogged efforts to serve as the midwife for a reformed, modern, but still conservative Russia. Stolypin did not shy from violence when he felt it necessary: the field courts-martial he introduced to crush unrest on the countryside summarily executed over a thousand individuals in 1906, permanently tarnishing his image among the liberal intelligentsia. Stolypin also forced a reform of the electoral law on July 3, 1907, that severely limited representation to the Duma among non-Russians and the less privileged. But once order had been restored and a more Russian and conservative parliament (the Third Duma) elected, Stolypin attempted to work with this body, despite his strong desire to uphold the tsar's power. Like more than one conservative before and after him, Stolypin attempted to build on Russian national feeling and patriotism to gather support for the government. For non-Russians, however, his policies appeared the first steps toward a new and more aggressive Russifying assault on their cultures. Stolypin may – with some exaggeration – be compared with Bismarck, with the enormous difference that Nicholas II was quite unwilling to concede significant power to his prime minister. Given Nicholas's attitude, one may doubt whether Stolypin could have succeeded in ushering in a modern "great Russia."[19]

Stolypin's plan for a stable, modern Russia was based economically on the creation of a class of prosperous farmers.[20] The Stolypin agrarian reforms, approved by the Duma in 1910, made it possible for individual peasants to gain as private property the dispersed strips of land they held in the commune and to consolidate them into a single plot. Credit was to be made available for the building of farmhouses, the digging of wells, buying of tools, and other expenses that peasant families would incur in setting up their own individual farms. The reform also made it possible to abolish the commune entirely if a majority of members (or two-thirds in the case of repartitional communes) so voted.

Stolypin called this reform – so radically foreign to the traditions of Russian agriculture – a "wager on the strong and sober." Did it have any chance of success? Some historians have argued that, given enough time, the reform could have produced a class of conservative supporters of the tsarist order. After all, by 1915 over a quarter of communal households had petitioned to leave the commune.[21] Others have pointed out that even after 1917, when the landlords had been chased out and their land seized by peasants, the commune continued to exist informally, but few of the newly formed "consolidated farms" did. Certainly after the Bolshevik revolution when landlord's estates were divided up among peasants, the individual farms (*khutory*) set up under the Stolypin reform were also attacked. There is much evidence that while some peasants did want to get out of the commune and strike out on their own, this individualist attitude provoked a great deal of social resentment among other peasants. All agree that for success, Stolypin's reform would have needed time, and with international tensions growing, time was running out.[22]

If the revolution of 1905 revealed the fragility in Russia's modernization since the Great Reforms, World War I and the 1917 revolutions showed the total fiasco of modernization under tsarist rule. Despite reforms and significant military expenditures since 1905, the Russian army remained inadequately trained and equipped. Even worse than the material situation of the Russian army was the state of its leadership: already in August 1914 the incompetence of Russian Generals Alexander Samsonov and Pavel Rennenkampf had at the very least exacerbated the scale of defeat at the Battle of Tannenberg. At the war's beginning, Russia lacked adequate supplies of artillery guns and shells. Russian industry did manage to switch over to military production and made good these inadequacies, but to do this, had to take resources from other sectors of the economy. Particularly troubling was the fragile condition of the railroad system (both track and rolling stock), motorized vehicles, and communications technology. All of these would be overwhelmed by the demands of war, with catastrophic results.

Russian finances could also not bear the strain of war; the Russian Empire went off the gold standard as soon as the war began. Fatally for Russia's budget, Nicholas II declared a prohibition on the sale of alcoholic beverages for the duration of the war, thereby depriving the Russian state of its largest single source of income. Prewar planners had not foreseen any shortages in food supply, and indeed grain production remained high until 1916. When food shortages did develop, more in the cities than in the army, it was due, not to poor harvests, but to supply bottlenecks, the breakdown in the transportation system, and the lack of consumer industrial goods to encourage peasants to sell grain. In the end the February 1917 disorders that brought down the tsarist regime had less to do with military defeats than with civilian hunger and the feeling that the government was hopelessly incompetent to deal with the problems of the war.[23]

Bolsheviks as Modernizers

Marxism is, above all things, a modernizing ideology. As Marx himself wrote as a young man in his *Theses on Feuerbach* (No. 11), "Philosophers have only interpreted the world in various ways; the point is to change it." This change was to be the working out of historical processes (especially economic ones) in a *scientific* manner. Lenin was a faithful follower of Marx in embracing both modernity and science (including a scientific understanding of history) as the proper – indeed only – way toward modernity. For Marx and the Bolsheviks, understanding the world was the first step toward changing it and moving toward a modern, socialist state.[24]

Russian Marxists had one big problem: Marx had assumed that the revolution would come first in the most advanced, industrialized countries – like England, France, or Germany. Marx always saw industrial workers as the bearers of revolution and despised the peasantry as backward and reactionary. In Russia, even in the second decade of the twentieth century, industrial workers made up a small percentage of the total population and were overwhelmingly outnumbered by peasants. Before 1914 Lenin had bitterly denounced the populists for arguing that revolution could be based on the peasantry, but after the 1917 revolution he suggested that industrial workers together with peasants would work to further revolutionary aims. But neither workers nor peasants would be the vanguard of revolution: for Lenin, already in his 1902 pamphlet *What Is to Be Done?*, the party would play that role.[25]

Not any social class but the Communist Party itself would push Russia toward modernity, whether it liked it or not, but in any case using the most scientific methods (i.e., Marxism) available. In its later decades the USSR boasted of having more scientists than any other country on earth. To quote historian David Holloway:

> the Soviet system itself was consciously constructed on the basis of a scientific theory and would be guided by that theory in its future development. The Soviet Union presented itself as the true heir to the Enlightenment project of applying reason to human affairs.[26]

The first years of communist rule were too chaotic for the formulation – much less the implementation – of any coherent plan of modernization. But the outline of such a plan is clear even in the earliest decrees which abolished private ownership of land (though de facto allowed peasants to take over landowners' estates), shut down the "bourgeois press" (i.e., liberal newspapers), established equal rights for all national and religious groups (thereby abolishing the special privileges that the Russian Orthodox Church had enjoyed), established a secret police (the Cheka), created a new military force (the Red Army), nationalized large-scale industry, and set up a one-party dictatorship. All of these measures were passed in the short period between November 1917 and June 1918. Thus by summer 1918 the main structures of the Soviet state that would last for over seventy years had been established: a centralized government controlling (at least in principle) the economy, a one-party dictatorship with a low degree of toleration for political dissent and possessing a secret police and army to defend itself from domestic and foreign enemies.

Up to this point in history, "modernization" had always been along liberal and capitalist lines. In western and central Europe, North America, and a few other spots on the globe, capitalist industrialization had gone hand-in-hand with constitutions, parliamentary democracy, and individual rights. Now the Bolsheviks wanted to create an entirely new kind of modernity, based on state control of the economy, a one-party system, and collective rather than individual social identities. There was no precedent for this radical attempt to change the course of history and, especially given the very difficult economic conditions in Soviet Russia after 1917, it is hardly surprising that this experiment was accompanied with a great deal of human suffering, especially in the crisis period 1917–21 and then again in the period of "crash industrialization" in the late 1920s and first half of the 1930s.

The "political modernization" of the communist state outlined above took mere months; economic and social transformations were to demand much more time, effort, and suffering. During the Civil War the struggle for mere survival prevented the communists from serious modernizing efforts. With the Civil War over, the New Economic Policy, or NEP (1921–8) was seen as a step backward from the communist point of view, as it allowed the return of despised traders, petty capitalists, and market forces. In practical fact, however, NEP could not be avoided. By 1921 industry had come to an almost total standstill, the railroads were in sore need of repair, mines were flooded and idle, and famine threatened millions of Russians. NEP allowed peasants to sell their produce on the open market after having paid a tax in kind. Small-scale traders, artisans, shopkeepers, and restaurants were allowed. The effect of this reform was rapid: by 1926 Soviet industry had reached and even exceeded output levels of the prewar period; grain production was also higher by 1926 than in 1913. This was not, however, the modernization expected by most communists. Aside from the negative social consequences, in particular the creation of a class of petty capitalists, the NEP-men, NEP allowed the market to influence the economy. For example, rather than concentrate on capital goods and heavy industry, the Soviet state had to expend resources on light industry (consumer goods) to produce industrial goods so that the peasantry would have a reason to sell their grain. This meant less investment in heavy industry and a slower growth rate, but even more distasteful for many communists was the simple fact of being subject to market forces at all. Thus when Stalin advocated crash industrialization, dismissing worries about the market, his ideas found a ready audience.

Modernization should not be understood only as economic development. To be sure, as Marxists, Lenin and his followers believed that the "substructure" (economic system) determined "superstructure" (culture, society, politics). During the 1920s, even before the Stalinist leap to crash industrialization, serious efforts were being made to create a new, modern, Soviet society. To do so would require a thoroughgoing rethinking of ethics, gender, the family, religion, literature, art, everyday life, education, even architecture and urban planning. To start with, Soviet citizens needed to be literate: a famous poster compared an illiterate to a blindfolded peasant about to step into an abyss. In the 1920s, despite tight government budgets, significant resources were expended on literacy campaigns so that by 1939 over 80 percent of Soviet citizens could read and write.

Mere literacy, however, was not enough. Soviet education attempted to instill in citizens a modern worldview free of "religious prejudices" (i.e., of religion) and full of science. Special groups like the "League of the Militant Godless" attacked religious belief – and sometimes believers – while trying to demonstrate that science could explain the world far better than religion. The Soviet authorities also tried to break down the monopoly of the middle-classes on higher education by establishing new preparatory courses for workers and peasants wishing to enter institutions of higher education. Predictably professors complained of under-prepared and disrespectful students, while the activist students often regarded the professors as bourgeois from another era or even as class enemies.[27]

The family and gender relations were a particular focus: it was obviously illogical and unscientific to allow half of the population (i.e., women) to remain outside public life, uneducated, and entirely burdened with bearing and raising children. Propagandizing women was also seen as one way to influence two social groups largely hostile to the communists: the peasantry and Muslims. Peasant women were exhorted to gain an education, raise their children as enlightened Soviet citizens, and reject patriarchal authority. Communist campaigns for Muslim women in central Asia to cast off and burn their veils (often in a public ceremony) had a similar purpose: to wrench women away from traditional society and claim them as modern Soviet citizens. The results of such campaigns were at best mixed. Muslim or peasant women who tried to join the party were often ostracized, physically abused, or even murdered.[28] As the communists themselves recognized, there was little room for compromise between traditional religious society – whether that be Muslim or Orthodox Christian – and modern communist ideology.

Among the many visions of modernity discussed in the 1920s was the shape of Soviet cities and the architecture within these cities. Urban planners envisioned utopian socialist cities that broke down the distinction between "country" and "city," enhancing citizens' health by providing ample parks and recreational areas. In keeping with communist ideas of liberating women from the burdens of housework, apartment complexes were designed with large communal kitchens and eating areas and only minimal space for food preparation in individual apartments. Numerous cheap cafeterias were set up, but the dreadful quality of the food served there provided material for many jokes of the era. The financial exigency of the 1920s prevented the construction of large-scale residence quarters, though some of these ideas took concrete shape after World War II in the new main building of Moscow State University, which combined offices, classrooms, dormitories, a swimming pool, and retail areas.

After Lenin's death a key question that the Communist Party had to answer was the status of NEP. That is, would this policy be continued for a long period, perhaps even decades more, or should it be regarded as a short "breathing space" before returning to more radical policies. The advocate for a long-term NEP was Nikolai Bukharin, while Trotsky headed the group opposing NEP as an unfortunate temporary retreat that should be overcome as soon as possible. In 1926 Stalin supported Bukharin's more gradualist approach against the "Left Opposition" headed by Trotsky. The following year, however, with the Left Opposition in disarray and its leaders expelled from the party, Stalin abandoned Bukharin's gradualist approach and himself took up a militant position far more radical than that of the erstwhile Left Oppositionists. While these disputes were political and personal, they also centered on how best to make the USSR a modern industrial state: by gradual, partly market-driven methods or through a state-driven crash industrialization. In the end, Stalin and crash industrialization won out over the more gradualist approach of the 1920s.

The launch of the first Five-Year Plan in 1928 meant in practical terms the end of NEP and the return to the communists' radical Enlightenment roots. Not the market or consumer demands but an all-encompassing plan based on rational calculations and involving all enterprises from the producers of raw materials to retail would propel the USSR toward the future. At least, this was the theory: one plan would eliminate wasteful competition and redundancy while allowing party priorities to be translated efficiently into reality. The goals set by the plan were very ambitious, demanding huge increases in a number of key economic areas from pig iron to oil to coal. For example, the production of coal, oil, iron ore, and pig iron were to be sharply increased, by a factor of two or three, in the space of five years. Later "targets" were even more ambitious and divorced from real circumstances.[29]

The First Five-Year plan was accompanied by collectivization in agriculture. Crash industrialization simply could not take place without control over the food supply. The brutality of collectivization stemmed primarily from the need to assure grain supply to the industrializing cities but also signaled a return to Marxist traditions of contempt for the peasant. Despite the much-propagandized alliance between worker and peasant symbolized by the hammer and sickle, there had never been much love lost between communists and peasants. After collectivization, however, it would be clear that peasants had no place whatsoever in

Soviet modernity. Even the word "peasant" (*krestianin*) disappeared from the Soviet vocabulary, replaced by *kolkhoznik* (collective farmer). The collective farm – large, mechanized, and efficient – would sweep away the peasantry and their retrograde culture: the "liquidation of the kulaks as a class" was just one aspect of the liquidation of an entire culture. But most of all, Soviet modernity would play itself out in cities, not the countryside.

The Modernizing Decade: 1930s

The decade starting with the Five-Year Plan (1928) and ending with the beginning of World War II (September 1939) can justifiably be termed "revolutionary." Not in a political sense: here nothing significant changed, as Stalin had already consolidated his personal power by 1928, but in economic and social terms. In many ways the economy of the USSR of 1928 was not so terribly different from the Russian Empire of 1913: most Soviet citizens lived on the countryside, industry had recovered to 1913 levels but had barely advanced beyond them; transport and agricultural methods remained backward. To be sure, the large estates of the landlords had been seized and divided up by the peasants in 1917, but this had the negative consequences for the overall economy (though not for peasants, who ate better) because there was now less grain for export. At the beginning of this period, the USSR was fifth among industrialized countries – more or less the same rank as in 1912 – but by the eve of World War II only the USA surpassed the Soviet Union in industrial output. While this decade was full of impressive economic achievement, it also witnessed enormous human suffering, with millions dislocated, working under miserable and dangerous conditions, living crowded in tiny and unsanitary apartments, and barely able to obtain the most basic food and clothing. Besides the human suffering, many later historians and economists have argued that the crash industrializing program, while impressive in the short run, saddled the USSR with a cumbersome economic system that was unable to develop normally in later decades. In this way Stalinist modernization planted the seeds of the eventual economic implosion of the USSR more than a half century later.

For the Five-Year Plan to succeed, three factors were crucial: sufficient labor, adequate bread for the industrial workers, and political stability (i.e., no strikes or protests against government policy). The cruel and brutal crash collectivization campaign of 1929–30 and the subsequent less violent but more thorough process leading to almost total collectivization of agriculture by the mid-1930s achieved all three of these goals. The campaign of "dekulakization" preemptively decapitated any peasant protest by arresting and exiling to Siberia and central Asia millions of the most prosperous peasants (including their families). This had the

FIGURE 4.1 Konstantin Zotov, "Every Collective Farm Peasant or Individual Farmer Now Has the Opportunity to Live Like a Human Being." 1934.
Source: Russian State Library, Moscow.

double advantage, from the Soviet point of view, of nipping possible rural dissent in the bud by depriving the countryside of leadership, and of providing labor for the cities (and, in many cases, slave labor for the Gulag). At the same time it demoralized the peasantry and deprived the countryside of the most dynamic individuals. Later Soviet problems with agricultural inefficiency can be traced back to the brutality of collectivization.

From the point of view of liberal economics (or simple humanity), dekulakization was a catastrophe, as many of those designated "kulak" destroyed their houses and slaughtered their farm animals for one last feast rather than cede their hard-earned property to the collective farm.[30] But looking at the matter with the icy gaze of Stalinist modernity, the kulaks needed to be "liquidated as a class" in order to clear the way for modern Soviet agriculture, which was to be characterized by large state-owned farms cultivated by machines. In 1929 a tractor was a rare sight in the Soviet countryside, and even in 1940 there were not enough for each collective farm. In order to use this resource more rationally the party set up Machine Tractor Stations (MTS) throughout the countryside. Along with the MTS party cells were established to report on local conditions and carry out propaganda work. The MTS, having control over crucial machinery for plowing, sowing, and harvesting, could also be used to reward or punish collective farms (by providing them with – or depriving them of – the machinery at crucial times). The MTS operated throughout the Stalinist period and were abolished only in 1958.

The industrialization drive took place in a heated atmosphere of mass enthusiasm or, if one prefers, of mass hysteria. Slogans like "There is no fortress that Bolsheviks cannot storm" abounded. It is not by coincidence that enormous mass festivals were orchestrated by the Soviet authorities at this time: the entire country was harnessed to "make good" its backwardness, to catch up and overtake western countries in a mere decade. At times enthusiasm swept away cool rational accounting, in particular production goals were pushed ever higher, at times to absurd levels. To take one already-mentioned example, the original First Five-Year Plan called for an almost doubling of coal production, from 35 to 68 tons. Then a later version of the plan raised the goal by a further 50 percent (actual output at plan's end in 1932 was 64 tons). As one branch of production enthusiastically pushed up its goal for the plan, others needed to do so both for political and economic reasons, to avoid lagging behind and to avoid production bottlenecks. The rush to increase output goals was in direct contradiction to the very purpose of central planning; that is, to oversee the entire economy and set production goals for each individual industry accordingly. At the same time enthusiasm fulfilled an important political – and psychological – need, as well as prodding workers to expend ever-greater efforts for the sake of production.

Crash industrialization brought with it unforeseen problems. Planners had expected that unemployment – an embarrassing problem during the NEP years – would be reduced but not disappear entirely. Instead almost immediately labor shortages developed. Factory managers scrambled to find workers; skilled machinists and others with factory experience could demand better wages and changed jobs frequently; in 1930 workers in the coal and iron industry changed jobs on average three times per year. One source of labor was the female population: increasingly women filled jobs both in industry and throughout the economy.[31] Another way to deal with labor shortages was to increase efficiency per worker.

Here propaganda and enthusiasm was combined with material prizes for efficient workers, as in the Stakhanovite movement, named for coal miner Aleksei Stakhanov who in 1935 produced 14 times his daily norm. Other workers were exhorted to follow Stakhanov's example; the most successful not only won praise and material rewards but in some exceptional cases were even invited to the Kremlin to meet Stalin and other high party dignitaries. Other workers viewed Stakhanovism as an attempt to squeeze more labor out of them for the same pay. Stakhanovites tended not to be generally popular; some were even murdered by their fellow workers.[32]

Stakhanovism was only one among a number of measures taken by the Soviet government to assure adequate labor supplies to the growing factories. The traditional seven-day week was abolished in 1931 and replaced with five days of labor followed by one day of rest. This had the double advantage of allowing plants to function without a break (not all workers had the same "sixth" day off) while abolishing Sunday (in Russian the same word as "resurrection") with its religious connotations. But this new week was unpopular and in 1940 the USSR returned to the traditional seven-day week. The need for skilled labor forced up the wage differential between skilled workers and unskilled laborers, to the disgruntlement of some communists. Stalin himself felt it necessary to specifically denounce egalitarianism in pay, *uravnilovka*, as "a petit-bourgeois prejudice."

Gradually labor conditions were tightened up, favoring enterprise over worker. Internal passports were introduced in December 1932 and withheld from collective farmers, who could now migrate to the cities only with special permission. Also in that year workers who failed to show up to work for a single day without reason could be dismissed. In 1939 "absenteeism" was defined down to appearing more than twenty minutes late to work and in 1940 failing to appear for work was made a criminal offence. Given the constant and acute labor shortages, one may doubt that factory directors often applied these strict measures, but the mere fact of their existence gave management one more tool against workers. In fact, though, the carrot was used more than the stick: workers who produced more than the norm were rewarded with special access to consumer goods, factory housing, and other perks.

Historians often use the word "gigantomania" when discussing the Stalinist modernization. Like the enthusiastic campaigns to ratchet up production goals, gigantic projects helped convince communists, the general populace, and the world that the USSR was truly constructing a new kind of modernity. Among such enormous projects were the Volga–White Sea Canal (built using mainly convict labor), the hydroelectric dam at Dneprostroi in Ukraine, which began producing electricity in 1934, and the huge metallurgical combine at Kuznetsstroi in western Siberia. Soviet cities were also to receive huge new buildings, foremost among them a new Palace of Soviets in Moscow that was to have been the world's

FIGURE 4.2   The Moscow Metro, one of the grand construction projects of the Stalin period.
Source: Bettmann/Corbis.

tallest structure, built on the banks of the Moscow River and – not coincidentally – requiring the destruction of the enormous 30-story tall cathedral of Christ the Savior. The cathedral was in fact destroyed but the palace never built, though the nearby Moscow Metro stop retained the name "Palace of the Soviets" until 1957, a kind of metaphor for the incomplete nature of Stalinist modernization.

The enormous Palace of Soviets was to be just one among a number of sky-scrapers that were to be built in the new Moscow. The proposed building fitted well with Lenin's call for a new kind of "monumental propaganda." Even without the palace, the face of Moscow changed hugely in the first three decades of Soviet rule. One of central Moscow's main streets, Okhotnyi Riad, was straightened, broadened, and renamed Gorky Street after the radical writer. Tsarist names and monuments were cleared away, and squares were remodeled to serve the needs of Soviet – soon Stalinist – marches, celebrations, and festivals. Red Square in Moscow became the focal point and model for such mass spectacles, with the party leadership observing the festivities from seats atop Lenin's Mausoleum, built next to the Kremlin Wall in the late 1920s. And of course Moscow grew enor-mously in the 1920s and 1930s, rapidly overtaking St Petersburg and topping four million just before World War II – almost quadrupling the 1920 figure.

Already in the 1920s there were plans to revolutionize the new socialist capital's architecture with skyscrapers, more modern urban design of streets and squares, as well as massive complexes incorporating apartments with cultural, culinary, and recreational establishments. Newsreels showed massive "clearing away of the past" – often including priceless churches – to broaden streets and allow for new construction. For the most part, however, the emblematic Stalinist high-rise buildings in Moscow such as Moscow State University and the Hotel Ukraine date from after World War II. One major innovation in the Moscow city fabric does date from the 1930s: in 1935 the first line of the Moscow metro opened, and by 1945 several lines were in operation. Another new and welcome addition to Moscow life in the 1930s was the opening of "the park of culture and relaxation," soon to be known as Gorky Park, near the city center. Here Muscovites could stroll, play sports, attend cultural events, and relax.[33]

The most famous "gigantic" project of all was the construction of the largest steel mill complex with an entirely new city around it: Magnitogorsk. Plans for the blast furnaces were modeled after those operated by US Steel in Gary, Indiana, and the city itself was to exemplify Stalinist modernity. Construction began in 1929 and a mere three years later a quarter of a million people made the city their home, including John Scott, a young American of radical views who had come to Magnitogorsk to help build socialism. Scott worked in the city as a welder for several years and wrote about his experiences in *Behind the Urals*, describing both the terrible working conditions and great hunger for education and eagerness for self-improvement that he witnessed among the Soviet people.

Magnitogorsk was located atop a huge deposit of iron (the city's name refers to the "magnetic" effect this deposit had on compasses) in the southern Urals, hundreds of miles from any major urban center, and equally distant from sources of coal, crucial for the production of iron and steel. Photos from the later 1930s show well-ordered apartment buildings and parks in the aptly named "socialist city," though we know that many other workers continued to live in poorly heated and unhygienic barracks while the bosses enjoyed exclusive cottages in their own part of town. The image of Magnitogorsk as a well-ordered, productive socialist city clashed with the reality of chaotic living conditions, an unstable labor force, frequent injuries and deaths on the job, and political repressions. For many Soviet citizens, however, the creation of this industrial city *ex nihilo* was a source of pride. The building of Magnitogorsk convinced many foreigners that the USSR had much to teach the West about modernizing.[34]

The communists' ambitions to transform humanity went far beyond economic development, though. Not just the economy or politics, but human attitudes and identities had to be changed. Historians find it difficult, of course, to delve into the human soul, but recent analyses of personal documents such as letters and diaries does show the sincere desire for what one historian has termed "self-transformation in terms of killing the Old Man and rearing the New Man within."[35] Individuals with "tainted social backgrounds" such as the children of priests, noblemen, or merchants, attempted to refashion themselves as collective-minded, optimistic, and future-oriented new Soviet people.[36] One successful "recasting" of an individual with questionable social background was Andrei Vyshinskii, born into a Catholic family in Odessa, son of a shopkeeper, and pre-revolutionary Menshevik. Despite his tainted past, Vyshinskii rose to become the Prosecutor General of the USSR in 1935, presided over the subsequent purges, and served as Soviet foreign minister 1949–53.

The impressive achievements in production hid less attractive aspects of everyday life in the Soviet Union. While industrial workers were not going hungry, obtaining basic foodstuffs demanded a significant investment of time and energy. Finding basic food and clothing meant standing in line, sometimes for hours. Clothing was dingy, of poor quality, and expensive. One of the reasons for the huge growth rates was the concentration of investment in heavy industry. Housing and light industry for consumer products, on the other hand, were starved of resources. While Soviet cities grew significantly, with urban dwellers doubling from 26 to 52 million between 1926 and 1937. At the same time housing stock remained nearly stagnant. Workers were typically housed in barracks and dormitories while many had to make due by renting "a corner" of a room, cordoned off by a cloth curtain. Only the luckiest or most privileged had an apartment for themselves. During the "Great Terror" of the late 1930s, one motivation to denounce one's colleagues or neighbors was simply to obtain their apartments, a practice common enough to be satirized in Mikhail Bulgakov's novel *Master and Margarita*.[37]

In many respects everyday life in the USSR of the 1930s resembled a Hobbesian nightmare: poor, nasty, brutish, and short. On the other hand, as Scott recounts in his memoirs, many Soviet citizens were willing to accept the brutal conditions of the present day as a necessary condition for a better future.[38] After all, early industrialization in England or the United States had involved a great deal of poverty and suffering, and in the USSR the process of industrial growth was being concentrated into a much shorter period. Stalinist festivals and other expressions of mass enthusiasm were designed to encourage the feeling that while today everyday conditions were admittedly inadequate, today's efforts would give birth to tomorrow's "radiant future."[39] Much later, after World War II, many Soviet citizens would proudly and fondly remember this difficult period as one full of hope, joy, and accomplishment paving the way for a radically new, just, and prosperous society.

Slogans and enthusiasm aside, the economic achievements of the first three Five-Year Plans (1928–41) were considerable. While the 20 percent annual growth rates promised by the plans did not materialize, economists estimate that the Soviet economy did grow by an unprecedented 12–14 percent per annum. To name just a few specifics, in the production of electricity the USSR rose from fifteenth in the world to third, output of pig iron had more than doubled, production of steel had tripled. By 1940 the USSR was second only to the USA in machine-building, tractors, trucks, and overall industrial production. Of crucial importance for communist ideology, the size of the industrial working class had tripled.

There were, however, some big losers in this rush to Soviet modernity. In particular the peasants, millions of whom were dispossessed and uprooted; additional millions died in the famine of 1932–3. The cruel truth was that Stalinist modernity simply excluded the peasantry. This was done formally by not issuing collective farmers internal passports in 1932, essentially condemning them to remain on the countryside. Cities had the priority on industrial goods and even foodstuffs; collective farms had to make do with what was left. Earnings for collective farmers were dependent on the farm as a whole making a surplus. When this did not happen (as was frequent), individuals staved off hunger with crops grown on their individual plots. The low level of productivity in agriculture remained a great weakness in the Soviet economy to the very end.

Another failure of modernization is less easy to document statistically. One may term it the "fading of utopian ideals" that many have seen occurring from the late 1930s. Increasingly party membership was a matter of careerism rather than enthusiasm or ideals. Family values, once derided as "bourgeois" and reactionary, were embraced by the Soviet state, which criminalized both abortion and male homosexual acts in the mid-1930s. The Soviet press and literature increasingly portrayed women in roles subservient to men and, while still working outside the home, placing more value on motherhood and child-rearing. Officers' ranks headed by Field Marshall ("Marshall of the Soviet Union") were reintroduced in the 1935. Finally a recent study has intriguingly argued that the purges of the late 1930s were essentially an expression of despair over the failure to rid Soviet society of "survivals of the old regime" during nearly 20 years of communist rule. The attempted elimination by police measures of "undesirable and suspect groups" labeled "'criminal contingents,' 'dangerous elements,' 'homeless elements,' 'kulak elements,' 'speculative elements' [etc.]" can hardly be squared with Marxism or the stated ideals of the October Revolution.[40] The turn toward violent measures to purge the USSR of these "undesirables" can be seen as a sign that the communist rulers of the USSR had begun to doubt the inherent strength and feasibility of the communist project.

Triumphs and Weaknesses of Modernization: The Acid Test of World War II

After 1945, and to this day, one oft-repeated justification of Stalinist crash industrialization in the 1930s was that without it, the Soviet Union would not have been capable of resisting the Nazi invaders in World War II. While such a broad assertion cannot be entirely verified or proven wrong by historical research, we can at least examine the assumptions upon which such an argument are based in light of existing economic and political data. On the one hand the cruelties of collectivization and the near-starvation of peasant populations certainly did not increase their desire to fight for the USSR. As we know, many peasants in the Ukraine and Belarus welcomed the Nazi soldiers, hoping for better living conditions than they had endured under Stalin. It is difficult to know for sure whether a more gradual approach to industrialization with fewer huge projects and crash programs would have allowed Soviet industry to develop sufficiently to ward off defeat, but some specialists have argued precisely that. In any case, we should not forget how close the USSR came to collapse in the autumn of 1941, in great part because of the miscalculations of Stalin and his monomaniacal refusal to believe that his ally since 1939 – Adolf Hitler – would turn on him (at least, not yet).[41]

Despite the economic development of the 1930s, the USSR remained per capita much less wealthy and considerably less industrialized than Nazi Germany. This meant that to fight the German war machine, the Soviet people had to suffer vastly more than the Germans. In the first year of all-out war, 1941–2, the Soviet military budget amounted to a staggering 43 percent of the entire GNP. And yet the Wehrmacht nearly succeeded in breaking through to Leningrad and Moscow in the first months of the war. Once it had recovered from the initial shock, however, the USSR had many advantages over the Nazi regime. The economic centralization and total state control over the economy that had been developed since 1928 served the war effort well: resources could be allocated to those military industries deemed most vital, and of course Soviet citizens were already accustomed to a dearth of consumer goods. The well-developed repressive apparatus (secret police, party surveillance, the encouragement of denunciations) and the lack of individual choice among citizens allowed a near-total mobilization of labor for the war. For example, almost all healthy men disappeared from the countryside, taking with them horses and machines for the war effort, forcing women to work under unimaginably difficult conditions. Food production declined in the war years, but again the repressive (and propaganda) apparatus prevented hunger from disturbing public order or morale.

As we have seen, in the 1930s special emphasis was made on developing industry in the Urals and other regions far from the western border. This strategy paid off during World War II when Magnitogorsk, for example, was able to continue and increase production for the war effort because of its location far from the front lines. Also, in 1941 Soviet engineers and plant managers proved very efficient in dismantling entire factories and evacuating them to the interior. In 1941–2, 30,000 evacuation trains with 1.5 million wagons were pressed into service, mainly in the frantic six months after the June 1941 attack. Another nearly million tons of industrial hardware was evacuated by ship. It is difficult to know exactly how much of a role these evacuated industries played in the final victory, but Soviet statistics claimed that in 1942, 47 percent of functioning industry in the east consisted of plant evacuated from Nazi-occupied areas. By the end of 1941 and especially in 1942 these plants were producing for the war effort. Already in 1942 the USSR was producing twice as many weapons as the Germans. These tanks, aircraft, rifles, artillery pieces, and ammunition would help the USSR turn the tide against the Germans in 1943.

By almost all economic indices, 1942 was the most difficult year. Using 1940 as the base year, GNP dropped by nearly one-third (from 92 to 66), agricultural output even more sharply (62 to 38), and the total value of goods sold in state retail stores plummeted to a mere third (84 to 34). At the same time the output of weaponry nearly doubled over that of 1940 (186), while light industry's output was cut in half (48).[42] Tax revenues dropped in 1942, and then picked up in subsequent war years. By 1945 the Soviet state was collecting almost 50 percent more taxes than in 1940 (a rise from 18 to 30.2 billion rubles), but GNP was still just 83 percent of 1940 figures, with agricultural production only 60 percent that of 1940. These cold figures show the success of the USSR in harnessing the entire economy to the war effort but cannot adequately show the sufferings of a population forced to work beyond exhaustion without adequate nourishment, clothing, or often even shelter. The scarcity of basic goods figures in the classic Soviet film *Ballad of a Soldier*, where a soldier on the front has a comrade take home to his beloved wife a precious gift: a bar of soap.

Unlike in America, the Soviet economy did not expand during the war. In 1945, production was only 92 percent of 1940 figures, with only armaments and machine building showing increases over 1940 (173 and 129 respectively). Production of coal and oil were both under 1940 figures (88, 68) though considerably improved over 1942 (43, 61). Given the international situation in the early 1940s and the planned nature of the Soviet economy, one might have expected Soviet planners to have worked out a contingency plan in case of war. In fact, no such plan existed and the transfer of industry from civilian to military uses did not always go smoothly. These difficulties were somewhat mitigated by the prewar economic buildup that had concentrated overwhelmingly on military industry and by the simple fact that Soviet industry was in any case inordinately (compared to western economies) heavy on military production. The absolute low point for production was reached in February 1942 (20–30 percent of June 1941 levels), in part because so much of the country was occupied by German troops. As evacuated industrial plant was set up and put into operation, however, production shot up.

As we know, Soviet consumers were used to very slim pickings on the retail front. But the war effort suppressed consumer production to unprecedented lows. In 1943, for example, only 10 percent of the 1940 amounts of outerwear (clothing) were produced, 14 percent of fabric, 7 percent of shoes, 8 percent of sugar. Even in 1945 these figures had hardly improved: 18 percent (of 1940) production in outerwear, 29 percent of fabric, 15 percent of shoes, 50 percent of flour, 25 percent of sugar. Ration cards were distributed according to one's work. Thus the ration for workers in strenuous jobs received (in late 1942) 600–1,200 grams of bread daily and 2.2–4.5 kilograms of meat or fish, 600–1,000 grams of fat monthly, while office workers had to make due with 400 grams of bread (daily) and monthly rations of 1,200 grams of fish or meat and 300 grams of fat. To make matters worse, the norms for rations, aside from bread, were rarely met. Hunger was nearly universal, and to stave off actual starvation many Soviet citizens planted potatoes in cottage gardens or other free land. The government tolerated an expansion of collective farmers' private plots (often cultivated at night because of the enormous labor demands on the farmers). The shortage of food made prices increase sharply – by war's end more than fivefold over1940 prices. Economists estimate that during the war, overall consumption had dropped by a third. In 1945, for instance, state cooperative stores carried less than half as much merchandise as in 1940.[43]

As bad as conditions were for Soviet citizens and soldiers during the war years, they would have been even worse without help from the western allies. Mere weeks after the Nazi invasion the US government began to supply lend-lease materiel to the USSR. Lend-lease took a number of forms, from aluminum and copper (essential for aircraft and other arms manufacture) to trucks to clothing to foodstuffs. The USA did not, for the most part, deliver weaponry to the USSR, but concentrated instead on raw materials, military transportation, communications equipment, and edibles. Among these goods were nearly a half-million trucks and "dzhipy" (a vehicle usually spelled "Jeep" by Americans), a million field telephones, 14 million pairs of boots, and some four million tons of foodstuffs. Millions of Russians remembered even decades later, for example, the cans of Spam that the USA had provided through lend-lease. It is unlikely that lend-lease was absolutely crucial for the Soviet war effort; the USSR would probably have won without it. Without the $11 billion of material supplied by the Americans and £420 million from the British, however, the war would have been longer and the sufferings that much greater.[44]

What accounted for the better performance of the Soviet war economy compared with that of Germany? At war's outset, the two economies were of roughly the same size, although including their occupied territories the Germans had somewhat of an edge. (Obviously per capita the Germans were much better off.) Many economists had predicted that the shaky Soviet economy would collapse entirely under the strain of war. In fact, the centralized, state-dominated nature of the Soviet economy made it easier to concentrate all resources on the war effort. State control over the collective farms meant that cities and soldiers would be better supplied with food than the collective farmers themselves. More than anything, however, the Soviet economy's advantage was its greater efficiency, in particular its success in mass-producing weaponry of all types (including tanks and aircraft) in record time. German arms may have been more sophisticated, but in the end the brute force of mass production crushed any advantage that may have brought. To state matters baldly, the USSR defeated the Germans because they put more men into uniforms, produced more weapons, and used these effectively.

There remains the question "Did Stalinist modernization win the war?" The one-party, repressive state dominating the entire economy and society could, indeed, harness social and economic power for the war effort more effectively than liberal democracies or even Nazi Germany. While Stalin is to a great extent responsible for the enormous initial losses in the war, once he pulled himself together he proved an effective war leader. Unlike Hitler, it needs to be remembered, Stalin did not overestimate his own military genius and usually followed the advice of military specialists. But generals who did not produce desired outcomes were unceremoniously punished: 30 were executed by firing squads in 1941 and 1942. Stalin and his generals felt no compunction about the massive squandering of human life on the front; even Hitler had to take more seriously public opinion over mass casualties. The Soviet political and economic system worked well during this time of crisis. But no economy or society can remain on a war footing forever and the Soviet system was in many ways less well suited to meet the challenges of peace.

Conclusion

Both tsars and communists felt the challenge of modernity. The Great Reforms of the 1860s and 1870s primarily aimed to create a modern Russia that would be capable of retaining its position as a European Great Power. Russia's defeat at the hands of the Japanese called into question the Russian Empire's modernity; the empire's collapse in the midst of World War I discredited it entirely. While the tsars, fundamentally premodern in their political and social conceptions, had never felt comfortable with modernity, for communists being at the avant-garde of history was absolutely central for their self-image. Unfortunately Russia in 1917 lagged far behind in literacy, urbanization, industrialization and other indices of modernity, and matters went from bad to catastrophic during the chaotic Civil War period (to 1921). In the 1920s, during NEP, allowing the economy to recover at least to prewar levels was the order of the day. But once Stalin had consolidated his personal power, the way for a mass drive toward communist modernity was open. The decade after 1928 witnessed astonishing – and brutal – changes in the Soviet economy and society. The success of the Soviet Union in defeating Nazi Germany is one indication that Stalinist modernity had succeeded, at least on the military front.

Military victory is not, however, the only measure of modernity. Other typical indices include literacy, urbanization, industrial production, public participation in politics. While by 1945 the Soviet literacy rate was around 80 percent, only around one-third of Soviet citizens lived in cities. Since 1928 industrial production had increased markedly and by 1945 the USSR was one of the two main industrial and military powers on earth, a position it would occupy for several more decades. But the living standards of Soviet citizens, though perhaps better in the late 1940s than 20 years earlier, can only be described as appalling when compared to those taken for granted by Americans or western Europeans. In particular it is difficult to reconcile the concept of modernity with the miserable conditions of the Soviet countryside where, by most measures, life was more difficult in 1945 than a generation earlier. Despite Lenin's famous statement that "Communism equals Soviet power plus the electrification of the entire country," most rural dwellers did not enjoy electricity in their homes in 1945.

Civil society, a crucial factor in modernity, was also very underdeveloped in the USSR. Censorship was heavy-handed, not only restricting information and free discussion, but demanding that journalism and literature serve the communist cause. As for public participation in the political process, the USSR obviously lacked free elections or a functioning parliament. The fact that millions belonged to the Communist Party by the 1940s is nearly irrelevant (though not treated that way by Soviet propaganda) as few of these individuals had any influence on policy-making. Women certainly played a far greater role in employment and public affairs in 1945 than in tsarist times, but women were under-represented within the Communist Party and completely absent from the highest level of Kremlin politics (the Politburo). Taking these different factors together, Soviet modernization must be characterized as peculiar and incomplete, an immensely strong state coupled with weak living standards and an almost absent civil society.

On another level the failure of Soviet modernization was even more complete. The October Revolution had aimed not simply to replace one regime with another, but to create a totally new kind of state and indeed a New Human Being. In 1945 the USSR was indeed an enormously strong state and considerably more economically developed than the Russian Empire had been. But despite the destruction of private property among peasants, the considerable weakening of religious belief, and the disappearance of numerous social categories (clergy, nobility, merchants), social stratification remained and had been considerably strengthened since the mid-1930s. The October Revolution aimed to usher in a new and better era in world history and, judged according to that standard, must be considered a failure.

Chapter 5
Belief

Beliefs help us make sense of the world. While science can explain how the world functions, belief tells us why we should care and how we should act within society. Science provides information but belief gives us meaning. In Russian history before the twentieth century belief meant mainly religious conviction. The tsars understood themselves as Christian rulers and their empire as a Christian state – "Holy Russia." But beliefs do not have to be based on religion or faith in a supreme being. Atheists, after all, often hold very strong beliefs about human society, morality, and behavior. Belief in this chapter will be understood in this broad sense, from religion to worldview, and even overlapping in some cases with ideology.

The connection between belief and ideology can be seen most obviously in the difference between perceptions of political legitimacy in the Russian Empire and the USSR. The tsar derived his political legitimacy from tradition, his position as a Christian ruler and, ultimately, from God directly. Lenin and Stalin based their political legitimacy on the belief that communism was the most progressive, modern, and humane sociopolitical ideology. Without wanting to minimize the enormous differences between the tsar's Christian faith and the communists' steadfast belief in their political ideology, both represent different versions of orthodoxy (in the broad, not specifically Christian, sense), and in both cases the government fostered its belief and restricted, forbade, and punished dissident views. For the tsars, "dissident beliefs" ranged from Old Believers to Jews to liberals to Marxists. For the communists, "dissidence" was even broader, including essentially every kind of religious faith and all political credos other than their own brand of socialism.

Both the Russian Empire and the Soviet Union tolerated many beliefs that they disliked. In both cases, however, there were limits to toleration (generally much

more narrow in the USSR than in tsarist Russia). Thus the Russian Empire tolerated Jews, Buddhists, Catholics, and even liberals – but outlawed some sects like
the self-mutilating *skoptsy* (who saw themselves as true Orthodox Christians) and
did not allow the tsar's subjects to be legally without religion (as in the German
konfessionslos). The USSR officially recognized freedom of religion and in practice
generally tolerated religious belief, though restricting its public practice and
penalizing believers in various ways. Some commentators have termed communism a "secular religion," a label that, I believe, obscures more than it explains.
More helpful, to my mind, is to view communist ideology as an "alternative
master narrative" to explain why we are here, where we came from, and whither
we should go. While traditional religion – especially Christianity and Judaism –
answer these questions by reference to God, communists made reference to
science, a Marxist view of historical progress, and the party's role in creating a
just and humane society here on earth.

In this chapter we will look into some of the "orthodox" and "dissident" (terms
that mean starkly different things, of course, before and after 1917) beliefs held
by large numbers of Russians and Soviet citizens. We will restrict ourselves mainly
to the Russian context simply for practical reasons: after all, even among Russians
(understood here as Russian-speakers) the variety of beliefs was enormous. Before
1917 Russians were overtly considered – in cultural and religious terms at least
– the bulwark of tsarist power but even after the revolution Russians continued
to dominate in the politics, economy, and culture of the USSR. Thus the beliefs
of the Russian-speaking population had a considerable, even dominant, effect on
cultural and social developments even to 1945.

Russian Orthodoxy, Dissenters, and Sects

Russia accepted Christianity not from Rome but from Byzantium at the end of
the tenth century, and this fact has marked Russia's history. While the Orthodox
Church differs little in dogma from the Roman Catholic Church, its practices,
customs, and rituals are strikingly distinct.

The Russian Orthodox Church forms part of the Orthodox community that
includes, among other people, most Ukrainians, Belarusians, Romanians, Serbs,
Bulgarians, Greeks, and Georgians. Because the Orthodox Church lacks a pope,
there is no one authority figure that has the final say on proper ritual and dogma.
In practice such matters tended to be decided by church councils at different
levels, making the church less uniform than the Roman Catholic Church, but at
the same time more flexible in its responses to local needs. One great difference
between the western (Roman Catholic) church and Orthodoxy is the far greater
autonomy afforded each individual national church (i.e., Russian, Romanian,

FIGURE 5.1   Cathedral of Christ the Savior. Moscow.
Source: Alexey Samarin/Shutterstock.

Serbian, Georgian) in the Orthodox world. But while specific practices and rituals might differ, all Orthodox believers see themselves as belonging to a single church.[1]

While Orthodox believers in Russia sometimes called themselves "Greek," the role of that language in parish churches was far less important than Latin was for Catholics. As a rule, Orthodox services are held in the vernacular, but in Russia a specific church language – Old Church Slavonic – was developed early on and continued to be used in churches in the twentieth century. While this language was not totally different from Russian, it was also not entirely comprehensible, in particular for uneducated peasants. Orthodox churches also permitted – in the Russian case, even required – their parish priests to marry (monks were subject to different rules, including chastity). As in other old regime states, the clergy formed its own legal estate (*soslovie*). But the fact that Russian Orthodox priests married and had children made this estate, at least to some extent, self-perpetuating in a way quite different from that of Catholic western Europe.

We must remember that throughout the imperial period, religious belief was less a matter of theology than of ritual. However, this strict distinction between ritual and faith is an artificial one. For Orthodox believers, the everyday, Sunday, and holiday rituals they carried out, fasts and feasts, foods and clothing, songs and prayers all formed a vital part of their religion. For this reason even minor changes in ritual – for example, crossing oneself with three fingers instead of two – were of crucial importance for traditional believers. Much more than Roman Catholicism or Protestant denominations of Christianity, Orthodoxy fuses ritual, belief, and dogma into a unified whole. The rationalist traditions of, say, Catholic Thomism or Jansenism are quite alien to Orthodox tradition. In any case, most Orthodox believers were peasant folk, illiterate and traditional in their beliefs and way of life. For them, religious ritual and tradition *was* their religious faith; the two could not be separated. Orthodox people made up a "sacred community" whose icons, chapels, and feasts helped order life for ordinary Russian people.[2]

On an everyday level, religious practice more than dogma set Orthodox believers apart from other Christians. For example, Orthodox Russian peasants could have been distinguished from, say, Catholic Poles, by the fact that Orthodox priests wore beards, had wives, and held services in Slavonic rather than in Latin. Russian churches on the countryside were small and generally unadorned – a fact that Russian officials on the western borderlands (present-day Belarus, Lithuania, western Ukraine) constantly bemoaned, in particular when comparing these modest structures with Baroque Catholic churches. Orthodox churches also lacked the musical instruments found in many Catholic or Lutheran churches. Considering the human voice to be God's instrument, Orthodox Church singing was always unaccompanied and hence lacked the organs so typical of large Catholic and Protestant churches. One could also tell an Orthodox church from Catholic or Protestant churches by the lack of pews: in Orthodox churches everyone stood – even the tsar and his family.

The Orthodox Church year was punctuated with fasts and festivals. The most important fasts were those before Christmas and Easter, the most important holidays. Orthodoxy placed more emphasis on Easter – Christ's resurrection – than on Christ's birth. Easter also marked the end of the harsh Russian winter and some of the Orthodox rituals no doubt built on ancient pagan practices. On Easter Orthodox Christians greeted (and greet) each other by saying, "Khristos voskrese!" ("Christ has risen!"), to which the proper response is "Voistinu vokrese!" ("Verily he has risen"). Special foods were eaten for the holiday, including *kulich*, a sweet bread made with plenty of butter and eggs, and *paskha*, made from sweetened cottage cheese combined with other delicacies. Both *kulich* and *paskha* symbolize the miracle of Christ's resurrection and the joy of the holiday.

Important holidays in the Orthodox calendar are proceeded by fasts. Indeed fasts play a far more important role in Orthodoxy than in other Christian denominations. Normally all Wednesdays and Fridays are fast days, though some weeks dispense with fasts altogether. Orthodox fasts are also stricter than those followed by Roman Catholics; for example, milk products are not allowed on fast days. Christmas is preceded by the long fast of Advent; and the festive meal, with 12 different foods eaten on Christmas Eve, while sumptuous, is without meat and milk products. In the Orthodox Church, as for other Christians, the long fast of Lent comes before Easter. In the Russian Orthodox tradition, Lent is preceded by a week of festivities, *maslennitsa*, during which pancakes with plenty of butter (*maslo*) are eaten. Both the fasts and the special foods eaten on holidays remind believers of God's bounty and dominion, connecting their religious faith with everyday life.

Like other Christian denominations, Orthodoxy has a monastic side. Traditionally the Russian Orthodox Church was divided into "white" clergy (parish priests), who were expected to marry (and their sons would then normally also take up a clerical career), and the "black" clergy or monks from among whom the church hierarchy (bishops, archbishops, metropolitan) would be taken. Monasteries played an important role in Russian history, in particular in bringing Russian culture to the "wild" lands on the fringes of Muscovy. Just as in western Europe in the Middle Ages, monasteries were often established far from the centers of civilization but in time often developed into important economic and cultural settlements. Among the most important monasteries were three bearing the special designation of "lavra": the Kievo-Pecherskaia lavra, Trinity-St Sergius in Sergiev Posad just north of Moscow, and Alexander Nevsky Lavra in St Petersburg. Thus the three most important Russian cities (Kiev is of course now Ukrainian, but for the Russian Empire and most Orthodox believers before 1917 it was the "cradle of Russian Orthodoxy") had their own special monasteries. There were Orthodox monasteries for both men and women (segregated, of course), and by the early twentieth century these housed more nuns than male monks. In the second half of the nineteenth century, numbers of monasteries and nunneries rose significantly, suggesting a rise in popular religiosity.[3]

In the seventeenth century a split had occurred in the Orthodox Church over efforts to correct (i.e., bring back in line with Greek originals) certain practices and rituals. Those who refused the new practices, for example to cross themselves with three fingers instead of two, were subject to ferocious persecution in the seventeenth century and did not receive de jure equal rights with other Christian believers until 1905. These so-called Old Believers were de facto generally tolerated, in particular in the western borderlands after 1863 as a "native Russian" population to counterbalance the Catholic Poles. Among the Moscow merchant community Old Believers were also common.[4] The term "Old Belief" included a great variety of different groupings and sects, the most important distinction being between the less radical *popovtsy*, who retained a clergy, and the more radical *bezpopovsty* (*bez* = "without"; *pop* = "Orthodox priest"), who worshiped on their own. In practice, the difficulty of ordaining priests in what amounted to an underground church meant that many communities lacked a permanent religious leader.

Besides the Old Believers, there were a number of so-called sectarians who considered themselves Orthodox but held views or carried out practices that were not accepted by the official church. Among them were the *Molokane* (from *moloko*, "milk," because they drank milk on certain fast days when this was forbidden to Orthodox believers), *Dukhobory* ("spirit fighters," who in some respects, including pacifism, resembled Quakers), *Khlysty* ("whips," who rejected any kind of church authority; their name comes from ecstatic ceremonies which including self-scourging), and *Skoptsy* ("castrators," who practiced self-mutilation, castration for men and the cutting off of nipples or breasts for women). As one may imagine, the last two sects were extremely small in number and severely persecuted by the Russian government.[5] *Dukhobory* ran into trouble with the authorities because of their refusal to submit to military service; the writer Lev Tolstoy helped them emigrate to Canada in the late 1890s, financing this with royalties from his novel *Resurrection*. Most sectarians, however, were less extreme (and less noticeable) and by the last third of the nineteenth century the Russian authorities no longer subjected them or Old Believers to persecution. All legal discrimination against sectarians and Old Believers was only abolished with the decree of religious toleration in April 1905.

The idea of a split between church and state, so important for the history of western Europe and North America, was never the tradition for Orthodox believers. While the Orthodox Church had its own hierarchy, headed by the Patriarch of Constantinople, it never enjoyed the secular political power of the western Papacy. Peter the Great had clashed with the Orthodox Church when pressing to Europeanize Russia in the late seventeenth century, and when the patriarch (head of the Russian church) Adrian had died in 1700, Peter left the position unfilled. In 1721 the apex of the church hierarchy (the patriarch) was abolished. In its place was created the Holy Synod, consisting of 10, later 12, clerics, and headed by a lay official, the Ober-Procurator, who resembled in his bureaucratic tasks the tsar's other ministers. True, the tsar had no influence over church dogma, and in specifically religious matters the clerical estate consistently defended its own prerogatives. The former historiographical view of significant government influence and interference in the affairs of the Orthodox Church has been shown by recent historiography to be very exaggerated. In fact, while the Orthodox Church was more closely linked with the state in Russia than, say, in France or the USA, the tsarist government rarely interfered in church affairs.[6] Still, liberal and radical Russians criticized the failure of the Orthodox Church to take a more independent stance against government policies; reforming intellectuals in the late nineteenth century often perceived a too-close embrace of the state as exerting a corrupting influence on the main religious task of the church. That this view was not quite fair is shown by the important charity work carried out by Orthodox clergy among needy workers in urban areas.[7]

This is not to say that the church remained unchanged during the half-century between the Great Reforms and revolution. For one thing, the church increased its power in such areas as family law; for example, regarding marriage. One had to be married within the church, which meant that marriages between, say, Catholics and Orthodox were generally not possible. Divorce also remained for the most part the province of the church and was exceedingly difficult to obtain, though as the twentieth century dawned more divorce petitions were granted than a generation or two earlier. The Russian state attempted to affect some aspects of church life during the Great Reforms by expanding the role of the parishioners (including parish councils) and reorganizing parishes for better efficiency. Unfortunately this reform was resisted by the church hierarchy, priests, and even parishioners. As the population grew, priests found themselves with ever larger congregations and without adequate salaries to raise their own families. The numerous small charges demanded by priests for services from baptisms to funeral services did little to endear Orthodox priests to their flock, but without such charges the priests simply could not made ends meet. In order to survive, many Orthodox priests also had to cultivate clerical allotments; that is, working the land like peasants. This was often seen as undignified and degrading.[8]

The educational level of Orthodox priests certainly rose in this period; by 1880 already 97 percent of priests had seminary degrees. But minor church officials such as deacons and sacristans tended to lag far behind, at times even making errors in basic prayers and catechism. Clerical education was reformed and modernized in the mid-nineteenth century and in many ways came to resemble the classical *Gymnasium* except, of course, for a stricter discipline and more emphasis on religious subjects. At the same time radical ideas common among Russian educated youths also spread in seminaries, leading in some cases to arrests and even the closing of "infected" seminaries for weeks and months, much to the government's consternation.[9]

For ordinary Russians, as we have mentioned, Orthodoxy permeated their everyday life, was an important part of their own perceived community, and ordered the year. As Chris Chulos has shown, peasant piety included beliefs and practices that often went beyond or even contradicted official church dogma. In the past, historians often spoke of "dual faith" (*dvoeverie*), arguing that "popular Orthodoxy" was derived from earlier pagan practices. Recent research has demonstrated the lack of evidence for such pagan influences and has pointed out that Russian peasants, if not always intellectuals or priests, saw beliefs in spirits at home, in the woods, or in streams and rivers as quite consistent with Orthodox tradition.[10] To quote one historian, in peasant life religion was "flexible and subversive."[11] Icons also played a special role in popular religiosity, much like the images of saints did in western Catholicism. Pilgrimages to holy sites and holy men also formed an important part of popular Orthodox piety.[12]

The Orthodox Church hierarchy tended to adopt very conservative positions and shy away from popular religiosity, but Orthodox faith and parish priests often played an important part in charity and social movements in the late imperial period. Activist priests both among peasants and, even more, among workers used the concepts of Orthodox community and Christian justice to work for social and political change. The most famous activist priest was Father Georgy Gapon who worked among the poor workers of St Petersburg. He became a celebrity for his role in organizing the march of unarmed worker-petitioners in St Petersburg on January 10, 1905, that would be met by tsarist bullets, going down in history as "Bloody Sunday." There is some irony in the fact that Gapon's own workers' organization was originally aimed to entice workers away from more seditious, socialist groupings. After the fiasco of "Bloody Sunday" the church authorities (the "Holy Synod") forbade any participation by clergy in any public funerals of those slain.[13] The irony of a priest-led, icon-bearing loyalist demonstration being shot down by tsarist police, with the priest himself subsequently denounced by church authorities nicely sums up some of the contradictions of "popular" and "official" versions of Orthodoxy in early twentieth-century Russia.

Relations between the Orthodox Church and educated Russians were often strained. The figure of the ignorant, drunken priest appears frequently in Russian literature and art. Many of the intelligentsia would have agreed with V. G. Belinskii's furious denunciation of the church and clergy in his "Letter to Gogol" (1847): "Does not the priest in Russia represent the embodiment of gluttony, avarice, servility, and shamelessness for all Russians?" One did not have to accept Belinskii's extreme views to perceive severe shortcomings in the Orthodox Church. Believers like the religious philosophers Vladimir Soloviev and Sergei Bulgakov, while criticizing atheist worldviews and western European positivism, were also troubled by inadequacies within the traditional Orthodox Church (though Soloviev never left the church and Bulgakov eventually returned to it). When the Orthodox Church excommunicated the Christian pacifist and writer Tolstoy in 1901, many took this as proof of the church's narrow and repressive attitude. To be sure, intellectuals throughout Europe during this period challenged religious authority, but in Russia the close connection between church and state made it even more difficult for a member of the intelligentsia to whole-heartedly embrace the Orthodox Church.

As we have seen, the Russian Empire practiced religious toleration, but this did not mean that all religions were considered equal. The Orthodox Church held a special place as the "ruling religion," as it was officially termed. The tsar had to be Orthodox, was crowned in an Orthodox ceremony, and was the official head of the church. Other Christian denominations and religions were tolerated, but not given equal rights with Orthodoxy. One indication of this is the fact that a subject of the tsar could convert to Orthodoxy from any religion but could not, for example, abandon Orthodoxy for Protestantism or Islam. "Toleration" essen-tially meant that one was expected to remain in the religion of one's birth. On the other hand there was a definite hierarchy of religions, from paganism on the bottom to Orthodoxy at the top, and one could usually "ascend" this hierarchy (e.g., convert from Islam to Protestantism), but not "descend" it (it was illegal to convert from any Christian denomination to a non-Christian religion, and Orthodox believers could not convert to Catholicism or other Christian denomi-nations). This situation changed only with the *ukaz* (edict) of religious toleration of April 1905, but even in the Duma period no clear agreement was reached as to whether conversion *out* of Christianity was to be permitted.

Not all Christians in the Russian Empire were Orthodox; nor were all Orthodox Russians. Ukrainians and Belarusians were mainly Orthodox and of course treated as Russians by the tsarist authorities. A more troublesome group were the Uniates, a religious group existing since the late sixteenth century (Synod of Brest, 1596). Accepting papal authority while retaining Orthodox rituals and practices (such as clerical marriage), Uniates resided mainly on the borderlands of Russia and Poland, today's Ukraine and Belarus. When the Russian Empire expanded west-ward during the Partitions of Poland (1772–95), hundreds of thousands of Uniates came under tsarist rule. For St Petersburg, the Uniate Church was little more than the bastard offspring of Catholic scheming and Orthodox weakness: the Russian authorities always regarded the Uniate Church as simply a ploy by the Poles to convert Orthodox people (i.e., Russians) to Catholicism. Following this negative attitude, most Uniates (especially among Belarusians) had been "reconverted" to Orthodoxy in the 1830s; a second mass conversion of Ukrainian Uniates would take place in 1875.[14] After that point the Uniate Church officially ceased to exist in Russia, but in fact many thousands continued secretly to follow its traditions, helped (illegally) by Uniate priests from neighboring Austrian Galicia. After 1905 most of these underground Uniates converted to Catholicism, the Uniate Church no longer existing institutionally in the Russian Empire.

The example of the Uniates gives us some indication of the great importance (in a negative sense) of Catholicism for the Russian Empire and its rulers. One may say with only slight exaggeration that while Protestantism was not taken seriously as a form of Christianity (being too rational and lacking mystical warmth), Catholicism was seen as a direct threat. In great part this stemmed from the almost inevitable equating of Catholicism with the Polish nation. Besides their political unreliability (from the Russian point of view), Poles were seen as dangerous purveyors of western ideas, including Catholicism. Russian officials worried constantly about Polish influences over "Russian" (Belarusian and Ukrainian) peasants, almost always describing the Polish priest as both better trained and far more militant than his more easygoing Orthodox counterpart. In many ways, the suspicious (not to say paranoid) attitude of Russian conservatives and the government toward the Catholics resembled the paranoia of this same group (with few exceptions) toward the Jews: for all their differences, both Jews and Poles-Catholics were seen as quintessentially "different," hostile, and fundamentally non-Russian.

In fact, during the last two or three decades of tsarist rule, increasing numbers of Jews were accepting Russian culture. By 1897 over 300,000 Jews lived outside the Pale, with the largest single community in St Petersburg. By that point thousands of Jewish parents were raising their children in Russian culture – in 1910, 42 percent of Jews in St Petersburg claimed Russian as their native tongue – and many more learned Russian as a second language. To be sure, the Jews in St Petersburg formed an unusual Jewish community, but the figure of the Russian-speaking young (and usually radical) Jew was by the early twentieth century very familiar in Russian journalism and literature. Jews were also prominent in the professions (such as medicine and the law) as well as among bankers and businessmen by the last decades of the nineteenth century. It is characteristic of Russian conservatives and officialdom that they were much more disturbed by modern Russian-speaking Jews than by their Yiddish-speaking, devout, traditional brethren. In part this stemmed from the significant number of young Jews in the revolutionary and liberal movements. But beyond this, modern Russian-speaking Jews were profoundly unsettling to many because their very identity, combining Russian culture and Jewish religion, violated the close connection between religion and nationality cherished by conservatives.[15]

Society between Science and Faith

While officially all subjects of the tsar had to profess a religion, among the intelligentsia – and especially among radicals – various forms of agnosticism and even atheism were not uncommon. Of course, many individuals combined religious faith with progressive political ideology or at least attempted to. For Marxist socialists the matter was simple: Marx had dismissed religion as "the opiate of the people," distracting them from working for change in the present world through promises of a better world to come. But the urge for a better world, here rather than later, certainly motivated Russian radicals: perhaps this is what Dostoevsky meant when he said that the Russian people's longing for "their own future universal church" was the basis of "our Russian socialism." Most liberals did not reject religion or Christianity, but at the same time often considered the Orthodox Church in its present form irrelevant to their spiritual needs or in need of significant reform.

Among radicals, atheism was more or less taken for granted. Not God but humanity was the focus of their worldview. Taking the Enlightenment view that knowledge could and should be used to improve human life in the here and now, the Marxists were typical of Russian radicals. Because knowledge was crucial in improving human conditions, belief in science – the process by which we arrive at knowledge – became almost deified in the radical mindset. Marx based his prediction of revolution on economic and sociological research that he carried out over decades. Lenin similarly spent much of his life in libraries reading and writing. Both were convinced that their politics were firmly grounded in science and scorned other radicals as "utopian"; that is, unrealistic and romantic.

It would be too narrow to identify the worship of science with the Marxists alone. From the 1860s onward, Russians spoke of "nihilism" as a political ideology. The word "nihilist" was coined by novelist Ivan Turgenev in his novel *Fathers and Sons* (1861), which contrasted the old generation of rather romantic and ineffectual liberals with the new generation that believed in nothing (*nihil* in Latin) that could not be proven by scientific methods. At first the word was used as an insult to brand radicals godless people without respect for Russia's past or traditions. But soon radicals like Dmitry Pisarev would proudly accept the title "nihilist" and openly declare that old, worn-out traditions, superstitions, and prejudices (he could not openly mention "religion" or "autocracy" among these, but everyone understood) should be mercilessly pounded and destroyed. The "nihilism" advocated by Pisarev and taken up by many young Russians was the opposite of cynicism or indifference. In fact the radicals believed very strongly in their own ideals of improving society through modern scientific work. Many young Russians of the educated class looked around themselves in the 1860s and after and saw poverty, superstition, repression, and injustice. They fervently believed that society could be reordered in a fairer way through the application of scientific principles to the economy, politics, and everyday life. Obviously such beliefs by their very nature contradicted and challenged the patriarchal, traditional, and religious tsarist regime.[16]

Life is, however, manifestly more than just rationality and science. Just as the rationalism of the enlightenment was followed by emotional release of the romantics in the late eighteenth century, within Russian radicalism the sober scientism epitomized by the Marxists battled with the more emotional (or at least less library-bound) political beliefs of populists and anarchists. The former group (in Russian *narodniki*, from the word *narod*, "the people") wanted to develop a revolutionary society out of what they saw as communist traditions within the Russian peasant commune. As we have seen, the commune held agricultural land in common and periodically redistributed it among peasants. The populists seized on the idea that communal ownership and redistribution of property according to need was a fundamental part of the Russian national character that could be developed into a modern egalitarian society. But just how this was to happen the populists never quite explained. Like the Marxists, they hated the cruelty and injustice of industrial capitalism, but unlike the Marxists, they thought that Russia could "leap over" the capitalist-industrial phase directly into an egalitarian, post-revolutionary society.[17]

The term "anarchism" was used in the later nineteenth century to describe (usually negatively) a broad array of sociopolitical radicals. Anarchism did not advocate "anarchy" in the sense of chaos, but it did oppose most forms of central government, advocating collectives and local decision-making in both economic and political matters. Here we need to distinguish two strands of "anarchism": the more ecstatic and violent brand exemplified by Mikhail Bakunin and the more organized, evolutionary version promoted by Petr Kropotkin. Bakunin's anarchism is perhaps best characterized by his own statement "The urge for destruction is also a creative urge." Radicals took this to mean that much dross of the past had to be destroyed and cleared away before a new society could be built. Bakunin's writings are vitally concerned with this process of destruction, far more than the admittedly less stimulating process of figuring out what to build.[18]

Kropotkin, on the other hand, had more to say about that process. Kropotkin's approach is nicely summed up in one of his books' titles: *Mutual Aid: A Factor of Evolution* (1902). While not rejecting violence out of hand (but also not mythologizing it like Bakunin who tended to glorify the violent act), Kropotkin argued that a better world would arise out of the cooperative spirit inherent in human nature. Rather than a world of "the survival of the fittest" (like nearly all social thinkers of the late nineteenth century, Kropotkin was influenced by Charles Darwin and Herbert Spencer's "social Darwinism"), human beings had natural tendencies toward sharing, helping one another, and cooperation: nurturing these natural human impulses would bring forth a higher level of human society. Both Bakunin and Kropotkin were born into important and well-to-do Russian noble families and both were forced to spend most of their lives abroad because of their radical views. Kropotkin lived to see the 1917 revolutions, returned to Russia, and was buried there in 1921, his funeral being one of the last mass non-Bolshevik political gatherings.[19]

Marxism and anarchism were not the only ideologies that attempted to base sociopolitical reform on a scientific worldview. For most educated middle-class people, both of these ideologies were too extreme, demanding an almost total rejection of the existing world and the creation of a new one. At the same time any thinking person in the Russian Empire could see very obvious flaws in the existing political and economic system. In western and central Europe these people might have joined reformist parties like the British Liberals or French Radicals. In Russia, without a parliament and where all political parties were illegal, no such possibility existed. Thus Russian liberals were forced either to support the radicals or simply bide their time, perhaps participate in local *zemstvo* activities, and put their energies into professional work. But here, too, science was seen as a guide for creating a better society.

In western Europe the middle-class worship of science had been codified, so to speak, into a philosophy of deed and belief known as positivism. The French thinker Auguste Comte is usually credited with the working out of this philosophy, based not on God but on the scientific method. Bazarov, with his constant scientific experiments and observations, could be seen as a radical Russian positivist. Generally, though, the positivists' political conclusions were not so radical, seeing slow and incremental change as the best way forward. In the Russian Empire positivism had its greatest impact among educated Poles, in the so-called Warsaw positivist school that developed after the repression of the 1863 Polish Insurrection. Recognizing that overt political or patriotic activity would be impossible under tsarist rule, the Warsaw positivists advocated educational and economic measures over political or armed struggle. Men like the novelist Bolesław Prus and journalist Aleksander Świętochowski called on the Polish nation – consisting at the time mainly of educated people of noble birth – to dedicate their lives to the education and economic betterment of all Poles, to integrating the large Jewish population living among them into the Polish nation, and to eliminating superstition and backwardness among the Polish peasantry. The Warsaw positivists were not atheists but they did apply their critical irony to certain aspects of the Polish Catholic Church and popular religious practices. Their fundamental outlook was nonreligious and enlightened, wanting to use reason, tolerance, and science to improve society.[20]

While many radicals and liberals either rejected religious belief or relegated it to the private, personal sphere, others glorified the irrational and the religious. The quintessential radical-turned-mystic was the novelist Fyodor Dostoevsky. As a young man in the late 1840s Dostoevsky had participated in radical circles, was arrested and exiled to Siberia. Here he underwent a spiritual crisis during which he found comfort and meaning in a return to Russian Orthodox religiosity. When Dostoevsky returned to St Petersburg in the late 1850s skeptical about western rationalism and convinced that only by returning to Christian religiosity could Russia (and Russians) find their way. More than any other great Russian novelist of the nineteenth century, Dostoevsky scorned western science and indeed the

west in general. He insisted that human freedom was based not on cold mathematical laws but indeed on the opposite: on emotion, suffering, love, and redemption. In *Notes from the Underground* (1864) Dostoevsky mocked the facile
scientism of Russian radicals, rejecting with horror their utopian visions of a
revolutionary future as a form of slavery. Dostoevsky's most thoroughgoing attack
on Russian radicalism, *Demons* (initially translated as *The Possessed*, 1872) is at
turns terrifying and hilarious, portraying Russian radicals as fools, schemers,
deluded dreamers, careerists, or simply evil and inhuman. Without God, the
radicals inevitably become destructive of society, others, and themselves: one of
the most sympathetic figures in the novel, Aleksei Kirillov, comes to the logical
(for Dostoevsky) conclusion that without God, the highest form of human
freedom is suicide – and acts consistently in line with this belief. Dostoevsky felt
that Russia, spanning Europe and Asia, had a peculiar mission in world history,
showing the west true Christian humility while spreading European-Christian
enlightenment in Asia. Dostoevsky was, of course, a creative writer, not a system-
atic philosopher or politician. The contradictions and simple incoherence of
certain of his beliefs reflect the complexity of the socioreligious problems faced
by the Russian intelligentsia in the later nineteenth century.[21]

Dostoevsky's return to religion may be seen as the harbinger of a larger trend.
Around the turn of the century an increasing interest in religion may be observed
among Russian intellectuals. One example would be the already-mentioned philosopher, Vladimir Soloviev. In a sense Soloviev tried to reconcile reason and
mysticism in his image of the beautiful "Sofia," or sacred knowledge. Soloviev was
vitally concerned with breaking down barriers – between Russian and western
Christianity, between scientific and religious worldviews, among human beings
in general. In his "Short Story of the Anti-Christ" Soloviev wrote of the twentieth
century (which he never experienced, dying in 1900) as "the epoch of the
last great wars and revolutions."[22] In the midst of these, the "great man" (or
"superman") publishes *The Open Way to Universal Peace and Prosperity*, which is
rapidly adopted as the solution to all world problems – except, peculiarly, the
name of Christ never appears in the work. Its author is, of course, the Anti-Christ,
a fact recognized by Pope Peter II at story's end as the western and eastern
churches merge, Christianity becomes one, and history comes to an end. Not
through human arrogance and earthly plans but by accepting God's grace is the
world saved.

Unlike Soloviev, who had never rejected Christianity, Sergei Bulgakov's life
went full circle from being born the son of a small-town priest to rejecting religious belief in favor of Marxism, and then, at the time of revolution, returning
to Christianity. At Moscow University in the 1890s young Sergei embraced
Marxism as the best solution to Russia's social and economic problems. By the
first years of the new century, however, he had become disillusioned with the idea

that Marxian science held the key to Russia's troubles. While not forsaking his burning interest in social reform, Bulgakov sensed that part of the problem was precisely in the narrowness of Marxist positivism. Moral behavior simply could not be reduced to economic categories and class conflict. For these reasons, Bulgakov abandoned Marxism and returned to Christianity in 1902. During the 1905 revolution Bulgakov supported the liberals, and then passed over to his own version of Christian Socialism, hoping through liberal reform to reconcile social justice, Christian truth, and Russian national traditions. Ultimately the strain between practical politics and mystical religion became too much and Bulgakov concentrated more and more on his religious and moral writings, finally being ordained an Orthodox priest in 1918.[23]

Bulgakov's most famous single work was his contribution to a collection of essays entitled *Vekhi* (Signposts) that appeared in 1909. *Vekhi* was itself a significant signpost in Russian cultural and intellectual history, marking a turn away from Marxism and positivist approaches and calling for a reexamination of (indeed, return to) Russian religious traditions. In articles with titles like "Philosophical Truth [*istina*] and the Intelligentsia's Truth [*pravda*]" (Nikolai Berdiaev), "Heroism and Askesis [*podvizhnichestvo*]" (Bulgakov), "Creative Self-Identity" (Mikhail Gershenzon), "Intelligentsia and Revolution" (Petr Struve), and "The Ethics of Nihilism" (Semyon Frank) the authors both embraced and severely criticized the Russian intelligentsia tradition. The moral indignation that had long characterized the intelligentsia, the authors argued, had to be mitigated by humility, a willingness to compromise (even with the tsarist government), and an acknowledgment (or even acceptance) of Russia's national and religious traditions. Atheist radicalism, which so often characterized the Russian intelligentsia, easily degenerated into dogmatic formulas that had nothing to do with the immediate problems of real Russian people. *Vekhi* urged progressive, educated Russians not to give up their passion for social reform but to rid themselves of their arrogance and feelings of superiority often based on an inadequate understanding of Russian realities, and learn from simple Russians. The individual essays differed greatly in their approach and solutions but were one – to quote the volume's preface, in "the recognition of the theoretical and practical primacy of spiritual life over the external forms of community."[24] In other words, not science but the spirit would save Russia.

The Orthodox Church should not be seen as utterly conservative or static. On the contrary, many clergymen were deeply troubled by the often bureaucratic and "official" nature of the church and saw the solution (or one solution) in the severing of the close link between Orthodox Church and Russian state. In August 1917, between the middle-class February and the Bolshevik October revolutions, the All-Russian Church Council opened in Moscow. This was the first such council to be held for over two centuries, since Peter the Great's creation of the Holy

Synod. The council was accompanied by large religious processions and other mass ceremonies involving tens of thousands of believers. One of the central goals of this council, as seen by its organizers, was to reestablish *sobornost'* – a concept that crops up in the Slavophiles, Soloviev, Bulgakov, and other Russian religious philosophers, indicating a mystical union of Russian people, tsar, and the Orthodox Church. As one step toward this, the council reestablished the office of patriarch (electing Bishop Tikhon to this office), which had been abolished by Peter. While the revolution swept away or made irrelevant many of the council's discussions, its convening did show that the Orthodox Church was in the midst of serious reform on the eve of the Bolshevik revolution.

The Triumph of Socialism and the Persistence of "Outdated Beliefs"

It goes without saying that Lenin did not agree with the views expressed either in the Church Council of August 1917 or in *Vekhi*. Just a few years before the collection's publication, Lenin had written in "Socialism and Religion" (1905), "Religion is a kind of spiritual moonshine in which the slaves of capital drown their human image, their demand for a life worthy of human beings." Lenin never softened in his disdain for religion or wavered in his complete devotion to the Marxist-scientific worldview. He also recognized that religious believers in general and the authors of essays collected in *Vekhi* would be among his strongest opponents (all *Vekhi* authors would die in exile).

Lenin and the communists were practical enough to recognize that most inhabitants of the Russian Empire in 1917 retained such "outdated beliefs" as religious faith, and in any case he believed that with education such "survivals" of the old order were doomed to extinction. While freedom of religion was officially guaranteed, religious leaders were extremely suspect in the eyes of the communists. In the Civil War many priests and bishops were arrested, exiled, or worse. The communists openly advocated and carried out "class justice"; that is, frequently more important than exact proof of an offense were the social origins of the accused. Priests (along with nobles, middle-class entrepreneurs, former tsarist officers, and capitalists, to name a few of the so-called former people) were specifically singled out as enemies of the revolution and actual or potential supporters of the Whites. In fact it is hardly surprising that many priests and bishops denounced the communists and allied with their enemies, given the verbal and physical attacks on churches, believers, and clergy by communists and Red Army soldiers.

Lenin's unrelenting contempt for spiritual life and religion was not, however, shared by all communists. In particular the first People's Commissar (i.e., minister) of Culture, Anatoly Lunacharsky, had published a two-volume work, *Religion and Socialism* (1908–11), in which he attempted essentially to espouse mysticism without actual belief in God. Lunacharsky's embrace of "myth" and "enthusiasm" were an attempt to tap into the fundamental psychological need of most humans for beliefs that go beyond materialism and scientific proof. It should be noted, however, that for all his ecstatic language, Lunacharsky rejected the idea of a transcendent God and of course was very far indeed from being an Orthodox Christian. Thus his ideas, while they exasperated Lenin, could not be accepted by Christian believers.

Another Bolshevik who attempted to bridge the gap between spirituality and Marxism was Aleksander Bogdanov, author of the scifi-utopian novel *Red Star* (1908). Bogdanov, by training a physicist, knew Lunacharsky well (they were brothers-in-law) and cooperated with him in establishing a school for Bolshevik workers on the Italian island of Capri (funded by the writer Maxim Gorky) after the revolution of 1905. Bogdanov and Lunacharsky advocated revolutionary "Godbuilding," essentially replacing God with the people and the quest for human perfection. Once again, such a heretical belief could hardly be accepted by any traditional religious believer (whether Christian, Jewish, or Muslim), but Bogdanov and Lunacharsky had touched on a very important psychological issue: if the communists were to be successful in "driving God out" of popular consciousness, God would have to be replaced by something. Marxist socioeconomic doctrine was simply too complex and arid (from a psychological point of view) to play this role. But Lenin, as ever, felt that Bogdanov and Lunacharsky's attempts to build a bridge between scientific Marxism and religious enthusiasm were useless and dangerous, merely confusing the issue and encouraging retrograde mental attitudes that would be better rooted out completely.

Still, the problem of popular belief remained. Ten years after the revolution, it has been estimated, 60 to 70 million Russians remained regular churchgoers and continued to be married in churches, baptize their children, and be buried with Christian rituals.[25] We must add to these millions more who attended mosques and synagogues. Even Communist Party members, it was complained, not infrequently were spotted attending religious services (they often blamed their wives for dragging them along). Despite festivals, antireligious education, and penalties for believers (ranging from losing one's job to being sent to the Gulag), religion persisted, often in a less public form but nonetheless resilient against all attacks. Even some forms of monasticism continued to exist, often in masked forms, in the 1920s and 1930s.[26]

In communist rhetoric on religion in the first years after the revolution, the attachment of women to old beliefs was often mentioned and deplored. Women, it was argued, remained more under the influence of the clergy (whether priests, imams, or rabbis), continued to follow religious rituals more than men, and were the key propagators of religious ideas to the younger generation. Thus if the party could weaken the hold that religion had on women, it would both open up a large portion of the population to communist ideals and would prevent the youth from being "poisoned" with religious ideas. It was hoped that by targeting women, the Communist Party could both weaken religion and spread their ideas among two of the most closed segments of the Soviet populace: the peasantry and Muslims.

Antireligious Campaigns

The communists' antagonism to spirituality and religion in general was intensi-fied in their hatred for the Russian Orthodox Church as not only a purveyor of outdated beliefs, but a crucial element of the tsarist system that the communists wished to destroy. A month after taking power, on December 4, 1917, the decree nationalizing all land swept away the church's landed property, including that belonging to individual priests. This decree was followed by others that made it illegal for the church to own property and ended all state subsidies to any religious organization. In January 1918 the teaching of religion in any school was made illegal and the provision that religion could be taught "privately" was understood to concern adults only. It thus became technically speaking illegal for parents to teach their children prayers or to instruct them in basic doctrines of faith. The nationalization of church property meant that church buildings could be seized by the state for use as clubs, warehouses, or for other functions. While many churches were let be and the prohibition against religious teaching of children in private was not frequently enforced, once the communists felt strong enough to move against these practices, they had the legal means to do so.[27]

The communists' overtly antireligious measures called forth an openly critical reaction from Patriarch Tikhon on February 1, 1918 (n.s.). In this public state-ment, the head of the Orthodox Church condemned the Bolsheviks for "sowing the seeds of hatred"; the immense prestige and popularity of the religious leader made the communists hold back from arresting him. While criticizing some com-munist laws, Patriarch Tikhon also called on the clergy to stay out of politics and to remain loyal to the secular government, refusing to cooperate with or bless the enemies of the communists (the Whites) for fear of encouraging fratricidal vio-lence. Once the Civil War was over, the communists felt strong enough to move against the Patriarch. The famine in southern Russia in 1921–2 gave the regime an excuse to attack churches, ostensibly to force recalcitrant priests to give up valuables that would be sold to assist famine victims.

Patriarch Tikhon was arrested on May 6, 1922, on the pretext that he had opposed such confiscations. The communists furthermore encouraged a split within the church, promoting the so-called renovationists ("Living Church")

FigURE 5.2 "Drunkenness on Holidays: A Survival of Religious Prejudices" (antireligion campaign).
Source: Hoover Institution Archives.

who stressed the social element of Christian teachings (initially in favor of selling church property to assist famine victims) and loyalty to the Soviet regime. The obvious favoritism that the communist regime showed the renovationists and their attacks on Tikhon, who was still accepted as Patriarch by most believers, discredited the renovationists. Even the death of Tikhon in 1925 and the official recognition of the renovationists as the legal Orthodox Church failed to help their position among believers, who often locked up churches and physically ejected Renovationist priests.[28]

While the renovationists had thrown in their lot with the communists, they were at least in many cases sincere Christians trying to make the best of a difficult situation. For more radical antireligious elements within the party, however, any compromise was out of the question. In 1925 a long-time militant atheist and supporter of Stalin wrote under the *nom de plume* Emelyan Yaroslavsky, edited a weekly magazine *The Atheist* (*Bezbozhnik*), and created the "League of the Militant Godless." The League, which counted over 100,000 members in 1928, brought together a variety of antireligious approaches. Some advocated education and dialogue to show the religious how illogical and scientifically unproven their beliefs were. Atheist "preachers" went out to the countryside to lecture against belief in God or debate with priests; these rallies were sometimes attended by thousands but were not always won by the atheists: peasants were reportedly unimpressed, indeed derisive, at one atheist's argument that "nature created itself." In general, the argumentation of the League must have seemed quite irrelevant to believers. For example, a "challenge" from the league argued that holy water, if left to stand, would develop the same microorganisms as water that had not been blessed. But why should the presence of microscopic creatures "with hair, horns, and tails" (sic!) shake one's faith?

The League of the Militant Godless sponsored antireligious publications, artwork, and even theater. Most of this fell flat. Most of the antireligious propaganda was being spread by urbanites to peasants, and the country folk had long mistrusted newfangled ideas coming from city slickers. Even more to the point, the atheists had little to offer believers in place of religion. It was one thing to say that God does not exist (after all, the Russian proverb admitted "God is far up, and the Tsar is far away"), but the replacement of God with abstractions like nature or science was unacceptable. Most of the party apparatus also did not respect the league, regarding it as meddling, inefficient, and frequently downright ridiculous. At times the league's festivals and attacks on religion (such as the blasphemous poster showing the Virgin Mary as pregnant and awaiting a Soviet abortion) simply enraged believers, party educators claimed, making it all the more difficult to garner support among the peasantry. The extreme tactics adopted by the league also alienated schoolteachers, many of whom remained religious but were seen as more open to logical argument (initially for science and perhaps later for communism) than the less educated masses.[29]

Antireligious propaganda and attacks were not limited to the Orthodox Church. Pope Benedict XV repeatedly expressed dismay over the arrest of bishops, the refusal of Bolshevik authorities to allow religious teaching for children, and the closing down of churches. While relatively few Catholics remained within the USSR before 1939, Catholic priests were subject to arrest and harassment as agents of a hostile foreign power. Young communists of Jewish origin attacked both religious beliefs and practices as absurd, going so far as to burst into synagogues on the sabbath or stand outside ostentatiously smoking (strictly forbidden on the sabbath) or even eating pork. Communist support among Muslims was so weak that local leaders dared not take Islam on directly, but imams and religious institutions were endlessly depicted as corrupt, ignorant, and inhumane. The attempt to woo Muslim women in Uzbekistan to cast off their veils in a public ceremony – the so-called *hujum* of 1927 – was generally admitted, even by communist authorities, to have been a failure. Most women who unveiled themselves were forced by public disapproval and violence to leave the region or go back to wearing the traditional garb.

With the end of NEP, antireligious policy hardened. Two of the strongest groups pressing for resolute action against religious peasants were the Komsomol (Young Communists) and League of Militant Atheists. Among those specifically targeted for arrest and exile during collectivization were village priests, in part because they often functioned as local leaders but also simply because of their symbolic value as an element of the noncommunist (if not openly anticommunist) past. A new slogan, "the Storming of Heaven," indicated a turn from the gradualist approach of the NEP period. During collectivization, priests and kulaks were seen as allies and denounced as such in the press. Along with mass arrests of priests came the symbolic confiscation of hundreds of church bells, the closing of the few remaining monasteries, and attacks on believers of all religions. New laws in 1929 not only forbade religious propaganda but made the teaching of atheism obligatory in school and defined priests as parasites on society who received income from their parishioners without working. It became increasingly hazardous to openly profess religious beliefs or to attend religious services. Many believers were subjected to various harassments; others even arrested. One indication of the effectiveness of these antireligious measures is the statistic that by 1930 four-fifths of village churches had been destroyed or shut down. By the early 1940s over 100 bishops, tens of thousands of Orthodox clergy, and thousands of monks and lay believers had been killed or had died in Soviet prisons and the Gulag.[30]

As motivation for the stepped-up antireligious policy from 1928, it seems clear that politics played a more important role than ideology. When writer Maxim Gorky in November 1929 wrote a letter to Stalin complaining of antireligious excesses and criticizing the crude methods used by the "Godless," Stalin seemed to agree. In his reply to Gorky, Stalin failed to mention any ideological justification for the antireligious attacks and even admitted that some methods of antireligious propaganda were silly and ineffective. But more important for Stalin than the crushing of belief was the destruction of an organization that could possibly oppose his own power: the church. It should also be remembered that the collectivization of agriculture involved the destruction of many rural churches, the arrest of priests, and the terrorization of the bulwark of Orthodox belief, the peasantry. After all, collectivization essentially destroyed traditional peasant life, and a vital part of that tradition was religious faith.

In the fervent atmosphere of socialist construction during the 1930s, antireligious measures and rhetoric blossomed. In 1930 two court trials of allegedly counterrevolutionary clergy took place, one in Leningrad and the other in Ukraine of the "Society for the Liberation of Ukraine." Membership in the League of the Militant Godless shot up to over five million in 1932, though party officials groused that only a small percentage were active. At the same time the Soviet state came to a kind of accommodation with Orthodox Metropolitan Sergii, who had issued a Declaration of Loyalty in 1927 and followed this up with a controversial pamphlet, *The Truth about Religion in the Soviet Union* (1930), in which he claimed that no religious persecution existed in the country. Sergii appeared to have been motivated by the sincere desire to persuade the communist government away from further persecution of believers, holding that compromise and loyalty to the present rulers was the only way to assure at least a modicum of acceptance for Orthodox believers.[31]

At the same time the renovationists who had cooperated with the Soviet authorities against Patriarch Tikhon remained active as the so-called Living Church. Sergii came from this background but later repented and rejected renovationist ideas. This group drew from a broad variety of individuals unhappy with the present church, including some with both extreme right (e.g., the pre-revolutionary group "Union of the Russian People" or Black Hundreds) and extreme left backgrounds. As their name implies, the renovationists hoped to renew the Orthodox Church, bring it more in line with present realities in the Soviet state, emphasize its social role, and in this way win the trust and support of the communist authorities. They also wanted to reduce the power of the "black clergy" (monks) for whom traditionally all ecclesiastic offices (bishops, metropolitans, etc.) had been reserved. In general they argued for a less hierarchical and more democratic inner church structure. While there were sincere motives among some who joined the renovationists, others were motivated by more petty aspirations for power and prestige. The fact that some renovationists denounced Orthodox priests who opposed them to the secret police tainted the entire movement. The communist authorities saw the Living Church mainly as a tool to weaken Orthodoxy and the taint of cooperation with the communists made it difficult for the renovationists to find acceptance among the peasant faithful. In 1946 the Living Church was finally disbanded.

The Survival of Religion under Soviet Rule

According to all constitutions of the USSR, Soviet citizens were allowed to follow their convictions in religious matters. In fact, as we have seen, religion was at best tolerated, and that within very narrow boundaries. Religion did not disappear entirely from public view, but increasingly retreated to private, personal, or underground venues. In particular communists were expected to shun religion, but being known as a believer could prevent one's acceptance to university or led to dismissal from a job (in particular, educators were expected by the 1930s to abjure religious faith).

Among the thousands of churches destroyed or converted to secular uses in the late 1920s and 1930s, perhaps the most famous was the Cathedral of Christ the Savior in Moscow. This enormous church, if architecturally undistinguished, had been built over a period of two generations, and was finally completed under Tsar Alexander III in 1883. The cathedral towered over the Moscow river near the Kremlin, impressive with its enormous marble panels and paintings of saints. The cathedral's huge size and its proximity to the Kremlin must have annoyed the communist government, but the cathedral was left mainly untouched for almost a decade and a half after the revolution. Then, on July 18, 1931, a short article appeared in *Pravda* announcing that the authorities had decided to build a new Palace of the Soviets. The article mentioned the address of the future palace without noting that the new building would rise on the site where the cathedral now stood. To build the new palace, it was clear that the cathedral would have to be demolished. On December 5, 1931, a series of explosions leveled the cathedral, though it took over a year to clear away the debris. In June 1933 Stalin signed an order to construct the world's largest building on the site: taller and heavier than the Empire State building (completed in 1931), topped by a 6,000 ton statue of Lenin. While the palace was never built, the destruction of the largest Orthodox cathedral in the world sent a clear signal to all believers of a newly militant antireligious policy.[32]

Christians were not, of course, the only ones affected by the antireligious repressions of the 1920s and 1930s. Jews found themselves in a peculiar position: at the same time a nationality and a religion. Because of the antisemitic excesses of the Bolshevik's opponents in the Civil War period, probably most Jews welcomed, if cautiously, Soviet rule. But rapidly their own religious practices and clergy came under attack. Yiddish publishing was allowed and even encouraged (though using a phonetic spelling system not accepted outside the USSR), but as a sacred tongue – and the language of Zionism – Hebrew was viewed with suspicion by the authorities. Just as with churches, many synagogues were shut down, often converted into communist clubs, like the Choral Synagogues in Minsk and Kharkov. Frequently the communist specifically used militant atheists of Jewish origin to attack the religion of their fathers. Rabbis, like other clergymen, were stripped of their rights as citizens and were often subject to harassment and arrest.[33]

While Jews were simultaneously a nationality and a religion, Muslims made up a number of national groups, mainly but not exclusively Turkic in ethnicity and language. Islam is more than a religion; it is a way of life that includes schools, courts, charities, and everyday practices. In the generation between revolution and World War II, most of these institutions were shut down and even the number of mosques declined radically: from 26,279 in 1912 to 1,312 in 1942.[34] Mullahs were "persuaded" to resign or were arrested for allegedly encouraging resistance to the Soviet government. Muslim women were encouraged to leave the isolation of their homes and participate in public affairs. Polygamy was outlawed as was the *zakah* (the contributions to charity every Muslim was required to make) and *kalym* (bride-price). Campaigns were undertaken against ritual prayer and fasting during Ramadan. Finally, in 1935, the Soviet government forbade Muslims from undertaking the *hadj* or pilgrimage to Mecca. Soviet measures against Islamic practices had a number of motivations: antireligious, national, and international. Besides the general distaste among communists for any religion, Islam seemed particularly dangerous as a possible source of contact with believers abroad. Within the USSR, the Soviet leadership worried about Pan-Turkic sentiments: the memory of the anti-Bolshevik Basmachi during the Civil War and the heresies of Sultan-Galiev remained strong.

As in other times of catastrophe, millennial sects cropped up. In certain ways, sects were better equipped to survive Soviet persecutions than were organized churches. Baptists had long existed, though on the edge of legality, even in imperial Russia. Following a brief period of toleration they ran into trouble with the authorities after 1929, when proselytizing was forbidden. But with their tight-knit communities, emphasis on reading the Scriptures, and experience with persecution, the Baptist communities continued to exist illegally in secret.

At the same time, despite the continued existence of the League of the Militant Godless, from the mid-1930s mainstream propaganda shifted away from direct attacks on religion (which might have the unwanted effect of making religion seem important) to more subtle approaches. Rather than deny the existence of God, Soviet culture glorified new gods: explorers, aviators, workers. To quote the very popular "March of the Jolly Guys" (1934): "We conquer space and time, We are the young masters of the world!" Soviet pilots competed to set new records. The most famous of them, Valerii Chkalov, flew over the North Pole not once but twice, becoming an international hero. Soviet athletes displayed their prowess in competitions and mass celebrations. The massive construction projects of the 1930s and the Stakhanovite competitions showed that human beings could change their world or, to put it another way, showed the triumph of science over belief.[35]

In the long run, violence and repression probably did less to weaken traditional religion than did economic and sociological changes among the Soviet populace. As peasants moved to the growing cities, the opportunity for religious worship was small, while the new city dwellers were attracted to many other forms of entertainment and community. Many towns were entirely without functioning churches by the late 1930s and larger cities often had only a handful. Of course, the Soviet authorities seldom allowed the building of new churches – the essentially Soviet city of Magnitogorsk had no churches at all. Even where churches could be found, in the towns churches did not play the same important role as crucial centers for community life that they had on the countryside. Perhaps Trotsky was right when he argued in 1923 ("Vodka, the Church, and the Cinema") that the cinema would help blot out religious belief among Soviet workers.[36]

By the end of the 1930s overt attacks on churches, synagogues, or mosques were becoming less common. After all, the majority of holy places had been destroyed or converted to other uses by that time and the number of clergy reduced significantly, with only four of the over 100 Orthodox bishops (as of 1930) still at their posts in 1939.[37] Religious believers could count on various forms of discrimination such as the rejection of their children's application for higher education and their barring from certain jobs. But clearly religious belief and spirituality had not been eliminated entirely. Even among the young there often remained a fascination for this now neglected part of the past. As we have noted, in the later 1930s there was a shift away from militancy and back to many forms of traditional behavior. But while many forms of traditional Russian identity – in the family (sacred motherhood), army (tsarist ranks and epaulets), popular culture (folk dances) were rehabilitated in the latter 1930s, religious belief never was. Within strict limits, religion could be tolerated, but it could never be accepted as a legitimate part of Soviet identity.[38]

The leaders of religious groups in the USSR reacted differently to these state repressions. Unlike private persons, they could not simply worship in private: their public position made it imperative to come to some kind of agreement with the existing political order. As we have seen, Metropolitan Sergii cooperated with the Soviet authorities from the late 1920s and remained at this post well into the 1940s. Sergii's position has been criticized both at the time (especially by the Orthodox Churches in exile) and later. Most likely Sergii hoped that by upholding the public role of the church he could help it weather the present terrible times. He also surely wished to preserve the traditions of the Orthodox Church against the renovationists of the Living Church. Other priests pretended to abandon their clerical calling but continued to administer to their parishioners spiritual needs in secret, risking their lives in the process. In other cases religious people without a priest simply organized their own ceremonies in secret, again risking arrest if the authorities were to find out.

It is impossible to estimate accurately the numbers of "underground faithful" worshiping in secret by the late 1930s. The church historian Dmitry Pospielovsky has suggested that one reason the Soviet regime tolerated the official church was to use it to keep tabs on unofficial religious associations.[39] The few remaining priests were forced to adopt such novel practices as mass baptisms, long-distance confessions, and performing funerals *in absentia*. Others pretended to give up their priestly calling while continuing to celebrate weddings and funeral rites in secret. In the late 1930s a second mass wave of arrests among clergy and lay believers took place in the context of the Great Terror. Thus on the eve of World War II the position of religious believers in the USSR appeared very grave, if not desperate.

——————— Compromising with Religion: World War II ———————

When World War II began, the USSR was allied with Nazi Germany. Following the Molotov–Ribbentrop Pact, the Red Army occupied what had been eastern Poland; this area became part of the Belarusian and Ukrainian SSRs, with the city Wilno (now Vilnius) and its surroundings given to Lithuania. With the incorporation of this territory, the USSR acquired for the first time a large Catholic population, along with many Jews and Orthodox believers. With the occupation of the Baltic countries in the following year, millions of other Catholics became Soviet citizens. Catholics were problematic for the communists for at least two reasons: they were often devoutly religious and they belonged to an international church headed by an explicitly anti-Soviet Pope. The fact that Catholic clergy and church hierarchy was heavily Polish did not help matters; the Poles were well known as both anti-Russian and anticommunist. In the short period before the Nazi invasion, mass arrests and deportations removed tens of thousands of former Polish and Baltic citizens from their homes. Among these were numerous clergy-men and believers. Antireligious spectacles were staged in schools whereby children were prompted to ask God for treats (and predictably nothing happened) and then to repeat the request to Stalin or the party, whereupon candies would shower down from above.

With the Nazi invasion of the USSR in June 1941 the position of religious believers changed suddenly. As we have seen, Stalin underwent a total breakdown and it was Metropolitan Sergii who immediately called on the faithful to defend their homeland in a widely (strictly speaking, illegally) disseminated pastoral letter that urged Russians to use all means to resist the foreign invader. Combining religious with national appeals, Sergii called on patriotic Russians to support the Soviet war effort because only the USSR could defend the Russian nation. The crisis of foreign attack immediately made Russian Orthodox believers and the church hierarchy allies with the Soviet government against the Nazi invaders. Collections in churches went to arm a tank column that was christened "Dmitrii Donskoi" after the medieval prince who defeated the Tatars. Metropolitan Aleksii of Leningrad remained in the city throughout the siege and pronounced many sermons on patriotic themes, comparing the present military struggle with the battles of Alexander Nevsky against the Teutonic Knights centuries earlier. Metropolitan Nikolai of Moscow spoke of the church's "holy hatred for the enemy," telling the faithful that the commandment "love their neighbor" did not apply to "the German murderers" and even spoke of Stalin as "our common father" in the struggle against the fascists.

The regime repaid this support with a lessening of restrictions. The League of the Militant Godless was abolished in 1942 and religious leaders were allowed freer expression of religious (cum patriotic) sentiments. The fact that churches in the territory under Nazi occupation were allowed to open encouraged Stalin to adopt a similarly benevolent position. In September 1943 the Soviet leader met with church leaders in the Kremlin, and the following month the Council for Affairs of Orthodox Church was set up. Other religions also received similar concessions, essentially trading loyalty to the regime for official recognition. A *sobor* (council) of church officials was allowed and Sergii was elected Patriarch of Moscow. Some 20,000 churches were allowed to reopen (showing the strength of underground faith) and several seminaries were allowed to train future clergy.[40]

The Soviet state and the Russian Orthodox Church reached agreements that in many ways would last until the end of the Soviet regime. This is not to say that religious persecution ended but merely that the position of the church and its relations with the Soviet state were at least significantly stabilized. The Soviet state would support the Orthodox Church, for example, in incorporating the Baltic bishoprics and Uniates after the war; in turn the head of the Orthodox Church (by war's end Patriarch Aleksii, Sergii having died in 1944) had to support, for example, Soviet claims that the Katyń massacre had been the work of the Nazis.

At war's end, many of the freedoms allowed the clergy were again withdrawn, in particular in publicizing their sermons and pastoral letters. But the basic agreement between Soviet state and Orthodox Church remained, restoring the right of the church to train – within strict limits – new priests, fill existing positions, and even open up new churches if sufficient interest and finances could be shown (obviously a rare event). The fundamental hostility of the Soviet state toward religiosity had not changed. Perhaps the very weakness of the Orthodox Church in 1945 compared to two or three decades earlier made the Soviet authorities more willing to agree to concessions.

Conclusion

The belief system of Soviet citizens in 1945, it seems safe to say, differed radically from that of subjects of the tsar in 1861. Even those who retained the belief in a transcendent God perceived the relation between God and human life in a quite different way. In 1861 the tsar's political legitimacy was derived from God: Christians, Jews, and Muslims alike said a prayer for the Russian ruler in churches, synagogues, and mosques weekly. At the end of World War II, religion had largely retreated from the public stage (despite a return during the war), retaining its place mainly in the private sphere. For many Soviet citizens, a secular worldview had made God seem old fashioned or simply irrelevant.

The process of secularization in the USSR was not, of course, unique to that country, though the violence of antireligious sentiments and practices was. During the same period in western and central Europe, church attendance declined and Orthodoxy among Jews was increasingly replaced by less stringent forms of religious practice. But the fact that the communist leaders regarded their atheism as a central part of a progressive, modern political ideology, combined with the deep religious believers of the majority of the population, made a clash of incompatible worldviews likely if not entirely inevitable. The destruction of the Russian peasantry went hand in hand with destruction of the traditional church. Once the victory over the peasantry had been assured, especially after the patriotic fervor of the remaining Orthodox hierarchy had been shown during World War II, compromise could be allowed. But religious belief never ceased to be perceived as a flaw, a personal weakness, or eccentricity by the Soviet regime.

Chapter 6

World

Where does Russia fit into the world? This is the fundamental question I will attempt to answer in this chapter. To do so, we will need to examine not just the foreign policy of Russia and the USSR – though this topic will take up a large portion of this chapter – but also to look at Russian attitudes on their place in the world. Throughout the nineteenth century Russia was one of the Great Powers of Europe, respected and feared, but rarely considered entirely "European." Western Europeans were (and to some extent still are) fond of quoting a remark attributed Napoleon, "Scratch a Russian and you find a Tatar." The quote, for all its pithiness, nicely sums up the ignorance of the west regarding Russia. After all, a major heroic phase of early Muscovite history had been the defeating of the Tatars and, as Christians (having accepted Christianity around the same time as the Poles or Hungarians), Russians resented such facile comparisons.

Throughout the imperial period Russia struggled to retain its great power status as Russian culture – especially novels, and then later music and opera – became better known abroad. During the first decades of Soviet rule the USSR was no longer a great power and was not even invited to major diplomatic conferences like those ending World War I. The USSR prided itself on its special mission, proudly presenting itself as a model for the world to follow rather than as a distant and backward place. All this is to say the unique geographical position of the Russian Empire and USSR, spanning two continents, found reflection in the mentality of both Russians and other Europeans as well as in the state's consistent struggle to maintain its position in the world.

Russia in Europe

The nineteenth century (to World War I) may justifiably be called the European era. Never before, nor after (thus far), did European culture, military strength, and political power have such an impact on the world. Identity as European was crucial for the self-definition and prestige of people from Dublin to Dvinsk, from Christiana to Athens. Thus arose the crucial question for Russians: "How European are we?" To be European meant to be progressive, strong, dominant, modern. By the mid-nineteenth century at least, European identity was also associated with the political and intellectual movements coming out of the French Revolution: liberalism, nationalism, secularism, even atheism. Certainly all Russians saw themselves as European in a broad sense: they were Christian, spoke a European language (unlike, arguably, the Hungarians or Finns), and their ruling house was connected by marriage to Danish, English, and various German royal lines. Yet Russian and European identities did not coincide completely, as one peculiarity of the Russian language indicates: when Russians said (and say) "in Europe," they nearly always mean "not in Russia." On the other hand, the word *Aziya* in Russian even today has a negative connotation of barbarism and backwardness.[1]

If Russians are not entirely European, what are they "really"? Perhaps the conservative poet Fedor Tiutchev (1803–73) said it best: "Russia cannot be understood intellectually / Nor measured by a common yardstick / She has a unique character / In Russia one can only believe." In this short poem Tiutchev, a sophisticated and cosmopolitan man who served in the tsarist diplomatic service in Munich and Turin, is expressing a core belief of the so-called Slavophiles: that Russia is unique, both in her (Russia is both grammatically and "emotionally" feminine in the Russian language) nature and in her world historical mission. The actual Slavophiles were a group of noblemen who in the decades immediately before emancipation developed a mystical-political philosophy, calling on the tsar to abolish serfdom, but arguing that the unique character of Russia and Russians made parliamentary democracy unsuitable for them. The Slavophiles condemned the Europeanizing reforms of Peter the Great, believing that these reforms made the Russian upper class superficially European but at the cost of their total alienation from the Russian peasant masses. The Slavophiles wanted reform in Russia – especially the abolition of serfdom – but they did not want constitutionalism. Rather they held that the deeply Christian nature of the Russian people and its tsar would allow, once superficial western reforms had been stripped away, a kind of mystical union between tsar and people. The original Slavophiles were excellent poets and writers, but not practical politicians: historian Andrzej Walicki's description of their philosophy as a "conservative utopia" rings true. However, their ideas – in particular the condemnation of Peter the Great's reforms, their emphasis on the Orthodox religion, and the insistence that Russia find its own identity in the world – were extremely influential. Among those who embraced such ideas were the writer Dostoevsky, the poet Tiutchev, and the Panslavs of the later nineteenth century.[2]

The more pro-European counterpart to the Slavophiles was found among those generally described as "westerners" (*zapadniki*; *zapad* means "the west"). This was never a compact group like the Slavophiles; rather it refers to a general orientation. One must note that in post-reform Russia westerners of various stripes always outnumbered Slavophiles. While most westerners, like the novelist Ivan Turgenev or the historian and politician Pavel Miliukov, embraced mildly leftist politics, many quite conservative Russians agreed with the idea that Russia was a solidly European country that would gradually develop economically and to some extent even politically along the lines already seen in Germany, France, and Britain. Westerners praised Peter the Great's reforms for ending Muscovite backwardness and linking Russia's destiny with the rest of Europe as an equal and respected member of the European state system. Westerners differed on just what form of government Russia should have, but liberal views were most prevalent. The general assumption was that with economic development, the spread of literacy, and the growth of prosperity, Russia would come to resemble other European countries more closely. Westerners were every bit as patriotic as Slavophiles, but saw Russia's proper place as a modern, strong European power rather than as a uniquely Orthodox Christian state.

As for ordinary Russians in the mid- to late nineteenth century, few were concerned about Russia's place in the world. To start with, they had little idea of peoples or countries outside their immediate village or region. Even in the early twentieth century, most Russians defined themselves first and foremost as Orthodox Christians. They knew that they were not Tatars (in pre-revolutionary usage, a synonym for "Muslim" as well as a specific ethnonym), Jews, or Catholics. Traditionally Russians referred to all foreigners as *nemtsy* – a word now meaning "Germans," but derived from the adjective *nemoi*, "mute." That is, foreigners were those who could not speak Russian. Foreigners tended to be lumped together, with English, Turks, and Japanese easily confused – a fact that made it difficult for Russian authorities to explain to peasant soldiers in World War I for what or against whom they were fighting.

Since the defeat of Napoleon, Russia had been one of the major European powers. The Congress of Vienna (1814–15) had set down the political order that would in many ways remain intact until 1914. To be sure, Russia's defeat in the Crimean War severely called into question Russia's Great Power status, but unlike the Ottoman Empire to the south, Russia was never seen as essentially moribund. Throughout the nineteenth century Russia remained, along with Britain and

France, among the most powerful European states. With the unification of Germany in 1871, the political order established at the Congress of Vienna was shaken but not destroyed. After all, Prussia – the nucleus of the newly united German Reich – had been a major participant in the "European Concert" since 1814. After 1871 Germany joined Russia, France, and Britain in the top echelon of European power, while Italy and Austria-Hungary were also among the European Great Powers, but distinctly of the second rank.

Throughout the nineteenth century, Ottoman power in Europe receded. In 1800 Ottoman rule extended north to the borders of the Habsburg Empire (later Austria-Hungary) and Russia, completely dominating the Balkan peninsula. By the late 1870s, however, Ottoman rule had shrunk considerably with the de facto independence of Romanians, Serbs, Bulgarians, and Greeks. Russia felt a special kinship with these Christian Orthodox communities in the Balkans; this kinship also provided the tsar with a convenient excuse to intervene in the region. Already in the first decades of the nineteenth century Serbia wrested power from its Ottoman overlords, though Serbian independence (strictly speaking, under Ottoman suzerainty) would be acknowledged as permanent only in 1830.[3]

The Russo-Turkish War of 1877–8 ended with an impressive victory for the Russian army that had marched through (present-day) Romania almost to the gates of Constantinople (now Istanbul). It appeared that Russia's military humiliation in the Crimean War a generation earlier was to be vindicated. In fact, however, the war had revealed serious weaknesses in the Russian army – particularly during the Battle of Plevna – but even worse, the initial gains of the Treaty of San Stefano were challenged by the western powers. The German chancellor Otto von Bismarck readily agreed to serve as an "honest broker" and called an international conference in his capital to discuss the "eastern question." The Congress of Berlin (1878) forced Russia to relinquish some of its gains and was bitterly resented by Russians, but it also acknowledged the independence of Romania and the sovereignty of Bulgaria. Russia's role as "protector of Orthodox Slavs" in the Balkans would remain a key element of national identity and foreign policy into the twentieth century.[4]

After 1878 Ottoman power in the Balkans was nearly completed wiped out, with the exception of eastern Thrace (still part of today's Turkey) and Albania. From the Russian point of view, the Balkans were its "sphere of influence," which it jealously guarded. For this reason Russia tended to support Serbia in its quarrels against Austria-Hungary, such as the so-called Pig War of 1906–9. From the perspective of Vienna, Russia's support for the Serbs was deeply resented both as interference in Austrian affairs and as an encouragement to the national movements among Slavs living under Austrian rule.

The Balkans, though close to Russia geographically and emotionally, remained a sideshow in European power politics. The center, both literally and metaphorically, was Germany. The unification of Germany elevated an important but sec-ond-rate power (Prussia) to the first rank, an elevation that Britain and especially France regarded with extreme misgivings and resentment. Previous to 1871, Prussia and Russia had been on excellent terms; after German unification rela-tions did not sour immediately – the Reinsurance Treaty between Germany and Russia was signed as late as 1887 – but the threatening potential German eco-nomic and military might gave Russia cause to consider other alliances. In the first generation after unification, German Chancellor Bismarck influenced Kaiser William I to avoid unnecessarily provoking Russian and British sensibilities. After William I's death in 1888 relations deteriorated under the brash new German ruler, Kaiser William II. The German threat was above all military and demo-graphic – Germany had, after Russia, the largest population of any country in Europe – but also economic. The German economy boomed in the decades after 1871 and Russian policy-makers were certainly well aware of Cicero's remark "Endless money forms the sinews of war."

The combination of Germany's potential military threat, Kaiser William II's bellicose rhetoric, and possibly the influence of Tsarina Maria Fedorovna (born Danish princess Dagmar) over her husband caused Tsar Alexander III to sign a military convention with France in 1892. This first rapprochement between France and Russia would blossom into a full-scale military alliance in 1894. France and Russia remained almost diametrically opposite in their domestic political systems: France was the only republic among the major powers, while Russia remained one of the few European countries without any sort of constitution at the end of the century. Geography and a mutual interest in forestalling possible German aggression brought the two dissimilar powers together.[5]

From the period of the Great Reforms to the turn of the century the Russian Empire's position in the constellation of European powers remained overall little changed. While the Crimean War had revealed serious military weaknesses in the Russian army, the much better showing of the Russian military in the Russo-Turkish War of 1877–8 indicated that Russia remained a power to be reckoned with. At the same time the growing power and wealth of the newly united Germany posed a threat to Russian security, in particular when combined with frictions over politics in the Balkans between Russia and Germany's close ally Austria-Hungary.

Russia as Empire

While Russia considered itself a major European power, geographically speaking most of Russian territory lay beyond the Ural Mountains, in Asia. Unlike the other major European empires of the later nineteenth century, the Russian Empire was geographically contiguous. While Russia, like other European imperial powers, expanded significantly in the second half of the nineteenth century, this expansion pressed outward from Russia's southern border in Siberia rather than expanding overseas like Britain, France, or Germany. Between the 1860s and the end of the nineteenth century the Russian Empire extended its rule over central Asian territories including the cities of Tashkent, Khiva, Merv, and Samarkand. Certain territories became Russian "protectorates" with the local rulers (like the Khan of Khiva and the Emir of Bukhara) remaining in place, but under Russian suzerainty.[6] The growth of Russian influence in central Asia was very disturbing to the British foreign policy establishment who were obsessed with the prospect of Russians pouring over the mountains of Afghanistan to threaten British rule in India. In fact the Russians lacked both the will and the military resources to pose a threat to any but the most unorganized and militarily weak principalities. Still, the so-called Great Game between Russia and Great Britain over influence in southern central Asia became the stuff of legends and worked to sour relations between the two countries at the turn of the century.

Compared with other European Empires (e.g., Belgian, French, British, German), the Russian Empire differed in nearly every respect except the most crucial: rule over non-Europeans by a European power. In certain respects Russian imperial rule was closer to that in the Ottoman and Habsburg Empires (Austria-Hungary after 1867). All three were contiguous land empires where the distinction between "metropole" (home) and "colony" was not always clear. None of these three empires experienced the kind of racial hierarchy perceived by British, French, or Belgian colonizers in Africa or Asia – after all, most of the tsar's non-Russian subjects were physically not distinguishable from Russians.[7] Furthermore, Russian policy had long been to coopt the ruling classes in non-Russian areas, whether these were Muslim Tatars, Protestant Germans, Orthodox Georgians, or (initially) Catholic Poles.[8] The relative lack of "race feeling" among Russians can be seen in the pride that the Russian national poet Alexander Pushkin expressed over his African great-grandfather who had been brought to Russia in Peter the Great's time.

In Russia's case, rule over other ethnic and religious groups had started at least from the time of Ivan the Terrible when the mainly Muslim city of Kazan was conquered and incorporated into Muscovy (1552). The name "empire" (*imperiia*) had been first applied to the Russian state by Peter the Great in the early eighteenth century. And while Russians ruled over millions of Muslims, Buddhists, and other Asians, the majority of the non-Russian population was European and Christian. In central Asia, where Muslims formed an overwhelming majority of the population, the Russian authorities did not make serious attempts to teach the local population Russian or – even less – to sponsor conversion to Russian Orthodoxy. Unlike the French Empire with its (at least rhetorical) *mission civila-*

trice (civilizing misssion) or the British efforts at education in India, the Russians seemed content to let local identities and rhythms of daily life persist. The fear of provoking violent resistence on the part of Muslims under Russian rule far outweighed any desire for Russification. Economic exploitation was not absent from Russian imperial rule in central Asia, but the export of cotton from central Asia to textile mills in European Russia would grow in importance in the Soviet period.

Some scholars have drawn a connection between domestic policy and Russian "imperialism."[9] As in other European countries, imperialism enjoyed considerable public support. Thus when General M. G. Cherniaev disobeyed direct orders and took Tashkent in 1865, it was impossible for Tsar Alexander II to punish or even reprimand the disobedient soldier.[10] Similarly the tsar was pressured by public opinion to intervene against the Turks in 1877 when the fellow Orthodox peoples (Serbs and Bulgarians) were under attack in the Balkans. And expansion of Russian influence into Manchuria and Korea in the 1890s seemed the fulfillment of a kind of Russian "Manifest Destiny," despite the knowledge in the Ministry of Foreign Affairs that both Britain and more immediately Japan were considerably annoyed by Russian meddling in east Asia. At the same time we should not forget that unlike in western or central Europe, the tsar ruled as an autocrat and did not have to worry about garnering parliamentary support. Thus it is difficult to see Russian expansion in central Asia or meddling in east Asian affairs as significantly influenced by public opinion, either pro or con. While the writer Dostoevsky did speak enthusiastically about Russia's role in bringing civilization to Asia, it seems unlikely that the government was particularly influenced by his or other Russians' enthusiasm for the Russian civilizing mission.[11]

Despite the expansion into Asia, the Russian state and public were always more concerned with Europe. The weakness of the Ottomans to the south allowed the Russian Empire to expand beyond the Caucasus Mountains already before mid-century. In the second half of the nineteenth century further Russian expansion, Muslim fears of living under Christian rule, and to some extent aggressive Russian policies caused the emigration of thousands of Muslims across the border to the Ottoman Empire. Similar migrations of large numbers of Muslims occurred as Ottoman rule contracted in the Balkans. By the late nineteenth century the Ottoman Empire was known as the "sick man" of European politics – but the balance of power demanded that this moribund power be kept on life support. In particular Britain watched carefully at every Russian move in the region, fearing a Russian conquest of the city they knew as Tsargrad, today's Istanbul. The Russians were interested in the Ottoman capital both for historical reasons – they had received Christianity from the city then called Byzantium in 988 – as well as for strategic considerations. Ottoman control of the Bosporus and Dardanelles straits bottled up Russian warships in the Black Sea – and could completely interdict shipping, including commercial vessels, in time of war. If the Russians were to gain control over the straits, their military and commercial potential would be considerably enhanced. Worried about the spread of Russian influence in central Asia, the British were adamantly opposed to any increase of Russian power over Ottoman territories.[12]

For Russian nationalists, expansion of Russian influence in the Balkans was a natural, even providential, mission that combined religion, culture, and state power. In his influential book *Russia and Europe* (1869) Nikolai Danilevsky argued that all Slavic peoples must be brought under Russian rule by the destruction of Habsburg and Ottoman Empires and the incorporation of Tsargrad (Istanbul) in the Russian Empire. The only major Slavophile who survived to the 1870s, Ivan Aksakov, added his voice to the so-called Panslavs, who demanded a more active role for Russia in defending the rights of Slavs in the Ottoman and Habsburg Empires.[13]

The Panslav influence on Russian foreign policy was mixed: the Russian Empire did intervene against the Turks in 1877 but one may argue that this step was based on power politics and public opinion, not Panslav writings. In any case the Panslav ideology suffered from a number of contradictions. The largest Slavic nations, Ukrainians and Poles, were respectively not recognized as a proper nation or despised as anti-Russian and Catholic. The implicit connection between Orthodoxy and Slavdom in most Panslav writings meant that Catholic Slavs like Slovaks, Czechs, and Croats simply did not "fit into the concept." And from a practical point of view the creation of a large Slavic state ruled from St Petersburg (or, more likely, from Moscow) would have to deal with the belt of non-Slavs (Romanians and Hungarians) that separated South Slavic peoples from Slavs to the north and east. But perhaps one should not demand consistency or logic from nationalist programs whose fundaments rest more on emotion than on reason. The significance of the Panslav program is less on the level of practical foreign policy and more an ideology that further developed Slavophile notions of Russia's proper place in Europe and the world.

———— Anxiety about Remaining "on Top": 1900–1917 ————

As the new century dawned, Russia was faced with a number of significant potential foreign threats. To the east the stunning modernization of Japan, with its Prussian-trained army, was worrisome. To the west, German economic and military strength continued to grow. Relations with Britain were strained over Russian expansion into central Asia and commercial rivalries in Persia. While the Russian economy was growing impressively, the new weaponry and the need to counter German strategic railroad building on the western frontier demanded ever greater military budgets. The increasing military budget of Austria-Hungary was also a concern. Partly in an effort to slow down the arms race and partly out of a sincere desire for peace, Tsar Nicholas II pushed for an international peace conference, which convened in the Dutch capital, The Hague, in 1899. The First Hague Convention set down rules of war and outlawed the use of poison gas, dumdum bullets, and the "launching of projectiles and explosives from balloons" (the verb "to bomb" had not yet been invented). A further conference in 1907 built on the first, in particular in extending rules of war to conflicts at sea. Unfortunately most of these rules were ignored or circumvented by both sides during World War I.

The extension of the Trans-Siberian railroad across Chinese territory in Manchuria, while seen as a triumph of foreign policy by some, severely disturbed the Japanese. The construction of a Russian naval base at Dalny (Port Arthur, Liaodong Peninsula) in particular could only be construed as a direct threat by Tokyo. The expansion of Russian commercial interests into Korea, a Japanese protectorate since 1895, further irritated the Japanese. Recognizing the potential for conflict with Russia, in 1902 Japan signed a military alliance with Great Britain that obliged the two states to neutrality in case of attack. Britain hoped thereby to discourage Russian aggression, but the Japanese were encouraged by the treaty to settle their scores with what they saw as outrageous Russian interference in their backyard. After Russia failed to withdraw troops from Manchuria, as it had promised to do, Tokyo decided to strike. On the night of February 8, 1904, without a formal declaration of war, the Japanese launched a surprise attack on the Russian base at Port Arthur, setting off the Russo-Japanese War.

While the initial Japanese attack did not succeed in taking the Russian base, it caused considerable damage to Russian warships anchored there. The Russians entered the war with enthusiasm and without seriously considering the possibility of a defeat at the hands of the "yellow monkeys," as the popular press termed Russia's opponents. Their optimism, based in part on typical early twentieth-century European racism, was ill-placed. The one competent Russian admiral in the Far East fleet, Stepan Makarov, was drowned when his flagship struck a mine while attempting to leave Port Arthur. After this catastrophe no serious attempts were made to engage the Japanese at sea until the arrival of the Baltic Fleet, which had traveled around the globe just in time for the Battle of Tsushima (May 27–8, 1905, n.s.) in which the obsolete Russian fleet was destroyed at the hands of the Japanese. Russian forces on land in Manchuria did not fare much better, being hampered by their hugely long supply lines and the fact that the Trans-Siberian Railroad was still not completed around Lake Baikal in Siberia. The Battle of Mukden (late February to early March 1905) raged for nearly three weeks and resulted in huge casualties on both sides (90,000 of a total force of 276,000 for the Russians; 70,000 of 270,000 for the Japanese). After a failed counterattack the Russians were forced to withdraw and no further significant land battles took place in Manchuria.[14]

By spring of 1905 both the Russians and the Japanese were reaching exhaustion, and massive civil unrest in Russia (the revolution of 1905) threatened the stability of the tsarist regime. The Japanese, despite their military victories, had exhausted their financial resources and were not prepared for a longer conflict. In response to a secret Japanese offer to negotiate, the two powers met under the auspices of American President Theodore Roosevelt at Portsmouth, New Hampshire, in August 1905. There a peace was worked out in which Russia had to acknowledge Korea as primarily within the Japanese sphere of interest. Russia was also obliged to cede to Japan both the southern half of Sakhalin Island and the lease on the Liaodong Peninsula, thereby giving up the base of Port Arthur to the Japanese. In part due to the skill of the Russian negotiator, Sergei Witte, Russia avoided having to pay the Japanese an indemnity. The Peace of Portsmouth was probably as favorable a resolution of the war as Russia could have obtained, considering the poor performance of the Russian army and navy in the conflict. The Russian public, however, tended to see matters differently. The defeat at the hands of a non-European power and the humiliating need to give up Russian territory (though mainly convicts lived on Sakhalin Island) gave conservatives and radicals alike a club with which to beat Sergei Witte.

The defeat at the hands of the Japanese forced the Russian military to consider what had gone wrong and how to prevent such disasters in the future. After the crushing of the revolution of 1905, in which troops played a significant role in putting down civil unrest, the army general staff set to work on a plan for broad reform. The result was a comprehensive report issued in 1908 calling for broad-ranging changes over a 10-year period, including the increase in numbers of machine guns and artillery, as well as the purchase of the first military aircraft. Large increases in the military budgets were approved by the Dumas, including the so-called Big Program of 1913 that called for a 40 percent increase in the size of the standing army. In the last full year before World War I, Russia spent 709 million rubles on the military, a sum unmatched by any other European state.[15]

Russia's opponent in any major war, it seemed clear, would be Germany, in particular as relations between Germany and Austria-Hungary became ever closer in the early twentieth century. Kaiser William II attempted to divert Russo-German relations back onto a more positive track by convincing his cousin Nicholas II to sign a defensive alliance at Björkö in the summer of 1905 when both were vacationing in the Baltic port on their yachts. When Nicholas's ministers heard of the agreement, however, they were horrified and pointed out to the tsar the incompatibility of defensive alliances with both France and Germany. The disgruntled Nicholas was thus forced to withdraw his agreement. The erratic behavior of William II and tensions in the Balkans did not augur well for continued peace, though no one expected a major European-wide war. On the positive side, in summer 1907 Russia and Great Britain signed an important diplomatic agreement that regulated the two powers' mutual relations in particular in regard to Afghanistan, Tibet, and Persia. In a real sense the Anglo-Russian Entente of 1907 ended the Great Game that had poisoned relations between the two countries and paved the way for the future Triple Alliance of Britain, France, and Russia during World War I.

The Balkans, populated mainly with Orthodox Slavic peoples, held a far more important place in Russian foreign policy and public opinion than mere power politics would have merited. With the Ottoman Empire almost entirely pushed out of Europe, Russia's main rival here was Austria-Hungary, among whose peoples were millions of Slavs (though mostly of the Roman Catholic religion). In 1908, with Russia still recovering from the disastrous war with Japan, Austria-Hungary decided to annex the province of Bosnia-Herzegovina, which it had occupied since the 1878 Congress of Berlin. Before taking this action, which Vienna knew well would be deeply unpopular among Serbs and Russians, the Austro-Hungarian minister of foreign affairs, Count Alois von Aehrenthal, met with his Russian counterpart, Alexander Izvolsky. Izvolsky agreed not to protest the annexation of Bosnia-Herzegovina, and Aehrenthal agreed to support Russia's demand that the Bosporus and Dardanelles (the straits connecting the Black and Mediterranean Seas) be opened to Russian warships. In the end, however, Austria went forward quickly with the annexation, making it impossible for Russia to prepare the ground diplomatically for a change of status of the Straits. Both the Russian foreign minister and the public felt betrayed; the Russian press published diatribes against the perfidious Austrians. In 1908 the Russian military was still too weak to countenance war, but the desire to strike back at Austria when possible was intensified.

Serbia was furious at the Austrian annexation of Bosnia-Herzegovina, home to a significant Serbian population, and felt outraged by Russia's failure to oppose the measure. Relations between Serbia and its much larger and richer neighbor to the north, Austria-Hungary, had gotten much worse since the latter imposed a customs blockade on Serbia in 1906, leading to the so-called Pig War (since that animal was one of Serbia's main exports to Austria). An agreement in 1909 opened up trade between the two countries again, but bad feeling persisted. Nor were Serbia's relations with its neighbors to the south and east much better. In 1912 the Balkan League consisting of Serbia, Bulgaria, Greece, and Montenegro attacked the Ottoman Empire, defeating the Ottoman troops and incorporating much of Macedonia and Thrace. Disagreements over the dividing up of the territory led to the Second Balkan War of 1913 in which the former allies, joined later by Romania and the Ottoman Empire, attacked Bulgaria. Serbia more than doubled in size after the Balkan Wars, to the great consternation of Austria-Hungary and the German Reich, who regarded the Balkan country as little more than a satellite of Russia.

Thus when the young Serbian nationalist Gavrilo Princip shot and killed the heir to the Habsburg throne, Grand Duke Franz Ferdinand, in the capital of Bosnia-Herzegovina in late June 1914, the stage was set for a full-scale European war. To be sure, no one expected the war immediately. But when, nearly a month later, Austria-Hungary presented Serbia with an ultimatum clearly designed to be unacceptable to any sovereign state, leaders throughout Europe realized with a shock that war was imminent. By August 6, when Austria-Hungary declared war on Russia, Europe was at war. German strategy was based on the so-called Schlieffen Plan, which aimed to prevent a two-front war by launching a massive attack on France in the first days of the war, knocking France out of the war, and then turning to Russia. The Schlieffen Plan assumed that Russia would be slow in mobilizing its forces and would not pose a serious threat for several weeks at least. The remarkable successes of the German army, which was only a few dozen miles from Paris by mid-August, caused the French to pressure their Russian ally into some kind of major attack to relieve pressure on the western front. The subsequent invasion of East Prussia on August 17 was a great shock to the Germans, who had not expected the Russians to be capable of such a large-scale operation just two weeks after the declaration of war. Once German troops had been brought from the western front, however, the Russians were soundly defeated at the Battle of Tannenberg in late August 1914. Russian troops would never threaten German soil again and already by autumn 1915 such important cities of the Russian Empire as Warsaw and Wilno (now Vilnius, capital of Lithuania) were in German hands.

The Russian troops fared somewhat better against the Austrians; Russia occupied eastern Galicia, a region populated mainly by Orthodox Ukrainians, for over a year. The Russian occupation regime did little to convince local Ukrainians – much less the Poles or Jews living there – of the desirability of long-term Russian rule. In particular the Russian authorities' mistreatment of Uniate clergy and their refusal to consider Ukrainians as anything but a branch of the Russian people alienated locals.[16] The Russian military authorities generally considered Jews as actual or potential spies (in part due to deeply ingrained antisemitism; in part because of the similarity of the German and Yiddish languages); hundreds of thousands of Jews were exiled to the Russian interior, as were smaller though still significant numbers of Poles and others.[17]

While all warring powers were shocked at the quick depletion of ammunition and the huge cost of the war, Russia was hit hardest of all. With a relatively weak industrial sector and railroad net, the Russian Empire found it impossible to satisfy both military and civilian needs. Indeed the inability of the minister of War, General Vladimir Sukhomlinov, to deal with ammunition shortages and chaotic administration led to his dismissal in June 1915. He was later accused of treason and while he was found not guilty, one of his close associates, Lieutenant Colonel Sergei Miasoedov was condemned and executed.

Now it seems clear that neither Sukhomlinov nor Miasoedov was guilty of more than incompetence, but at the time the idea of widespread treason seemed a plausible explanation for Russian military reversals. As we now know, however, the weaknesses of the Russian state were entirely domestic: poorly supplied and trained (though brave) soldiers, a weak railroad network that was constantly breaking down under the strain of war, and incompetence in the upper ranks of the Russian military, which was further exacerbated by Nicholas's persistent interference in military affairs about which he understood little. In any case, while the supply of weaponry and ammunition for the troops improved from 1915, conditions on the home front grew steadily worse. Russians in both cities and the countryside were suffering cold and hunger, and the government seemed quite unable to explain just why the war should continue.

The collapse of the tsarist regime in February 1917 was brought on not by foreign intrigue but by the miserable conditions under which Russians were living, combined with a perception that the Russian government was unable or unwilling to bring the war to an end. The Bolshevik takeover in October also cannot be blamed on German intrigues, though the arrival of the Bolshevik leader, Vladimir Ilych Lenin, to Petrograd in April 1917 did owe something to the Germans. Stranded in Switzerland during the war years (he had nearly been arrested and interned in Austrian Poland in August 1914), Lenin accepted a German offer of a railroad carriage to cross Germany in order to get back to Russia. Knowing well Lenin's antiwar sentiments and radical ideology, the Germans hoped thereby to weaken the Russian desire to continue the war effort. Russian support for the war was almost nonexistent by fall 1917 but, it must be admitted, it was Lenin who pushed through (against the desire of some of his closest colleagues in the Bolshevik/Communist Party) the Treaty of Brest-Litovsk (March 1918) that actually ended the war on the Eastern Front.

USSR Confronts the World to 1935

When the Bolsheviks, led by Lenin, took over Russia in October 1917, they promised an entirely new political order, including a completely novel foreign policy. To quote a history of Soviet foreign policy published in 1986, "For the first time in the history of mankind, an entirely new foreign policy appeared, one that served not exploiters but the working class…"[18] The initial actions and proclamations of the new People's Commissariat of Foreign Affairs, headed by Lev Trotsky, were certainly new and very shocking to traditional diplomats. To start with, Trotsky published the secret agreements that the tsarist and provisional governments had reached with the allies. In particular the agreement that Russia would receive control over the Straits as a war prize was extremely embarrassing to politicians who had assured their electorate that the war was not being fought for sordid reasons like territorial expansion. The Soviet state also repudiated all tsarist foreign debt, impoverishing thousands of middle-class investors in western Europe who had purchased tsarist bonds. And, of course, the Bolsheviks immediately began negotiating with the Germans to pull Russia out of the war, rejecting the tsarist and Provisional Government's agreements with the allies.

The tragicomic negotiation of the peace with Germany, where Trotsky harangued German diplomats and generals about the inevitability of world revolution, vividly showed the difference in style and substance between traditional diplomacy and the Bolshevik version. As was clear both to Trotsky and to the Germans, he was just playing for time – and time was, in the short run, on the Germans' side. Fed up with the Soviet negotiators' behavior, the Germans issued an ultimatum: either sign a peace or face the resumption of military action. Despite furious discussions among the Bolshevik leadership (see chapter 1, "Politics," pp. 36–7), in the end they agreed to sign the very harsh Treaty of Brest-Litovsk in March 1918. While the treaty "gave away" enormous amounts of territory along the former western frontiers of the Russian Empire, in reality it simply confirmed the fact that the Bolsheviks had no control over those regions. In pushing his colleagues to sign a draconian peace with the Germans, Lenin was gambling that with increasing numbers of American troops arriving in France, the Germans could not win the war. Lenin's gamble paid off.

Immediately after October 1917 the communists expected revolution to spread throughout Europe, probably starting in industrial Germany, to sweep away the necessity for diplomacy in the traditional sense. With the failure of revolutions in various parts of Germany, Finland, Hungary, and elsewhere in 1918–19, the communists needed to work out a more lasting form of foreign policy. In a sense Soviet foreign policy until the mid-1930s represented a "figuring out" of how to reconcile the interests of the USSR as a state and the interests of world revolution. Marx had not foreseen that any such contradiction would arise, as he assumed that once it took hold in one country, the revolution would spread rapidly throughout the world. The Soviet view of their place in the world was also complicated by the power struggle between Trotsky and Stalin in the 1920s. Trotsky represented the more "Orthodox" view that a primary focus had to remain on spreading revolution around the world, summed up in the slogan "permanent revolution." Stalin, on the other hand, while not overtly denying the need to spread revolution, became associated with the more modest slogan "socialism in one country." In other words, in the short term at least Soviet policy had to concentrate on building and strengthening socialism in the USSR. Then, when the opportunity arose, the Soviet Union would be better able to exert its influence – and export revolution – around the world.

From the start, the allied governments viewed the Bolshevik revolution with dismay and hoped for the quick demise of Lenin and his party. Indeed even before the October 1917 revolution the allies had done what they could to prevent the return of socialists like Trotsky and Lenin to Russia, one reason why Lenin had to accept German help in order to get back to Petrograd. During the Civil War the western powers did contribute weapons, money, and some troops to the Whites. But public disapproval in the west of anything that would prolong the war, combined with the lack of unity among the White forces, meant that this assistance did not make a significant difference in the outcome of the Civil War.

The so-called Allied Intervention began with a British landing at Arkhangelsk to protect military stores warehoused there – after all, the British did not want this materiel to fall into German hands. The initial 1,200 British troops who arrived in August 1918 were later augmented by several thousand Americans. But there was no effort to use these troops directly against the communists, and Arkhangelsk is, after all, several hundred miles from Petrograd. Before the Civil War played out, the French had landed some units at Black Sea ports, and first Japanese troops, then American troops in tens of thousands, were sent to the Far East around Vladivostok.[19]

The most significant episode of foreign "intervention" in the Civil War, however, involved Czechoslovak prisoners of war (POWs) trying to return home via the Trans-Siberian Railroad. When the Bolsheviks came to power tens of thousands of soldiers from the Austro-Hungarian army were languishing in POW camps in Russia. In March 1918 an agreement was signed between the Soviets, Czechoslovak leaders, and representatives of the allies to transport Czechoslovak soldiers around the world, starting with a journey to the Pacific Ocean via the Trans-Siberian railroad, to join a unit in France that would contribute to the allied war effort against Germany. As trains of Czechoslovak soldiers were making their slow way across Siberia, a fight broke out in Cheliabinsk, apparently when a trainload of Czech and Slovak soldiers found itself next to cars full of Hungarian POWs. When Trotsky ill-advisedly gave the order that any Czech POW found armed would be shot on sight, the Czechoslovaks, fearing for their own safety, disarmed local Soviet authorities and for all practical purposes took over vast stretches of the Trans-Siberian Railroad line. But the Czechoslovak soldiers did not have any firm ideological commitment to the Whites; they mainly wanted to get out of Russia and back home. At first the so-called Czech Legion cooperated with the White ruler of Siberia, Admiral Alexander V. Kolchak, but soon realized Kolchak's weakness and handed him over to the Bolshevik authorities in early 1920. By the end of that year most of the Czech and Slovak soldiers had left Russia for their newly created homeland, Czechoslovakia.[20]

A decisive year for the new Soviet state and its foreign policy was 1920. The Civil War had ended and the effort to spread communism to western Europe through Poland was defeated by the Polish army in August 1920. By this point, Soviet attempts to rally leftist forces in the Baltic provinces and Finland had also been defeated; in most of these countries the Communist Party was forced underground. Clearly the Bolshevik takeover in Russia was not going to be the spark to set off a worldwide communist conflagration. The Soviet state needed more lasting institutional means of spreading communist ideology and assuring Soviet Russian interests in the world, two goals that did not always mesh. Soviet foreign relations were also complicated by the pervasive view that the western "capitalist" world was bent on destroying the world's only socialist state. While the western powers certainly viewed Soviet Russia with grave mistrust, they were too divided and concerned with their own affairs to be plotting the USSR's demise.

While Soviet Russia had been in the throes of the Civil War, a new diplomatic order had been set up in Europe. The various treaties ending the war signed in and around Paris in 1919 entirely changed the map of Europe, in particular in the region between Germany and Russia. While the Germans were humiliated by the Treaty of Versailles, the Bolsheviks were not even invited to the conference. All along Russia's western border new boundaries were drawn and new states created from Finland to Czechoslovakia (the latter lacking, however, a common border with the USSR until 1944). The main purpose of the postwar treaties was to punish the Central Powers (Germany and Austria-Hungary) and to prevent future German aggression. But an important secondary consideration was to prevent the spread of Bolshevism. From the start, this new diplomatic order aimed to isolate and weaken Soviet Russia. The western powers, in particular France, hoped that the newly independent Poland would serve as a bulwark against communist influence from Russia. For this reason, Polish–Soviet relations in the interwar were always strained, the USSR supporting Lithuania in its claims for Vilnius (Wilno) and secretly helping to finance Belarusian and Ukrainian underground movements against Polish rule in interwar eastern Poland. The diplomatic isolation of the USSR thus stemmed both from its own ideology and from the western powers' desire to create a *cordon sanitaire* protecting the rest of Europe from the "communist virus."

In the 1920s the main instrument of Soviet foreign policy was the Comintern – short for "Communist International," sometimes known as the "Third International." The Comintern was founded at a meeting of several dozen, mainly tiny, left-wing parties held in Moscow in March 1919. The aim of the Comintern was simple: to spread communist revolution and to oppose the bourgeois world order, which was specifically conceived as including socialist parties like the by-now mainstream German SPD. In order to join the Comintern, a party had to agree to Lenin's Twenty-One Conditions, which pledged them to oppose moderate parties, to not participate in coalition governments, and to press forward toward revolution. In practice, belonging to the Comintern meant toeing the Soviet party line.[21]

The Comintern set up a variety of organizations bringing together, to name a few, communist athletes, peasants, youth, and labor unions, to help spread the idea of communism among different social groups. It also took a very strong stance against imperialism, which both helped gain members for the communist cause among Africans and Asians who lived under colonial rule and also served as a club with which to beat the main imperialist powers, Great Britain and France. While the Comintern was successful in setting up pro-Soviet communist parties throughout Europe and in several Asian countries, it antagonized existing governments who rightly saw the organization as aiming to interfere in the internal affairs of every country. The Comintern's harsh delineation between socialists and communists also made very difficult any effective resistance to the growing threat of right-wing extremism in the 1920s and early 1930s.

The Comintern represented the left-wing, radical face of Soviet foreign policy. At the same time, however, the Soviet state needed at least provisional relations with capitalist countries until the revolution came. Thus Soviet foreign policy went in two contradictory directions: for a total undermining of the capitalist world and for short-term cooperation with that same hostile world. These contradictions would in certain ways persist to the end of the USSR, but were most acute in the 1920s and early 1930s. One sign that Soviet Russia could also participate in traditional diplomacy were the treaties signed in 1920 and 1921 with newly independent countries that had in 1914 formed part of the Russian Empire: Finland, Estonia, Latvia, Lithuania, and Poland. These treaties did not establish good relations with these countries but at least ended the open or covert state of war previously existing between most of them and Soviet Russia. Trade agreements were also reached with Great Britain, Norway, Austria, and Italy.

All of these treaties were relatively small steps and the traditional diplomatic world continued to shun Soviet Russia, which for example was not invited to join the League of Nations. This attitude began to change in the early 1920s out of the pragmatic realization that Soviet rule in Russia was not going away soon and that Russia, while at present weak, would once again be a major player on the international stage. The first major victory for pragmatism was the Treaty of Rapallo, signed by Soviet Russia and Germany in April 1922. For all their economic and ideological differences, Germany and Russia had one big thing in common: they were both pariahs on the international stage. Rapallo essentially wiped away the terms of Brest-Litovsk, with both countries renouncing any further territorial or financial claims on the other. A secret clause allowed the German military to train in Russia, a violation of the Treaty of Versailles. The triumph of the Soviet people's commissar for foreign affairs, Georgy Chicherin, in working out the details of Rapallo with the Germans undermined the prestige of the Comintern and its chief, Grigory Zinoviev.

After Lenin's death in 1924 and in the later 1920s as Stalin consolidated his power, both pragmatic diplomacy and the Comintern continued to coexist. In 1925 Stalin supported the idea of "socialism in one country," originally proposed by Nikolai Bukharin, not giving up the idea of world revolution but laying more stress on defending the one existing socialist country. Despite the often belligerent public stance of the Comintern, the actual instructions given to communist parties outside the USSR tended toward caution, recognizing the doubtful effectiveness of such small groups and fearing reprisals from foreign governments in the case of failed coups or violent attacks. For example, Great Britain established diplomatic relations with the USSR in 1924 but broke off these relations three years later when the press published a letter from the Comintern to the British Communist Party advocating working for revolution in Ireland and within the British Army. Even worse was the disaster of the Chinese communists. The Comintern supported – at least rhetorically – the Chinese Communist Party but when the nationalist Kuomintang, led by Chiang Kai-Shek, destroyed the Chinese communist organizations with great bloodshed in 1927, the USSR was helpless to intervene.[22]

The British breaking off of relations and the Chinese disaster in 1927 led to a full-scale war scare within the USSR. Press accounts and mass meetings led Soviet citizens to believe that the capitalist world was planning an imminent attack. While some Soviet leaders may indeed have feared an attack, it seems likely that this war scare was also exaggerated as part of the anti-Trotsky campaign being waged by Stalin and his supporters. Trotsky had consistently opposed "socialism in one country" as a concession to capitalism, so it was to Stalin's advantage to show that defense of the USSR was a burning need far outstripping the spreading of revolution abroad. In November 1927 Trotsky, along with the former head of the Comintern, Zinoviev, were expelled from the party.

The following year, coinciding with the beginning of the First Five-Year Plan and the collectivization of agriculture, Soviet foreign policy veered back towards the radicalism of the Comintern. In 1928 the Comintern issued a statement arguing that capitalism was entering its final phase and all communist parties should adopt an uncompromising ultraradical line. No cooperation with mainstream socialist parties was to be allowed; indeed these were termed "social fascists," implying that there were really no significant differences between non-communist socialists and the extreme right wing. This ultraradical policy not only alienated governments throughout Europe but made impossible any cooperation between socialist parties and the communists, thereby facilitating Adolf Hitler's takeover in 1933. When Hitler came to power the obvious falseness of the "social fascist" label was exposed. While under previous German governments of the Weimar Republic (1919–33) communists had been at times jailed, refused government employment, and subject to physical attack at the hands of right-wing groups, once Hitler came to power, thousands of left-wing political activists – socialists and communists alike – were arrested, beaten, and sometimes killed. Thousands more fled abroad, in some cases ending up in Moscow where they would perish during the purges.

The disastrous consequences of the ultraleft stance of the Comintern led to a complete policy reversal and significant downgrading of the Comintern's role in Soviet foreign policy. In 1935, at the seventh and final world congress of the Comintern, the overthrow of capitalism was officially repudiated as the organization's main goal and the rhetoric of "social fascism" was discarded and replaced with the idea of the "Popular Front." The Popular Front ideology called on communists to work together with all parties of the left to prevent the triumph of fascism.[23] This new and more pragmatic stance allowed the participation of communists in Léon Blum's Popular Front government in France, formed in 1936 and also paved the way for communist cooperation with other groups opposing Franco's takeover of power in Spain. But, as we will see, relations between communists and other leftist groups was not always simple.

Russia Abroad: Émigrés

In the decade or so after the October 1917 revolution, some three million Russians left their homeland, unable or unwilling to live under Soviet rule. The émigrés often belonged to the educated middle classes or even the aristocracy. The cliché about Parisian taxi drivers in the 1920s being Russian princes is of course exaggerated, but not so far from the truth. Among the most famous émigrés were Ivan Bunin, the first Russian to receive the Nobel prize for literature, another later Nobel prize winner, Vladimir Nabokov, historian and Kadet politician Pavel Miliukov, astronomer Otto Struve, composer Igor Stravinsky, and choreographer George Ballanchine. Among the émigrés were Russian Jews like historian and writer Simon Dubnov. Along with these celebrated scientists and artists thousands of engineers, doctors, teachers, and other specialists left Russia after 1917, a huge loss for the Soviet regime.

Émigré communities were set up in cities as diverse as Shanghai, Los Angeles, Berlin, Paris, and Belgrade. A Russian university functioned for a time in Prague, and Russian publishing houses brought out thousands of books, journals, and newspapers in various cities. The emigrants tended to regard themselves as the true Russia as opposed to the communists who, they thought, had betrayed the ideals and cultural continuity of their native land. They brought up their children speaking Russian, patronized or established Russian Orthodox Churches, and attempted to continue Russian traditions and culture in exile. Initially many hoped that the Bolshevik regime would quickly collapse, but after the White defeat in the Civil War only the most optimistic exile could expect to return home soon. In the 1920s the "Change of Milestones" (*smenovekhovstvo*) movement developed, arguing that, despite ideological differences, Russians abroad should accept the fact of communist rule in Russia and return home. For most, however, this was not a possibility: they despised the communist ideology and feared for their safety in the USSR.[24]

Trying to make sense of Russia's and their own place in the world, émigré thinkers, most important among them Nikolai Trubetskoi and P. N. Savitsky, developed the ideology known as Eurasianism. The Eurasians, writing mainly in the 1920s, argued that Russia belonged neither to Europe nor Asia but, in part because of the Tatar invasion and rule from the thirteenth to fifteenth centuries, formed its own unique mode of development. This emphasis on Russian uniqueness linked them with the Slavophiles, but the latter never saw anything positive coming out of the centuries of Mongol rule. It is quite likely that the Eurasians, writing as émigrés in a period when their native country was in many ways cut off from the rest of Europe, found a kind of psychological compensation in the idea of Russian uniqueness deriving from the country's unique geographical position and historical development. The Eurasians regarded the triumph of communism in Russia as a regrettable but necessary event to push forward the country's modernization, though it must be said that few of these thinkers actually returned to Soviet Russia. Eurasianism provided a new way of looking at Russian history as uniquely spanning two continents while not belonging entirely to either one.[25] In the 1920s, the decade when Eurasianism was born, these ideas provided hope for a return to Russia's pre-1914 greatness after what seemed like catastrophic defeats for Russian power and prestige. In the post-Soviet period Eurasian concepts have once again received considerable attention, in particular as an answer to the perplexing problem of post-Soviet Russian identity.

Among the largest and most important centers for the Russian emigration were Paris, Berlin, and Kharbin, though significant émigré communities developed in dozens of other cities from Prague to Shanghai to San Francisco. Paris was the unchallenged "capital" of the Russian émigrés in the interwar period, with dozens of émigré organizations, hundreds of daily and weekly journals, Russian-language schools, and even a "people's university" (*Russky narodny universitet*). While most Russian exiles in Paris were far from rich, among them were also some who managed to salvage some part of their wealth, and moderately prosperous middle-class people like the writer Ivan Bunin who was awarded the Nobel prize in 1933. The excellent command of French among scholars like the historian and erstwhile Kadet-party leader Pavel Miliukov gave French journalists and government figures a ready source of non-Soviet information on Russia – though the exiles' views on communist Russia seldom had much impact on foreign policy. Among the thousands of Russians residing in Paris in the 1920s and 1930s were famous writers like Bunin, Nadezhda Teffi, and Alexander Kuprin, philosophers like Nikolai Berdiaev, journalists, workers, ex-tsarist officers, and many other now forgotten individuals. Already by the 1930s hope for a return to Russia – at least to a Russia they could recognize as home – was fading for most émigrés in Paris. Increasingly their children, and even more their grandchildren, would identify themselves as French.[26]

Due in part to its relative proximity to Russia, Berlin became a very major center of exiles in the 1920s and into the 1930s. Until the early 1930s it remained fairly easy to travel to and from the USSR, and many artists and writers from Soviet Russia stopped in Berlin – sometimes for lengthy stays – on their way to and from Moscow or Leningrad. German historian Karl Schlögel has described Russian Berlin as a place where exiled Russian monarchists, liberals, and Mensheviks could brush shoulders with communists and their sympathizers. The Soviet embassy in Berlin, centrally located on the main street Unter den Linden, even extended invitations to members of the émigré community, hoping in this way both to encourage Russians to return home or, failing that, to recruit spies. As in Paris, dozens of newspapers and journals in the Russian language were published in Berlin, ranging from the semifascist *Call* (*Prizyv*) to the SR *Days* (*Dni*) to the pro-Soviet *On the Eve* (*Nakanune*). Writer Vladimir Nabokov spent nearly the entire interwar period in Berlin, from 1922 to 1937, publishing there his novel *The Gift* (*Dar*), in which the young writer offended many by ridiculing pre-revolutionary writer Nikolai Chernyshevsky. Political disputes among Russian émigrés could also turn violent, as when Nabokov's father, a liberal Kadet, was assassinated by a right-wing fanatic who was actually aiming at Nabokov's party leader, Pavel Miliukov. By the mid-1930s Russian Berlin was on the wane, having been dealt a serious blow by Hitler's coming to power in 1933.[27]

Far to the east, a unique center of "Russia abroad" developed in the Manchurian city of Kharbin. The city had been founded only at the very end of the nineteenth century during the construction of the Chinese Eastern Railroad that linked the Trans-Siberian with Khabarovsk and Vladivostok on the Pacific.[28] In 1917 the city was home to some 70,000 persons, of whom around 60 percent had come there from the Russian Empire. After the revolution and Civil War, thousands more Russians came to Kharbin after fleeing the USSR, giving the city in 1929 a population of some 60,000 Russians (by then outnumbered by around 100,000 Chinese inhabitants). Unlike Paris and Berlin, Russian Kharbin was a relatively compact city unto itself, but as in those European cities, the Manchurian city was witness to significant scholarly, literary, and political developments. Kharbin was unusual in its geographic location and its uneasy existence under Chinese sovereignty. By the late 1920s around half of the city's Russian population held Soviet passports (required for anyone wishing to seek employment on the railroad). With the Japanese occupation of the city in 1932 and increasingly strained relations between the USSR and Japan, the Russian presence in Kharbin became less and less tenable. By the mid-1930s tens of thousands of Russians had left the city for the USSR, and many other thousands such as historian Nicholas Riasanovsky and literary scholar Simon Karlinsky emigrated to California and other western cities. Certain traces of Russian emigrant life abroad persist to the present day, but its heyday was over by 1939.

Another kind of "Russia abroad" developed after the expulsion of Trotsky from the USSR in 1929. For the next decades, from exile in Turkey, France, Norway, and finally Mexico, Trotsky indefatigably wrote, received visitors, and denounced Stalin for perverting the revolution. Among other things, while in exile Trotsky wrote and published *The Permanent Revolution* (1929), *History of the Russian Revolution* (1930), *The Revolution Betrayed* (1936), *Stalin School of Falsification* (1937), and his memoirs, *My Life* (1930). After the Comintern turned its emphasis away from the spread of world revolution, Trotsky and his sympathizers formed in 1938 a "Fourth International" in protest to the pragmatic trend in Soviet foreign policy. Always denounced in the USSR as a traitor to the revolution (any connection to Trotsky could lead to arrest and worse during the purges), in exile, Trotsky remained critical but continued to believe in the positive outcome of developments in the USSR. His critical voice provided an alternative to radicals dissatisfied with Stalinism, though of course only outside the USSR. One may question just how influential Trotsky was in the 1930s but clearly Stalin perceived him, even in Mexican exile, as a threat. On August 20, 1940, an agent sent by Stalin struck Trotsky from behind with an ice pick, crushing his skull; Trotsky died the next day.[29]

The Threat Turns Real: 1935–1945

The initial reaction in Moscow to Hitler's taking of power (January 1933) had been positive, seeing the National Socialist Chancellor as an indication that the bourgeois capitalist world was collapsing. By the end of the year, however, after the destruction of the German Communist Party, the burning of the Reichstag, and Hitler's elimination of all opposition, Stalin could see just how wrong that assessment had been. As anyone with even a passing acquaintance with *Mein Kampf* or the Nazi leader's speeches could attest, Hitler was obsessed with communism almost as much as with the Jews. Indeed in Hitler's feverish rhetoric it is often difficult to distinguish the two: communists and Jews go hand in hand in the Nazi leader's paranoid ravings. One reason for middle-class support of Hitler was his staunch anticommunism. Hitler's loathing for communism, his determination to rearm Germany, and his repeated statements on the need for German expansion to the east ("Lebensraum") were a direct threat to the USSR's very existence.

As we have seen, in 1935 the Comintern began to advocate a policy of cooperation with all parties who opposed "fascism." It was the communists, in fact, who lumped Hitler and Mussolini together under this label; the National Socialists in Germany never called themselves fascists. If this policy of a "popular front" was too late to prevent the extreme right-wing from taking power in Italy and Germany, it at least helped the moderate socialist Léon Blum stave off the right wing threat in France.

At the same time, even before Hitler's rise to power, the USSR had attempted to secure its western frontier by signing with its western neighbors (with the exception of Finland) the so-called Litvinov protocol (named after the Soviet commissar for foreign affairs), promising to renounce war. In 1932 nonaggression pacts were signed with France, Finland, Poland, Estonia, and Latvia; in latter years these agreements were further developed. In 1933 the USA finally recognized the USSR, the last major power to do so, and the following year the USSR joined the League of Nations. Ironically, just as the threat of Hitler arose, the USSR was becoming increasingly integrated into the world diplomatic system.

From his first days in power Hitler exhibited extreme hostility toward the Soviet state. The secret military cooperation that had taken place since Rapallo was ended, and the staff of the Soviet Embassy in Berlin found their movements carefully scrutinized. In November 1936 Germany signed the Anti-Comintern Pact with Japan, with Italy joining the next year. This pact was specifically aimed against the USSR and posed the threat of attack from both east and west. Tensions with Japan had somewhat abated after the sale of the Chinese Eastern Railway to the Japanese satellite Manchukuo in 1933, but clashes between Red Army and Japanese troops continued, escalating into real battles in 1938 and 1939. The victory of the Red Army, led by General Georgy Zhukov, over the Japanese at a series of battles in Mongolia between May and June 1939, commonly known as Khalkhyn Gol, convinced the Japanese military that a plan to press on to invade Siberia was untenable. The Japanese would turn their attentions to Southeast Asia and not threaten Soviet territory again.[30]

In the west a great test for the western democracies and the newly moderate Comintern came when Spanish general Francisco Franco led his troops in revolt against the elected left-wing Spanish government in 1936. The Spanish Civil War pitted the pro-government republicans, along with liberals, socialists, and other leftists, against the rebels, led by Franco and supported by the church, landowners, and other conservatives. The western democracies refused to support the republicans and even harassed those volunteers – like English writer George Orwell and Americans in the Abraham Lincoln brigade – who wanted to contribute to the republican cause. Unlike the hesitant western powers, the German and Italian governments openly supported Franco. After some delay the USSR intervened in favor of the republicans, though this support in troops and materiel never matched that of Germany and Italy. The Soviet intervention in the Spanish Civil War was also marred by the activities of the NKVD (secret police) there against foreign anarchists and Trotskyists. With Franco's triumph in 1939, the Soviet intervention in Spain was discredited as divisive and ineffectual.[31]

Meanwhile Nazi Germany was going from strength to strength. In 1938 Hitler annexed Austria, the so-called *Anschluss*, and bullied British Prime Minister Chamberlain into the Munich Agreement, essentially forcing the Czechoslovak government – which was not consulted – to give up territory along its western borders. Forced to relinquish these border regions, the so-called Sudetenland with their sophisticated defenses, to Germany, Czechoslovakia found itself vulnerable to any German threat. By spring 1939 Czechoslovakia had been destroyed by the Nazis, with German troops occupying the western part of the country and the German puppet Slovakia set up in the east. The obvious next target for Hitler's aggression was Poland, and both France and Germany warned Hitler that any move on that country would mean war. But after so many empty warnings, why should Hitler believe this one?

The apparent unwillingness of the western powers to challenge Hitler made a deep impression on Stalin, whose character in any case tended toward paranoia. The inaction of Britain and France suggested that they wished Hitler to gain strength in order to turn on the USSR. The deep suspicion that Stalin felt toward the western powers, in particular Britain, made any mutual agreement against Hitler exceedingly difficult. And, to be fair, it must be admitted Britain and France would have been very glad to see Hitler and Stalin destroy each other. The western leaders could not conceive of an agreement between the two dictators because of the profound ideological differences between them. Yet there were signs of a softening – at least in public rhetoric – of the hostility between Nazi Germany and the USSR. In April 1939 Hitler failed to denounce the USSR as usual in his annual foreign policy speech. The following month the pro-western (and Jewish) head of Soviet diplomacy, Maxim Litvinov, was replaced by Stalin's flunkie, Viacheslav Molotov. Unknown to the world, Molotov and the Nazi foreign minister, Joachim Ribbentrop, were negotiating a nonaggression pact, which was signed in Moscow on August 23, 1939.

The Molotov–Ribbentrop Pact can truly be called a "diplomatic bombshell." Now that Hitler no longer had to worry about Soviet reprisals in case of war with Poland, everyone recognized that a Nazi attack on that state was imminent. Secret protocols set down the division of Poland between Germany and the USSR, as well as delineating spheres of influence in the Baltic. This freed the USSR to demand Bessarabia back from Romania (see below) and, supplemented with a further agreement in September, allowed the USSR a free hand in the Baltic. In return the USSR agreed to pay Nazi Germany 31.5 million Reichsmarks in nonferrous metals and gold. For many, the Molotov–Ribbentrop Pact seemed an outrageous act of political cynicism. But leaving moral questions aside – we are, after all, considering two of the greatest mass murderers in history – Stalin's decision to ally the USSR with Germany can be seen as based on cool calculations. Stalin distrusted the western powers (especially Churchill) and was certain they hoped for a showdown that would destroy or severely weaken both Nazi Germany and the USSR. Stalin was well aware of Hitler's maniacal hatred for communism but the Soviet leader felt that given two or three more years to build up the army, the USSR could better hold off the Nazi onslaught.

The expected attack on Poland came on September 1, 1939. Despite courageous resistance, the Polish army crumpled under the massive air and land assault by the Wehrmacht. On September 17, after waiting cautiously to see how the western powers would react and to gauge the ability of the Poles to resist, the Red Army invaded Poland from the east. According to Soviet propaganda, this was a liberation, aiming to include oppressed Ukrainians and Belarusians in their respective Soviet republics. But few were misled, least of all the tens of thousands of Poles, Jews, and others, particularly of the middle-class, specifically targeted for NKVD arrest and exile to Siberia and central Asia.[32]

Stalin knew well that peace with Germany would not last forever, so he moved forward to secure the western border of the USSR as much as possible. After solidifying his hold over eastern Poland Stalin demanded that Finland withdraw its border to the west, which would have meant abandoning the carefully constructed defense line named after the Finnish head of state, Marshal Carl Mannerheim. When the Finns demurred the Red Army attacked in November 1939 and, despite their valiant resistance, the Finns were obliged to cede the demanded territory, including the city of Viipuri (Vyborg) to the USSR. In March 1940 it was Romania's turn to give up territory, this time the province of Bessarabia, which before 1914 had belonged to the Russian Empire. And in summer 1940 the three Baltic republics of Estonia, Latvia, and Lithuania were coerced into sham elections that brought communist majorities to power, which promptly petitioned for entrance into the USSR. All the time Stalin continued to deliver raw materials to Germany as agreed, though the Germans were not so quick to reciprocate and provide the USSR with manufactured goods.[33]

The defeat of France and the air attack on Britain made Stalin fear that he might soon be left alone to face Hitler. He knew very well that Hitler would turn on him as soon as he could, but hoped to use the time gained by the alliance with the Nazis to build defenses and prepare for war. By spring 1941 there were many indications that Hitler planned to attack that year, and yet Stalin persisted in seeing any intelligence suggesting an imminent attack as disinformation planted by the British. Even when a communist working in the German Embassy in Tokyo, Richard Sorge, provided microfilms showing that an attack was in the works, Stalin rejected the veracity of the information. While Stalin did allow his generals to prepare a plan for defense, he strictly forbade any further troop build-up or building of further defenses, not wanting to give the Germans any possible provocation for attack.[34]

The long-awaited attack came in the early morning hours of June 22, 1941, when the Wehrmacht and Luftwaffe smashed into the USSR in a coordinated mass attack along a front hundreds of miles long. The Red Army was caught by surprise, many aircraft were destroyed on the ground, and at first it appeared that the USSR would collapse under the shock of the attack. Within several weeks German troops had overrun most of the Belarusian and Ukrainian SSRs, and by

Figure 6.1   Iraklii Toidze, "The Motherland Calls!" 1941.
Source: Hoover Institution Archives.

September they were threatening Moscow and Leningrad. Upon receiving news of the attack on the USSR, Operation Barbarossa, Churchill pledged the aid of Britain and the two countries rapidly patched up relations. From Washington, Roosevelt watched nervously, unable to engage American troops because of strong isolationist sympathies, and extended lend-lease aid to the USSR. When the Japanese launched their surprise attack on the naval base at Pearl Harbor near Honolulu, Hitler inexplicably declared war on the USA, making the USA and USSR wartime allies.[35]

One of the most contentious issues among the wartime allies was Poland. The Polish government in exile in London, remembering Stalin's role in the destruction of their country as Hitler's ally, could hardly be enthusiastic about cooperation with the USSR. In any case, Stalin made rather clear that he regarded the USSR's 1940 western border – that is, after incorporating considerable Polish territory – to be beyond discussion. But under pressure from the British and recognizing the primary need to defeat Hitler, the London Poles maintained chilly but correct relations with the Soviet authorities. With their help, the thousands of Poles who had been captured as POWs or arrested after the Soviet invasion and transported to the interior of the USSR in 1939–41 were allowed to leave via Iran. Many of them participated in the war effort as part of General Anders's Polish army. And then in April 1943 retreating Nazi armies uncovered mass graves of thousands of Polish officers. The London Poles had long been frustrated by the inability or unwillingness of the Soviet authorities to explain the fate of many young officers who remained unaccounted for. They now realized that their worst suspicions had been realized. When they asked for a Red Cross investigation of the graves, the USSR angrily broke off relations and prepared to create its own Polish government. Though long denied in the USSR, it was well known at the time and now beyond any reasonable doubt that the thousands of Polish officers found buried at Katyń had been executed by the NKVD in the spring of 1940.[36]

Two allied conferences brought together the three main leaders of the anti-Hitler forces – Roosevelt, Churchill, and Stalin – and aimed to coordinate efforts between the three main warring powers and to set down the contours of the postwar world. At the first, held in Teheran in late 1943, the big three agreed to support the partisans led by Tito in Yugoslavia, promised the opening of a second front in western Europe (long an angry demand of Stalin), set the borders of Poland between the Oder-Neisse River in the west and the Curzon Line in the east, and pledged Soviet support for the war against Japan once Hitler had been defeated. Stalin's insistence on borders for Poland that amounted to moving the state some 150 miles westward did not bode well for the postwar period, but the allies were too concentrated on the immediate need to defeat Hitler to ponder overly much on the fate of the Poles. The formation of a United Nations organization after the war was also agreed upon at Teheran.

The second wartime conference was held in February 1945 at Yalta, on the Crimean Peninsula in the Black Sea. Holding the conference on Soviet territory was a triumph for Stalin, though hard on the ailing American president who had barely two months to live. At Yalta the Polish question was again raised, with Stalin insisting on the need for a friendly Polish state to prevent further German aggression on the USSR. In the end, the Curzon Line – roughly the 1940 Soviet western border – was agreed on as Poland's eastern frontier, with the Polish state receiving territory from Germany as compensation for those lands lost in the east. The powers agreed that an unconditional surrender would be demanded of Germany, which would be divided into occupation forces and obliged to undergo demilitarization and denazification measures. Stalin reaffirmed his commitment to attacking Japan within 90 days of war's end in Europe. At Yalta the Big Three further discussed the organization of the United Nations, whose founding conference would take place in San Francisco the following June.[37]

May 9, 1945, marked the end of World War II – known in the USSR as the "Great Fatherland War" – for the Soviets. The Soviet Union was among the victorious powers but lay in ruins. Between 20 and 30 million Soviet citizens had been killed, entire cities and regions laid waste by the Nazi soldiers, with the survivors hungry and in millions of cases without a roof over their heads. But the Soviet Union was now a world power, far more important on the world scene than the Russian Empire had ever been. Two world powers emerged from World War II – the USA and the USSR. As soon as the surrender agreement had been signed with Nazi Germany, Roosevelt's successor as US president, Harry Truman, stopped lend-lease shipments to the USSR. The mutual suspicions between Stalin and the western powers quickly came out into the open. Despite the immense respect and prestige the USSR had gained for its role in defeating Germany, Stalin continued to see his country as surrounded and threatened by the capitalist world. The use by the Americans of a new, frightful weapon – the atomic bomb – against two Japanese cities did nothing to reassure Stalin.[38] Thus the world went from war to "Cold War" almost without pausing.

Conclusions

Throughout its history, Russia has felt itself to be both European and "not-quite-European." On the edge of the European continent and stretching nearly halfway round the world, Russia was a unique European and world power. While most of the Russian Empire and USSR's territory lay to the east of the Ural Mountains in Asia, the great bulk of the population and the capital city were located in Europe. More importantly Russian culture and identity had grown up in close contact with Europe, while Asia, either in the form of the Ottoman Empire or

China, were distant and exotic places from the perspective of St Petersburg or Moscow. Even after 1917, when Moscow proclaimed itself the center for a new socialist world, Soviet foreign policy was much more concerned with Europe than with the rest of the world.

From the acceptance of Christianity in its eastern rite in the late ninth century, Russian identity has always been associated with Europe. This does not mean, however, that Russians always felt themselves entirely comfortable with that association. From Peter the Great onward, even highly cultured Russians often felt a sense of inferiority – or at least a lack of proper respect – vis-à-vis European culture. The Slavophile versus Westerner controversy from the early nineteenth century onward reflected differing understandings of this European connection. Should Russia, as the Slavophiles argued, reject western models and embrace a pre-Petrine, religious model for future development? Or, following the Westerners, did Russia have to go through the same economic and political developments as the rest of Europe? Even under communist rule, while ostensibly following an internationalist ideology, the conflict between Trotsky's internationalist "permanent revolution" and Stalin's "revolution in one country" retained echoes of the westerner versus slavophile debates.

In foreign policy, too, Russia was a unique European power. Expanding in central Asia in the last decades of the nineteenth century, it strayed close to Britain's perceived sphere of interest north of British India. Expanding its commercial interests into Manchuria and Korea around the turn of the century, Russia offended Japan and helped spark the humiliating Russo-Japanese War of 1904–5. And despite these Asian entanglements, Russia always perceived its primary interests on the European continent and in particular in relation to the growing threat of Germany. Two wars with Germany would destroy the tsarist order and come close to toppling Stalin. But in the end the victory over Hitler lent Stalin and Soviet communism a legitimacy and prestige in the world they had never before attained. In 1945 Soviet citizens could truly feel that the USSR had outgrown any kind of inferiority complex toward the European west and that it was time for the West to learn from Moscow.

Chapter 7

Culture

The term "culture" refers to a wide variety of phenomena from education to folklore to literature to scientific research to music and the visual arts. Obviously no comprehensive coverage of Russian or Soviet culture could be made in a single book, much less a textbook chapter. Here my aim is more modest: to provide an outline to some of the most important, influential, or innovative aspects of Russian culture from the mid-nineteenth to the mid-twentieth century. In the decades before World War I, Russian culture – in particular novels and music – became far better known in the west than ever before. Within Russia, culture very frequently had a political or ideological function: in an autocracy where political discussion was severely circumscribed, a poem, novel, or painting could indirectly criticize the existing order.

After the revolution the political function of art would be harnessed to the glorification of the Soviet Union, but at least initially and in many ways through the 1920s, Soviet artists and writers engaged in a number of fascinating cultural experiments. In the 1930s the experimental side of Soviet culture almost disappeared and was replaced by often heavy-handed and formulaic propaganda. At the same time advances in literacy under Soviet rule meant that more and more people could take part, if passively, in Soviet cultural life. Popular culture like film and song both educated and entertained and, especially during World War II, played an important political and patriotic role.

─────── Tsarist Education: Strengths and Weaknesses ───────

Even in modern democratic societies, the role of the school is much debated: should it aim to form sober, industrious, patriotic citizens or free-thinking, critical individuals? In imperial Russia there was no question – from the government's point of view, at least – of schools *aiming* to create free thinkers, and yet Russian officialdom harbored profound suspicions that education almost inevitably led in that direction, away from a loyal, religious worldview and toward atheism and nihilism. It had been, after all, a former university student who in 1866 attempted to assassinate Tsar Alexander II, and from the 1860s onward students were nearly always prominent among radicals and socialists. At the same time a modern state requires general literacy and ever-increasing numbers of highly trained specialists. As usual, the needs of modernity clashed with Russia's old regime, patriarchal society. Another important problem for Russian education was the Russian Empire's chronic lack of funds. While funding for education rose steeply between 1863 and 1914, even at the end of the imperial period not all Russian children attended school and illiteracy continued to be widespread.[1] Among non-Russians, with the exception of a few groups like Jews, Germans, and Baltic peoples, illiteracy was even higher.

Three separate school systems taught literacy and simple mathematics, mainly to peasant children. These were run by the Ministry of Education ("Ministry of People's Enlightenment," to use the sonorous Russian phrase), the Orthodox church (Holy Synod), and local *zemstva*. By the early twentieth century, there were over 80,000 elementary schools, nearly four times the number of 20 years before. Of these, the largest single number were parish schools run by the Holy Synod, but the *zemstva* schools were better funded. A typical one-class peasant school taught religion, Russian, calligraphy, arithmetic, and singing. In cities pupils might also learn geography, history, geography, and drawing. The course at a primary school was generally three years, though by the early twentieth century many primary schools offered an extra, fourth, year, recognizing the utility of further learning. Between 1860 and 1913 the number of pupils in elementary schools rose by a factor of 16 (from 600,000 to nearly 10 million). Of these, over nine million were studying in elementary schools (grades 1–4) while a total of 127,400 students were enrolled in higher education of all types. As more Russians attended school, even if only for two or three years, literacy rates rose. In 1897 only 21 percent of all Russians were literate, but urban males had a literacy rate almost three times as high (56 percent), while rural women were very unlikely in 1897 to be able to read or write (10 percent literacy rate).[2]

The Russian government's attitude toward education paralleled its overall conflicted feelings about modernizing: while recognizing the necessity of education for economic development, Russian officials were uneasy about the social and political impact that a more educated populace might have. The government's uneasiness with education may be seen in the so-called Tolstoy system, named after the notoriously reactionary minister of education under Tsar Alexander II (1866–80), Dmitry Tolstoy. Tolstoy worked to expand education in Russia, but only under careful bureaucratic supervision. In particular he insisted that secondary education be dominated by classical gymnasia where the study of ancient languages (Greek and Latin) formed a major part of the curriculum. Requiring these languages as a prerequisite for university study meant that less-privileged Russians and in particular peasants had almost no chance of being admitted to higher education. Progressive Russians argued that the classical gymnasium was a German import that would only stymie Russia's modern development. Not Greek or Latin, they argued, but history, science, and mathematics were needed for the younger generation. Of course Tolstoy's system was precisely aimed against the study of natural science that was seen as encouraging a materialistic, atheist worldview.[3] Though Tolstoy retired as minister of education in 1880, his elitist and antimodern conception of education was revived with a vengeance under Tsar Alexander III. The best expression of this desire to prevent education from encouraging social mobility was found in an 1887 circular which stated that "children of drivers, footmen, cooks, laundrymen, [and] small traders" should be specifically denied entrance to secondary education.[4] And indeed, secondary education was dominated by the children of nobles, clergy, and officials. In 1897 only one peasant in a thousand attended secondary school; a peasant studying at a university was even rarer.

In the decades after serf emancipation, as Ben Eklof and other specialists have shown, peasants showed a growing interest in getting an education for their children. The practical utility of literacy and a basic knowledge of arithmetic was appreciated by peasant parents. At the same time many peasant children did not finish the "full" three-year course or even enroll in the first place. A survey taken in Nizhny Novgorod district in 1909 to find out reasons for the nonenrollment of children cited among the most important reasons poverty, the lack of warm clothing, the need to keep care of younger siblings, the distance of school from home, and negative parental attitudes. By the early twentieth century most children did attend school for some period of time, but even in 1911 only about 10 percent of peasant children completed the entire three-year course. Apparently once the rudiments of literacy and arithmetic had been learned, many parents saw no further need to persist in education.[5]

Schoolteachers were ill paid and often without adequate preparation. Even in schools funded by the *zemstva*, teachers and curricula were subject to surveillance and petty harassment by the local authorities. The combination of poor pay and general lack of respect caused many to regard teaching as a stopgap profession, to be abandoned when a better opportunity arose. For this reason teachers tended to be very young: in rural schools, the majority of teachers were under 30 and barely 10 percent over 40 years of age. The teacher in a rural school, often young and female, was often a lonely individual unable to marry for lack of funds and longing for a chance to escape the countryside for the city.

Even in the cities teachers were ill paid and lacked social prestige, but there at least they had more possibilities for banding together to demand more respect and better working conditions for their profession.[6] The need for a more sophisticated level of literacy meant that schools were better developed in urban areas. Townspeople were also more likely to have more education themselves and to push their children toward secondary and even higher education. With few exceptions, the secondary schools in the Russian Empire were located in towns. At century's end, when the number of elementary schools was approaching 100,000, secondary schools could be counted in the hundreds: in 1899 there were 191 classical gymnasia, 53 pro-gymnasia, and 115 "real" schools with a more practical, science-based curriculum. In general, entrance to a university was limited to graduates of the classical gymnasia, but in some cases others could be admitted after passing a strict exam.

So far we have spoken only of Russian education: but what about the half of the empire's population that spoke other languages? Starting at the top, in 1863 there were three non-Russian universities in the empire, in Helsinki, Dorpat (today's Tartu, in Estonia), and Warsaw. By 1890 the Warsaw "Main School" (*Szkoła Główna*) had been turned into a Russian and Russifying university, the erstwhile German university in Dorpat had been Russified and renamed Iurev, and only the University of Helsinki continued to offer a university course in a language other than Russian (at that point mainly in Swedish). In Muslim regions local school systems teaching Arabic and religious subjects were tolerated, including higher schools like medrasas. Similarly most Jewish boys learned to read (in the Hebrew script) in *hedarim* (sing. *heyder*) under the supervision of *melamdim* who, like Isaac Bashevis Singer's father in pre-1914 Warsaw, often knew no non-Jewish languages. Laws requiring Jewish teachers (*melamdim*) to know and teach Russian were widely circumvented. At the same time, however, increasing numbers of Jews were successfully entering the Russian-language school system despite government quotas from the 1880s to limit their numbers in gymnasia and higher education.

In the Baltic provinces by the end of the nineteenth century, Latvian and Estonian children could learn to read in their native languages in privately financed elementary schools. Lithuanian literacy, on the other hand, could not be taught legally because until 1903 the government demanded that the language be printed in Cyrillic letters, a demand that literate Lithuanians, many of them Catholic priests, firmly rejected. Thus Lithuanian literacy had to be taught illegally, if at all. Similarly hundreds and perhaps even thousands of "secret schools" taught children to read in Polish despite the threat of arrest and fines. Finally Ukrainian and Belarusian children could receive education if at all only in the Russian language as the central government continued to insist that their native tongues were only dialects of Russian.

A Society in Upheaval?
Russian Culture in the Late Nineteenth Century

In nineteenth-century Russia literature was more than entertainment – it provided Russian society with figures that became almost as real as actual human beings, showed modes of behavior to be emulated or avoided, and provided the outside world – through translations – with a window onto Russia. Modern Russian literature started with Alexander Pushkin (1799–1837), but his poetry never broke through the translation barrier to become well known in other languages. The surreal world of Nikolai Gogol (1809–52), with clocks striking 13, noses detaching themselves from their owners and making brilliant careers, and featuring amusing scoundrels of various stripes, was more successful – though mainly after the writer's death – in becoming part of world literature. The phrase "dead souls" from Gogol's eponymous novel has entered a number of languages to mean nonexistent people who show up on bills, reports, and statements – to earn some trickster money, of course. But it was only in the 1860s that the Russian novel really hit its stride, in particular with the "big three" Russian novelists: Ivan Turgenev (1818–83), Fyodor Dostoevsky (1821–81), and Lev Tolstoy (1828–1910). To these three we must add a fourth novelist, less known outside Russia, but possibly the most influential of them all within Russian society with his novel *What Is to Be Done?* (1863), Nikolai Chernyshevsky (1828–89).

Without a parliament and with strict censorship, fiction gave Russians one way to read about and discuss current political topics. While fictional works, too, could be rejected by the censors, it was far safer to put political ideas in the mouth of a fictional character than to advocate them on one's own. The first of the great Russian novels of the 1860s and 1870s was Turgenev's *Fathers and Sons*, which was first published in 1862, immediately after the emancipation law. The novel contrasts the younger generation of college friends Evgeny Bazarov and Arkady Kirsanov with the latter's father and Uncle Pavel. The clash between generations is not between conservative and liberal, but between liberal gentlemen of the old generation and young radicals exemplified by the ultrascientific and, we suspect, atheistic Bazarov. Since the novel's first publication, controversy has ranged over whether the humorless but hardworking and dedicated Bazarov was meant as a positive or negative character. Certainly for the older generation – exemplified by the exquisitely dressed and coiffed Uncle Pavel – Bazarov represented all that was wrong with youth: sneering, disrespectful, in short, a "nihilist." The word "nihilist," based on the Latin *nihil* (meaning "nothing") and referring to individuals who disdained traditional beliefs and advocated radical politics, was popularized in Russian and other languages by this novel. Bazarov rejects tradition, good manners, even music (mocking Arkady's father for his love for the cello), but it would not be correct to say that he believes in nothing. Bazarov believes in science: throughout the novel he constantly observes nature, dissects frogs, and carries out medical experiments. He wishes to be a doctor, which indicates some kind of social commitment. And while conservatives and modern liberals like Uncle Pavel may have found him repulsive, thousands of young radicals admired his scientific outlook and lack of sentimentality.

If Bazarov, the archetypical "nihilist," provided young radicals with a positive role model, Chernyshevsky's 1863 novel, *What Is to Be Done?*, set down an entire program of action. It is difficult for present-day readers to appreciate the impact of this novel with its flat characters, ridiculous scenes (as when the heroine jumps out of a window to flee her parents' repressive house, landing in the waiting arms of a chivalrous male comrade), and absurdly convoluted plot. But Russian readers were entranced by the novel, including one Vladimir Ulianov, later Lenin, who would give one of his most important political pamphlets the same title. The publication of Chernyshevsky's *What Is to Be Done?* was due to the incompetence of the censorship authorities, almost literally a case of its "falling through the cracks," when two censors each believed the other had rejected the manuscript. Once published, the novel was a huge success but was almost immediately banned, the censors punished, and Chernyshevsky arrested and sent to Siberia. The author, one of the most attractive personalities among major figures of Russian culture, lived out the rest of his life in exile, being allowed to return to Astrakhan on the Volga River only in 1883 and returning to his native Saratov only to die.[7]

What Is to Be Done? bore the subtitle "Stories about new people." Its main character, Vera Pavlovna, escapes her parents' narrow-minded petit-bourgeois household with the help of a male comrade, Lopukhov, with whom she enters into a fictitious (and never consummated) marriage to avoid problems with the police, and sets about rescuing prostitutes and other impoverished women by setting up a sewing collective. Lopukhov predictably falls in love with Vera but gallantly (or comradely) refuses to press himself on her when he realizes that she loves another. Lopukhov then disappears, to reappear later in the novel after a long stay in America (for the purposes of the novel, a modern and progressive place). For all its unlikely plot, improbable personages (among them the ultraradical Rakhmetev, who sleeps on a bed of nails to toughen himself), and unbelievable coincidences, the novel gave many young and idealistic Russians a model for action and the hope that dedicated individuals could change the world for the better.

One contemporary who was not impressed by Chernyshevsky's novel was Fyodor Dostoevsky. Exiled to Siberia for participating in a radical group, Dostoevsky returned to St Petersburg in 1859 as a Christian and conservative. For Dostoevsky, Chernyshevsky's novel, like all utopian schemes, fundamentally contradicted human nature by depriving humanity of freedom. Dostoevsky's counterargument to *What Is to Be Done?*, *Notes from the Underground* (1864), features a bilious and rather ridiculous narrator who admits his own human foibles but insists that he would rather suffer on his own terms than become a mindless automaton in the "Crystal Palace" of modernity. Contemporary readers would have recognized the Crystal Palace from Chernyshevsky's novel, where in a dream Vera Pavlovna visits the structure outside London. For her, the Crystal Palace symbolizes a progressive and modern world, but for Dostoevsky the building was part of an industrialized world where free will and human feelings had been blotted out by an impersonal and all-knowing state. Ten years later, Dostoevsky was to further develop his loathing for utopian schemes and the radicals who proposed them in his novel *The Demons* (earlier translated as *The Possessed*).

Turgenev was a westernizing liberal, Dostoevsky a slavophilic conservative, but Lev Tolstoy's politics played – until the end of his life – a much smaller role in his art. Rather Tolstoy's major novels *War and Peace* and *Anna Karenina* are far more interested in exploring human relationships both in society and between the sexes. *War and Peace*, written in the 1860s and first published (like most of the novels discussed here) in serial form, portrays Russian society (the Russian word *mir* means both "high society" and "peace") during the Napoleonic War. In the novel Tolstoy's characters, most of them belonging to aristocratic society, come to feel their identity as Russians amidst the struggle against the French invader in 1812. The novel vividly combines actual historical events (the Battle of Borodino, burning of Moscow, etc.) with Tolstoy's memorable fictional heroes Pierre Bezukhov and Andrei Bolkonsky. The novel ends with a long "second epilogue" in which Tolstoy develops his theory of historical causation, trying to document how freedom and necessity play off one another in historical events.

Anna Karenina, though nearly as long as *War and Peace*, has a much narrower focus. Its initial line has become proverbial: "Happy families are all alike; every unhappy family is unhappy in its own way." In the novel, the happy family grows out of the love between Kitty Shcherbatskaya and Konstantin Levin, the unhappy one is of course Anna's own. Anna's attempt to escape a miserable home life and frigid husband through a love affair with a dashing young officer, Count Vronsky, ends up destroying everyone involved. In the novel, Tolstoy grapples with the fundamental issues of love and sexual attraction, laying bare the hypocrisy of his own society where men's infidelities were tolerated, even expected, but a "fallen woman" was cast out of society entirely. Later Tolstoy was to develop the topic further in a total condemnation of all sexual attraction and relations in the novella *Kreutzer Sonata* (1889).

As he aged, Tolstoy's commitment to social justice intensified and he even dared challenge the government directly, as in his "I cannot remain silent" essay published in 1908. Not only did Tolstoy label the government as repressive and cruel; he even suggested that the Orthodox Church had failed to play its part in working for reconciliation. Tolstoy's disagreements with the church had already led to his excommunication in 1901. But Tolstoy was not a consistent political or philosophical thinker. He advocated a mixture of pacifism, asceticism (no sex!), and anti-industrial, antimodern rhetoric. He was deadly accurate in his criticism of careerism and the superficial strivings that take up much of human life, as in "The Death of Ivan Ilych" (1886) where the title character, a successful jurist and judge, recognizes too late the emptiness of his own life, and screams for days in a death agony before finally reconciling himself to the inevitable and expiring. When the great writer died in 1910, not just Russia but the world mourned him.[8]

Born more than three decades after Dostoevsky and Tolstoy, Anton Chekhov (1860–1904) differed from the great novelists in his social origins, education, and approach to literature. Chekhov could rightly claim to be a son of the people, as his father had been born into serfdom. His initial forays into literature were taken to help earn money while a medical student, and later Chekhov famously quipped, "Medicine is my lawful wife, and literature is my mistress." It is indicative of Chekhov's modest character that he never published a novel, but excelled in the dramatic genre and short stories. Unlike Tolstoy and Dostoevsky, Chekhov is never exalted and priestlike. Rather his works are full of modest people, unfulfilled dreams, and the sadness of individuals living in a world they can neither quite grasp nor change. His famous story "The Lady with the Little Dog" (1899; the Russian title has only two words: "Dama s sobachkei") portrays a couple who find true love with each other while remaining locked in unhappy marriages. The play *The Cherry Orchard* (1904) tells the story of a Russian aristocrat who, unable to adjust to post-reform economic realities, is forced to sell her estate, including its beloved cherry orchard, to a former serf. Chekhov's characters often seem unable to deal with the rapid pace of modern life, while longing for change and fulfillment, they lack the drive or ruthlessness to reach their goals. But for all their weakness and passivity, the people who fill Chekhov's stories and plays are instantly recognizable as the human beings we encounter every day – or when looking in the mirror.[9]

Literature was not only a major part of Russian culture; it also formed the way Russians thought about themselves. For educated Russians, Anna Karenina, Bazarov, or Nina Pavlovna were every bit as real as people they knew in everyday life. Literature provided a model (or, in the example of Anna Karenina, anti-model) for behavior in society; it also let Russians indirectly discuss the burning political and moral issues of the day. Writing and reading were not just pastimes or aesthetic pursuits: they were deeply moral and political actions. This strong connection in Russian culture between literature and sociopolitical commitment before the revolution in many ways paved the way for the much narrower and more propagandistic socialist realism that would be declared as the only proper form of literature in the USSR from the early 1930s.

Like literature, Russian music also "took Europe by storm" in the second half of the nineteenth century. The coming together of five young musicians just before the Great Reforms did much to revolutionize Russian symphonic music. The Five, or the "Mighty Handful" (*Moguchaia kuchka*), as they came to be known – Mily Balakirev, César Cui, Modest Mussorgsky, Alexander Borodin, and Nikolai Rimsky-Korsakov – none formally trained as musicians, were united in their desire to create a new kind of Russian music, based on native tunes and traditions. The native component can be seen in some of their most famous pieces' titles, like "The Great Gate of Kiev" and "The Hut on Chicken Legs" (referring to the dwelling of the witch Baba-Yaga from Russian folklore) in Mussorgsky's "Pictures at an Exhibition" (1874) and Borodin's "On the Steppes of Central Asia" (1880). The slightly younger Pyotr Tchaikovsky went even further in incorporating Russian elements and Russian history in his music, most famously in the opera version of Pushkin's *Eugene Onegin* (1879) and in the 1812 Overture (1882). By the early twentieth century Russian music, composers, and musicians were increasingly well known in the European musical scene. Indeed the first perform-ance of Igor Stravinsky's "Rites of Spring" (1913) not only took place in Paris – almost causing a riot as fights broke out between supporters and detractors – but the work much more frequently goes by its French title ("Le Sacre du printemps") than the original Russian. By the eve of World War I, in music as in literature, Russian culture was well integrated with the rest of Europe.[10]

Science and Technology

Late nineteenth-century Europe, at least its growing middle classes, was in love with science. As we have seen, in Russia too young people especially were attracted by materialist philosophies – it was not by chance that Arkady Kirsanov in *Fathers and Sons* replaced the novel his father was reading with Ludwig Büchner's mate-rialist classic *Kraft und Stoff* (Force and Matter). The attraction of Marxism for young Russians was also a reflection of their desire to apply scientific methods to burning social and political problems of the age.

Russian science had boasted distinguished specialists, usually working in the various imperial universities, already before the 1860s. But both the number and the quality of Russian science would improve markedly from the Reform Era onward. For one thing, more Russians were studying science and technology. Rather like the shock of Sputnik for Americans in 1957, the defeat in the Crimean War was attributed in part to the failure of Russian science. Conservatives tended to view natural science with suspicion; it was radicals like Chernyshevsky, Nikolai Dobroliubov, and Dmitry Pisarev who embraced it wholeheartedly. Still, the government recognized that a modern state needed trained scientists, so grudgingly allowed the universities more autonomy under the reformist University Statute of 1863. One aspect of the new statute had a direct impact on science education. Previously those studying natural sciences enrolled in a university's Faculty of Physics and Mathematics and gained a broad, but superficial, knowledge of a variety of branches of science. Under the new university statute, specialized departments of mathematics, physics, chemistry, biology, and so on, were set up. Thus students majoring in physics, for example, would not have to complete courses and exams on botany. Special fellowships were set up to pay for promising young scientists to complete their studies (essentially to do their doctorates) in Germany and other European countries. Again, conservatives grumbled about the political risk of exposing young people to western ideas, but the practical need for trained specialists and university professors of science in Russia overwhelmed such concerns.

One of the most popular fields of study at nineteenth-century Russian universities was medicine. Physicians saw themselves not just as healers but – like Bazarov – as scientists, vitally interested in increasing their knowledge of how human and animal physiology functions in order to better serve their patients and their fatherland. While women were not allowed to study at Russian universities, special parallel courses were set up for them in 1869, and three years later Professor V. I. Guerrier of Moscow University was allowed to open a special university-level program known as the Higher Courses for Women. Natural sciences and mathematics played an important part in the courses' curriculum, and many young women were inspired to become medical doctors. Soon special medical courses were opened for women – first at the Medical and Surgical Academy in 1872 – and many young Russian women went abroad, especially to France and Switzerland, to obtain their medical degrees.[11]

When Dmitry Tolstoy became minister of education in 1866 he both reduced university autonomy and deemphasized the role of science in the curriculum. His policies aimed to reduce the number of lower-class students at universities but ended up failing, in great part because neither professors nor the students as a whole supported such elitism. Most students were not wealthy; in the 1870s between two-thirds and three-quarters of students at Odessa, Kazan, and Kiev universities needed financial assistance. Ironically Tolstoy's attempts to squeeze out less well-off students may have had the effect of strengthening student solidarity as richer students pooled resources with their poorer colleagues, shared books, and generally created a student identity that was fundamentally progressive, scientific, and antigovernment.[12]

Research and learning did not take place only in the universities. Since the early eighteenth century the St Petersburg Academy of Sciences had sponsored research in various fields including astronomy, anthropology, mathematics, and geology. And "science" (*nauka*) in Russian meant not only natural sciences but also the study of history and literature. The Academy of Sciences also published scholarly journals and sponsored research, textbooks, and celebrations such as the centennial of the death of Russian scientist, poet, and historian Mikhail Lomonosov in 1865. There were also private organizations like the Society of Admirers of Natural Science, Anthropology, and Ethnography, founded in 1864 in Moscow, the Moscow Mathematical Society, and the so-called Free Economic Society, which in particular supported research to improve the quality of Russian agricultural efficiency, such as A. M. Butlerov's extremely popular book on apiculture (*Bees: Their Life and the Basic Rules of Rational Apiculture*). The Russian Geographic Society had existed since 1846 and sponsored a number of geographic, ethnological, and historical expeditions and research. One of its most energetic members N. M. Przhevalsky (properly Mikołaj Przewalski, as he was born in a Polish family) undertook expeditions to central and eastern Asia, even reaching the outskirts of Tibet. His name is known to zoologists and horse-lovers who know that "Przewalski's horse" (*equus przewalski*), inhabiting Mongolia and central Asia, is the only living wild (as opposed to feral, like mustangs in the American west) horse.

Several scientists born in the nineteenth-century Russian Empire achieved world fame and are still well known, even outside scientific circles. Perhaps the single most famous of all is chemist Dmitry Mendeleev (1834–1907), author of the Periodic Table of the Chemical Elements. Mendeleev was born into a poor family, either the fourteenth or seventeenth child according to different sources. Like many other Russian students, Mendeleev was of the clerical *soslovie*: his grandfather had been a priest and his father had studied at a theological academy. Mendeleev's career as a scientist almost exactly parallels the fortunes of post-reform Russia; having studied in St Petersburg and Heidelberg in the 1850s, he became the first professor of chemistry at St Petersburg's Technological Institute in 1862 (and gained the same title at St Petersburg University the following year). Already in 1869 he proposed what would come to be known as "Mendeleev's Law," arguing for recurring ("periodic") characteristics (inertness, volatility, etc.) according to molecular weight. He would spend the rest of his life expanding on this insight and working on his Periodic Table of the Chemical Elements, which may be seen in any chemistry classroom around the world.

On a practical level, in 1893 Mendeleev became Director of the Bureau of Weights and Measures and worked on new standards for manufacturing vodka (the Russian government would introduce a state monopoly on distilling and selling the beverage in 1894). Throughout his life Mendeleev combined research in pure science with an interest in applying scientific knowledge to practical problems, while also participating in educational efforts and urging better material conditions for young Russian scientists. On a political or philosophical level Mendeleev rejected the most extreme theses of the "nihilists," insisting that religion and science were compatible and that science in no way threatened Russian traditions, whether cultural or religious. In the end Mendeleev was a cautious westerner, still very Russian with his impressive beard and Orthodox religious beliefs, but recognizing that in order to be strong and prosperous, Russia needed to participate in the scientific culture of Europe and the world.[13]

Two Russian scientists received the Nobel prize before 1914, in both cases for Physiology-Medicine. Microbiologist Ilya Mechnikov (1845–1916) was awarded the prize in 1908 for his work on the human immune system and methods of immunization against disease. Even more famous a century later is physiologist and psychologist Ivan Pavlov (1849–1936), whose work on conditioned reflexes gave us "Pavlov's dog." He demonstrated that dogs conditioned to expect food at the ringing of a bell began to salivate upon hearing the bell, even in the absence of food. Pavlov had a long and rich life. Born more than a decade before the serf emancipation in the provincial city of Riazan, he began his higher education – typically for a boy of the clerical *soslovie* – at Riazan Ecclesiastical Seminary, but in 1870 transferred to the University of St Petersburg. Pavlov's career did not take off at once; after completing his doctoral degree in 1883 he spent two years in postdoctoral research in Germany (Breslau and Leipzig). He then applied unsuccessfully for positions at universities in St Petersburg and Siberian Tomsk in 1889–90 before being selected in 1890 to organize and run the new Institute of Experimental Medicine in the capital. He would remain there until his death nearly 50 years later. Pavlov published widely, both in physiology (his *Lectures on the Work of Digestive Glands*, 1897, won him the Nobel prize in 1904) and in pharmacology. When the revolution came in 1917 Pavlov was already an elderly figure of world renown. He was one of the few famous scientists to remain in Russia under Soviet rule, continuing his research and courageously defending acquaintances who had been arrested in the dark period after Sergei Kirov's assassination in 1934. His laboratory in St Petersburg became a museum after his death.

Another world-class scientist from the Russian Empire who deserves mention is Maria Skłodowska (1867–1934), better known by her married name, Marie Curie. Skłodowska was born in Warsaw in the immediate aftermath of the failed Polish insurrection of 1863. As a girl she helped other children learn to read Polish, an action punishable by prison at the time. Unable to pursue studies beyond a secondary level in the Russian Empire, like many other ambitious young women Maria traveled to Paris to continue her education (her sister Bronisława was already there studying medicine). There she met her future husband and research partner, Pierre Curie, and together with him made important discoveries on the nature of radioactivity. While she lived out the rest of her life in France, she never lost her attachment to her native Poland, even naming the first new chemical element she discovered "polonium." She and Pierre shared an initial Nobel prize (in physics) in 1903. After his death Marie was honored as the first person to receive a second Nobel prize (in chemistry) in 1911.[14]

The development of the modern and scientific study of history is also a phenomenon of the later nineteenth century. In Russia scientific history began with Sergei Soloviev (1820–79), whose indefatigable labors in the archives produced the immense and even today useful *History of Russia from Ancient Times* in 29 volumes. Soloviev's student at Moscow University, Vasily Kliuchevsky (1841–1911), continued the master's work while shifting the emphasis from political and institutional history toward geographical and economic factors, as in his study of the historical process of deforestation in Russia. His lectures at Moscow University were immensely popular, requiring the largest lecture halls to hold auditors, many of whom were not even students. Like most Russian scholars, he was a liberal in his political sentiments, joining the Kadet party after 1905.[15]

Historical studies were not just popular among ethnic Russians. With the world's largest Jewish community in 1900, the Russian Empire also witnessed a blossoming of Jewish history. These Jewish historians, building on German-Jewish models, collected materials and wrote – in Russian, Yiddish, even Hebrew – on their people's past in the Russian Empire. Because Jewish history was not taught in Russian universities, most of these scholars had to eke out a living as teachers or writers. The most famous among them, Simon Dubnov (1860–1941), published an immense variety of studies on Jewish national identity and the role of Jews in Russian history. He wrote in both Russian and Yiddish, and his *History of the Jewish People* (in 10 volumes) was translated into a number of languages, including English. Dubnov was also active in Jewish politics, arguing for "autonomy"; that is, the maintenance of Jewish culture, languages, and traditions (though not necessarily religious orthodoxy; he was himself not a believer) while participating in all aspects of the host country's economic, political, and cultural life. As a middle-class liberal, he viewed the Bolshevik revolution as a tragedy, and left Russia in 1922. The last 20 years of his life were spent in Germany and Latvia, where he was murdered in 1941 by a Latvian militiaman while being herded into a ghetto outside Riga.[16]

Russian scholarship and science, for all the repressions of state policy and censorship, were rich and growing in the half-century after the emancipation of the serfs. In science, technology, and the humanities, Russian institutions and their scholars were recognized as among the best in the world. At the same time most poor and illiterate Russians had no capability to know or appreciate these great scholars. But less exalted aspects of modernity were beginning to reach peasant Russia, too. It is to these forms of popular culture that we turn next.

Peasant Culture Becoming Mass Culture: Liubok, Chapbooks, Press

In 1863 the vast majority of Russian peasants were illiterate, but 50 years later chances were better than even that a young male peasant would be capable of reading at least simple texts. Technological improvements in printing, paper-making, and lithography enabled savvy businessmen to tap into the broad peasant market for cultural goods. Pedlars brought in their packs books (usually easy-to-read adventure stories or tracts on religious subjects), pictures to adorn peasant huts, and other such cultural goods. While more sophisticated people scorned the lurid colors of the pictures and the crude plots of the books, for many provincial people these were real cultural advances.

One of the most widespread genres of popular reading was the so-called *lubok* (pl. *lubki*). Strictly speaking, the *lubok* was an illustration, originally printed from wood blocks or copper plates. With the coming of lithography to Russia in the first half of the nineteenth century, it became possible to mass-produce these images, which often had some kind of caption, a kind of early cartoon. From the 1860s, the *lubok* developed into a small illustrated pamphlet or book, sometimes retelling a religious story or saint's life, but increasingly on a secular theme. According to cultural historian Jeffrey Brooks, four categories of stories domi-nated in the majority of *lubki*: "folklore, chivalrous tales, instructive works, and tales about merchants."[17] Among the titles of turn-of-the-century Russian chap-books discussed by Brooks are *The Lion Who Raised the Tsar's Son*, *The Story of Frantsyl Ventsian and the Beautiful Queen Rentsyvena*, *The Glorious Knight Antipka*. *A Humorous Story from Village Life*, and *Anecdotes and Legends about Peter the Great*. The stories could be based at least in part on legends about tsars and their family, or simply indulged in exoticism, as in the story of Frantsyl and Rentsyvena, whose cover showed a turbaned and mustachioed gentleman kissing a dark-haired beauty. Humor also played a part in these stories as in *The Glorious Knight Antipka*, the joke being that Antipka is a typical peasant woman's name. The nature of the knight's exploits is hinted at by the cover showing a peasant woman beating a supine man with a hefty rod.

Nationalism and national identity were also reflected in these popular works. By reading in Russian, peasants were participating in a community larger than their village, the first step towards perceiving themselves as part of a larger nation. In the chapbooks, Russian identity could take a number of forms. For example, in *Yapancha, the Tatar Horseman*, when the Muslim hero is defeated by Ivan the Terrible, he swears allegiance to the tsar, converts to Orthodoxy, and becomes a Russian. But native Russians could also be faced with the loss of their national identity at the hands of pernicious foreigners, as in *A Prisoner of the Turks* or *Slavery Among the Asiatics*. And national minorities living in the Russian Empire also made appearances in these books, from the exotic (though vicious) Turkmen in *Slavery Among the Asiatics* to Gypsies (Sinti and Roma) in a number of tales, to Cossacks and Jews. In general, as one might expect, Russian heroes tended to be contrasted with shifty and dangerous non-Russians.

In some ways popular culture or "folk art" was adopted into or merged with "high culture" in late nineteenth-century Russia. This was part of a larger trend in Europe and North America in which separate elite and popular cultures came together – at least to some extent – in a modern mass culture. For example, there was an increasingly large market for traditional handcrafted wooden toys and furniture. Artists like Mikhail Larionov, Kazimir Malevich, and Nataliia Goncharova adopted simple peasant styles in their visual art. Composers like Tchaikovsky and Igor Stravinsky took peasant tunes as inspiration for their symphonies. Various kinds of decorative arts, from painted wooden spoons to lacquer boxes (most famously painted in the village of Palekh), became widely distributed not only in peasant homes but in those of the middle and upper classes. Perhaps the most famous symbol of Russia, the nesting Matryoshka doll, while using peasant motifs, was actually a product of the industrial age, first appearing in the 1890s, possibly inspired by Japanese souvenirs.[18]

Mass culture was not, of course, limited to the peasantry. After all, in the decades before 1914 hundreds of thousands of peasants flocked into the industrializing cities and became town folk. The growing mass-circulation press specifically catered to their needs. Advances in paper-making around mid-century made the mass production of very cheap newsprint possible. This, combined with the increasing share of a newspaper's profits coming from advertisements rather than the price paid by readers meant that by the early twentieth century one could purchase a newspaper for just a kopeck. While more expensive newspapers catering to the more educated classes, like *Novoe Vremia* (New Times, a conservative daily) or *Sankt-Peterburskie Vedomosti* (St Petersburg News, a liberal paper), provided sophisticated political and cultural news from around the world, most newly literate Russians were more interested in reading about scandals and violence. The popular press was happy to satisfy these urges. In the Black Sea port of Odessa, cheap dailies like *Odesskii listok* offered readers stories about the dangers of nightlife in the city, crimes of passion, and exposés about shysters, prostitution, and suicides.[19]

Middle-class people were certainly not immune to a taste for the lurid and sexual. Two of the most popular post-1905 novels, *Sanin*, by Mikhail Artsybashev, and *The Keys to Happiness*, by Anastasiia Verbitskaia, openly – not to say lasciviously – discussed sexuality outside marriage, frankly depicting characters who used sex as a means of getting what they wanted or simply for pleasure. Artsybashev's novel was written from the point of view of a heterosexual man who unabashedly enjoyed sex, including with young peasant girls; Verbitskaia's heroines openly viewed sex as a commodity that could be exchanged for material goods and a fine life. Both novels showed mainly heterosexual relationships, but Mikhail Kuzmin's *Wings* (1907) depicted the life of an openly and enthusiastic homosexual man who rejected the very concept of the "natural" (or "unnatural") in sexual life. Conservatives were of course horrified at this casual approach to sensuality but readers flocked to purchase the novels. After the Bolshevik revolution all three "decadent" novels were banned.[20]

Mass culture in late imperial Russia went far beyond the written word. The beginnings of commercial sports can be seen in this period, in particular with great enthusiasm for football (American "soccer"), bicycle racing, wrestling, and tennis. In many cases it was not the social elite but the middle and working classes who were the most enthusiastic fans of spectator sports. In the final decades before World War I, we also see increased tourism (the word spreading from English to other languages, including Russia, at this time) and the development of the Black Sea coast as a tourist center. Finally cinema houses were opening in all major cities of the Russian Empire by 1900 and before 1917 Russian viewers could watch not only typical farces and adventure epics on the silver screen, but also screen versions of classics such as *War and Peace*, Dostoevsky's *The Gambler*, and Verbitskaia's *Keys to Happiness*.[21]

——————— Visual Arts Reflecting Social Change ———————

The visual arts and artists in imperial Russia were also caught up in social movements. Many artists used their work to depict the poor and oppressed, much as writers like Dostoevsky wrote about the fringes of society. Paintings drew attention to social injustice and the miserable living and cultural standards endured by the Russian masses. Of course, artists also painted aristocrats in their exquisite homes and depicted heroic scenes from Russian folklore and history. Between the 1860s and 1917 Russian visual art passed from a predominantly realist style to increasingly stylized and even nonrepresentational forms. And visual art expanded beyond painting to include photography, "magic lantern" shows, and finally cinema. All of these art forms were both influenced by and reflected the social and political realities that surrounded them.

Perhaps the most famous of all Russian realist artists was Ilya Repin (1844–1930), born to a modest family near the city of Kharkiv in what is now Ukraine and originally apprenticed to an icon painter. Repin's talents gained him a place at the Imperial Academy of Arts in St Petersburg. In the 1870s he painted his first major work, *Volga Barge Haulers*, depicting a group of men attached like animals to a vessel they are pulling up the Volga River. The weary, resigned faces of the haulers speak of physical suffering and brutalization. In 1878 Repin joined a group of young realist artists, the "Wanderers" (*peredvizhniki*), who rebelled against academic conventions in art. These artists arranged exhibitions throughout the empire (hence their name), showing their paintings that often depicted the sufferings of the lower classes as well as scenes from Russian history. The 1880s, it will be recalled, were a time of political reaction in Russia; the paintings of the wanderers functioned as a silent protest at political repressions. One of Repin's most famous paintings, *They Did Not Expect Him* (in Russian only three syllables: "Ne zhdali," 1884) shows a haggard and thin young man entering a middle-class household and the shocked faces of two women, probably his mother and sister. Viewers of the painting would have understood that the man had just returned from exile in Siberia. In later years Repin's works took on a more impressionistic caste, as in his exultant painting *The October Manifesto of 1905*.

Like many other realists of his generation, Repin was fascinated by historical topics. One of his early works (1871) shows Peter the Great interrogating his son Aleksei, the grim face of the father ominously pointing to the future tragedy, when Aleksei will die under torture. Another Repin painting, an enormous canvas that now hangs in the Tretyakov Gallery in Moscow, shows the aftermath of a famous and fateful event in Russian history, when in a fit of rage Ivan the Terrible struck his eldest son and killed him. The grief-crazed father embraces the bloody head of his son, the murder weapon barely visible in the foreground of the painting. By depicting two of the most famous tsars as murderers of their own sons, Repin indirectly challenged the legitimacy of autocratic rule. The artist also painted more positive scenes from Russian history, like the rambunctious *Reply of the Zaporozhian Cossacks to Sultan Mehmed IV of the Ottoman Empire*, in which a group of Cossacks (easily identifiable by their mode of dress and especially their shaved heads with one long strand of hair) pen a clearly insulting missive to the Ottoman ruler. While the Cossacks were challenging the Ottoman ruler, Russian viewers of the painting no doubt interpreted the free soldiers' independent stance in a more general way as glorifying the dignity and freedom of common men over repressive rulers.

Over his long career Repin also painted dozens of portraits, including Tolstoy, Mendeleev, the composer Modest Mussorgsky, businessman and art lover Pavel M. Tretyakov, and even Nicholas II himself. His painting of the marriage of Nicholas II (1894) with Alexandra show sumptuously attired Orthodox priests, clad in gold cloth, the couple standing as if at attention at the key moment in the Orthodox wedding ceremony when crowns are placed on the newly weds' heads,

FIGURE 7.1   Ilya Repin, *Reply of the Zaporozhian Cossacks to Sultan Mehmed IV of the Ottoman Empire* (oil on canvas).
Source: State Russian Museum, St Petersburg, Russia/The Bridgeman Art Library.

the entire scene in a palatial hall observed by dozens of well-dressed people. In 1901 Repin was commissioned by the government to paint a ceremonial portrait of the State Council, an appointed body that advised the tsar. The painting was completed just before the Russo-Japanese war and shows dozens of elegantly dressed elderly gentlemen meeting in a luxuriously appointed room. One of the studies for this painting, a portrait of the infamous reactionary Pobedonostsev, reflected Repin's (and liberal Russia's) abhorrence of the man and his politics: the portrait shows an old man in court uniform with folded hands, looking like a menacing corpse.[22]

Repin's speciality was the depiction of humanity, with expressive facial features revealing misery, grief, joy, or suffering. One of his contemporaries, Isaac Levitan (1860–1900), hardly painted people at all, specializing instead in landscapes. Levitan's canvases show the unspectacular but deeply moving landscape of Russia, with birch trees, lakes, deserted roads, and rivers. As his name suggests, Levitan was of Jewish background and his grandfather had been a rabbi. After attending a traveling exhibition of the wanderers' paintings Levitan got in contact with the group and joined them in 1891. His paintings like *The Vladimirka* (1892) or *Over Eternal Peace* (1894) create a mood of peacefulness and longing, in part by using lines (roads, rivers) that stretch beyond the painting's edge, pulling the viewer's gaze forward and making us wonder what lies beyond. Social problems and

FIGURE 7.2   Vasily Vereshchagin, *An Allegory of the 1871 War*. 1871 (oil on canvas).
Source: Tretyakov Gallery, Moscow, Russia/The Bridgeman Art Library.

human misery rarely appear in Levitan's works; indeed his paintings seldom include human figures at all. The power of his compositions rather lies in the deeply felt love for the Russian countryside. A shy and retiring man, Levitan became friends with writer Anton Chekhov at whose house in the Crimea he died.

Another aspect of Russian painting of the later nineteenth century was exoticism, best exemplified in the central Asian canvases of Vasily Vereshchagin (1842–1904). In his twenties the young artist did military service in Turkestan, and then traveled to India and Tibet, all the time gathering sketches and material for future paintings. He accompanied the Russian army during the Russo-Turkish War of 1877–8 and was seriously wounded. He became the most famous Russian painter of battles, but his pacificist tendencies were always clear. His early work *The Apotheosis of War* (1871) shows an enormous pyramid of skulls in a vast wasteland being picked clean by flocks of birds. A later painting, *Defeat: Service for the Dead*, based on what the artist had experienced during the Russo-Turkish war of 1877–8, depicts a lone military officer and an Orthodox priest, apparently saying a prayer, in a vast field. Only upon careful inspection of the painting does one notice that the field is a vast graveyard full of the corpses of fallen soldiers over whom the priest pronounces a funeral prayer.

Vereshchagin's paintings from central Asia did much to acquaint Russians with this newly acquired part of the empire. He produced paintings showing the magnificent if decaying buildings of Samarkand, like the *Tomb of Timur* (1869) and portraits of the exotic-looking beturbaned inhabitants of central Asia. The governor general of Turkestan, Konstantin Kaufman, was impressed enough by the young artist that he allowed him to travel freely throughout the territory, which had only a few years earlier been incorporated into the Russian Empire. Vereshchagin's "Turkestan Series" of over 200 drawings and paintings was later exhibited in Moscow and St Petersburg to tens of thousands of viewers.[23]

Technological breakthroughs in preserving visual images threatened traditional forms of art in the later nineteenth century. Most important among these new technologies were the photograph and the moving picture. The photographer Sergei Mikhailovich Prokudin-Gorsky (1863–1944) was a pioneer in both portrait and landscape photography and even developed a technique to add color to photographs, creating astonishingly lifelike images. Starting in 1907, Prokudin-Gorsky spent eight years traveling around the empire (in a specially equipped railway carriage paid for by Nicholas II) documenting the diverse landscapes and peoples of the empire.[24]

The first moving pictures in Russia were shown as curiosities in music halls, shops, cabarets, and nightclubs, but by 1908 there were several movie theaters in St Petersburg and other Russian cities. Initially risqué farces seem to have predominated, at least to judge by titles like *The Female Samson*, *Help Me Fasten this Corset!*, and *The Mother-in-Law in the Harem*, all from the period 1908–14. But soon audiences tired of moving pictures as a curiosity and demanded better developed plots and more elaborate productions. Since films in this period were all silent (i.e., without the spoken word; they were always accompanied by music supplied by live musicians in the theater), the products of the German and French film industries could easily be imported to Russia. Russian studios produced some 400 movies in the years before World War I, and these competed for audience interest with titles from France, Scandinavia, and even America. Foreign-made films dominated, with about 80 percent of Russia's domestic market before the war. But there were also Russian feature films like a film version of Pushkin's *Queen of Spades* that competed with adventure stories like *The Scalped Corpse*. The box-office blockbuster, however, was a film version of the notorious novel *The Keys to Happiness*. Film was also turned to documentary usage; for example for the three hundredth anniversary of the Romanov dynasty in 1913. Some of the early pre-1917 footage was incorporated into the late Soviet feature by Stanislav Govorukhin, *Tak zhit' nelzya* (1990; roughly "No Way to Live"), which suggested that life for most Russians in 1914 was better than in the late 1980s.[25]

Culture could also be used to express patriotic ideals. This tendency became particularly pronounced during World War I all over Europe. Moviegoers could take in the semipornographic *Wilhelm in the Sultan's Harem*, which mocked the German Kaiser and his ally the Ottoman Sultan. Entertainments featuring heroic episodes from Russian history, folk songs, and balalaika bands were organized to benefit the wounded and other victims of war. Posters mocked the enemy, showed atrocities committed by the Germans, and showed Russian victories. Even more personal than posters were postcards, a relatively new form of communication. During the war, it has been estimated, millions of postcards were printed up and sent. These illustrated a variety of military and patriotic themes: Cossack horsemen decapitating a German soldier ("Happy New Year – A Successful Blow!"), a large hairy beast wearing the distinctive German helmet, benevolent Russian nurses, or a Russian peasant soldier shooting down the German eagle. Patriotic art was also featured in a new use for posters: those urging citizens to buy war bonds. One of the most famous, by Leonid Pasternak (the poet's father), showed a weary soldier mopping his brow with the caption "Aid to War Victims." The development of poster art as a means of education and propaganda during the war would be further employed by the communists after 1917.[26]

Bolshevik Revolution in Culture

Coming to power in late 1917, the Bolsheviks had very definite ideas about culture. Following Marxist teachings, they were convinced that culture was part of "superstructure" that grew up heavily influenced by the "substructure" of the economic realities of a given time and place. Thus imperial Russia's cultural scene would have to differ sharply from that of the new communist Russia. Culture was to belong to all citizens, not just to an elite, and it was one of the communists' jobs to spread that culture. At the same time culture was a tool to change social and political attitudes, to show people how to live, and to spread communist ideology. Culture was not something neutral for the communists: it was either good or bad. There was an inherent elitism in their program to lift cultural standards (one could even say "to improve the masses' cultural taste"), but it was also a democratic impulse, wanting the best of culture for the entire population, not just for a small and privileged segment of it.

While it was only in 1920 that the party set up a "Department of Agitation and Propaganda" from which the word *agitprop* was derived, the phenomenon of using culture to propagate the Bolshevik message had been used nearly from the start. For example, during the Civil War the communists had issued brightly colored posters urging peasants to support them, spreading the idea that a victory for the Whites would mean renewed slavery under the landowners. Other posters with texts in a number of languages but impressive primarily in their visual aspect, showed the communists as the friend of the Ukrainian peasant (against the Polish landlord) and respecting Muslim peoples and their cultures.[27] Most impressive of all, Agitprop trains visited the countryside, bringing striking images on posters (designed to be understood by the illiterate), motion pictures, and live plays. Agitprop trains often had their own printing presses so they could print up and leave behind posters. The communists also set up *agitpunkty* – "agitation points" – at major railroad stations. Here people could come and read newspapers, hear lectures, and watch moving pictures. At a chaotic time when travelers could be stranded for hours and even days, the *agitpunkty* were effective at spreading among ordinary people the ideas and aspirations of the communists.

The press was also used as a tool of revolution. In the days after the October revolution the presses of many bourgeois newspapers were simply seized. With an extreme shortage of paper due to wartime conditions, the communists also denied paper shipments to any journal or newspaper they thought might be hostile. By autumn 1918, the non-Bolshevik press had ceased to exist; henceforth the party would guide the editorial stance of all publications. Numerous newspapers aimed at different readerships: for city dwellers, peasants, women, teachers, the military, and so on. But during the Civil War, the harsh economic conditions and lack of paper meant that many newspapers consisted of a single or two sheets, and these were not published every day. Then there was the problem of distribution: throughout the early years and also well into the 1920s local party leaders complained that they were not receiving adequate numbers of journals and newspapers. Compared with the pre-revolutionary press, Soviet papers were dull and poorly produced. No longer could one find stories about murders and scandals, the stuff of boulevard journalism before 1917. Now readers had to be content with higher-minded material about the achievements of socialism, discussion of world politics, and the occasional criticism of local or national leaders (usually in the context of their arrest).

The Bolsheviks developed the poster into a serious art form, combining images, text, and striking design. Many of the early posters were designed to be easily understandable even without reading the text. One early poster showed a peasant man blindfolded, about to walk over a cliff. The legend read, "The illiterate is like a blind man; failure and misfortune await him everywhere." The fat, leering capitalist in a tuxedo needed no explanation (though for the literate a text further explained the nature of capitalism). Radiant suns over schools or peasant women symbolized the great strides made under communism. Famous poets like Vladimir Mayakovsky contributed to posters urging citizens to join shock brigades. Other posters showed the economic strides made in a year, introduced citizens to the members of the Communist Party leadership, or produced in graphic form the decisions of party congresses.[28]

While images played an important role in spreading the communist message, from the first the party dedicated itself to eradicating illiteracy. As Lenin had said, "The illiterate person stands outside of politics," which the communists found an intolerable situation. Thus spreading literacy was a primary goal of communist rule. It is estimated that in 1918 about two-thirds of urban workers could read and write, but in the countryside and among women, literacy rates were much lower; among some nationalities, like Chechens, literacy was extremely rare.

The People's Commissariat of Enlightenment (Narkompros) saw as its primary goal full literacy throughout the country, not just for Russians but for all nationalities. The liquidation of illiteracy was to be carried out on a number of levels. Nadezhda Krupskaia, Lenin's wife and an educational activist, called for a network of *likpunkty* (liquidation [of literacy] points), small schools open to all who wanted to learn their letters. But in the chaotic Civil War years, results were mixed or worse. Only with the consolidation of communist power in late 1919 and 1920 did the anti-illiteracy campaign really get off the ground. A decree of December 26, 1919, declared that in order to allow "the entire population of the Republic to participate consciously in the political life of the country" a number of Soviet institutions, from the Red Army to the Komsomol (young communists' league) to the *Zhenotdel* (women's department) and of course including the Narkompros would all work together to eliminate illiteracy. The decree required citizens from 8 to 50 years of age who could not read or write to attend literacy courses, but also freed them from work two hours daily for this purpose. Literate citizens could be "drafted" to serve as literacy teachers. Most strikingly the degree made refusing to study or to teach a criminal offense.[29]

The Soviet rulers also tried to make it worthwhile to be literate by producing a wide variety of reading materials from the classics, to simplified explanations of the basics of Marxism, to works of popular science. But it would not be until the late 1920s that production of reading matter would catch up with the pre-1914 levels, mainly because of the dire economic situation of the USSR in its first years. There was also the problem of what to print. Surveys showed that most readers wanted light material, adventures, and novels, not political tomes or classics like Pushkin. To some extent a compromise was reached with the "red detective story" like *Mess-Mend: Or a Yankee in Petrograd* (1923–5) featuring black magic (used by the American bad guys), decadent capitalism, a proletarian revolution in America, and of course memorable stock characters like "Laurie Lane" and "taciturn Ned." The communists' admiration for science was used in the science-fiction genre, and historical novels also made their appearance (often lionizing anti-tsarists rebels of the past like Stenka Razin and Bolotnikov. Unfortunately the near collapse of the economy during the Civil War and financial stringency during NEP meant that printed material was in short supply and the communist authorities favored political tracts over entertainment.[30]

Among the most famous Russian writers of the 1920s (and to this day) was the duo Ilya Faynzilberg and Evgeny Petrov, who wrote under the pen name "Ilf and Petrov." They introduced to Russian literature the memorable hero/antihero Ostap Bender. In *The Twelve Chairs* (1928) Bender and various hapless confeder-

НЕГРАМОТНЫЙ тот-же СЛЕПОЙ
ВСЮДУ ЕГО ЖДУТ НЕУДАЧИ И НЕСЧАСТЬЯ·

FIGURE 7.3 Aleksei Radkov, "The Illiterate Is Just as Blind. Disaster Awaits Him Everywhere" (anti-illiteracy poster). 1920.
Source: Hoover Institution Archives.

ates scour the Russian provinces for a set of dining-room chairs, one of which is thought to contain precious jewels sewn into its upholstery. Along the way, the story mocks monarchists (and disturbingly suggests that they are still plotting – though ineffectually – against Soviet power), bureaucrats, chess players, priests, and nearly every aspect of everyday life a decade after the revolution. While the novel never challenges the legitimacy of communist rule, neither does it hide the hypocrisy and thievery that continue to characterize everyday life. The novel's success led to a sequel, *The Golden Calf*, even though at the end of the first novel

Ostap Bender was killed off (he is resurrected for the second). Ilf and Petrov's novels, especially *The Twelve Chairs*, remained popular throughout the Soviet period and were also made into several film versions (including, in the west, by American director Mel Brooks, whose parents were born in Kiev, then in the Russian Empire).

Films were an obvious choice for communist propaganda. The moving picture was still enough of a novelty to attract mass audiences; it was appropriate for both literate and illiterate audiences, and was the quintessence of modernity. Most early Soviet movies were *agitki*, short documentaries showing revolutionary events or leaders. But many old films, mainly of foreign origin, were discovered on the shelves of closed movie houses; it was titles like *The Cabinet of Doctor Caligari* and *The Skull of the Pharaoh's Daughter* that Russians were watching in the first years after the revolution. By the mid-1920s, however, the Soviet film industry, from studios to distribution to movie houses, was taking shape. One of the first successful longer films (as opposed to short *agitki*) was *The Little Red Imps* (1923), about two Ukrainian youngsters and an American black (!) during the Civil War in Ukraine. Another early classic was the 1924 film *Mr. West in the Land of the Bolsheviks*, which parodied the American cops-and-robbers genre while giving it a Soviet twist.[31]

In the second half of the 1920s, however, increasing numbers of increasingly sophisticated films were made in the USSR, including Sergei Eisenstein's master-pieces *Strike* (1924) and *Battleship Potemkin* (1925). On a more popular level, *Katka the Reinette Apple Seller* (1926) turned the camera on the contradictions of NEP life in Leningrad, juxtaposing fat traders, flapper girls in garish lipstick, and smoky casinos where *nepmen* and their molls danced the foxtrot. Just as the rest of the economy was gradually recovering under NEP, so too was the film industry. But even in 1928 only 123 films were released and 300 million tickets sold – this at a time when in the USA 100 million people attended the movies weekly.[32]

While many poets and writers had left Russia rather than live under commu-nist rule, others stayed, either by chance or by conviction. The poet Vladimir Mayakovsky not only welcomed the revolution but wrote poems celebrating it, like "150,000,000" and "Poem about [my] Soviet Passport." Writers tried to come to grips with the new Soviet realities, like Boris Pilnyak in his *Naked Year* (1921), which described the devastations of the Civil War period. Others tried to come up with an entirely new style of writing to reflect the new proletarian dictatorship under Soviet rule. The "Proletkult" (short for proletarian culture) tried to come up with a new, fully proletarian brand of literature cleansed of bourgeois influences. But their actual achievements in writing were minimal and the concept of proletarian culture itself was criticized by Trotsky. Even Lenin had rather traditional tastes in literature, preferring classical poetry to the modern "proletarian" stuff.

Figure 7.4   Film poster for Sergei Eisenstein's *Battleship Potemkin*, 1925.
Source: Alamy/RIA Novosti.

Historian Sheila Fitzpatrick has characterized cultural policy in the 1920s as the "soft line," noting that in the immediate post-revolutionary years the communists wished to woo the intelligentsia rather than antagonize it further. A great deal of cultural experimentation was allowed, within certain limits. Commissar of People's Enlightenment Anatoly Lunacharsky exemplified this line: a dedicated communist, he also supported avant-garde artists and writers. Lunacharsky opposed narrowly defined political demands on culture and its creators, pursuing instead a policy of "whoever is not against us, is with us." Lunacharsky's openness to a relatively broad approach to culture could not survive in the feverish atmosphere of the "great leap" of the late 1920s. His resignation from the Commissariat of People's Enlightenment in 1929 was one indication that culture, too, was to be harnessed directly to the project of building a modern socialist state.[33]

Socialist Realism

In the early 1930s, as Stalin consolidated his power, there was a turn back to more traditional forms of power, gender relations, and social hierarchy. Art, too, became more conservative not so much in its choice of topics, but its style and moralism. While Russian literary and visual culture had always had a social and political mission – as the work of Chernyshevsky or Repin shows – now art was to faithfully serve the narrow demands of the party. Institutionally, too, the writer's profession became more narrowly defined – in particular after 1932 by membership to the Writers' Union – and the leeway for artistic experimentation or nonstandardized subjects became much more narrow. By the late 1930s it would have been impossible to publish a novel like *The Twelve Chairs* with its conman hero. Critics have parodied the Soviet novel of the 1930s and 1940s as "Boy meets tractor," and writers were expected to portray in proper socialist-realist form the struggles for production, overcoming pernicious foreign influences, and defeating the "survivals" of capitalist mentalities.[34]

Socialist realism was declared to be the sole proper approach to literature and art at the meeting of the Writers' Congress in 1934, Stalin's cultural henchman Andrei Zhdanov appeared before the writers to inform them of their present and future tasks under socialism. Zhdanov noted that Stalin had called writers "engineers of the human soul" and explained that such a lofty calling also placed grave responsibilities on writers. Zhdanov characterized the writer's duties as follows:

> it means knowing life so as to be able to depict it truthfully in works of art, not to depict it in a dead, scholastic way, ... but to depict reality in its revolutionary development. ... the truthfulness and historical concreteness of the artistic portrayal should be combined with the ideological remolding and education of the working people in the spirit of socialism. This method in literature and in literary criticism is what we call the method of socialist realism.[35]

Zhdanov's speech deserves quotation as an excellent example of the "wooden language" used by Soviet bureaucrats: heavy, wordy, repetitive, without nuance. But the general idea was clear enough: writers were to be engaged in the struggle for socialist construction and should portray that struggle not simply in a documentary way, but in a positive manner that would indicate to the reader how they *should* act, not just how people *did* act. So, for example, a socialist-realist novel might well show a factory boss who was incompetent, even corrupt. In the end, however, the honest workers and the party would root this negative character out and punish him. Love stories were not taboo, but they too had to be inserted in the context of revolutionary struggle as in the exchange between a pair of young people who after affirming their love for each other admit that there is one thing they love even more: the party.

A late Soviet joke summed up socialist realism (in art this time) very well: there was a competition to depict a general who had lost his right eye and arm in battle. The first artist painted the general with all organs and limbs intact: he was shot for "idealism." The second artist depicted the general as in life, without a right eye or arm: he was shot for "formalism." The third artist's painting showed the general from the left side: he was awarded the Stalin prize. While fictional, the joke showed the constraints artists and writers were put under but also suggested that with some ingenuity they could produce memorable, or at least acceptable, art.

Socialist realism further developed, if in a particular and narrow direction, the social consciousness shown in the realist painters of the 1870s like Repin and the realist writing style of writers like Tolstoy or Chekhov. Two of the most famous socialist realist novels were actually published before the official doctrine was proclaimed by Zhdanov. Dmitry Furmanov's novel *Chapaev* tells the story of a valiant but politically uneducated officer during the Civil War and the process of his political education. Fyodor Gladkov's *Cement* (1924) tells the story of a young man, Gleb Chumalov, in the years after the Civil War, the frictions between him and his newly revolutionized wife, and the difficulties of rebuilding the factory where he had been employed before the war, which he returns to find in a state of ruin. In both novels one finds action, intrigue, and memorable heros (Chapaev himself, in *Cement* Gleb) and villains (in *Chapaev* the White officers; in *Cement* Engineer Kleist who originally turns Gleb over to the Whites, though later in the novel Kleist is "converted" to being a hardworking supporter of the revolutionary regime). Both novels were made into successful films, and the film version of *Chapaev* (1934) is said to have been one of Stalin's favorite films.

Another early socialist-realist novel was Nikolai Ostrovsky's *How the Steel Was Tempered* (1932–4). In this semi-autobiographical novel Ostrovsky portrayed a young worker's experiences through the Civil War as a model communist worker and as an inspirational example to other young people, despite his physical handicap. Ostrovsky himself had lost his vision before he began to compose the novel; he died at the end of 1936, 32 years old. But by the later 1930s and after, the Soviet novel became increasingly formulaic and dull. Like everyone else, writers feared the consequences of appearing out of step with the times. Thus Soviet novels of the late 1930s and 1940s tended to play it safe, emphasizing heroic figures later parodied by novelist Vladimir Voinovich, like the character who removed his own appendix (successfully) while leading a polar expedition. The risks of publishing anything can be seen in the case of Alexander Fadeev, whose 1945 novel *The New Guard* won the Stalin prize in 1946 but was nonetheless subsequently denounced in the press, forcing the author to rewrite the novel several times.

Socialist realism started as a literary method but was soon extended to other arts, including the visual arts. One of the icons of socialist realism in sculpture is Vera Mukhina's *The Worker and the Collective Farmer* (1937) holding the emblematic hammer and sickle (respectively) in a dynamic forward-thrusting motion. But here, too, endless workers and resolute collective farmers eventually made for dull art. By the late 1930s, the industrial worker was nearly always male, burly, and standing in the front of the image, towering over the female collective farmer.

The Stalinist "Cult of Personality" also used the forms of socialist realism. This cult would reach its apex after World War II, but already by the mid-1930s Soviet daily life was full of poems, paintings, books, and songs extolling the wisdom, justice, and kindness of Stalin.[36] Stalin was almost inevitably connected with Lenin who, being dead, could not protest (allegedly during these years Stalin threatened Lenin's wife, Nadezhda Krupskaia, that if she expressed any criticism, he would "find a new widow for Lenin"). In the posters of the 1930s, produced in the thousands, one sees the benevolent, kindly Stalin overseeing the construction of socialism. One famous poster showed Stalin working late at his night desk with the legend "Stalin in the Kremlin thinks about each of us." Portraits of Stalin became *de rigueur* as artists vied for new ways of glorifying the great man. One of the most famous, showing Stalin in conversation with war minister Kliment Voroshilov (1938), the towers of the Kremlin and smokestacks of Moscow behind them, gave the impression of a benevolent Stalin deep in conversation with his lieutenant about the welfare of the Soviet people.[37] The growth of the Cult of Personality was combined with the blotting out – from history books and often from life – of those who had clashed or disagreed with Stalin, Trotsky foremost among them.

Conclusion

Between the Great Reforms and World War II, Russian culture included such diverse phenomena as painting and scientific research, literature and film, peasant art and realist painting. One significant difference between Russian culture and that of the west was the very strong political commitment felt by artists and exhibited in their works. Russia (and all the more, the Soviet Union) lacked a strong tradition of "art for art's sake." The use of literature as a forum to discuss politics and social issues during the imperial period developed after 1917 into socialist realism, the use of literature (and later all art) to further the revolutionary cause. For most Russians, probably, culture was most important for its entertainment value, whether as a beautiful picture, an amusing movie, or a moving poem. But whether in the 1860s or 1930s, Russian writers and artists used their art to reflect on the society surrounding them and also to shape the future.

The transformation of elite and peasant cultures into a more unified "mass culture" in this period was a common trend throughout Europe and North America. Higher literacy rates meant that on the eve of the revolution more Russians were reading than ever before. Publishing, both books and periodicals, was crucial for the communists who perceived an urgent need to inform the population on a variety of topics, from the basics of Marxism to world politics to scientific discoveries. But culture in all of its forms – cinema, literature, science, posters, paintings, poetry, music – would soon be harnessed to the task of building socialism. The cultural experimentation of the 1920s gave way to a more narrow understanding of writers and artists as "engineers of human souls" whose works needed to educate and propagandize, not just entertain. The narrow and instrumental use of culture set down in socialist realism can, however, be seen as the *reductio ad absurdum* of the pre-revolutionary tendency to emphasize the socio-political role of culture.

Conclusion

Changes and Continuities, Russia-USSR: 1861–1945

Between the emancipation of the serfs in 1861 and the triumph over Nazi Germany in 1945, the politics, economics, everyday life, and culture of Russians changed immeasurably. The changes affected nearly all aspects of life, politics, economy, society, and culture. Russia went from autocracy to socialism, from backward agriculturally based economy to industrialization, from patriarchal conservative family life to increased role of women in society, from a mainly religious and preliterate culture to a secular society. On the international scene Russia in 1861 was one among several major European powers whose poor performance in the Crimean War, however, led some to question its future as a major international player. In 1945 the USSR's military might was unchallenged from the Pacific to Berlin and many feared that a Soviet-dominated Europe was if not inevitable, then at least a distinct possibility. The booming industry that had made the military victory possible had mainly been built since 1930 and this striking economic growth seemed to augur a future rise in living standards.

It would be tempting to focus only on the differences between Russia in 1861 and the USSR in 1945. Yet the changes were often superficial and many of the problems that the tsarist governments had wrestled with before 1917 remained, in one form or another, at the later date. For instance, while the level of industrialization had risen considerably by 1945, agriculture remained inefficient and a constant drain on the economy. Furthermore, industry was geared heavily toward capital goods and the military with little concern for producing items for consumer use. The state-driven command economy had functioned well in building up heavy industry and military production but had not significantly improved everyday living standards for most Soviet citizens. Political ideology had changed enormously but most Soviet citizens in 1945, just like subjects of the tsar in 1861, lacked real influence over the political system. The Supreme Soviet was no more of a democratic institution than the tsar's State Council had been. Freedom of speech and publication was even more limited at the end of our period than at its beginning, in great contrast to the situation in most of Europe. On a very basic level, the great-grandchild of a woman born in 1860 would not enjoy more civil liberties and, unless quite exceptional, would live under conditions quite unacceptable to citizens of western Europe or North America. Much had changed, to be sure, but even serf emancipation, industrialization, revolution, and two major wars had not entirely remade Russia.

The Search for Modernity

One of the themes of this book has been modernity, broadly defined as a literate, secular, industrial society enjoying a fair amount of civil liberties, with the majority of the population living in urban areas and working in culture, industry, or administration (office jobs) – but not in agriculture. Modernity is also reflected in a sophisticated educational system and a high level of technology. A modern state is able to defend itself militarily and enjoys influence and prestige on the world stage. In all of these categories we can see that over our period the Russian/Soviet state underwent modernization of a partial and one-sided nature. True, in 1945 the USSR was militarily strong and enjoyed respect on the world stage, but its victory over Nazi Germany has been at the cost of tens of millions of citizens, partly because of Nazi barbarity but also due to a patent disregard for casualties shown by the Red Army commanders and most of all by Stalin himself. True, the Soviet Union had a well-developed system of university and technical education, often boasting that more engineers and scientists lived in the USSR than in any other country. But the general level of Soviet science, with few exceptions, could not compete with institutions and scientists in the west. Furthermore, the level of technology in everyday life was much lower than in the west and this gap would grow in ensuing decades.

Societies do not modernize voluntarily: circumstances force them to take these painful measures. Russia's defeat in the Crimean War forced Tsar Alexander II to embark on sweeping reforms that had been thought about for decades, if not generations. Alexander II could not simply sweep away the old order, in particular as he was the very symbol of that order. Rather he had to find compromises with the existing society and economy. Thus serfdom was ended, former serfs received land, but they had to pay for that land, and remained dependent upon the peasant commune, unable freely to leave the countryside. Politically Alexander could not afford to alienate the landowners entirely; economically he had to take money from the former serfs to pay off the landowners, and from fear of social unrest felt compelled to tie the peasants to the rural commune, or at least to restrict somewhat their departure from it.

If in liberating the serfs the tsarist regime compromised with economic realities, in politics there was no compromise at all. While the elective local institutions, the *zemstva*, were set up to help deal with practical local issues like education, health, and building roads, their prerogatives remained very narrow, and rapidly tsarist administrators like provincial governors clashed with *zemstvo* institutions. While censorship was somewhat mitigated and the legal system improved, Alexander refused to consider the election of even a consultative legislature. Thus into the twentieth century Russia remained an autocracy, refusing to allow even wealthier, better-educated citizens to participate in governance and thereby alienating Russian society from tsarist rule.

Still, for all the contradictions of the Great Reforms, they did succeed in setting the stage for the first wave of industrialization a generation later, essentially "taking off" in the 1890s. During these early decades of industrial development, large factories sprung up in Moscow, St Petersburg, and elsewhere, and Russia's growth rate exceeded that seen anywhere hitherto. Hundreds of thousands of peasants flocked to the cities – the communes usually being happy to let them go, as there was a labor surplus on the countryside – and became industrial workers. At the same time universities in the Russian Empire were expanding and thousands were receiving training as physicians, lawyers, engineers, teachers, and other educated professionals. Russian journalism and publishing grew with increased literacy. With these changes came ever more vocal demands for political change, demands that the tsars consistently refused to consider. The wave of terrorism that killed Alexander II in 1881, and a second, more widespread period of violence against tsarist authority in the first years of the twentieth century revealed the frustrations of Russian society at the uneven rate of change in their country.

World War I showed the frailty of Russian modernity. The primary goal of the Great Reforms had been to preserve Russia's status as a great power, which essentially meant creating an effective modern military. Yet in World War I the Russian army, despite its huge size, made a poor showing. After the short-lived successes against the Germans in East Prussia the Russian army constantly lost ground against the Germans and, to a lesser extent, the Austro-Hungarian army. Only the German concentration of forces on the western front prevented Russian military defeat in 1915 or 1916. The Russian state was also unsuccessful in organizing and channeling patriotism into support for the present regime. While the British royal house could (and did) embark on a campaign of patriotic self-definition, for both personal and ideological reasons the Romanov tsar was quite unable to do so. Instead the combination of poor military performance, widespread shortages of basic foodstuffs, and the perception of treason and mismanagement at the highest levels of the state led to the implosion of Romanov power in February 1917.

The year 1917 was a crucial year both for what happened and for what did not. Tsarist power was swept away in February and the Bolsheviks seized control of the country in October. Why were Russian liberals not successful at holding power once it had passed to their hands with the first revolution? One could argue that they were at once "too modern" and "not modern enough": too modern for Russia because of their cosmopolitanism and political sophistication, making them want a parliamentary democracy for which Russia was unprepared, but not modern enough in their refusal to recognize the danger posed by the extreme left and in their unwillingness to limit civil liberties as a temporary measure during a time of instability and heightened political tensions. Continuing the unpopular war with an army incapable of winning was also a mistake. One way or the other, however, it seems clear that Russia could not have sustained its liberal government for long: both a lack of democratic tradition and the huge material difficulties facing any post-tsarist government would probably have led to an authoritarian solution.

Russia's new rulers from October 1917, the Bolsheviks, were resolute in their ambition to make their homeland modern: in a specifically Marxist and socialist guise. At first, however, the communists could do little more than defend their hold on power. The violence and instability of the Civil War (1918–20) did not create authoritarian tendencies within the party, but surely exacerbated them. The Soviet communists, disappointed in their hopes for world revolution, nonetheless saw themselves as possessing a unique truth that showed *the* correct path toward modernity. While tactics and short-term measures could be debated, the final goal of communism could not be questioned. The tactical retreat of NEP, allowing the economy to recover the devastations of war and revolution, had no political counterpart. Once Stalin had sufficiently consolidated power, he could and did push for a radical leap forward also on the economic front.

The changes of the 1930s were probably more thoroughgoing and brutal than in any decade of Russian history before or since. Millions of peasants were forced onto collective farms, entire industrial cities were built, millions left the countryside for urban work, never to return. In the artificially exacerbated famines of 1932–3, millions of Kazakhs, Ukrainians, Russians, and people of other nationalities perished as a direct result of Moscow's policies. The Gulag grew enormously as kulaks, "Trotskyites," "wreckers," and millions of other real or imagined enemies of Soviet power were arrested, jailed, and in many thousands of cases, executed. The trauma of this unprecedented level of violence dealt by a state onto its own citizens was to leave long-lasting scars. Arrests and executions made Soviet citizens, in particular those in responsible positions, loath to express critical opinions, even when such criticism would be crucial for improving efficiency. Better to keep one's head down and not stick out than to show initiative and independent thinking – and risk being cut down by the next purge.

It is difficult, even after several decades, to be objective about the changes of the 1930s. We can, however, see that between 1929 and 1939 Soviet society changed radically. True, most Soviet citizens continued to live in rural areas, a statistic not consistent with traditional definitions of "modernity." True, life in Soviet cities was often crude, uncomfortable, and difficult. But foundations had been laid for further more positive development and the progress achieved in a short decade was remarkable. We cannot objectively answer the question whether the USSR would have been able to withstand the Nazi onslaught in 1941 without the forced pace of economic modernization in the previous decade. On the other hand the industrial plant created in that cruel decade certainly helped the USSR stop, expel, and defeat the Germans, though at enormous human expense.

It is more difficult to gauge the changes in society over this period. Women played a much larger role in the professions, administration, and public life, and yet old attitudes that men should dominate at home (and not be bothered with housework and raising children) had not disappeared. At the highest level of Soviet politics, practically no women were to be seen. In the professions, certain jobs from teachers to physicians came to be dominated by women, while other, better-paid and more prestigious positions like professors and surgeons were overwhelmingly male. While women had been prominent among radicals in the pre-revolutionary period, only a single woman ever reached the highest circle of political power – the Politburo – in the entire history of the USSR. While women were far more likely to work outside the home, men rarely shared equally domestic chores and child-rearing responsibilities. Furthermore the huge and disproportionately male casualties in World War II meant that Soviet women would have a difficult time finding a husband in the postwar period.

Religious belief probably still played a large role in the lives of most Soviet citizens, but its public role had certainly declined. Official disapproval and fear of retribution combined with the scarcity of clergymen and places to worship made it far more difficult for parents to convey their religious beliefs and practices to the younger generation. At the same time official propaganda trumpeted the impending triumph of communism, a kind of paradise on earth that made religious promises of afterlife seem outdated and false. Clearly, however, the power of religion and spirituality had not disappeared entirely, as is shown by the Soviet government's decision to use the Orthodox Church to strengthen patriotism during the "Great Fatherland War."

Changing Identities

A key element of human psychology is identity; in other words the answer to the question "who are you?" Identities can be based on a number of factors: religion, locality, nation, social class, education, political views, even sexual preference. Starting with the last factor named, one can confidently state that an openly gay identity was a rare occurrence throughout this period. Both traditional religious morality and, after an initial period of hesitation and toleration, Soviet law and social practice severely condemned homosexuality in any form. The heterosexual family continued to be seen as the norm, though after 1917 and with increased urbanization the typical Russian family of, say, the 1930s, was smaller than that of 50 years earlier. Women continued to carry out most of the work at home, such as cleaning and preparing meals, even while holding full-time jobs in offices and factories.

Social class in imperial Russia depended to a great extent on *soslovie*, the legal category into which one was born. Thus one might have visiting cards printed identifying oneself as "Ivan Ivanovich Ivanov, nobleman" or "Petr Petrovich Petrov, merchant of the first guild." Peasants of course made up the largest *soslovie* and the majority of all Russians before the revolution and they would have identified themselves socially as neither noble landowners nor urban dwellers, but as "simple folk," peasants or poor town dwellers. The Great Reforms weakened *soslovie* without destroying it entirely, but another identity based more on education than on birth was also developing: that of the intelligentsia. By defining themselves by their education and work rather than their origins, members of the intelligentsia were pioneering a more modern form of identity. For most Russians, however, the most important distinction would have remained between those who worked the land and those with soft hands who apparently (from a peasant's point of view) did no work at all.

Political identities were not widely developed in Russia before 1917. That is, very few Russians, and even fewer non-Russian subjects of the tsar, would have defined themselves in political terms, as conservative, liberal, socialist, or anarchist (to name just a few of the choices). Still, the educated minority often did think in political terms and defined themselves accordingly. Differences in outlook and tactics between different interpretations of socialism, liberal, conservatism, and nationalism were increasingly debated in particular after 1905. In the Soviet period matters became far more simple: especially after the ban on party factions in 1920, one could openly identify with only one political position: that of the Communist Party. The population was divided between "party" and "nonparty" people and it was quite superfluous to ask which party. The lack of a free press and the omnipresence of the party's security apparatus made the development of alternative political identities impossible.

Religion was far more important than politics in the Russian Empire. All subjects of the tsar had to belong to a religious community, whether that be Christian, Pagan, Buddhist, Jewish, or Muslim. Religion influenced one's outward appearance, everyday life, even what one ate. Religious identity was thus very strong before 1917 and, despite all efforts of the communists, remained so at least to the 1940s. Before the 1920s, when individuals were often not entirely sure what language they spoke or what nationality they belonged to, there was seldom any doubt about the religion they adhered to. With the spread of education and as a result of antireligious campaigns, by the 1940s national identities had begun to compete with or even eclipse religious self-definition.

The interplay between religion, locality, and nation in forming identity during this period of intensifying nationalism is of particular interest. Modern nationalism tends to emphasize the role of language and downplay religion, but in the Russian Empire religion was the most common factor of self-identification. Slavic peasants in what is now Belarus and Ukraine when asked about their native tongue during the census of 1897 did not always know how to respond. But they had no doubt as to their adherence to the "Russian faith" (Orthodoxy) or "Polish faith" (Catholicism). By the end of the nineteenth century the spread of literacy helped to increase the depth of national identity. Estonians and Latvians, for example, organized schools, choirs, and clubs based on nationality. Poles, Armenians, and Georgians enjoyed a long-established tradition of literary language and national culture, and during this period national self-consciousness spread increasingly beyond just the privileged classes. Still, in many places identities continued to be based overwhelmingly on one's village and religion and not on some larger imagined "nation." In central Asia language remained far less important for identity than religion and the distinction between nomads and sedentary people.

After 1917 the Soviets proclaimed the end of any restrictions on national cultures or languages and, once firmly in power, moved to establish nationality as a very major factor in administration and Soviet identity. Before 1917, nationality had no legal status at all and even the tsarist bureaucracy had a hard time determining an individual's national identity (e.g., to decide whether someone should be subjected to anti-Polish measures). Throughout the 1920s the Soviet authorities worked to codify languages and to divide up the population according to ethno-linguistic characteristics, culminating in the introduction of the passport system in 1932, which required that each Soviet citizen have one (and only one) nationality. Thus ironically the internationalist USSR helped develop – even create – national feeling among its citizens.

Culture and Ideologies

Modern societies are usually described as secular; that is, they explain the world more through science than religion. As we have seen, for the vast majority of the tsar's subjects, religion, not science, gave meaning and order to life. Yet, already in pre-revolutionary Russia, a scientific worldview already predominated among the intelligentsia and much of the middle class. The great cultural gap between educated Russians and the Russian masses (not to even mention the large non-Russian percentage of the population) stymied the development of civil society and made very difficult any quick transition to any kind of liberal democratic rule. The ideologies that the Russian intelligentsia embraced in the generations after the Great Reforms reflect this cultural-ideological gap: on the one hand progressive Russians were well acquainted with European modernity – economic, cultural, social, political – and wanted to replicate this modernity in their own homeland. On the other hand the great majority of the population neither knew nor desired sweeping political or cultural change; their desires were more simple: more land and prosperity. The different worldviews held by the intelligentsia and the masses pushed the former toward radical "from the top down" solutions to perceived deficiencies in the existing political and economic status quo.

Soon after the Great Reforms the gap between intelligentsia and peasant culture and ideology became apparent, in particular during the "crazy summer" of 1874 when thousands of idealistic young radicals "went to the people," aiming to spread their ideas among the peasantry. The peasants' negative response helped split the radical movement and encourage a small but extremely dedicated group to embrace terrorism as a political tactic. The terrorist "Land and Freedom" group succeeded in assassinating Alexander II in 1881, but the tsar's death did not usher in the hoped-for social revolution. Repression over the final two decades of the nineteenth century pushed the radical movement underground, but the terrorist methods of "Land and Freedom" – assassination of political figures and other servitors of the tsarist state – were embraced in the early twentieth century by the Socialist Revolutionary party. Even more significantly much of the middle-class intelligentsia refused to condemn violent attacks on tsarist ministers, seeing them as a means of forcing the tsarist state to compromise with society and agree to political reforms.

The acceptance of terrorist violence against the state by a significant part of educated Russian society reflects their impatience with the pace of modernization in Russia as well as the failure of the tsarist government in co-opting the middle class. The noncondemnation of violence was also based on a firm belief in the immorality of the present regime based as it was on privilege (by birth, not accomplishment), tradition, and autocracy. Perhaps if the last two tsars had been men of broader vision and understanding, Russian history would have taken a different turn. And yet it is difficult to see an entirely peaceful transition from autocracy to even limited democratic rule. The impatience for political change (and even more, the *kind* of change) among the intelligentsia did not find broad support among the masses, and the tsarist regime was strong enough to defend itself from liberal demands. Strong enough, that is, until the crisis of World War I.

Tsarism collapsed mainly from internal weaknesses and its broad lack of support in early 1917. The unfortunate Provisional Government that ruled Russia – after a fashion – from February to October 1917 demonstrated very well the strengths and weaknesses of the intelligentsia. These were sincerely liberal men in an exceedingly illiberal situation. Saddled with an unpopular war, lacking a functioning political system, and unsure of their own political legitimacy, it was perhaps inevitable that they would be swept away by more ruthless political actors. The Bolsheviks certainly did not lack ruthlessness, but even they found that the political exigencies of the Civil War period pushed them toward more radical political and economic policies than they would otherwise have adopted. Thus by the early 1920s Soviet Russia – soon to be the USSR – was a one-party state in which political expression was severely restricted and where the economy was overwhelmingly in the hands of the state.

The Bolsheviks exhibited one familiar characteristic of the pre-revolutionary Russian intelligentsia – their ideology foresaw sweeping, radical change in the country whether the population wanted it or not. Marxism as interpreted by the Communist Party of the Soviet Union was by definition the most progressive ideology for human development; thus any opposition to it could only be explained by ignorance or evil intentions. The economic and cultural development of the USSR from the 1920s to 1945 was impressive indeed, but throughout the period (and indeed all the way to "the end" in 1992), the party never quite trusted the Soviet people to make its own decisions or influence its own future. In any case the brutality of collectivization and crash industrialization in the 1930s, combined with the millions of arrests of real or suspected "enemies" in the same decade, did little to win mass support, though it was effective in stifling dissent. At the same time the radical changes of the 1930s created a cadre of communists who firmly believed that the present dislocations and even violence were but the birthing pains of a new and better world. In 1945 they would point to the USSR's victory over Nazi Germany as vindication for the painful changes of the 1930s.

─────────────── Technology and Everyday Life ───────────────

The world changed enormously between 1861 and 1945, perhaps nowhere more obviously than in the field of technology and everyday life. In 1861 railroads had only begun to link together the vast country; in 1862 Moscow and St Petersburg were linked up to western European railroad networks through Warsaw. By 1914 one could travel by rain from one end of the empire to the other, from Helsinki to Moscow, across the Urals and through Siberia, and on to the Pacific Ocean. Not just the well-to-do, but growing numbers of common people took journeys by train; it became common for young people to go to the city to look for work, and then return bringing town fashions and ways of thinking. The railroad also aided permanent migration such as that of thousands of land-hungry peasants from European Russia and Ukraine to Siberia.

Changes in technology did not immediately have a great impact on the lives of most inhabitants of the Russian Empire, who continued for the most part to live in small peasant huts, eat the same meager diet, and amuse themselves with games and songs that would have been familiar to their grandparents. By the late nineteenth century, however, technological advances had begun to penetrate even to the countryside. Even more significantly more and more peasants had spent at least some time in towns and came home with stories – not always believable for the folks back home – about multistory buildings, elegant shops, exotic foods, even trams and automobiles. True, it was a rare village that had electricity, but increasing numbers of peasants had at least seen electrical lighting in towns. Even if most Russians continued to subsist on porridge and bread, the quintessentially Russian samovar had made its way to the village and even peasants regularly drank tea with sugar – a practice far less common in the first half of the nineteenth century. Clothing changed, too. By the late nineteenth century few Russians spun their own cloth, finding manufactured material both cheaper and more attractive.

Technological change meant that human and animal power was increasingly – if slowly – being replaced by machine power. Trains took the place of horse-drawn stages, though well into the twentieth century one would have to rely on a horse-drawn carriage to get to the station. In cities workers made their way to work first on foot, then in streetcars pulled by horses, then in electric trams, and finally in autobuses powered by the internal combustion engine. Throughout the period covered in this book – indeed, in many ways to the end of the twentieth century – automobiles were luxury items reserved for the elite, but by the early twentieth century in larger cities of the Russian Empire cars were no longer rare. On a more practical level, tractors and harvesting machines (e.g., from the American firm International Harvester) could be purchased in Russia, though only a few landlords had sufficient land and property to make them practical. More modestly bicycles – Russian still uses the old-fashioned word *velocipede* – made their way to Russia, partly as practical machines for transportation but even more as a means of diversion and sport.

Some of these new machines put humans out of work – for example, trains reduced the need for long distance coach drivers – but even more jobs were created by them. Telegraph offices required trained operators (nearly always men), telephone switchboards – direct dialing would come much later – needed operators (usually young women). Department stores that opened in middle-sized and larger towns sought staff that dressed and spoke "properly" and yet could subsist on a quite modest wage. Office jobs expanded and by the early twentieth century the typewriter was ubiquitous and usually "operated" by a young woman.

The first three decades of Soviet rule continued these technological advances or, more precisely, took the technology of the pre-1917 period and applied it more broadly throughout the country. The devastation of World War I, famine, and the Civil War stymied the development and spread of technology, but this process resumed again in the 1920s and 1930s. While the hugely expanding Soviet cities of the 1930s would have seemed primitive to westerners, for many of their inhabitants, fresh from the countryside, they seemed amazingly modern, with indoor plumbing and electricity. Rural modernization lagged far behind, but at the same time increasing numbers of tractors and harvesters were being delivered to the countryside by the end of our period. A mixture of old and new characterized the USSR in 1945: on the one hand more and more Soviet citizens were experiencing miracles of modern technology like automobiles, electric light, telephones, and running water. On the other hand, for many collective farmers these advances remained far away and for many city dwellers forced to share a single room with several families, any talk of technological advances would have seemed absurd.

Technological change had its most radical effect, perhaps, on the military. Weapons, tactics, military training changed utterly from the mid-nineteenth century to World War II. Armies grew in size and the needed weapons and ammunition became much more costly. The demands of a modern military force was, as we have seen, one of the main motivations behind the Great Reforms. During World War I the financial demands of fighting a modern war helped bring down the tsarist state. The crash industrialization program of the 1930s was often justified as necessary not just to improve living standards, but also to prevail in the case of a war. World War I had brought onto the scene numerous new technologies of war, from poison gas to airplanes to tanks, that would be used to even more deadly effect in World War II. Some of the weapons developed and used by the USSR during World War II, such as the Katyusha rocket launcher and T-34 medium tank, were recognized as among the best available. Thus the USSR also contributed to military technology in the 1940s.

Roads Not Taken, and Why

In closing, we return to a question frequently asked about Russia's historical development from the late imperial through the Soviet to our own days: Why did Russia not develop into a prosperous, free, and democratic country in this period? First of all, we must note that the question is rather unfair: Why should Russia necessarily follow the historical path of Britain or the USA? Still, given the success of economic and political transformation in the twentieth century in countries as diverse as South Korea, Germany, Japan, and Chile, the question is not entirely without merit. To start with the obvious: Russia in the twenty-first century is arguably more prosperous and free – if not precisely democratic in a western sense – than at any time in its history. The question then becomes, why did developments in Russia in these fields lag behind, say, Germany or Spain? Let us consider some political, cultural-sociological, and economic factors that may suggest tentative answers to these questions.

Politically Russia was more conservative than any other European state in the nineteenth century. Only in 1905 was the tsar forced to issue a kind of constitution (which he resolutely refused to acknowledge as such) and allow the creation of a legislature (whose functioning he consistently stymied). During the scant 10 years of its existence, the State Duma and the tsar's government were nearly constantly at loggerheads; perhaps if Peter Stolypin had not been assassinated in 1911, he could have developed a *modus vivendi* with the legislature. In any case most Russians were unimpressed by the Duma's activity, and in the one fairly free election in Russia in the early twentieth century – for the Constituent Assembly, held in late November 1917 (o.s.) – two-thirds of the total vote went to parties (the Socialist Revolutionaries and Bolsheviks) who were hardly wedded to the principles of western-style democracy. In any case the ruling Bolsheviks – whether led by Lenin or Stalin – did not embrace the rule of law or parliamentary niceties, basing their vision of a future Soviet Russia on their own revision of Marx's historical-sociological teleology. The violence of collectivization and the first Five-Year Plans, exacerbated by the political purges of the late 1930s, did much to spread fear and suppress independent expression – or even thought. In general the USSR did everything to control society rather than allow the development of an autonomous civil society along western lines. The mass arrests of the 1930s served as a reminder of the dangers of not following the party line.

"Political culture" is an imprecise and risky term that runs the risk of trotting out national stereotypes in the place of enlightenment. "Russians" do not all think the same way, nor were all (or even the majority) of the tsar's subjects and Soviet citizens Russian by ethnicity or language. Still, some comments may be hazarded. First of all in the period 1861–1945 there was just over a decade of semimodern politics in the sense of parliamentary elections, parties, and fairly open political debate. Even in 1917 the majority of Russians (and other subjects of the tsar) were illiterate, though in local (not national, much less international) terms, and had little conception of the rule of law or the workings of parliamentary democracy. For the great majority, simply keeping body and soul together remained a struggle; their lives were guided by practical issues and religious faith. To be sure, given a generation or two of growing education and prosperity, there is every reason to believe that Russian society might have developed a functioning civil society and democratic order. But this period of peaceful development was never given to Russia in the first half of the twentieth century: the destruction of World War I and Civil War was followed by a brief decade of relative peace before the upheavals of collectivization and crash industrialization, followed closely by the crushing exertions and devastations of World War II. Peace and prosperity may not be an absolute prerequisite for democratic development, but severe economic, political, and military upheaval are seldom auspicious conditions under which to build democratic institutions.

Economically Russia was also at a disadvantage when compared to other major powers. The country's size is only apparently a positive factor: for most practical purposes, the long borders meant having to expend valuable resources on defense and the great distances made it difficult and expensive to govern the country. These distances also made trade more difficult; for many farmers not close to a rail line it simply made no economic sense to produce more than they could consume. And Russia was much poorer than any of the western powers; indeed by some measures poorer than Italy and Spain circa 1900. Russia lacked domestic capital and investment to industrialize and had to rely to a significant measure on foreign capital in its first industrialization spurt of the 1890s. The poverty of most Russians also meant that the domestic market was underdeveloped: even if they wanted more goods, they usually lacked the means to purchase them.

When, after revolution, Civil War, and NEP, the communists got around to launching their industrialization of the USSR, their priorities were quite different from that of most liberal economists – or consumers. Not clothing, tools, or other everyday items but heavy machinery for further industrialization and military production received the greatest impetus. Thus from the start Soviet industrialization saw the everyday citizen and consumer – if at all – as a secondary issue. Soviet industrialization was first and foremost designed to serve the needs of the state. While this kind of emphasis may have helped the USSR win World War II (though this is also debatable), it undoubtedly saddled the country with inflexible and bureaucratic industrial plants that had little reason to respond to consumer desires or to adopt new technologies. Looking ahead to the later part of the twentieth century, this emphasis on heavy industry, huge factories, and central planning made the USSR unable to develop or take advantage of computer technology. After 1992 the post-Soviet Russian economy had to scramble to make up these lost decades.

In the end, though, history is about what happened – not what should or could have taken place. In the 84 years from the emancipation of the serfs and the end of World War II, Russia changed enormously. In 1861 westerners tended to see the country as backward, even barbaric, and barely European. In 1945 the USSR had defeated Europe's most dynamic economy, Germany, and was one of only two world superpowers. Illiteracy was by 1945 mainly a thing of the past and the

USSR was training more scientists and engineers than any other state. While economic conditions lagged behind western norms, millions of Soviet citizens could discern significant material improvement in the past decades and – more importantly – had great hopes that prosperity would grow rapidly in the postwar years. As for political freedoms, it was also hoped that the defeat of the fascist enemy would allow the Soviet state to lessen restrictions on public expression, which had to some extent already been done during the war itself. Perhaps the exertions and misfortunes of the 1930s, sufferings during the war itself, and victory over the Nazis would allow the USSR to become a less repressive and most prosperous country? But the answer to that question, and that fascinating story, belongs to another book.

Timeline of Important Events

1815	Congress of Vienna, Russia gains Kingdom of Poland
1830–1	"November Uprising" of Poles against Russian rule
1854–6	Crimean War
1855–81	Reign of Alexander II
1860	State Bank founded
1861–76	The Great Reforms
1862	Turgenev, *Fathers and Sons*
1863	Chernyshevsky, *What Is to Be Done?*
1863	University statute reforms Russian higher education
1863–4	"January Uprising" of Poles against Russian rule
1864	Dostoevsky, *Notes from the Underground*, *Demons*
1865	General Michael Cherniaev takes Tashkent
1867	Russia sells Alaska to USA
1865–9	Tolstoy, *War and Peace*
1869	N. Danilevsky, *Russia and Europe*
1871	Vereshchagin, "The Apotheosis of War"
1872	Special higher education courses for women set up in Moscow
1875	Uniates in Russian Empire converted to Orthodoxy
1875–7	Tolstoy, *Anna Karenina*
1877–8	Russo-Turkish War
1878	Congress of Berlin
1881	Assassination of Alexander II
1881	Attacks on Jews ("pogroms") in Southwest (Ukrainian) provinces
1881–94	Reign of Alexander III

1883	State Peasant Land Bank established
1884	Repin, "They Did Not Expect Him"
1885	State Noble Land Bank established
1891	Widespread Famine
1892	Levitan, "The Vladimirka"
1894	Franco-Russian military alliance
1894–1917	Reign of Nicholas II
1897	Russia adopts gold standard
1899	First Hague Convention called by Nicholas II
1901	Lev Tolstoy excommunicated from the Orthodox Church
1903	Prohibition of printing Lithuanian in Latin letters dropped
1903	Kishinev Pogrom
1904	Ivan Pavlov receives Nobel prize for Physiology-Medicine
1904–5	Russo-Japanese War
1905	October Manifesto promises political reform
1905	Lenin, "Socialism and Religion"
1905	Periodical publications in Yiddish and Ukrainian allowed
1905–7	Revolution throughout the Russian Empire
1906–9	"Pig War" between Serbia and Austria
1906–11	Peter Stolypin Prime Minister
1906–17	Duma period
1907	Anglo-Russian Entente signed
1907–14	Stolypin agrarian reform
1908	Austria annexes Bosnia-Herzegovina
1908–11	Anatoly Lunacharsky, *Religion and Science*
1909	*Vekhi* ("Signposts")
1910–14	Stolypin Agrarian Reform
1911	Marie Curie-Skłodowska is first person to receive a second Nobel prize (in chemistry)
1912–13	Balkan Wars
1914–18	World War I
1916	Anti-Russian uprising in Turkestan
1917 February	Tsar forced to abdicate by liberal revolution
1917 February–October	"Provisional Government"
1917 July	Universal suffrage granted to all Russian citizens
1917 October	Bolshevik Revolution

1917 October 26	Land Decree confiscates church and noble land
1917 November	Declaration of the Rights of the Peoples of Russia
1918	Lenin, *State and Revolution.*
1918 February	Soviet Russia adopts Gregorian (western) calendar
1918 February	Patriarch Tikhon pronounces anathema on Soviet regime
1918 March	Treaty of Brest-Litovsk
1918–20	Civil War / War Communism
1919	Paris Peace conference creates new map of east-central Europe Comintern created in Moscow
1920	Soviet authorities set up "Department of Agitation and Propaganda" (Agitprop)
ca. 1920 to ca. 1933	Policy of *korenizatsiia*
1921 February–March	Kronstadt Rebellion
1921 March	Tenth Party Congress
1921–8	New Economic Policy (NEP)
1922 April	Treaty of Rapallo
1922 May	Arrest of Patriarch Tikhon
1922 December	Formation of USSR
1923	*The Little Red Imps* shows in Soviet cinemas
1924 March	Death of Lenin
1924	Gladkov, *Cement*
1925	Eisenstein, *Battleship Potemkin*
1925	"League of the Militant Godless" founded
1927	28 percent of students in higher education are female
1927	Metropolitan Sergii issues conciliatory "Declaration of Loyalty"
1928	Ilf and Petrov, *The Twelve Chairs*
1929	Trotsky expelled from USSR
1928 October	First Five-Year Plan begins
1929	Teaching of atheism in schools made compulsary
1929–31	Collectivization of Agriculture
1930s	Crash Industrialization throughout USSR
1932–3	"Terror Famine" in Ukraine, southern Russia, Kazakhstan
1933–4	Recriminalization of (male) homosexual acts
1934	Zhdanov announces new artistic method, "Socialist Realism"
1934	Film version of *Chapaev* opens in Leningrad

1934	Creation of Jewish Autonomous Region of Birobidzhan
1935	USSR embraces "popular front" against fascism
1936	Abortion outlawed
1936–9	USSR supports Republican forces in Spanish Civil War
1937	Mukhina, *The Worker and the Collective Farmer*
1939 summer	Battle of Khalkin Gol, Soviet victory over Japan
1939 August	Molotov–Ribbentrop Pact
1939 September	World War II begins
1939 November– March 1940	Soviet war against Finland ("Winter War")
1939–40	Mass Arrests and deportation of Poles from former eastern Poland
1939–45	Mass murder of Jews (Holocaust, Shoah)
1940 summer	Baltic States absorbed into USSR
1940–1	Mass arrests and deportations in Baltic republics
1941 June 21–22	Nazi Germany invades USSR ("Operation Barbarossa")
1941	Deportation of Volga Germans to central Asia
1941–2	Evacuation of industrial plant from western regions of USSR to the east
1943 April	Nazi troops discover mass graves of Polish officers at Katyń
1943 November– December	Teheran Conference
1944	Deportations of Crimean Tatars, Chechens, Ingush, and others
1944–7	Exchange of population (esp. Poles and Ukrainians)
1945 February	Yalta Conference
1945 May 9	World War II ends for USSR

Notes

---------------------------- Chapter 1 ------------------------------

1　On the causes for serf emancipation and the formulation of policy, see Daniel Field, *The End of Serfdom: Nobility and Bureaucracy in Russia, 1855–1861* (Cambridge, Mass., 1976).

2　Steven L. Hoch, "The Banking Crisis, Peasant Reform and Economic Development in Russia, 1857–1861," *American Historical Review*, vol. 96, no. 3 (June 1991), pp. 795–820.

3　On the atmosphere during the year of emancipation, see Daniel Field, "The Year of Jubilee" in Ben Eklof, John Bushnell, and Larissa Zakharova, eds., *Russia's Great Reforms, 1855–1881* (Bloomington, Ind., 1994), pp. 40–57.

4　Terence Emmons and Wayne S. Vucinich, eds., *The Zemstvo in Russia: An Experiment in Local Self-Government* (Cambridge, UK, 1982).

5　John L. H. Keep, *Soldiers of the Tsar* (Oxford, 1985), pp. 351–81.

6　For a good overview, see W. Bruce Lincoln, *The Great Reforms* (DeKalb, Ill., 1990).

7　For one account of the first phase of this growing alienation between intelligentsia and Russian state, see Nicholas V. Riasanovsky, *A Parting of Ways: Government and the Educated Public in Russia, 1801–1855* (Oxford, 1976).

8　Adam Ulam, *Russia's Failed Revolutions: From the Decembrists to the Dissidents* (London, 1981), pp. 66–128.

9　Petr A. Zaionchkovskii, *The Russian Autocracy in Crisis, 1878–1882* (Gulf Breeze, Fla., 1979).

10　Richard S. Wortman, *Scenarios of Power: Myth and Ceremony in Russian Monarchy* (Princeton, NJ, 2000), vol. 2, pp. 161–305.

11　Dominic Lieven, *Nicholas II: Twilight of the Empire* (New York, 1994).

12　Anna Geifman, *Thou Shalt Kill: Revolutionary Terrorism in Russia, 1894–1917* (Princeton, NJ, 1993).

13 Steven G. Marks, *Road to Power: the Trans-Siberian Railroad and the Colonization of Asian Russia* (Ithaca, NY, 1991).

14 J. N. Westwood, *Russia Against Japan, 1904–15: A New Look at the Russo-Japanese War* (Houndsmills, Basingstoke, 1986).

15 The best overview of these years is Abraham Ascher, *The Revolution of 1905* (Stanford, Calif., 1992), 2 vols.

16 Abraham Ascher, *P. A. Stolypin: The Search for Stability in Late Imperial Russia* (Stanford, Calif., 2001).

17 Geoffrey A. Hosking, *The Russian Constitutional Experiment: Government and Duma* (Cambridge, UK, 1973).

18 D. E. Showalter, "Manoeuvre Warfare: The Eastern and Western Fronts, 1914–1915" in Hew Strachan, ed., *Oxford Illustrated History of the First World War* (Oxford, 1998), p. 46.

19 Mark Von Hagen, *War in a European Borderland: Occupations and Occupation Plans in Galicia and Ukraine, 1914–1918* (Seattle, Wash., 2007).

20 Peter Gattrell, *A Whole Empire Walking: Refugees in Russia during World War I* (Bloomington, Ind., 1999).

21 Eric Lohr, *Nationalizing the Russian Empire: The Campaign against Enemy Aliens during World War I* (Cambridge, Mass., 2003).

22 Norman Stone, *The Eastern Front 1914–1917* (New York, 1975).

23 On the erosion of Nicholas's moral authority as tsar during World War I, see Orlando Figes and Boris Kolonitskii, *Interpreting the Russian Revolution: The Language and Symbols of 1917* (New Haven, Conn., 1999), pp. 9–29.

24 Pavel Miliukov, *Political Memoirs, 1905–1917* (Ann Arbor, Mich., 1967), pp. 377–8.

25 E. N. Burdzhalov, *Russia's Second Revolution: The February 1917 Uprising in Petrograd* (Bloomington, Ind., 1987).

26 Richard Abraham, *Alexander Kerensky: The First Love of the Revolution* (New York, 1987).

27 Alexander Rabinowitch, *The Bolsheviks Come to Power: The Revolution of 1917 in Petrograd* (New York, 1976). For an excellent detailed account of the collapse of the Russian army in the course of 1917, see Allan K. Wildman, *The End of the Russian Imperial Army* (Princeton, NJ, 1980, 1987), 2 vols.

28 For a fictionalized, highly anti-Lenin, but very readable account of Lenin's coming to Russia in 1917, see Aleksandr Solzhenitsyn, *Lenin in Zurich* (London, 1976).

29 Evan Mawdsley, *The Russian Civil War* (Boston, 1987). A very readable account of the revolution and Civil War published only a few years after the events described and still valuable as a historical source is William Henry Chamberlain, *The Russian Revolution, 1917–1921* (New York, 1935), 2 vols.

30 Orlando Figes, *Peasant Russia, Civil War: The Volga Countryside in Revolution 1917–1921* (London, 1989).

31 Piotr Wandycz, *Soviet–Polish Relations, 1917–1921* (Cambridge, Mass., 1969).

32 Paul Avrich, *Kronstadt, 1921* (Princeton, NJ, 1970).

33 Anne Gorsuch, "NEP Be Damned! Young Militants in the 1920s and the Culture of Civil War," *Russian Review*, vol. 56, no. 4 (October 1997), pp. 564–80.

34 Moshe Lewin, *Lenin's Last Struggle* (New York, 1968).

35 James Harris, "Stalin as General Secretary: The Appointments Process and the Nature of Stalin's Power" in Sarah Davies and James Harris, eds., *Stalin: A New History* (Cambridge, UK, 2005), pp. 63–82.

36 Moshe Lewin, *Russian Peasants and Soviet Power: A Study of Collectivization* (New York, 1975).

37 Robert Conquest, *The Harvest of Sorrow: Collectivization and the Terror Famine* (Oxford, 1986).

38 Robert Conquest, *Stalin and the Kirov Murder* (Oxford, 1989); Matt Lenoe, "Did Stalin Kill Kirov and Does It Matter?" *Journal of Modern History*, vol. 74 (2002), pp. 352–80.

39 J. Arch Getty, *Origins of the Great Purges: The Soviet Communist Party Reconsidered, 1933–1938* (Cambridge, UK, 1985); J. Arch Getty and Robert T. Manning, eds., *Stalinist Terror: New Perspectives* (Cambridge, UK, 1993); J. Arch Getty and Oleg V. Naumov, *The Road to Terror: Stalin and the Self-Destruction of the Bolsheviks, 1932–1939* (New Haven, Conn., 1999).

40 Paul Hagenloh, *Stalin's Police: Public Order and Mass Repression in the USSR, 1926–1941* (Washington, DC, 2009).

41 Robert Conquest, *The Great Terror: A Reassessment* (New York, 1990).

42 Anne Applebaum, *Gulag: A History* (New York, 2003).

43 Jan T. Gross, *Revolution from Abroad: The Soviet Conquest of Poland's Western Ukraine and Western Belorussia* (Princeton, NJ, 1988).

44 Allen Chew, *The White Death: The Epic of the Soviet-Finnish Winter War* (Washington, DC, 1990).

45 Gabriel Gorodetsky, *Grand Delusion: Stalin and the German Invasion of Russia* (New Haven, Conn., 1999).

46 Harrison Salisbury, *The 900 Days: The Siege of Leningrad* (New York, 1969).

47 Antony Beevor, *Stalingrad* (New York, 1998).

48 John Erickson, *Stalin's War with Germany* (New Haven, Conn., 1999), 2 vols.

Chapter 2

1 Gregory Freeze, "The *Soslovie* (Estate) Paradigm in Russian Social History," *American Historical Review*, vol. 91, no. 1 (1986), pp. 11–36.

2 Elise K. Wirtschafter, *Structures of Society: Imperial Russia's "People of Various Ranks"* (DeKalb, Ill., 1994).

3 Stephen F. Frank, *Crime, Cultural Contact, and Justice in Rural Russia, 1856–1914* (Berkeley, Calif., 1999).

4 Jane Burbank, *Russian Peasants Go to Court: Legal Culture in the Countryside, 1905–1917* (Bloomington, Ind., 2004).

5 On peasants coming to Moscow, see Joseph Bradley, *Muzhik and Muscovite: Urbanization in Late Imperial Russia* (Berkeley, Calif., 1985).

6   Reginald Zelnik, ed., *A Radical Worker in Tsarist Russia: The Autobiography of Semen Ivanovich Kanatchikov* (Stanford, Calif., 1986).

7   Mark Steinberg, *Moral Communities: The Culture of Class Relations in the Russian Printing Industry, 1867–1907* (Berkeley, Calif., 1992).

8   Rose Glickman, *Russian Factory Women: Workplace and Society, 1880–1914* (Berkeley, Calif., 1984).

9   Leopold Haimson, "The Problem of Social Stability in Urban Russia, 1905–1917," *Slavic Review*, vol. 23, no. 4 (1964), pp. 619–42; vol. 24, no. 1 (1965), pp. 1–22.

10 Michael F. Hamm, ed., *The City in Late Imperial Russia* (Bloomington, Ind., 1986), p. 2.

11 The best overview of the Russian peasant's *longue durée* is provided by David Moon, *The Russian Peasantry 1600–1930: The World the Peasants Made* (London, 1999).

12 Christine D. Worobec, *Peasant Russia: Family and Community in the Post-Emancipation Period* (DeKalb, Ill., 1995), provides an excellent overview. For a contemporary educated Russian's "scientific" description of a typical Russian peasant, see Olga S. Tian-Shanskaia, *Village Life in Late Tsarist Russia*, ed. David L. Ransel (Bloomington, Ind., 1993).

13 Orlando Figes, *Peasant Russia Civil War: The Volga Countryside in Revolution 1917–1921* (London, 2001).

14 Catriona Kelly and David Shepherd, eds. *Constructing Russian Culture in the Age of Revolution: 1881–1940* (Oxford, UK, 1998), p. 302.

15 Viktor P. Danilov, *Rural Russia under the New Regime* (London, 1988); James Heinzen, *Inventing a Soviet Countryside: State Power and the Transformation of Rural Russia, 1917–1929* (Pittsburgh, 2004).

16 For an engaging social history of the Russian peasantry in the 1920s and 1930s, see Sheila Fitzpatrick, *Stalin's Peasants: Resistance and Survival in the Russian Village after Collectivization* (Oxford, 1994).

17 A very readable and thought-provoking overview of the complicated relations between social classes, nationality, and politics in imperial Russia is provided by Geoffrey A. Hoskin, *Russia: People and Empire 1552–1917* (Cambridge, Mass., 1997).

18 Edith W. Clowes, Samuel D. Kassow, and James L. West, eds., *Between Tsar and People: Educated Society and the Quest for Public Identity in Late Imperial Russia* (Princeton, NJ, 1991).

19 Richard Pipes, *The Russian Revolution* (New York, 1991), pp. 121–52.

20 Richard Pipes, ed., *The Russian Intelligentsia* (New York, 1961).

21 Richard Wortman, *The Development of a Russian Legal Consciousness* (Chicago, 1976); Andrzej Walicki, *Legal Philosophies of Russian Liberalism* (Oxford, 1987).

22 Louise McReynolds, *The News under Russia's Old Regime: The Development of a Mass-Circulation Press* (Princeton, NJ, 1991); Beth Holmgren, *Rewriting Capitalism: Literature and the Market in Late Tsarist Russia and the Kingdom of Poland* (Pittsburgh, 1998).

23 Jane Burbank, *Intelligentsia and Power: Russian Views of Bolshevism, 1917–1922* (Oxford, 1986).

24 Michael David-Fox, *Revolution of the Mind: Higher Learning among the Bolsheviks, 1918–1929* (Ithaca, NY, 1997); Nicholas Lampert, *The Technical Intelligentsia and the Soviet State* (New York, 1979).

25 Daniel Beer, *Renovating Russia: The Human Sciences and the Fate of Liberal Modernity, 1880–1930* (Ithaca, NY, 2008).

26 Vera Dunham, *In Stalin's Time: Middleclass Values in Soviet Fiction* (Cambridge, UK, 1976).

27 William G. Wagner, "Paradoxes of Piety: The Nizhegorod Convent of the Exaltation of the Cross, 1807–1935" in Valerie A. Kivelson and Robert H. Greene, eds., *Orthodox Russia: Belief and Practice under the Tsars* (University Park, Penn., 2003), pp. 211–38.

28 Laurie Bernstein, *Sonia's Daughters: Prostitutes and Their Regulation in Imperial Russia* (Berkeley, Calif., 1995), p. 46.

29 Ruth Dudgeon, "The Forgotten Minority: Women Students in Imperial Russia, 1872–1917," *Russian History/Histoire Russe*, vol. 9, no. 1 (1982), pp. 1–26.

30 Irina Paperno, *Chernyshevsky and the Age of Realism: A Study in the Semiotics of Behavior* (Stanford, Calif., 1988).

31 Barbara Engel, *Mothers and Daughers: Women of the Intelligentsia in Nineteenth-Century Russia* (Cambridge, UK, 1983).

32 Richard Stites, *The Women's Liberation Movement in Russia* (Princeton, NJ, 1978).

33 Laurie S. Stoff, *They Fought for the Motherland: Russia's Women Soldiers in World War I and the Revolution* (Lawrence, Kans., 2006).

34 Elizabeth A. Wood, *The Baba and the Comrade: Gender and Politics in Revolutionary Russia* (Bloomington, Ind., 1997).

35 A. Kollontai, "Make Way for the Winged Eros" in William G. Rosenberg, ed., *Bolshevik Visions: First Phase of the Cultural Revolution in Soviet Russia*, 2nd edn. (Ann Arbor, Mich., 1990), vol. 1, pp. 84–94.

36 Douglas T. Northrop, *Veiled Empire: Gender and Power in Stalinist Central Asia* (Ithaca, NY, 2004).

37 Wendy Z. Goldman, "Women, Abortion, and the State, 1917–36" in Barbara Evans Clements, Barbara Alpern Engel, and Christine D. Worobec, eds., *Russia's Women: Accommodation, Resistance, Transformation* (Berkeley, Calif., 1991), pp. 243–66.

38 Scott W. Palmer, *Dictatorship of the Air: Aviation Culture and the Fate of Modern Russia* (Cambridge, UK, 2006), pp. 251–2, 273.

39 Petr A. Zaionchkovskii, *Pravitel'stvennyi apparat samoderzhavnoi Rossii v XIX v.* (Moscow, 1978); Daniel Orlovsky, *The Limits of Reform* (Cambridge, UK, 1981).

40 Walter Pintner, Walter MacKenzie, and Don Karl Rowney, eds., *Russian Officialdom: The Bureaucratization of Russian Society from the Seventeenth to the Twentieth Century* (Chapel Hill, NC, 1980).

41 Theodore Von Laue, *Sergei Witte and the Industrialization of Russia* (New York, 1963). Witte's self-justifying but fascinating memoirs have also been published in English translation: *The Memoirs of Count Witte*, trans. and ed. Sidney Harcave (Armonk, NY, 1990).

42 Milovan Djilas, *The New Class: An Analysis of the Communist System* (New York, 1958).

43 Mikhail S. Voslenskii, *Nomenklatura: Anatomy of the Soviet Ruling Class* (London, 1984). While this work concentrates mainly on a later period, it also argues for the *nomenklatura* as a principal class in the USSR from the 1920s.

44 Wendy Z. Goldman, *Women, the State, and Revolution: Soviet Family Policy and Social Life, 1917–1936* (Cambridge, UK, 1993).

45 Dan Healey, *Homosexual Desire in Revolutionary Russia: The Regulation of Sexual and Gender Dissent* (Chicago, 2001).

46 Bruce Adams, *The Politics of Punishment: Prison Reform in Russia 1863–1917* (Dekalb, Ill., 1996).

47 Joan Neuberger, *Hooliganism: Crime, Culture, and Power in St. Petersburg* (Berkeley, Calif., 1993).

48 Alan M. Ball, *And Now My Soul Is Hardened: Abandoned Children in Soviet Russia, 1914–1930* (Berkeley, Calif., 1994).

49 Moshe Lewin, *The Making of the Soviet System: Essays in the Social History of Interwar Russia* (New York, 1985).

50 Paul Hageloh, *Stalin's Police: Public Order and Mass Repression in the USSR, 1926–1941* (Washington, DC, 2009); David Shearer, *Policing Stalin's Socialism: Repression and Social Order in the Soviet Union, 1924–1953* (New Haven, Conn., 2009).

51 The stories of "repressed women" and fervent supports of Soviet power are brought together in Sheila Fitzpatrick and Yuri Slezkine, eds., *In the Shadow of Revolution: Life Stories of Russian Women from 1917 to the Second World War* (Princeton, NJ, 2000). For the life of one individual whose experience in the Gulag transformed him into a true believer, see Thomas Lahusen, *How Life Writes the Book: Real Socialism and Socialist Realism in Stalin's Russia* (Ithaca, NY, 1997).

52 Patricia Herlihy, *The Alcoholic Empire: Vodka and Politics in Late Imperial Russia* (Oxford, 2002).

53 Laura L. Phillips, *Bolsheviks and the Bottle: Drink and Worker Culture in St. Petersburg, 1900–1929* (DeKalb, Ill., 2000).

54 Louise McReynolds, *Russia at Play: Leisure Activities at the End of the Tsarist Era* (Ithaca, NY, 2003).

55 Diane Koenker and Anne E. Gorsuch, eds., *Turizm: The Russian and East European Tourist under Capitalism and Socialism* (Ithaca, NY, 2006).

56 Robert Edelman, *Serious Fun: A History of Spectator Sports in the USSR* (Oxford, 1993).

Chapter 3

1 Henning Bauer et al., eds., *Die Nationalitäten des Russischen Reiches in der Volkszählung von 1897* (Stuttgart, 1991), cited in *Handbuch der russischen Geschichte* (Stuttgart, 1992), vol. 3, p. 1748.

2 Theodore R. Weeks, "'Us' or 'Them'? Belarusians and Official Russia, 1863–1914," *Nationalities Papers*, vol. 31, no. 2 (June 2003), pp. 211–24.

3 For the implications of such a hierarchy in both imperial and Soviet times, see Yuri Slezkine, *Arctic Mirrors: Russia and the Small Peoples of the North* (Ithaca, NY, 1994).

4 For an interesting attempt to contrast Polish and Russian "paths to European history," see Klaus Zernack, *Polen und Russland: Zwei Wege in der europäischen Geschichte* (Berlin, 1994).

5   I have tried to develop these ideas more fully in my *Nation and State in Late Imperial Russia: Nationalism and Russification on the Western Frontier, 1863–1914* (DeKalb, Ill., 1996).

6   Ingeborg Fleischhauer, *Die Deutschen im Zarenreich: Zwei Jahrhunderten deutsch-russischer Kulturgemeinschaft* (Stuttgart, 1986).

7   On Baltic Germans' attempts to deal with modernization in the pre-1914 period, see Heide W. Whelan, *Adapting to Modernity: Family, Caste and Capitalism among the Baltic German Nobility* (Cologne, 1999).

8   For a stimulating if somewhat popularized narrative of this "Great Game" between Britain and Russia, see Karl E. Mayer and Shareen Blair Brysac, *Tournament of the Shadows: The Great Game and the Race for Empire in Central Asia* (New York, 2006).

9   Jeff Sahadeo, *Russian Colonial Society in Tashkent, 1865–1923* (Bloomington, Ind., 2007).

10 Theodore R. Weeks, "Managing Empire: Tsarist Nationalities Policy" in Dominic Lieven, ed., *The Cambridge History of Russia*. Vol. 2: *Imperial Russia, 1689–1917* (Cambridge, UK, 2006), pp. 27–44.

11 David MacKenzie, *The Lion of Tashkent: The Career of General M. G. Cherniaev* (Athens, Ga., 1974).

12 Seymour Becker, *Russia's Protectorates in Central Asia: Bukhara and Khiva 1865–1924* (London, 2004).

13 Alexei Miller, *The Ukrainian Question: The Russian Empire and Nationalism in the Nineteenth Century* (Budapest, 2003).

14 Edward Allworth, *Central Asia: 130 Years of Russian Dominance, A Historical Overview*, 3rd edn. (Durham, NC, 1994).

15 Edward C. Thaden et al., *Russification in the Baltic Provinces and Finland, 1855–1914* (Princeton, NJ, 1981).

16 Theodore R. Weeks, "*Russification*: Word and Practice 1863–1914," *Proceedings of the American Philosophical Society*, vol. 148, no. 4 (December 2004), pp. 471–89.

17 Adeeb Khalid, *The Politics of Muslim Cultural Reform: Jadidism in Central Asia* (Berkeley, Calif., 1998).

18 Jeremy Smith, *The Bolsheviks and the National Question, 1917–1923* (New York, 1999).

19 Richard Pipes, *The Formation of the Soviet Union, Communism and Nationalism, 1917–1923*, rev. edn. (Cambridge, Mass., 1964).

20 Terry Martin, *The Affirmative Action Empire: Nations and Nationalism in the Soviet Union 1923–1939* (Ithaca, NY, 2001).

21 Yuri Slezkine, "The USSR as a Communal Apartment, or How a Socialist State Promoted Ethnic Particularism," *Slavic Review*, vol. 53, no. 2 (summer 1994), pp. 414–52.

22 Serhy Yekelchyk, *Stalin's Empire of Memory: Russian–Ukrainian Relations in the Soviet Historical Imagination* (Toronto, 2004).

23 Ginzburg tells her story in her moving memoirs, *Journey into the Whirlwind* (New York, 1967) and *Within the Whirlwind* (New York, 1981).

24 Various interpretations of the 1932 "terror famine" are present in recent historiography. Speaking generally, one may say that Ukrainian historians see the famine as a

genocide against their people, and conservative historians such as Conquest tend to agree. See David Marples, *Heroes and Villains: Creating National History in Contemporary Ukraine* (Budapest, 2007), pp. 35–77. The two cases are set down well in Robert Conquest, *The Harvest of Sorrow: Collectivization and the Terror Famine* (Oxford, 1986); and Robert W. Davies and Stephen G. Wheatcroft, *The Years of Hunger: Soviet Agriculture, 1931–1933* (Basingstoke, 2004). An excellent overview of the Kazakh case is given in Niccolò Pianciola, "Famine in the Steppe: The Collectivization of Agriculture and the Kazak Herdsmen 1928–1934," *Cahiers du Monde russe*, vol. 45, no. 1–2 (January–June 2004), pp. 137–92.

25 Terry Martin, "The Origins of Soviet Ethnic Cleansing," *Journal of Modern History*, vol. 70 (1998), p. 823.

26 Jan T. Gross, *Revolution from Abroad: The Soviet Conquest of Poland's Western Ukraine and Western Belorussia* (Princeton, NJ, 1988).

27 V. Stanley Vardys and Romuald J. Misiunas, eds., *The Baltic States in Peace and War, 1917–1945* (University Park, Penn., 1978), pp. 139–72.

28 Robert Conquest, *The Nation Killers: The Soviet Deportation of Nationalities* (London, 1978).

29 For one case study of postwar "population exchanges," see Theodore R. Weeks, "Population Politics in Vilnius 1944–1947: A Case Study of State-Sponsored Ethnic Cleansing," *Post-Soviet Affairs*, vol. 23, no. 1 (2007), pp. 76–95.

30 The subject of violence and ethnic cleansing carried out by both Poles and Ukrainians during World War II remains very painful and controversial. For an even-handed approach, see Timothy Snyder, *The Reconstruction of Nations: Poland, Ukraine, Lithuania, Belarus, 1569–1999* (New Haven, Conn., 2003), pp. 154–201.

31 For a critical examination of one aspect of the "Jewish myth" – that Jews dominated in revolutionary parties, see Erich Haberer, *Jews and Revolution in Nineteenth-Century Russia* (Cambridge, UK, 1995).

32 John D. Klier, *Russia Gathers Her Jews: The Origins of the "Jewish Question" in Russia, 1772–1825* (DeKalb, Ill., 1986).

33 For an overview of the history of Jews in this region (primarily but not exclusively in the Russian Empire), see Israel Bartal, *The Jews of Eastern Europe, 1772–1881*, trans. Chaya Naor (Philadelphia, Penn., 2002). More specifically on the Russian Empire and the later period, see Heinz-Dietrich Löwe, *The Tsars and the Jews: Reform, Reaction, and Antisemitism in Imperial Russia, 1772–1917* (Chur, Switzerland, 1992).

34 Verena Dohrn, "The Rabbinical Schools as Institutions of Socialization in Tsarist Russia, 1847–1873," *Polin*, vol. 14 (2001), pp. 83–104.

35 Irvin Michael Aronson, *Troubled Waters: The Origins of the 1881 Pogroms in Russia* (Pittsburgh, 1990).

36 John D. Klier and Shlomo Lambroza, eds., *Pogroms: Anti-Jewish Violence in Modern Russian History* (Cambridge, UK, 1992).

37 Benjamin Nathans, *Beyond the Pale: The Jewish Encounter with Late Imperial Russia* (Berkeley, Calif., 2002).

38 For a very readable, illustrated history of Jewish life, politics, and culture in the Russian-Soviet context, see Zvi Gitelman, *A Century of Ambivalence: The Jews of Russia and the Soviet Union, 1881 to the Present* (New York, 1988).

39 On the Polish example, see Theodore R. Weeks, *From Assimilation to Antisemitism: The "Jewish Question" in Poland, 1850–1914* (DeKalb, Ill., 2006).
40 Henry Abramson, *A Prayer for the Government: Ukrainians and Jews in Revolutionary Times, 1917–1920* (Cambridge, Mass., 1999).
41 Zvi Gitelman, *Jewish Nationality and Soviet Politics: The Jewish Sections of the CPSU, 1917–1930* (Princeton, NJ, 1972).
42 Robert Weinberg, *Stalin's Forgotten Zion: Birobidzhan and the Making of a Soviet Jewish Homeland: An Illustrated History, 1928–1996* (Berkeley, Calif., 1998).
43 Yuri Slezkine, *The Jewish Century* (Princeton, NJ, 2004), p. 224.

--- Chapter 4 ---

1 For a stimulating discussion of diverse aspects of "modernity" in the Russian and Soviet context, see David L. Hoffmann and Yanni Kotsonis, eds., *Russian Modernity: Politics, Knowledge, Practices* (New York, 2000).
2 Quoted in Ronald Suny, *The Soviet Experiment: Russia, the USSR, and the Successor States* (Oxford, 1998), p. 235.
3 Arcadius Kahan, *Russian Economic History: The Nineteenth Century* (Chicago, 1989), p. 30.
4 Steven G. Marks, *Road to Power: The Trans-Siberian Railroad and the Colonization of Asian Russia* (Ithaca, NY, 1991).
5 Kahan, *Russian Economic History*, p. 34. In general on railroads in tsarist Russia, see J. N. Westwood, *A History of Russian Railroads* (London, 1964). Donald Treadgold, *The Great Siberian Migration: Government and Peasant in Resettlement from Emancipation to the First World War* (Princeton, NJ, 1957).
6 Yanni Kotsonis, "'No Place to Go': Taxation and State Formation in Late Imperial and Early Soviet Russia," *Journal of Modern History*, vol. 76 (September 2004), pp. 531–77; *idem*, "'Face to Face': The State, the Individual, and the Citizen in Russian Taxation, 1863–1917," *Slavic Review*, vol. 63, no. 2 (2004), pp. 221–46.
7 Peter Gatrell, *The Tsarist Economy 1850–1917* (New York, 1986), p. 228.
8 Boris Ananich, "The Russian Economy and Banking System" in Dominic Lieven, ed., *The Cambridge History of Russia*, vol. 2: *Imperial Russia, 1689–1917* (Cambridge, UK, 2006), pp. 402–25.
9 Richard Wortman, *The Development of a Russian Legal Consciousness* (Chicago, 1976).
10 Jörg Baberowski, *Autokratie und Justiz: Zum Verhältnis von Rechtsstaatlichkeit und Rückständigkeit im ausgehenden Zarenreich, 1864–1914* (Frankfurt, 1996).
11 Simon Dixon, "The Orthodox Church and the Workers of St. Petersburg, 1880–1914" in Hugh McLeod, ed., *European Religion in the Age of the Great Cities, 1830–1930* (London, 1995), pp. 119–41; and Page Herrlinger, *Working Souls: Russian Orthodoxy and Factory Labor in St. Petersburg, 1881–1917* (Bloomington, Ind., 2007).
12 Michael Hamm, ed., *The City in Late Imperial Russia* (Bloomington, Ind., 1986).
13 Paul R. Gregory, *Before Command: An Economic History of Russia from Emancipation to the First Five-Year Plan* (Princeton, NJ, 1994), pp. 14–36.

14   Theodore Von Laue, *Sergei Witte and the Industrialization of Russia* (New York, 1963).

15   Wayne S. Vucinich, *The Peasant in Nineteenth-Century Russia* (Stanford, Calif., 1968); Teodor Shanin, *The Awkward Class: Political Sociology of Peasantry in a Developing Society: Russia 1910–1925* (Oxford, 1972).

16   David Moon, *The Russian Peasantry 1600–1930: The World the Peasants Made* (London, 1999), pp. 11–36.

17   Boris Mironov, "The Development of Literacy in Russia and the USSR from the Tenth to the Twentieth Centuries," *History of Education Quarterly*, vol. 31 (1991), p. 235.

18   Robert Blobaum, *Rewolucja: Russian Poland 1904–1907* (Ithaca, NY, 1995).

19   Abraham Ascher, *P. A. Stolypin: The Search for Stability in Late Imperial Russia* (Stanford, Calif., 2001).

20   "Modernization from Above: The Stolypin Land Reform" in Judith Pallot and Denis J. B. Shaw, *Landscape and Settlement in Romanov Russia 1613–1917* (Oxford, 1990), pp. 164–92.

21   A. Gerschenkron, "Agrarian Policies and Industrialization: Russia 1861–1917" in H. J. Habakkuk and M. Postan, eds., *The Cambridge Economic History of Europe*, vol. 6: *The Industrial Revolutions and After: Incomes, Population and Technological Change (II)* (Cambridge, UK, 1965), p. 795.

22   Peter Waldron, *Between Two Revolutions: Stolypin and the Politics of Renewal in Russia* (DeKalb, Ill., 1998).

23   Peter Gatrell, *Russia's First World War: A Social and Economic History* (London, 2005).

24   Andrzej Walicki, *Marxism and the Leap to the Kingdom of Freedom: The Rise and Fall of the Communist Utopia* (Stanford, Calif., 1995).

25   My interpretation of *What Is to Be Done?* as a rejection of a broad-based and democratic socialist party in Russia is a traditional (and broadly accepted) one, but this view has been challenged recently in Lars T. Lih, *Lenin Rediscovered:* What Is to Be Done? *in Context* (Leiden, 2006).

26   D. Holloway, "Science, Technology and Modernity" in Ronald Suny, ed., *The Cambridge History of Russia*, vol. 3: *The Twentieth Century* (Cambridge, UK, 2006), p. 549.

27   Daniel Peris, *Storming the Heavens: The Soviet League of the Militant Godless* (Ithaca, NY, 1998).

28   Gregory J. Massell, *The Surrogate Proletariat: Moslem Women and Revolutionary Strategies in Soviet Central Asia, 1919–1929* (Princeton, NJ, 1974).

29   Alec Nove, *An Economic History of the USSR*, 2nd edn. (Harmondsworth, Middlesex [UK], 1989), p. 189.

30   The stories of "dekulakized" men and women figure in two important recent works on this period: Sheila Fitzpatrick and Yuri Slezkine, eds., *In the Shadow of Revolution: Life Stories of Russian Women from1917 to the Second World War* (Princeton, NJ, 2000); and Orlando Figes, *The Whisperers: Private Life in Stalin's Russia* (New York, 2007).

31   Wendy Z. Goldman, *Women at the Gates: Gender and Industry in Stalin's Russia* (Cambridge, UK, 2002).

32   Lewis H. Siegelbaum, *Stakhanovism and the Politics of Productivity in the USSR* (Cambridge, UK, 1988).

33 Monica Rüthers, *Moskau bauen von Lenin bis Chruščev: Öffentliche Räume zwischen Utopie, Terror und Alltag* (Vienna, 2007); Karl Schlögel, *Terror und Traum: Moskau 1937* (Munich, 2008).

34 Stephen Kotkin, *Magnetic Mountain: Stalinism as a Civilization* (Berkeley, Calif., 1991).

35 Jochen Hellbeck, *Revolution on My Mind: Writing a Diary under Stalin* (Cambridge, Mass., 2006), p. 75.

36 Sheila Fitzpatrick, *Tear Off the Masks! Identity and Imposture in Twentieth-Century Russia* (Princeton, NJ, 2005).

37 Lewis Siegelbaum and Andrei Sokolov, *Stalinism as a Way of Life*, abridged ed. (New Haven, Conn., 2004); Sheila Fitzpatrick, *Everyday Stalinism: Ordinary Life in Extraordinary Times: Soviet Russia in the 1930s* (New York, 1999).

38 John Scott, *Behind the Urals* (Bloomington, Ind., 1989 [originally published 1942]).

39 Karen Petrone, *Life Has Become More Joyous, Comrades: Celebrations in the Time of Stalin* (Bloomington, Ind., 2000).

40 Paul Hagenloh, *Stalin's Police: Public Order and Mass Repression in the USSR, 1926–1941* (Washington, DC, 2009), pp. 325–6.

41 John Barber and Mark Harrison, *The Soviet Home Front, 1941–1945: A Social and Economic History of the USSR in World War II* (London, 1991).

42 These figures are from Bernd Bonwetsch, "Der 'Grosse Vaterländische Krieg': vom deutschen Einfall bis zum sowjetischen Sieg (1941–1945)" in *Handbuch der Geschichte Russlands*, ed. M. Hellmann, K. Zernack, and G. Schramm (Stuttgart 1992), vol. 3, p. 953.

43 Mark Harrison, *Soviet Planning in Peace and War, 1938–1945* (Cambridge, UK, 1985).

44 Robert H. Jones, *The Roads to Russia: United States Lend-Lease to the Soviet Union* (Norman, Ok., 1969).

--------------------------- Chapter 5 ---------------------------

1 John Meyendorff, *The Orthodox Church: Its Past and Its Role in the World Today* (Crestwood, NY, 1981).

2 Vera Shevzov, *Russian Orthodoxy on the Eve of the Revolution* (Oxford, 2004).

3 For an excellent overview of the Russian Orthodox church from Peter the Great to 1917, see the articles by Simon Dixon and Chris Chulos in Michael Angold, ed., *The Cambridge History of Christianity*. Vol. 5: *Eastern Christianity* (Cambridge, UK, 2006), pp. 325–70.

4 Roy R. Robson, *Old Believers in Modern Russia* (DeKalb, Ill., 1995).

5 Laura Engelstein, *Castration and the Heavenly Kingdom: A Russian Folktale* (Ithaca, NY, 1999).

6 Gregory L. Freeze, "Handmaiden of the State? The Church in Imperial Russia Reconsidered," *Journal of Ecclesiastical History*, vol. 36, no. 1 (January 1985), pp. 82–102.

7 Page Herrlinger, *Working Souls: Russian Orthodoxy and Factory Labor in St. Petersburg, 1881–1917* (Bloomington, Ind., 2007).

8   For a famous account of the hardships of an ordinary Orthodox priest, first published in 1858, see I. S. Belliustin, *Description of the Clergy in Rural Russia: The Memoir of a Nineteenth-Century Parish Priest*, translated with an interpretive essay by Gregory L. Freeze (Ithaca, NY, 1985).

9   Gregory L. Freeze, *The Parish Clergy in Nineteenth-Century Russia: Crisis, Reform, Counter-Reform* (Princeton, NJ, 1983); Laurie Manchester, *Holy Fathers, Secular Sons: Clergy, Intelligentsia, and the Modern Self in Revolutionary Russia* (DeKalb, Ill., 2008).

10 Leonid Heretz, *Russia on the Eve of Modernity: Popular Religion and Traditional Culture under the Last Tsars* (Cambridge, UK, 2008).

11 I thank Professor Christine Worobec for this pithy and insightful remark.

12 Chris J. Chulos, *Converging Worlds: Religion and Community in Peasant Russia, 1861–1917* (DeKalb, Ill., 2003).

13 Jennifer Hedda, *His Kingdom Come: Orthodox Pastorship and Social Activism in Revolutionary Russia* (DeKalb, Ill., 2008), esp. pp. 126–52.

14 Theodore R. Weeks, "The 'End' of the Uniate Church in Russia: The *Vozsoedinenie* of 1875," *Jahrbücher für Geschichte Osteuropas*, vol. 44 (1995), pp. 1–13; and idem, "Between Rome and Tsargrad: The Uniate Church in Imperial Russia" in Robert B. Geraci and Michael Khodarkovsky, eds., *Of Religion and Empire: Missions, Conversion, and Tolerance in Tsarist Russia* (Ithaca, NY, 2001), pp. 70–91.

15 Jacob Frumkin, Gregor Aronson, Alexis Goldenweiser, eds., *Russian Jewry (1860–1917)* (New York, 1966), gives an excellent self-portrait of the community.

16 Franco Venturi, *Roots of Revolution: A History of the Populist and Socialist Movements in Nineteenth-Century Russia* (Chicago, 1983), pp. 325–8.

17 Andrzej Walicki, *The Controversy over Capitalism: Studies in the Social Philosophy of the Russian Populists* (Oxford, 1969).

18 Arthur P. Mendel, *Michael Bakunin: Roots of Apocalypse* (New York, 1981); John Randolph, *The House in the Garden: The Bakunin Family and the Romance of Russian Idealism* (Ithaca, NY, 2007).

19 Caroline Cahm, *Kropotkin and the Rise of Revolutionary Anarchism, 1872–1886* (Cambridge, UK, 1989).

20 Leszek Kolakowski, *The Alienation of Reason: A History of Positivist Thought* (Garden City, NY, 1968); Stanislaus Blejwas, *Realism in Polish Politics: Warsaw Positivism and National Survival in Nineteenth-Century Poland* (New Haven, Conn., 1984).

21 Joseph Frank, *Dostoevsky: The Stir of Liberation, 1860–1865* (Princeton, NJ, 1986). Frank's multivolume work provides not only a detailed biography of the writer but an extraordinarily insightful and fascinating portrait of the age.

22 Vladimir Solovyov, *War, Progress, and the End of History: Three Conversations, Including a Short Story of the Anti-Christ* (Hudson, NY, 1990), pp. 159–91.

23 Catherine Evtuhov, *The Cross and the Sickle: Sergei Bulgakov and the Fate of Russian Religious Philosophy, 1890–1917* (Ithaca, NY, 1996).

24 *Vekhi: Landmarks*, trans. and ed. Marshall S. Shatz and Judith E. Zimmermann (Armonk, NY, 1994), p. xxxvii.

25 Roger W. Pethybridge, *One Step Backwards, Two Steps Forward: Soviet Society and Politics in the New Economic Policy* (Oxford, 1990), p. xi.

26 Jennifer Jean Wynot, *Keeping the Faith: Russian Orthodox Monasticism in the Soviet Union, 1917–1939* (College Station, Tex., 2004).
27 Glennys Young, *Power and the Sacred in Revolutionary Russia: Religious Activists in the Village* (University Park, Penn., 1997).
28 Edward E. Roslof, *Red Priests: Renovationism, Russian Orthodoxy, and Revolution, 1905–1946* (Bloomington, Ind., 2002).
29 Daniel Peris, *Storming the Heavens: The Soviet League of the Militant Godless* (Ithaca, NY, 1998.
30 Dmitry V. Pospielovsky, *A History of Marxist-Leninist Atheism and Soviet Antireligious Policies* (New York, 1987), vol. 2, pp. 47–90.
31 William B. Husband, "Soviet Atheism and Russian Orthodox Strategies of Resistance, 1917–1932," *Journal of Modern History*, vol. 70 (March 1998), pp. 74–107; Gregory L. Freeze, "The Stalinist Assault on the Parish, 1929–1941" in Manfred Hildermeier, ed., *Stalinismus vor dem Zweiten Weltkrieg: Neue Wege der Forschung* (Munich, 1998), pp. 209–32.
32 Ryszard Kapuściński, *Imperium* (New York, 1994), pp. 95–108.
33 Nora Levin, *The Jews in the Soviet Union since 1917* (New York, 1988), vol. 1, pp. 259–81.
34 Geoffrey Hosking, *The First Socialist Society*, 2nd edn. (Cambridge, Mass. 1993), p. 239.
35 William Husband, *"Godless Atheists": Atheism and Society in Soviet Russia, 1917–1932* (DeKalb, Ill., 2000), is excellent in detailing the clash between religious and communist ideals in this period.
36 L. Trotsky, "Vodka, the Church, and the Cinema" in William G. Rosenberg, ed., *Bolshevik Visions* (Ann Arbor, Mich., 1990), vol. 2, pp. 106–10.
37 Nathaniel Davis, *A Long Walk to Church: A Contemporary History of Russian Orthodoxy*, 2nd edn. (Boulder, Colo., 2003), p. 11.
38 Paul Froese, *The Plot to Kill God: Findings from the Soviet Experiment in Secularization* (Berkeley, Calif., 2008).
39 Dmitry V. Pospielovsky, *The Russian Church under the Soviet Regime, 1917–1982* (Crestwood, NY, 1984), pp. 163–91.
40 Geoffrey A Hosking, *Rulers and Victims: The Russians in the Soviet Union* (Cambridge, Mass., 2006), pp. 200–203; Daniel Peris, "'God Is Now on Our Side': The Religious Revival on Unoccupied Soviet Territory during World War II" in Michael David-Fox et al., eds., *The Resistance Debate in Russian and Soviet History* (Bloomington, Ind., 2003), pp. 138–67.

Chapter 6

1 For European views of Russia, see Martin Malia, *Russia under Western Eyes: From the Bronze Horseman to the Lenin Mausoleum* (Cambridge, Mass., 1999).
2 Andrzej Walicki, *The Slavophile Controversy: History of a Conservative Utopia* (Notre Dame, Ind., 1989).

3 Barbara Jelavich, *Russia's Balkan Entanglements, 1806–1914* (Cambridge, UK, 1991).

4 Charles Jelavich, *Tsarist Russia and Balkan Nationalism: Russian Influence in the Internal Affairs of Bulgaria and Serbia, 1879–1886* (Berkeley, Calif., 1958).

5 George F. Kennan, *The Fateful Alliance: France, Russia, and the Coming of the First World War* (New York, 1984).

6 Seymour Becker, *Russia's Protectorates in Central Asia: Bukhara and Khiva 1865–1924* (London, 2004).

7 For more on racism in Russia, see Eli Weinerman, "Racism, Racial Prejudice, and Jews in Late Imperial Russia," *Ethnic and Racial Studies*, vol. 17, no. 3 (1994), pp. 442–95.

8 For a stimulating comparison of these understudied empires, see Mark von Hagen and Karen Barkey, eds., *After Empire: Multiethnic Societies and Nation-Building: The Soviet Union and the Russian, Ottoman, and Habsburg Empires* (Boulder, Colo., 1997).

9 Dietrich Geyer, *Russian Imperialism: The Interaction of Domestic and Foreign Policy, 1860–1914* (New Haven, Conn., 1987).

10 David MacKenzie, *The Lion of Tashkent: The Career of General M. G. Cherniaev* (Athens, Ga., 1974), pp. 51–98.

11 Heinz Gollwitzer, *Europe in the Age of Imperialism 1880–1914* (New York, 1969), pp. 44–50.

12 Ronald P. Bobroff, *Roads to Glory: Late Imperial Russia and the Turkish Straits* (London, 2006).

13 Michael Boro Petrovich, *The Emergence of Russian Panslavism, 1956–1870* (New York, 1956).

14 J. N. Westwood, *Russia against Japan 1904–05: A New Look at the Russo-Japanese War* (Basingstoke, 1986); David Wells and Sandra Wilson, eds., *The Russo-Japanese War in Cultural Perspective, 1904–1905* (New York, 1999).

15 Allan K. Wildman, *The End of the Russian Imperial Army*. Vol. 1: *The Old Army and the Soldiers' Revolt (March–April 1917)* (Princeton, NJ, 1980), pp. 72–3.

16 Mark Von Hagen, *War in a European Borderland: Occupations and Occupation Plans in Galicia and Ukraine, 1914–1918* (Seattle, Wash., 2007).

17 Peter Gatrell, *A Whole Empire Walking: Refugees in Russia during World War I* (Bloomington, Ind., 1999).

18 A. A. Gromyko and B. N. Ponomarev, eds., *Istoriia vneshnei politiki SSSR 1917–1985*, 5th edn. (Moscow, 1986), vol. 1, p. 5.

19 Robert Jackson, *At War with the Bolsheviks: The Allied Intervention in Russia, 1917–20* (London, 1972). On the American intervention in Siberia, see David S. Foglesong, *America's Secret War against Bolshevism: United States Intervention in the Russian Civil War 1917–1920* (Chapel Hill, NC, 1995).

20 Jon Smele, *Civil War in Siberia: The Anti-Bolshevik Government of Admiral Kolchak, 1918–1920* (Cambridge, UK, 1996).

21 Kevin McDermott and Jeremy Agnew, *The Comintern: A History of International Communism from Lenin to Stalin* (New York, 1997).

22 Conrad Brandt, *Stalin's Failure in China, 1924–1927* (Cambridge, Mass., 1958).

23 Jonathan Haslam, *The Soviet Union and the Struggle for Collective Security in Europe, 1933–1939* (New York, 1984), pp. 53–9.

24 Hilde Hardeman, *Coming to Terms with the Soviet Regime: The "Changing Signposts" Movement among Russian Émigrés in the Early 1920s* (DeKalb, Ill., 1994).
25 Nicholas V. Riasanovsky, "The Emergence of Eurasianism," *California Slavic Studies*, vol. 4 (1967), pp. 39–72.
26 For a number of "case studies" on the major centers of Russian emigration, see Karl Schlögel, ed., *Der grosse Exodus: Die russische Emigration und ihre Zentren 1917 bis 1941* (Munich, 1994).
27 Marc Raeff, *Russia Abroad: A Cultural History of the Russian Emigration, 1919–1939* (Oxford, 1990); Karl Schlögel, *Berlin, Ostbahnhof Europas: Russen und Deutsche in ihrem Jahrhundert* (Berlin, 1998).
28 David Wolff, *To the Harbin Station: The Liberal Alternative in Russian Manchuria, 1898–1914* (Stanford, 1999).
29 Isaac Deutscher, *The Prophet Outcast: Trotsky, 1929–1940* (Oxford, 1963).
30 Adam B. Ulam, *Expansion and Coexistence: Soviet Foreign Policy 1917–1973*, 2nd edn. (New York, 1974), pp. 209–79.
31 Edward H. Carr, *The Comintern and the Spanish Civil War* (London, 1997).
32 An excellent collection of memoirs of this period is Irina Grudzińska-Gross and Jan T. Gross, eds., *War through Children's Eyes: The Soviet Occupation of Poland and the Deportations, 1939–1941* (Stanford, Calif., 1981).
33 Albert L. Weeks, *Stalin's Other War: Soviet Grand Strategy, 1939–1941* (Lanham, Md., 2002).
34 Gabriel Gorodetsky, *Grand Delusion: Stalin and the German Invasion of Russia* (New Haven, Conn., 1999).
35 Chris Bellamy, *Absolute War: Soviet Russia in the Second World War* (New York, 2007).
36 Anna M. Cienciala, Natalia S. Lebedeva, and Wojciech Materski, eds., *Katyn: A Crime Without Punishment* (New Haven, Conn., 2007).
37 Lloyd C. Gardner, *Spheres of Influence: The Great Powers Partition Europe, from Munich to Yalta* (Chicago, 1993).
38 David Holloway, *Stalin and the Bomb: The Soviet Union and Atomic Energy, 1939–56* (New Haven, Conn., 1994).

──────────────── Chapter 7 ────────────────

1 Patrick L. Alston, *Education and the State in Tsarist Russia* (Stanford, Calif., 1969); James C. McClelland, *Autocrats and Academics: Education, Culture, and Society in Tsarist Russia* (Chicago, 1979).
2 Figures from Arcadius Kahan, *Russian Economic History: The Nineteenth Century* (Chicago, 1989), pp. 170–76.
3 Allen Sinel, *The Classroom and the Chancellery: State Educational Reform in Russia under Count Dmitry Tolstoi* (Cambridge, Mass., 1973).
4 Quoted in J. N. Westwood, *Endurance and Endeavour: Russian History 1812–1992*, 4th ed. (Oxford, 1993), p. 194.
5 Ben Eklof, *Russian Peasant Schools: Officialdom, Village Culture, and Popular Pedagogy, 1861–1914* (Berkeley, Calif., 1986).

6   Christine Ruane, *Gender, Class, and the Professionalization of Russian City Teachers, 1860–1914* (Pittsburgh, 1994).

7   Irina Paperno, *Chernyshevsky and the Age of Realism: A Study in the Semiotics of Behavior* (Stanford, 1988).

8   For an interesting analysis of major nineteenth-century Russian writers as ideologues, see Nicholas Rzhevsky, *Russian Literature and Ideology: Herzen, Dostoevsky, Leontiev, Tolstoy, Fadeyev* (Urbana, Ill., 1983).

9   Walter Bruford, *Chekhov and His Russia: A Sociological Study* (London, 1947).

10 Richard Taruskin, *On Russian Music* (Berkeley, Calif., 2009); Francis Maes, *A History of Russian Music: From* Kamarinskaya *to* Babi Yar (Berkeley, Calif., 2002).

11 Christine Johanson. *Women's Struggle for Higher Education in Russia, 1855–1900* (Montreal, 1987).

12 Samuel Kassow, *Students, Professors, and the State in Tsarist Russia* (Berkeley, Calif., 1989); Susan K. Morrissey, *Heralds of Revolution: Russian Students and the Mythologies of Radicalism* (Oxford, 1998).

13 Michael D. Gordin, *A Well-Ordered Thing: Dmitrii Mendeleev and the Shadow of the Periodic Table* (New York, 2004).

14 Barbara Goldsmith, *Obsessive Genius: The Inner World of Marie Curie* (New York, 2005).

15 Robert Byrnes, *V. O. Kliuchevskii, Historian of Russia* (Bloomington, Ind., 1995).

16 Sofiia Dubnova-Erlikh, *The Life and Work of S. M. Dubnov: Diaspora Nationalism and Jewish History* (Bloomington, Ind., 1991).

17 Jeffrey Brooks, *When Russia Learned to Read: Literacy and Popular Literature 1861–1917* (Princeton, NJ, 1985), p. 68.

18 Andrew L. Jenks, *Russia in a Box: Art and Identity in an Age of Revolution* (DeKalb, Ill., 2005).

19 Roshanna P. Sylvester, *Tales of Old Odessa: Crime and Civility in a City of Thieves* (DeKalb, Ill., 2005).

20 Laura Engelstein, *The Keys to Happiness: Sex and the Search for Modernity in Fin-de-Siècle Russia* (Ithaca, NY, 1992).

21 Louise McReynolds, *Russia at Play: Leisure Activities at the End of the Tsarist Era* (Ithaca, NY, 2003).

22 Elizabeth K. Valkenier, *Ilya Repin and the World of Russian Art* (New York, 1990).

23 Vahan D. Barooshian, *V. V. Vereshchagin: Artist at War* (Gainesville, Fla., 1993).

24 Robert H. Allshouse, ed., *Photographs for the Tsar: The Pioneering Color Photography of Sergei Mikhailovich Prokudin-Gorskii Commissioned by Tsar Nicholas II* (London, 1980).

25 Denise J. Youngblood, *The Magic Mirror: Moviemaking in Russia, 1908–1918* (Madison, Wis., 1999).

26 Hubertus F. Jahn, *Patriotic Culture in Russia during World War I* (Ithaca, NY, 1995).

27 Stephen White, *The Bolshevik Poster* (New Haven, Conn., 1988), pp. 18–64.

28 Victoria Bonnell, *Iconography of Power: Soviet Political Posters under Lenin and Stalin* (Berkeley, Calif., 1997).

29 Peter Kenez, *The Birth of the Propaganda State: Soviet Methods of Mass Mobilization* (Cambridge, UK, 1985), pp. 75–8.

30 Jeffrey Brooks, "The Breakdown in Production and Distribution of Printed Material, 1917–1927" in Abbott Gleason, Peter Kenez, and Richard Stites, eds., *Bolshevik Culture: Experiment and Order in the Russian Revolution* (Bloomington, Ind., 1985), pp. 151–74.

31 Denise J. Youngblood, *Soviet Cinema in the Silent Era, 1918–1935* (Ann Arbor, Mich., 1985); idem, *Movies for the Masses: Popular Cinema and Soviet Society in the 1920s* (Cambridge, UK, 1992).

32 Richard Stites, *Russian Popular Culture: Entertainment and Society since 1900* (Cambridge, UK, 1992), p. 60.

33 Sheila Fitzpatrick, *The Commissariat of Enlightenment: Soviet Organization of Education and the Arts under Lunacharsky, October 1917–1921* (Cambridge, UK, 1970).

34 Katerina Clark, *The Soviet Novel: History as Ritual* (Chicago, 1981).

35 Quoted in Nicholas Luker, ed., *From Furmanov to Sholokhov: An Anthology of the Classics of Socialist Realism* (Ann Arbor, 1988), p. 19.

36 Boris Groys, *The Total Art of Stalinism: Avant-Garde, Aesthetic Dictatorship, and Beyond* (Princeton, NJ, 1992).

37 Evgeny Dobrenko and Eric Naiman, eds., *The Landscape of Stalinism: The Art and Ideology of Soviet Space* (Seattle, Wash., 2003).

Select Bibliography

Allworth, Edward. *Central Asia: 130 Years of Russian Dominance, A Historical Overview.* 3rd edn. Durham, NC, 1994.

Applebaum, Anne. *Gulag: A History.* New York, 2003.

Aronson, Irvin Michael. *Troubled Waters: The Origins of the 1881 Pogroms in Russia.* Pittsburgh, 1990.

Ascher, Abraham. *P. A. Stolypin: The Search for Stability in Late Imperial Russia.* Stanford, Calif., 2001.

Ascher, Abraham. *The Revolution of 1905.* 2 vols. Stanford, Calif., 1988.

Avrich, Paul. *Kronstadt, 1921.* Princeton, NJ, 1970.

Bacon, Elizabeth. *Central Asians under Russian Rule: A Study in Cultural Change.* Ithaca, NY, 1966. (Based on a visit 1933–4.)

Balzer, Harley. *Russia's Missing Middle Class.* Armonk, NY, 1996.

Barber, John, and Mark Harrison. *The Soviet Home Front, 1941–1945: A Social and Economic History of the USSR in World War II.* London, 1991.

Barkey, Karen, and Mark von Hagen, eds. *After Empire: Multiethnic Societies and Nation-Building: The Soviet Union and the Russian, Ottoman, and Habsburg Empires.* Boulder, Colo., 1997.

Becker, Seymour. *Nobility and Privilege in Late Imperial Russia.* DeKalb, Ill., 1985.

Bernstein, Laurie. *Sonia's Daughters: Prostitutes and Their Regulation in Imperial Russia.* Berkeley, Calif., 1995.

Blank, Stephen. *The Sorcerer as Apprentice: Stalin as Commissar of Nationalities, 1917–1924.* Westport, Conn., 1994.

Bonnell, Victoria. *Roots of Rebellion: Workers' Politics and Organizations in St. Petersburg and Moscow 1900–1914.* Berkeley, Calif., 1983.

Bradley, Joseph. *Muzhik and Muscovite: Urbanization in Late Imperial Russia.* Berkeley, Calif., 1985.

Brooks, Jeffrey. *When Russia Learned to Read: Literacy and Popular Literature 1861–1917.* Princeton, NJ, 1985.

Brovkin, Vladimir. *Behind the Front Lines of the Civil War: Political Parties and Social Movements in Russia, 1918–1922*. Princeton, NJ, 1994.

Brovkin, Vladimir. *Russia after Lenin: Politics, Culture, and Society, 1921–1929*. New York, 1998.

Brower, Daniel. *Turkestan and the Fate of the Russian Empire*. London, 2003.

Brown, Kate. *A Biography of No Place: From Ethnic Borderland to Soviet Heartland*. Cambridge, Mass., 2004.

Burbank, Jane, and David L. Ransel, eds. *Imperial Russia: New Histories for the Empire*. Bloomington, Ind., 1998.

Byrnes, Robert. *Pobedonostsev*. Bloomington, Ind., 1968.

Carr, E. H., and R. W. Davies. *Foundations of a Planned Economy, 1926–1929*. 2 vols. London, 1969, 1978.

Carrère d'Encausse, Hélène. *Decline of an Empire: The Soviet Socialist Republics in Revolt*. New York, 1979.

Clark, Katerina. *Petersburg, Crucible of Cultural Revolution*. Cambridge, Mass., 1995.

Clements, Barbara. *Bolshevik Feminist: The Life of Alexandra Kollontai*. Bloomington, Ind., 1979.

Clowes, Edith, Samuel D. Kassow, and James L. West, eds. *Between Tsar and People: Educated Society and the Quest for Public Identity in Late Imperial Russia*. Princeton, NJ, 1991.

Conquest, Robert. *The Great Terror: A Reassessment*. New York, 1990.

Crisp, Olga. *Studies in the Russian Economy before 1914*. New York, 1976.

Danilov, V. P. *Rural Russia under the New Regime*. London, 1988.

David-Fox, Michael. *Revolution of the Mind: Higher Learning among the Bolsheviks, 1918–1929*. Ithaca, NY, 1997.

Daniels, Robert V. *Russia: The Roots of Confrontation*. Cambridge, Mass., 1985.

Davies, Robert W. *The Industrialization of Soviet Russia*. 3 vols. New York, 1986.

Davies, Sarah, and James Harris, eds. *Stalin: A New History*. Cambridge, UK, 2005.

Dunham, Vera. *In Stalin's Time: Middleclass Values in Soviet Fiction*. Cambridge, UK, 1976.

Edmondson, Linda, and Peter Waldron, ed. *Economy and Society in Russia and the Soviet Union, 1860–1930*. New York, 1992.

Eklof, Ben, John Bushnell, and Larissa Zakharova, eds. *Russia's Great Reforms*. Bloomington, Ind., 1994.

Emmons, Terence. *The Formation of Political Parties and the First National Elections in Russia*. Cambridge, Mass., 1983.

Engelstein, Laura. *The Keys to Happiness: Sex and the Search for Modernity in Fin-de-Siècle Russia*. Ithaca, NY, 1992.

Erickson, John. *The Road to Berlin*. Boulder, Colo., 1983.

Evtuhov, Catherine. *The Cross and the Sickle: Sergei Bulgakov and the Fate of Russian Religious Philosophy, 1890–1917*. Ithaca, NY 1997.

Field, Daniel. *The End of Serfdom: Nobility and Bureaucracy in Russia, 1855–1861*. Cambridge, Mass., 1976.

Figes, Orlando. *Natasha's Dance: A Cultural History of Russia*. New York, 2002.

Figes, Orlando. *A People's Tragedy: The Russian Revolution 1891–1924*. London, 1996.

Fitzpatrick, Sheila. *Everyday Stalinism: Ordinary Life in Extraordinary Times: Soviet Russia in the 1930s*. New York, 1999.

Freeze, Gregory L. *The Parish Clergy in Nineteenth-Century Russia*. Princeton, NJ, 1983.

Fuller, William. *Civil-Military Conflict in Imperial Russia, 1881–1914*. Princeton, NJ, 1985.

Gatrell, Peter. *The Tsarist Economy, 1850–1917*. New York, 1986.

Geifman, Anna. *Thou Shalt Kill: Revolutionary Terrorism in Russia, 1894–1917*. Princeton, NJ, 1993.

Gerschenkron, Alexander. *Economic Backwardness in Historical Perspective*. Cambridge, Mass., 1962.

Geyer, Dietrich. *Russian Imperialism: The Interaction of Domestic and Foreign Policy, 1860–1914*. New Haven, Conn., 1987.

Gillard, David. *The Struggle for Asia 1828–1914: A Study in British and Russian Imperialism*. London, 1977.

Gitelman, Zvi. *Jewish Nationality and Soviet Politics: The Jewish Sections of the CPSU, 1917–1930*. Princeton, NJ, 1972.

Gleason, Abbott. *Young Russia*. New York, 1980.

Goldman, Wendy Z. *Women at the Gates: Gender and Industry in Stalin's Russia*. Cambridge, UK, 2002.

Gorodetsky, Gabriel. *Grand Delusion: Stalin and the German Invasion of Russia*. New Haven, Conn., 1999.

Gregory, Paul R. *Before Command: An Economic History of Russia from Emancipation to the First Five-Year Plan*. Princeton, NJ, 1994.

Gross, Jan T. *Revolution from Abroad: The Soviet Conquest of Poland's Western Ukraine and Western Belorussia*. Princeton, NJ, 1988.

Hagenloh, Paul. *Stalin's Police: Public Order and Mass Repression in the USSR, 1926–1941*. Washington, DC, 2009.

Haslam, Jonathan. *The Soviet Union and the Struggle for Collective Security in Europe, 1933–39*. New York, 1984.

Healy, Dan. *Homosexual Desire in Revolutionary Russia: The Regulation of Sexual and Gender Dissent*. Chicago, 2001.

Heretz, Leonid. *Russia on the Eve of Modernity: Popular Religion and Traditional Culture under the Last Tsars*. Cambridge, UK, 2008.

Herlihy, Patricia. *The Alcoholic Empire: Vodka and Politics in Late Imperial Russia*. Oxford, 2002.

Hirsch, Francine. *Empire of Nations*. Ithaca, NY, 2005.

Hoffmann, David L. *Stalinist Values: The Cultural Norms of Soviet Modernity, 1917–1941*. Ithaca, NY, 2003.

Holquist, Peter. *Making War, Forging Revolution*. Cambridge, Mass. 2002.

Hosking, Geoffrey A., ed. *Church, Nation and State in Russia and Ukraine*. Houndsmills, Basingstoke, UK, 1991.

Husband, William. *"Godless Atheists": Atheism and Society in Soviet Russia, 1917–1932*. Dekalb, Ill., 2000.

Jahn, Hubertus F. *Patriotic Culture during World War I*. Ithaca, NY, 1995.

Jelavich, Barbara, *A Century of Russian Foreign Policy*. Philadelphia, 1964.

Kahan, Arcadius. *Russian Economic History: The Nineteenth Century.* Chicago, 1989.

Kappeler, Andreas. *The Russian Empire: A Multiethnic History.* New York, 2001.

Kassow, Samuel. *Students, Professors, and the State in Tsarist Russia.* Berkeley, Calif., 1989.

Keep, John L. H. *The Russian Revolution: A Study in Mass Mobilization.* London, 1976.

Kelly, Catriona, and David Shepherd, eds. *Constructing Russian Culture in the Age of Revolution: 1881–1940.* Oxford, 1998.

Kenez, Peter. *The Birth of the Propaganda State: Soviet Methods of Mass Mobilization.* Cambridge, UK, 1985.

Kennan, George F. *The Fateful Alliance: France, Russia, and the Coming of the First World War.* New York, 1984.

Khalid, Adeeb. *The Politics of Muslim Cultural Reform: Jadidism in Central Asia.* Berkeley, Calif., 1998.

Kingston-Mann, Esthere, and Timothy Mixter, eds. *Peasant Economy, Culture, and Politics of European Russia, 1800–1921.* Princeton, NJ, 1990.

Koenker, Diane, William Rosenberg, and Ronald Suny, eds. *Party, State, and Society in the Russian Civil War: Explorations in Social History.* Bloomington, Ind., 1989.

Kotkin, Stephen. *Magnetic Mountain: Stalinism as a Civilization.* Berkeley, Calif., 1995.

LeDonne, John P. *The Russian Empire and the World 1700–1917: The Geopolitics of Expansion and Containment.* Oxford, 1997.

Lewin, Moshe. *Russian Peasants and Soviet Power: A Study of Collectivization.* New York, 1975.

Lieven, Dominic. *Empire: The Russian Empire and Its Rivals.* New Haven, Conn., 2000.

Lincoln, W. Bruce. *The Great Reforms.* DeKalb, Ill., 1990.

Lindenmeyr, Adele. *Poverty Is Not a Vice: Charity, Society, and the State in Imperial Russia.* Princeton, NJ, 1996.

Litvak, Olga. *Conscription and the Search for Modern Russian Jewry.* Bloomington, Ind., 2006.

Lohr, Eric. *Nationalizing the Russian Empire: The Campaign against Enemy Aliens during World War I.* Cambridge, Mass., 2003.

Macey, David. *Government and Peasant in Russia, 1860–1906.* DeKalb, Ill., 1987.

Mackenzie, David. *Imperial Dreams, Harsh Realities: Tsarist Russian Foreign Policy, 1815–1917.* Fort Worth, Tex., 1994.

Malia, Martin. *The Soviet Tragedy.* New York, 1994.

Mally, Lynn. *Culture of the Future: The Proletkult Movement in Rev Russia.* Berkeley, Calif., 1990.

Manning, Roberta. *The Crisis of the Old Order in Russia.* Princeton, NJ, 1982.

Marks, Steven G. *Road to Power: The Trans-Siberian Railroad and the Colonization of Asian Russia.* Ithaca, NY, 1991.

Martin, Terry. *The Affirmative Action Empire: Nations and Nationalism in the Soviet Union, 1923–1939.* Ithaca, NY, 2001.

Morrissey, Susan. *Heralds of Revolution: Russian Students and the Mythologies of Radicalism.* Oxford, 1998.

Nahaylo, Bohdan, and Victor Swoboda. *Soviet Disunion: A History of the Nationalities Problem in the USSR.* New York, 1990.

Naiman, Eric. *Sex in Public: The Incarnation of Soviet Ideology*. Princeton, NJ, 1997.

Nathans, Benjamin. *Beyond the Pale: The Jewish Encounter with Late Imperial Russia.* Berkeley, Calif., 2002.

Neuberger, Joan. *Hooliganism: Crime, Culture, and Power in St. Petersburg*. Berkeley, Calif., 1993.

Northrop, Douglas T. *Veiled Empire: Gender and Power in Stalinist Central Asia*. Ithaca, NY, 2004.

Nove, Alec. *An Economic History of the USSR*. 2nd edn. Harmondsworth, Middlesex [UK], 1989.

Phillips, Laura L. *Bolsheviks and the Bottle: Drink and Worker Culture in St. Petersburg, 1900–1929*. DeKalb, Ill., 2000.

Pipes, Richard. *The Formation of the Soviet Union, Communism and Nationalism, 1917– 1923*. Rev. ed. Cambridge, Mass., 1964.

Pospielovsky, Dmitry V. *The Russian Church under the Soviet Regime, 1917–1982*. Crestwood, NY, 1984.

Rabinowitch, Alexander. *The Bolsheviks Come to Power: The Revolution of 1917 in Petrograd*. New York, 1976.

Raleigh, Donald. *Provincial Landscapes: Local Dimensions of Soviet Power*. Pittsburgh, 2001.

Rieber, Alfred. *Merchants and Entrepreneurs in Imperial Russia*. Chapel Hill, NC, 1982.

Sahadeo, Jeffrey. *Russian Colonial Empire in Tashkent, 1865–1923*. Bloomington, Ind., 2007.

Sanborn, Joshua. *Drafting the Russian Nation*. DeKalb, Ill., 2003.

Schimmelpenninck van der Oye, David. *Toward the Rising Sun*. DeKalb, Ill., 2001.

Seaton, Albert. *Stalin as Military commander*. New York, 1976.

Shanin, Teodor. *Russia, 1905–1907: Revolution as a Moment of Truth*. New Haven, Conn., 1986.

Shanin, Teodor. *Russia as a "Developing Society."* New Haven, Conn., 1985.

Shatz, Marshall, and Judith Zimmerman, eds. and trans. *Vekhi = Landmarks*. Armonk, NY, 1994.

Shevzov, Vera. *Russian Orthodoxy on the Eve of Revolution*. Oxford, 2004.

Siegelbaum, Lewis H., Andrei Sokolov, and Sergei Zhuravlev, eds. *Stalinism as a Way of Life: A Narrative in Documents*. New Haven, Conn., 2000.

Slezkine, Yuri. *Arctic Mirrors: Russia and the Small Peoples of the North*. Ithaca, NY, 1994.

Smith, Jeremy. *The Bolsheviks and the National Question, 1917–23*. New York, 1999.

Smith, Steve A. *Red Petrograd: Revolution in the Factories, 1917–1918*. New York, 1983.

Steinberg, Mark. *Proletarian Imagination: Self, Modernity, and the Sacred in Russia 1910– 1925*. Ithaca, NY, 2002.

Steinberg, Mark, and Heather Coleman, eds. *Sacred Stories: Religion and Spirituality in Modern Russia*. Bloomington, Ind., 2007.

Stites, Richard. *Russian Popular Culture: Entertainment and Society since 1900*. Cambridge, UK, 1992.

Stites, Richard. *The Women's Liberation Movement in Russia*. Princeton, NJ, 1978.

Stone, Norman. *The Eastern Front 1914–1917*. London, 1975.

Suny, Ronald, and Terry Martin, eds. *A State of Nations: Empire and Nation-Making in the Age of Lenin and Stalin*. Oxford, 2001.

Suny, Ronald, ed. *Transcaucasia, Nationalism, and Social Change*. Ann Arbor, Mich., 1983.

Thaden, Edward, ed. *Russification in the Baltic Provinces and Poland, 1855–1914*. Princeton, NJ, 1981.

Thurston, Robert. *Life and Terror in Stalin's Russia, 1934–1941*. New Haven, 1996.

Thurston, Robert, ed. *A People's War: Popular Responses to World War II in the Soviet Union*. Champaign-Urbana, Ill., 2000.

Tian-Shanskaia, Olga S. *Village Life in Late Tsarist Russia*. Ed. David L. Ransel. Bloomington, Ind., 1993.

Tucker, Robert. *Stalin in Power: The Revolution from Above*. New York, 1990.

Tumarkin, Nina. *Lenin Lives! The Lenin Cult in Soviet Russia*. Cambridge, Mass., 1983.

Ulam, Adam B. *Expansion and Coexistence: Soviet Foreign Policy, 1917–1973*. 2nd edn. New York, 1974.

Viola, Lynn. *Peasant Rebels under Stalin: Collectivization and the Culture of Peasant Resistance*. New York, 1996.

Von Geldern, James, and Louise McReynolds, eds. *Entertaining Tsarist Russia*. Bloomington, Ind., 1998.

Von Hagen, Mark. *Soldiers in the Proletarian Dictatorship: The Red Army and the Socialist State*. Ithaca, 1990.

Von Laue, Theodore. *Sergei Witte and the Industrialization of Russia*. New York, 1963.

Vucinich, Alexander. *Social Thought in Tsarist Russia: The Quest for a General Science of Society, 1861–1917*. Chicago, 1976.

Walicki, Andrzej. *The Slavophile Controversy: History of a Conservative Utopia*. Notre Dame, Ind., 1989.

Ward, Chris. *Stalin's Russia*. 2nd edn. London, 1999.

Weeks, Theodore. *Nation and State in Late Imperial Russia: Nationalism and Russification on the Western Frontier, 1863–1914*. DeKalb, Ill., 1996.

Weiner, Amir. *Making Sense of War: The Second World War and the Fate of the Bolshevik Revolution*. Princeton, NJ, 2001.

Weiner, Douglas. *Models of Nature: Ecology, Conservation, and Cultural Revolution in Soviet Russia*. Bloomington, Ind., 1988.

Wildman, Allan K. *The End of the Russian Imperial Army*. 2 vols. Princeton, NJ, 1980, 1987.

Wirtschafter, Elise K. *Structures of Society: Imperial Russia's "People of Various Ranks."* DeKalb, Ill., 1994.

Wood, Elizabeth A. *The Baba and the Comrade: Gender and Politics in Revolutionary Russia*. Bloomington, Ind., 1997.

Worobec, Christine, *Possessed: Women, Witches, and Demons in Imperial Russia*. DeKalb, Ill., 2001.

Wortman, Richard. *The Development of a Russian Legal Consciousness*. Chicago, 1976.

Young, Glennys. *Power and the Sacred in Revolutionary Russia: Religious Activists in the Village*. University Park, Penn., 1997.

Youngblood, Denise J. *Movies for the Masses: Popular Cinema and Soviet Society in the 1920s*. Cambridge, UK, 1992.

Index